DISPLACEMENT URBANISM

Politics of Bodies and Spaces of Abandonment and Endurance

Edited by
Giovanna Astolfo and Camillo Boano

First published in Great Britain in 2026 by

Bristol University Press
University of Bristol
1-9 Old Park Hill
Bristol
BS2 8BB
UK
t: +44 (0)117 374 6645
e: bup-info@bristol.ac.uk

Details of international sales and distribution partners are available at bristoluniversitypress.co.uk

© Editorial selection and matter © Giovanna Astolfo and Camillo Boano; individual chapters
© their respective authors 2026

The digital PDF and ePub versions of this title are available open access and distributed under the terms of the Creative Commons Attribution-NonCommercial-NoDerivatives 4.0 International licence (https://creativecommons.org/licenses/by-nc-nd/4.0/) which permits reproduction and distribution for non-commercial use without further permission provided the original work is attributed.

DOI: 10.51952/9781529242348

British Library Cataloguing in Publication Data
A catalogue record for this book is available from the British Library

ISBN 978-1-5292-4232-4 paperback
ISBN 978-1-5292-4233-1 ePub
ISBN 978-1-5292-4234-8 OA Pdf

The right of Giovanna Astolfo and Camillo Boano to be identified as editors of this work has been asserted by them in accordance with the Copyright, Designs and Patents Act 1988.

All rights reserved: no part of this publication may be reproduced, stored in a retrieval system, or transmitted in any form or by any means, electronic, mechanical, photocopying, recording, or otherwise without the prior permission of Bristol University Press.

Every reasonable effort has been made to obtain permission to reproduce copyrighted material. If, however, anyone knows of an oversight, please contact the publisher.

The statements and opinions contained within this publication are solely those of the editors and contributors and not of the University of Bristol or Bristol University Press. The University of Bristol and Bristol University Press disclaim responsibility for any injury to persons or property resulting from any material published in this publication.

Bristol University Press works to counter discrimination on grounds of gender, race, disability, age and sexuality.

Cover design: Liam Roberts Design
Front cover image: Calais, France. Giovanna Astolfo, 2016

This book is dedicated to everyone who is escaping capture.

Contents

List of Figures and Tables vii
Notes on Contributors x
Acknowledgements xvi

Introduction 1
Giovanna Astolfo

1   Framing Displacement Urbanism 17
           Giovanna Astolfo and Camillo Boano

PART I   Extraction

2   Displacement, Two Ways: Necroeconomic Navigations 55
           in the Peri-Urban Global Southeast
           Elliott Prasse-Freeman

3   Producing *Zoé*: The Camp as a Form of Extraction 72
           in Castel Volturno
           Sofia Moriconi

PART II   Expulsion

4   Planning and Design of Rural-to-Urban Resettlements 91
           for Fast Urbanization in Suzhou, Yangtze River Delta
           Paola Pellegrini and Jinliu Chen

5   Between Augmented Disposability and Deferred 115
           Disposal: A View from Istanbul
           Francesco Pasta

PART III   Exhaustion

6   Displaced and Evicted Migrant Women: Informal 137
           Settlement as a Mechanism of Resistance and
           Territorial Self-Management
           Yasna Contreras Gatica

7	Shifting Geographies of Presence: Territorial Biographies and Forced Displacements Entanglements Within the Kurdistan Region of Iraq *Layla Zibar*	160
8	Beyond Shelter: Makeshift Inhabitation in Displacement in Greater Paris *Stefano Mastromarino*	189

PART IV Extinction

9	Place Wounding and Becoming-Extinction in Baghdad after the 2003 US-led Invasion *Sana Murrani, Dhirgham Alobaydi, and Ula Merie*	209
10	Top-Down Disaster Preparedness and Grassroots Environmental Endurance in 2010s Turkey *Eray Çaylı*	230

PART V Endurance

11	Beyond Destitution and Deprivation: Interrogating the Modalities of Endurance by Self-Settled Refugees in Arua City, Uganda *Peter Kasaija*	247
12	Calais as a Zone of Care: Reimagining an Urban Migration Hub Between France and the United Kingdom *Kieran Tam and Irit Katz*	273

Conclusion: The Impossible Task　　291
Camillo Boano

Index　　297

List of Figures and Tables

Figures

3.1	Castel Volturno is situated on the coast, almost equidistant from two established urban areas	75
3.2	Buildings in Castel Volturno inhabited by day labourers	76
3.3	Location of the main Kalifoo Grounds in the Castel Volturno area	78
3.4	Gathering of people in one of the humanitarian spaces of Castel Volturno	82
4.1	The transformation of the rural land east of the city of Suzhou, where the Suzhou Industrial Park was realized since 1994. The area in 1969 (top); the same area in 2022 (bottom)	96
4.2	The comparison of an ancient village south of Suzhou, Tongli, with the last large resettlement community built in the Suzhou Industrial Park (SIP), Lotus Village	97
4.3	Aerial view facing south from the roof of a high-rise in Nanhuan New Community, Gusu District, Suzhou	100
4.4	Aerial view facing north of Xujiabang neighbourhood, SIP, Suzhou	100
4.5	The first resettlement neighbourhoods built at the western edge of SIP (the large dashed line). Xujiabang and Xiayuan are within the dashed outline between two main roads, the Eastern Ring Road and the Suzhou-Hangzhou Expressway. Satellite view capturing the situation in 1969, with the perimeter of the main rural resettled villages (top); the same area in 2022 (bottom)	101
4.6	The remaining houses along the canal of a rural village included in Nanhuan resettlement community	102
4.7	Photo of Xujiabang neighbourhood	106
4.8	Example of a neighbourhood with the same characteristics in Suzhou, view from the road	106

5.1	Fikirtepe, 2023: 'The right time, the right man': Erdoğan's electoral poster in the area scheduled to be redeveloped in Phase 3	122
5.2	Fikirtepe, 2022: the existing texture in Fikirtepe in the area that will be redeveloped in Phase 2	122
5.3	Fikirtepe, 2023: a closed-down real estate office turned into a second-hand shop	123
5.4	Municipal and informal waste collectors compete for access to the rubbish bins	127
5.5	Fikirtepe, 2022: Mandıra caddesi, Fikirtepe's high-street, had its entire northern flank razed	128
6.1	Metropolitan area of Iquique-Alto Hospicio	140
6.2 and 6.3	*Tugurios:* overcrowded central housing	144
6.4	Residential trajectories. Woman A: Colombian migrant from Buenaventura	148
6.5	Residential trajectories. Woman B: Bolivian migrant from Sucre	149
7.1	Arbat strip	162
7.2	Shifting Kurdish borders	167
7.3	Iraq National Housing Programme	168
7.4	1970s collectives built for relocation purposes	171
7.5	1980–87 collectives: confinement model	173
7.6	'Protected enclave' set by the allied forces in 1991 (top); leaflets used during operation Provide Comfort, 1991 (left); and safe routes within protected enclaves (right)	175
7.7	Location of UN Habitat SRP interventions, 1995–2003	177
7.8	The expansion of ISIS control and the concentration of ethnic groups in both Syria and Iraq	180
7.9	Ashti IDP Camp	182
7.10	Kawergosk Refugee Camp, KR-I	182
7.11	1975–2022 documented forced displacement receiving sites in the Kurdistan region of Iraq	184
9.1	Blast walls in the centre of Baghdad	213
9.2	Fortified Green Zone and official buildings behind the walls	214
9.3	Sadr City neighbourhood showing the ad hoc development of properties	218
9.4	Informal housing (*ashwaiat*) on the outskirts of Baghdad	222
9.5	Deliberate acts of deforestation of a former date palm farm	223
9.6	One of the 25 camps set up in the Kurdish Region, Kabarto Yazidi IDP camp in Duhok, north of Iraq	224

| 11.1 | Snapshot of refugee demographics for Arua City in numbers and gender | 252 |

Tables

| 6.1 | Differences between displacement and forced eviction for women migrants | 153 |

Notes on Contributors

Giovanna Astolfo is Associate Professor of Urban Design in Development at the Bartlett Development Planning Unit (DPU), University College London. She is an urban researcher with an architectural theory and practice background. At DPU, she combines funded research, research-based teaching, and action learning from several contested and ungovernable urban geographies in Southeast Asia, the Amazon region, South America, West Africa, Southern, Eastern Europe, and the United Kingdom, with a focus on non-conventional urbanisms, continuous displacement and migration, spatial violence, and housing justice. Further non-funded research interests are related to the ethics of design, and the role of architecture and urbanism within the current socioecological devastation, which informs the pedagogical dimension of her taught programme. Prior to focusing entirely on teaching and research, she worked as an architect in between studies, in architectural offices in Venice, São Paulo, and London, on situated projects for the reimagination of vacant buildings and demilitarization of border zones.

Camillo Boano researches urban design critique and the philosophies of architecture. He is Full Professor of Architectural and Urban Design at the Politecnico di Torino. He has practised architecture in conflict, emergencies, and urban informality in different contexts and has worked on radical pedagogy and collective processes. He currently investigates in Latin America, the Middle East, and the Black Mediterranean. Among other works, he is the author of *The Ethics of a Potential Urbanism: Critical Encounters Between Giorgio Agamben and Architecture* (2017), *Progetto Minore. In alla ricercar della minorità nel Progetto architettonico ed urbanistico* (2020) and, with Cristina Bianchetti, *Lifelines Politics, Ethics, and the Affective Economy of Inhabiting* (2022).

Dhirgham Alobaydi is Chair in the Department of Architecture Engineering at the University of Baghdad. Many of his research projects and publications have focused on the morphological developments of Iraqi cities, particularly the urban forms and structures of historic nuclei. He has conducted several studies and reports focusing on understanding the role of Iraqi local communities in preserving their intangible cultural heritage, including rituals, practices, expressions, knowledge, and skills that communities recognize as part of their cultural heritage. His recent publications examine the role of streets and the syntactic properties of urban grids in creating successful urban places and well-connected communities. His work has included the design of planning processes to enhance the education and communication functions of cities. He received Doctor of Philosophy and Master of Architecture degrees, with a focus on urban planning, from the University of Kansas.

Eray Çaylı is Professor of Human Geography with a Focus on Violence and Security in the Anthropocene at the University of Hamburg. He holds a PhD from University College London (2015). His research and teaching focus on the spatial politics of violence and disasters by interweaving anthropology, geography, architecture, and visual culture. Alongside the numerous journal articles he has written and special issues he has guest edited on the subject, his major publications include the monographs *Victims of Commemoration: The Architecture and Violence of Confronting the Past in Turkey* (2022) and *Climate Aesthetics: Essays on Anthropocene Art and Architecture* (in Turkish, 2020), and the anthology *Architectures of Emergency in Turkey: Heritage, Displacement and Catastrophe* (2021). Prior to his current appointment at Hamburg, he worked for more than a decade at UK-based universities including University College London and the London School of Economics and Political Science. He is a member of the *Journal of Visual Culture*'s editorial collective.

Jinliu Chen is a Lecturer and Researcher affiliated with Suzhou City University, holding a PhD from the University of Liverpool, UK. His research focuses on advancing knowledge in urban studies and promoting sustainable practices in urban environments. He has published extensively in esteemed journals, including 'Tourism Management', 'Cities', 'Sustainable Cities and Society', 'NPJ Heritage Science', and 'Applied Geography.' His innovative approaches, such as using GIS-based analyses for sustainable urban renewal strategies, demonstrate his commitment to enhancing urban living conditions through research-driven insights. Additionally, he has won over 20 urban design competitions and received several awards. Through his work, he has contributed significantly to the discourse on sustainable urban practices and well-being.

Yasna Contreras Gatica is a geographer and Associate Professor, Universidad Austral de Chile, Geography Department. Yasna is a feminist geographer and co-founder of the Migrant Housing IG-Platform. She holds a PhD in architecture and urban studies from the PUC Chile. As part of the project Geographies of Conflict and Social Cohesion (ANID/FONDAP/15130009), she investigates mechanisms of exclusive access to housing and land in Chile for immigrant women and families. With ANID funds, she also examines the concept of informal territory from the exposure to socio-environmental injustices and disaster risks of those who live in precarious settlements within Chile and in the Latin American region (ANID Fondecyt Regular 1261116). She researches the migratory trajectories of immigrant women from the region and Afro-descendant women who reveal the reproduction of new interterritorial violence. She also explores how the processes of gentrification, land usurpation, displacement, and eviction violate the rights of migrants and immigrants. She works with communities living in Chilean informal settlements, especially women leaders, who build self-managed projects. Since 2023, she has formed the ANID Geography and Urbanism Study Group.

Peter Kasaija is a PhD researcher at the Urban Action Lab (UAL), Department of Geography, Geoinformatics and Climatic Sciences, Makerere University, Kampala. He is currently finalizing his research on power relationships that underpin informal sanitation infrastructures. He has more than ten years' extensive teaching and research experience within the field of urban development. His specific interests include urban informality, urban environmental change/transitions, housing, poverty and inequality, climate change adaptation/resilience, urban migration and protracted displacement, inclusive governance, and planning. He is collaborating with colleagues on various fieldwork-based courses conducted under partnerships between Makerere University and international research institutions, including the Norwegian University of Science and Technology – NTNU (Norway), the Development Planning Unit (DPU) (UK) and the University of Manchester (UK). He is also working with other urban development practitioners (including state agencies, civil society, and other urban development professionals) towards promoting research-based decision-making, and multi-actor knowledge co-production and exchange, in addition to harnessing synergies across different fields and levels of urban development expertise.

Irit Katz is Associate Professor of Architecture and Urban Studies at Cambridge's Department of Architecture, and a Fellow of Christ's College. Her work focuses on built environments shaped in extreme conditions, with a particular emphasis on spaces of displacement, conflict, spatial injustice, and environmental changes. It builds on her experience as a practising architect and incorporates a variety of methods, including spatial ethnography, participatory and visual methods, policy analysis, archival research, and a strong engagement with cultural and political theories. Her research covers historic and contemporary contexts, looking at various forms of human settlement and inhabitation – including urban, rural, camps, and other environments – as ever-changing spatial constellations through which political negotiations and cultural transformations are staged and reworked. Her latest book, *The Common Camp: Architecture of Power and Resistance in Israel-Palestine* (2022), was published by the University of Minnesota Press.

Stefano Mastromarino is a PhD candidate and Research Assistant at The Bartlett's Development Planning Unit, UCL, funded by the ESRC (UK). In the same department, he is also involved in the AHRC-funded project 'Reframing arrival infrastructures'. Formerly a research intern at the Ipraus Lab in Paris for the development of the platform 'Architecture et précarités', he studied Architecture at Politecnico di Torino, ENSA Paris-Belleville and TU Dortmund. Besides academia, he has been involved in various forms of migrant support and activism in France, Italy, and the United Kingdom, and worked as a UASC Support Worker for a non-profit organization providing housing and aid services to young people seeking asylum in the United Kingdom. His research looks at makeshift refuges amid protracted displacement in Italy. Specifically, he is exploring inhabitation practices and institutional forms of 'overcoming' and sheltering in the migrant refuge 'Khandwala' in Trieste and the so-called 'Ghetto di Borgo Mezzanone', a settlement mostly inhabited by migrant agricultural workers in the outskirts of Foggia.

Ula Merie is Senior Lecturer at the University of Babylon. She holds a PhD in post-colonial architecture from the Sheffield School of Architecture, focusing on the architecture of the post-war period and utopianism. Ula is a researcher at the Heritage Borders of Engagement Network/NTU, a representative for Iraq in the Epidemic Urbanism Initiative, a Research Fellow at the Academic Research Institute in Iraq (TARII), an Associate at the GIGA Institute for Middle East Studies, and Principal Investigator of the project UA – Urban Acupuncture: A Strategy of Catalytic Interventions: Ta'ziz Science Cooperations 2023–2025, The German Academic Exchange Service (DAAD) in partnership with Universität Kassel, Beirut Arab University, Alexandria University. Her research explores architectural humanities (history and theory), the architecture of home and heritage, the history and theory of architecture in post-war cities, spatial justice, conflicted identities, politics, ethics, gender equality, and the contestation of urban environments, ranging from public to private, under the umbrella of design and power.

Sofia Moriconi is Postdoctoral Fellow at the Federico II University of Naples, Italy. Her research interests concern the encounter between humanitarian spaces and urban processes, the production of territories linked to racialized and diverse subjectivities, and affirmative urban politics. She is a humanitarian activist and holds a PhD in urban planning from the same university. She has recently published the paper 'Humanitarian assemblages in Naples: How humanitarian space is absorbing urban leftover'.

Sana Murrani is an associate professor in spatial practice with a background in architecture and urban design. She is the Arts/Health Research Lead at the School of Arts, Design and Architecture at the University of Plymouth, United Kingdom. Sana's main research falls within the field of architecture, in particular the imaginative negotiations of spatial practices and social justice. She focuses on highlighting the impact of transient conditions of war, conflict, and displacement on people's creative spatial responses to sudden changes in their built environment and the making (or remaking) of the concept of home and collective imaginary housing for the future. Sana is the founder of the Displacement Studies Research Network and co-founder of the Justice and Imagination in Global Displacement research collective, working at the intersection between displacement, design, imagination, and justice. Her latest book is *Ruptured Architecture: Spatial Practices of Refuge in Response to War and Violence in Iraq 2003–2023* (2024). Written in the face of spatial wounding and the many injustices suffered by the Iraqi people, the book articulates the dual nature of rupturing as both a sign of trauma and a powerful act of resistance, examining how these forces shape homes, urban environments, and border spaces.

Francesco Pasta is an Istanbul-based urbanist and researcher focusing on community-led planning, displacement, and the spatial politics of urban transformation. He holds a PhD in Urban Planning, Design and Policy from Politecnico di Milano, where he examined development-induced displacement in Istanbul. From 2013 to 2016, he worked in Southeast Asia with the Asian Coalition for Housing Rights, the Community Architects Network, and affiliated practices as a community architect and coordination assistant. Since 2023, he has coordinated community planning initiatives in post-earthquake Antakya with Architecture Sans Frontières–UK and local partners. He is currently a Research Associate at the Istanbul Urban Observatory (IFEA) and an IPC-Mercator Research Fellow at the Istanbul Policy Centre, where he investigates how community-led planning can inform policy for just post-disaster reconstruction in Turkey.

Paola Pellegrini is an associate professor at the School of Architecture and Design of the American University of Beirut. She holds a bachelor's and a master's degree in Architecture and a PhD in Urbanistica from the Università IUAV di Venezia, Italy. She was an associate professor at the Design School of Xi'an Jiaotong – Liverpool University, Suzhou, China, a visiting associate in Urban Planning and Design at the Harvard Graduate School of Design, Cambridge MA, a visiting professor at the Universidade Estadual Paulista, Faculdade de Arquitetura, Artes e Comunicação, Brazil, and an adjunct associate professor at the Politecnico di Milano and at the Università IUAV di Venezia. Paola is a chartered architect in Italy, and has always combined academic work with multi-scalar professional practice. Thanks to a long international career and multiple research experiences, Paola has a broad knowledge of the urban, architectural, and social dimensions of the built environment and has published extensively in international journals and books. Her recent academic research explores sustainable urban regeneration, especially high-density residential neighbourhoods and resettlements.

Elliott Prasse-Freeman is an assistant professor and Presidential Young Professor in the National University of Singapore's Department of Sociology and Anthropology. He has conducted long-term fieldwork in Myanmar. His most recent book, *Rights Refused* (2023), focuses on Burmese subaltern political thought as adduced from an extended ethnography of activism and contentious politics in the country's semi-authoritarian setting.

Kieran Tam recently completed an MPhil in architecture and urban design at the University of Cambridge; his thesis was titled 'Beyond Humanitarianism: From States of Violence to Futures of Care in Northern France'. He was awarded the Dalibor Vesely Prize and RIBA Dissertation Medal Commendation for his research and design project on the migrant humanitarian crisis in Northern France, drawing primarily from three months of volunteer experience and situated research in Northern France relying on sensory ethnography and participatory methods. He is an advisory committee member for Calais Food Collective, a grassroots organization advocating for food and water autonomy for people on the move, with which he spent a year working on the ground.

Layla Zibar is a postdoctoral researcher affiliated with the Department of Architecture – Urban Design, Urbanism, Landscape, and Planning unit at Sint-Lucas Brussels/Ghent Campuses, KU Leuven University, Belgium. Her academic and professional interests focus on exploring the intricate connections between crises, forced displacement urbanisms, humanitarian interventions, post-conflict recovery, transitional and transformative justice, and the lived experiences of displaced individuals. She also works as an independent research consultant/academic trainer for (post-)war recovery, reconstruction, and house, land, and property rights (HLP) complex issues. Layla has a dual PhD degree in architecture and urbanism (2023) from BTU (DE) and KU Leuven (BE), an MSc in urban design, community development, and architectural engineering (Cairo University, Egypt, 2016), and a BA in architectural engineering (Aleppo University, Syria, 2010).

Acknowledgements

This book – like all editorial and collective endeavours – has had a long gestation. We have been shaping its structure and framework since 2021.[1] Originally conceived with four parts in mind, the book evolved into five, with a section on endurance replacing an initial part on exception. This change allowed us to welcome more voices, geographies, and perspectives, expanding the ways displacement is understood as urbanism.

The project was inspired by and developed in parallel with other reflections and publications on themes such as inhabitation, lifelines, home-making, and infrastructures of care (see Boano and Astolfo, 2020; Boano and Bianchetti, 2022; Astolfo, 2023; Boano et al, 2024; Astolfo et al, 2024).

Displacement Urbanism has grown into a process-driven book, bringing together a diversity of perspectives on displacement. While we propose a general framework, the chapters are not bound to a single monographic style. Instead, they operate as individual yet interconnected contributions, each offering a step towards collectively shaping a multifaceted understanding of displacement urbanism.

This book is not a conclusive output, but part of an ongoing process of co-producing research, advocacy, and capacity-building, initiated and led by the editors. It brings together early-career and senior scholars, activists, and migrant-scholars working at the forefront of displacement issues, through both institutional and personal partnerships.

We are deeply grateful to all the friends, colleagues, and contributors who have generously shared their experiences, ideas, and enduring support. The extended timeline of the project enabled more collaborators to join, and more space for new conversations and future projects to emerge.

During this long period, other books were published on displacement and its spatial, architectural, or planning dimension. They include: S. Pasquetti, and R. Sanyal (eds) *Displacement: Global Conversations on Refuge* (Manchester University Press, 2020); P. Adey, J.C. Bowstead, K. Brickell, V. Desai, M. Dolton, A. Pinkerton, and A. Siddiqi (eds) *The Handbook of Displacement* (Springer, 2020); S. Soedberg, *Urban Displacements: Governing Surplus and Survival in Global Capitalism* (Routledge, 2021); G. Baeten, C. Listerborn, M. Persdotter, and E. Pull, *Housing Displacement: Conceptual and Methodological Issues* (Routledge, 2021); L. Beeckmans, A. Gola, A. Singh, and H. Heynen, *Making Home(s) in Displacement: Critical Reflections on a Spatial Practice* (Leuven University Press, 2022); K. Strauss, *Geographies of Displacement/s* (Routledge, 2023); A.I. Siddiqi, *Architecture of Migration: The Dadaab Refugee Camps and Humanitarian Settlement* (Duke University Press, 2023); L. Lessard-Phillips, A. Papoutsi, N. Sigona, and P. Ziss, *Migration, Displacement and Diversity: The IRiS anthology Paperback* (Oxford University Press, 2023); S.A. Lichtman, and J. Traganou, *Design, Displacement, Migration Spatial and Material Histories* (Routledge, 2024); A.J. Knudsen, and S. Tobin, *Urban Displacement: Syria's Refugees in the Middle East* (Berghahn Books, 2024); T. Mayer, and T. Tran, *Displacement, Belonging, and Migrant Agency in the Face of Power* (Routledge, 2024); G. Jónsson, *Urban Displacement and Trade in a Senegalese Market: An Anthropology of Endings* (UCL Press, 2024); A. Sioli, N. Awan, and K. Palagi (eds) *Architectures of Resistance: Negotiating Borders Through Spatial Practices* (Leuven University Press, 2024); and the ongoing *Displacement Urbanism* podcast series by Romola Sanyal.[2] With them all – indirectly – we were able to think our contribution, constructing a constellation of possible thoughts.

We are grateful to everyone who has shared their experience, interest, and knowledge in the different chapters, at conferences, in email exchanges and through conversations. A special thanks goes to Harriet Allsopp for the thoughtful and careful support during the final curation process; to Ayesha Khalil during the initial stages of reading and commenting; to Catherine Sharp, Open Access Funding Manager at University College London; and to the Bristol University Press editorial team, particularly Emily Watt, for their support.

Notes

[1] See https://youtu.be/rFYvYgaw6kw?si=6cMUn40fJEQteD2h
[2] www.lse.ac.uk/geography-and-environment/research/displacement-urbanism-podcast

Introduction

Giovanna Astolfo

Displacement Urbanism is an examination of how we make sense of the co-constitutive relation of displacement and urbanization today. What does it mean that we live in a time of global protracted and overlapping displacement? What does it mean that displacement is integral to planetary urban (re)production? Can displacement offer a different understanding of the urban? These are important questions about what constitutes urban space and its relation to processes, conditions, and subjects. Disregarding whether a single answer is possible, this book advances a set of intersecting arguments. The first argument is that displacement remains embedded within – and constitutive of – the racial capital logics of accumulation and extraction that are the basis of the current mode of spatial production, its resulting inequalities, and the climate collapse. From Myanmar to Chile, from France to Uganda, from Italy to China, and across other many geographies, displacement is a form of urbanization on its own, as it produces spaces, landscapes, and territories that are imbricated in the management and control of lives – their exposure, incorporation, abandonment, and slow death. Intersecting biopolitics with theories on extraction and surplus production, the book presents displacement urbanism as a political technology that produces disposable and displaceable subjects.

The second argument is that the scale of extraction and expulsion has reached a global normalized level. It is the planetary scale of displacement that makes us think of it in a twofold way, as both an exo-endogenous force (a product of capitalism, a political technology and something immanent to urbanization) and a condition of life (disposability/displaceability). In this context, deploying the term 'displacement urbanism' has the advantage of locating the spatial and temporal condition of displacement within the complex and interrelated processes of global-scale economic and political organization with endless local and subjective variations. Such definition enables us to look across cases, spatialities, temporalities, and effects in an effort to put the universal and singular, the generalized and the embodied, in a meaningful conversation – necessarily stretching them over histories of colonialism, capitalism, racialization, extraction, and precarization.

The third and final argument advanced by the book is that the above is not sufficient to capture the complexity of lived experiences. If, on the one hand, displacement generates precarity, erosion, and debility, on the other hand, people continue to make lives in displacement. They gesture toward a critical presence by doing and undoing, by giving up and resisting. In this sense, framing displacement and urbanism as mutually integral allows for the possibility of questioning the apparent opposition between being displaced and making place. The book is a call to look at contexts and conditions of displacement beyond the idea of subtraction and absence – of a place, of a home, of a future. Across 12 chapters, the book unpacks the relation between the new normal global ontological condition of being displaced and the agent-full embodied action of making place, replacing, and emplacing bodies, communities and objects through stories, cases and spatial narratives. In so doing, the book offers a composite representation of displacement urbanism that holds together different agencies – oppression and liberation, exhaustion and endurance, uninhabitability and inhabitation – as conditions of possibility.

To clarify, the book employs the term 'displacement' to refer to a wide variety of phenomena, ontological conditions, and states of possibility to understand and analyse the politics and poetics of life in displacement. From relocation to gentrification to campization, the book moves beyond and away from disciplinary confinements and normative language. It leaves it to the different chapters to return the depth of the meaning of displacement, borrowing from distant literatures and learning from life. In the same way, the book employs the term 'urbanism' beyond its disciplinary territories to understand the complexity of processes and the socio-economic, cultural, and technical factors that go beyond the space/time assemblages and the contested nature of spaces.

Intersecting political economy, accumulation, and extraction theories with biopolitics, it examines and structures the relation of displacement and urbanism through different cycles of capital production applied to spaces and lives: extraction, expulsion, exhaustion, extinction, and endurance. Each cycle foregrounds displacement urbanism as a political technology that renders spaces, and by extension lives, disposable and displaceable in racialized and gendered ways. The disposable/displaceable subject is one who lives in a condition of perpetual displacement, as a way of being managed, continually reabsorbed by, and ultimately disposed of according to the logic of racial capital. Yet, beyond the inherent limits of different bio and necropolitical readings – which are discussed in Chapter 1 – the disposable/displaceable subject is also capable of escaping capture.

On the structure of the book and its chapters
Part I: Extraction

Extraction refers to the process of extraction of value from capital, land, and life that employs displacement as a central feature. It examines displacement urbanism as related to the instrumentalization and material destruction of specific lives. Extraction is centred around the idea of disposability/displaceability as annihilation, meaning the rendering bodies disposable (no longer needed to the reproduction of capital relations) and their consequent erosion, abandonment, and slow death. It refers to those situations in which displacement leads to the actual or sociopolitical death of bodies; to those contexts where life – including human life – has become increasingly surplus to capital, to the point where it cannot be reinscribed into logics of production. This is the case of workers in the extractive industries in Myanmar; and the case of the necro-agro-economy of the Southern Italian *caporalato*.

Chapter 2, by Elliott Prasse-Freeman, foregrounds the politics of displaceability, reflecting on the notion of postcolonial 'necroeconomy', where surplus workers are necessary for capital until the moment when their lives also become an object of extraction. Focusing on Myanmar's peri-urban assemblages, the chapter delves into what the author defines as a 'simple displacement squeeze': a situation where labourers end up self-exploiting in a manner that goes beyond the limits of bodily sustainability, through using pharmaceuticals to keep their bodies going or relying on multiple sources of debt. When bodies break down or land prices increase, displacement follows. The chapter shows how the interaction of two dispossession machines – driven by force and by the market – co-constitute one another and combine to build the built environment itself.

Chapter 3, by Sofia Moriconi, explains how, through the paradigmatic example of Castel Volturno, Italy, the simultaneous presence of a displaced population, cheap racialized labour, and abandoned houses creates the ideal conditions for the reproduction of exploitative and extractive systems. At the centre of this process are two characteristics: the condition of *zoé* (less than human life) to which the displaced are confined; and the continuous racialization of this form of life. It is precisely the element of race and those practices that racialize the workforce that build the premises for the endurance of exploitation and extraction, and for capital reproduction: the more the human differs from the 'white-heterosexual male', the more their work can be devalued. The case of Italian agribusiness epitomizes all of this, with little hope in sight.

Taken together, Prasse-Freeman's and Moriconi's chapters offer two distinct approaches to the necroeconomy to untangle the intricate relationships between labour, extraction, and displacement, as well as the spaces they produce, intersecting excess and survival. Both focus on migrant and displaced labourers, who neither capture the value they produce nor manage to transform their lives into stable ones, ultimately living 'out of place' and subsisting on the bare minimum for survival. Here, operations of capital intersect with, and even disregard, the continuum of life and death.

For Moriconi, it is the physical concentration of *zoé* (bare lives) – migrant cheap labour – and ruined buildings that plays a specific role in capital operations. It absorbs the excess of labour through racialization thus preventing delocalization. Excess is precisely what defines the territory: the interplay of human marginalization and physical decay reveals the copresence of multiple surpluses – excess labour and excess built environment, both of which require absorption, creating a dynamic where both human and physical resources are continuously exploited and ultimately discarded in ongoing cycles of extraction.

For Prasse-Freeman, cheap labour in and around Yangon is often just a parasitic presence, suggesting that people may be more valuable to capital when they are no longer alive. Pushed to the limit of survival by pharmaceutical sustainment to continue (self-)extraction, at some point bodies reach a breaking point. They stop reproducing themselves because they are so altered by the demands of capital that they become disabled. When this happens, debt starts, marking the beginning of the cycle of dispossession and displacement.

The potential for mobilization and repoliticization remains an open question, highlighting the need for future exploration of whether marginalized groups in places such as Castel Volturno or the periphery of Yangon can move into positions of strength and create a 'common politics of the displaceable', as Prasse-Freeman suggests.

Part II: Expulsion

This part returns to the notion of disposability/displaceability, but it examines its reincorporation into the logics of capital. Not all displaceable lives are deemed disposable or expendable – some are reabsorbed into the logics of racial capital production and accumulation because there is still an opportunity to extract value from them. Expulsion refers to all those contexts where people are moved around, made precarious through instability, but not annihilated. This part takes an approach to displacement based on the framework of accumulation by dispossession, or accumulation by displacement, thus examining cases of planetary gentrification and dispossession in China and Turkey.

Chapter 4 by Paola Pellegrini and Jinliu Chen offers a close reading of the case of Suzhou Industrial Park in the Yangtze River Delta. Here, displacement is explored as a governmental territorial strategy. It is framed through the relation between state-driven economic growth and the continuity of planning models devoted to capital extraction and population control.

Chapter 5 by Francesco Pasta centres on Fikirtepe, a neighbourhood in Istanbul. He discusses protracted mega projects of urban renewal and large-scale redevelopments and how the disposability–redevelopment nexus complexifies our understanding of urban disposability, framing it as a form of resistance where practices of recycling, upcycling, and downcycling adapt remaindered spaces to continue to extract value from waste.

In this part, destruction takes centre stage alongside expulsion, showcasing how it can be generative while sitting at the core of displacement urbanism. Creative destruction can either involve the remaking of entire cities and neighbourhoods, as in China, or buildings, as in Turkey. In both contexts, state propaganda and the illusion of economic growth and development are deeply intertwined with creative destruction processes. However, a key contrast between the two lies in the role, voice and agency of the people, all of which are notably absent in the chapter on the Suzhou Industrial Park, with individuals being represented as having limited power to resist disposability. In the case of Istanbul, in contrast, reflections point to urban disposability as a dynamic, generative, and stratified condition that is continuously remade, both as a driver of urban change and a context for everyday living.

Framed through the paradigm of expansion through expulsion, Pellegrini and Chen's analysis offers yet another lens on China's contemporary urbanization. They argue that the state-led model of urban development instrumentalizes land and people alike – treating land as disposable and populations as displaceable – in the pursuit of economic growth. This framing underscores displacement not as a side-effect but as a systemic strategy, sanctioned through planning regimes and legitimized by appeals to the public interest, which help pre-empt dissent. The chapter offers two key contributions. First, it foregrounds the rural–urban dichotomy as a central axis of dispossession, highlighting how rural populations remain structurally excluded from the urban value they help produce, thereby reinforcing their marginality. Second, it critiques the urbanity produced by this model: a built environment marked by alienation, repetition, and disregard for local specificity or community identity. Ultimately, the chapter exposes displacement as generative destruction as both a material and symbolic process. Yet, it leaves open the question of whether – and how – displacement as historical erasure might be acknowledged, compensated, or redressed.

Pasta's chapter examines displacement through urban disposability as a socio-spatial strategy in which areas marked for redevelopment are deliberately stigmatized and allowed to deteriorate to justify real estate-driven renewal. In this framing, buildings are rendered valuable through their destruction, becoming expendable assets in cycles of capital accumulation.

However, Pasta introduces the idea of augmented disposability, where delays and failures in redevelopment produce not just precarity, but temporal and spatial interstices – suspended periods where life persists. In these in-between moments, residents do not simply wait to be expelled; instead, they repair, maintain, and rework the space to their own ends. These practices challenge the narrative of disposability, revealing a social life within obsolescence and complicating linear accounts of displacement, and participating into the long durée of disposability, reworking it to different ends.

Part III: Exhaustion

This part centres on the original biopolitical reading of displacement and the camp, revisited through more recent approaches that point to issues of debility, wearing down, and erosion. Here, disposability/displaceability is once more at the centre of discourse and is intended both as suspension and immobilization, as well as hyper-mobilization. Exhaustion refers to all the forms of slow violence that are perpetrated through displacing and moving people around. This part focuses on the slow wearing out of migrants and refugees across Chile, France, and the Kurdistan region of Iraq.

Chapter 6 by Yasna Contreras Gatica explores how migrant women in northern Chile experience and respond to displacement by self-managing informal spaces, raising questions about housing as a human right in the context of urban inequality. Chapter 7 by Layla Zibar examines displacement and campization in the Kurdistan region of Iraq, showing how it is tied to long-term political and spatial transformations. Emphasis is placed on understanding the region's territorial biography, using both historical and ethnographic approaches. Chapter 8 by Stefano Mastromarino looks at Paris, where Black refugees inhabit displacement and reshape urban life through spaces of transit, abandonment, and resistance, challenging conventional notions of urbanity.

The juxtaposition of three distinct and distant territories in this part reveals how erosion and abandonment manifest across diverse geographies. In the Kurdistan region of Iraq, the enduring legacy of conflict and displacement has shattered communities and produced a landscape of despair. In Paris, urban life oscillates between care and hostility, where refugees and migrants navigate daily marginalization alongside moments of solidarity. In Chile's Grande Norte, migrant women and mothers struggle for safety and belonging amid the pressures of gentrification and informality. Across these cases, exhaustion emerges as a shared condition shaped by systemic political, social, and economic forces.

Each chapter highlights territories caught in ambivalent tensions: between removal and refuge, destruction and repair, hope and despair. Whether in metropolitan cities or borderless regions such as Kurdistan, exhaustion is to be understood through a politico-economic lens as the continuous possibility for extraction and reabsorption, where continuous displacement and dispossession make people hypermobile, fragile, precarious, and debilitated – as Scott (1988, quoted by Zibar in this book) puts it, 'converted into economically fragile subjects' and hence 'better object of political control'. Exhaustion emerges as a result of the continuous displacements, placements, and replacements that bring territories as much as subjects to a point of breakdown. It deeply intersects with the suffering, pain, and trauma felt by bodies and territories alike.

Through focusing on the spatial figures of *tugurios* and *campamentos*, Contreras Gatica's narrative reveals a complex tapestry of urban inequality where women become displaceable subjects through various structural forces, including market pressures, state negligence, conflict, and profit-seeking by small landowners. While the quest for shelter and security entails multiple movements and a state of hypermobility, for these women displacement also becomes a project – an insurgent practice of making home in the face of adversity. As one of them argues, '[We, the displaced and evicted] are in the process of building your city.'

By treating the territory itself as both the object and subject of the narrative, Zibar's chapter excavates the entanglement of shifting powers – be they religious, tribal, or humanitarian – in determining waves of removal, replenishment, hosting, protecting, and homemaking in the Kurdistan region of Iraq. This region exists within unrecognized borders, its landscape shaped by endless cycles of rejection and reception to the point of exhaustion. Zibar's gesture of 'rewriting presence' through archaeological and historical excavation becomes a means of reclaiming agency and the visibilization of experiences that is often overlooked.

Mastromarino's chapter delves into the intricate interstitial spaces of greater Paris, where refugees inhabit displacement and navigate across emergency and endurance in their journey to Calais and the United Kingdom. Displacement urbanism, in this context, is depicted not as an exception but as the quotidian reality of being abandoned, eroded, and left behind. Different spatial subjectivities emerge, which challenge and question conventional notions, meanings, and substance of settlement, pointing toward a politics of unsettling, nomadism, uprootedness, and opacity. In this sense, displacement may be seen as 'a new form of urbanity' – one that embraces fluidity and complexity rather than fixed boundaries and identities.

Part IV: Extinction

This part reflects on disposability/displaceability related to the creation of uninhabitable spaces, shatter, or waste zones – areas of ruination, segregation, neglect, and abandonment where territorial destruction, 'wounding', and more-than-human death entangle. Here, displacement becomes associated with different forms of spatial violence, whether ecological assaults, multiple disasters, or war beyond repair; but the law also comes to the fore in all its violence. The induced extreme precarity inherent to the displaceability of inhabitants connects directly with spatial logics of territorial and ecological violence and with processes of nationalism, identity, and law enforcement. In turn, extractive forms of violence are legitimated in the name of climate change, ecological reparation, and disaster preparedness. This part focuses on war-wounded territories in Iraq and ecologically disposable communities in disaster-hit Turkey.

Chapter 9 by Sana Murrani, Dhirgham Alobaydi and Ula Merie focuses on Baghdad's post-2003 US invasion displacement urbanism, mobilizing the idea of place wounding and referring specifically to political agendas, socio-spatial patterns of trauma (ethnic and religious divides), and the environmental crisis unfolding across the country. It explores how these have generated a complex palimpsest of temporality and protractedness of displacement in the city. With the use of very grounded material developed in years of engagement with the city, the chapter positions displacement urbanism in the tensions between spatial injustices and urban violence, intersecting with landscape, housing, and master-planning as complicit in the promotion of a post-war city.

Chapter 10 by Eray Çaylı explores how the Disaster Law recently issued in Turkey served to impose forms of displacement, mobilizing images of ecologies and preparedness. The chapter specifically looks at two self-built neighbourhoods from opposite ends of Turkey: a racialized working-class neighbourhood in Istanbul and another on the banks of the Tigris River in Amed/Diyarbakır. Through a critique of the architecture of state policy imposition, Çaylı makes visible the experiences of displacement by state-endorsed colonial-rooted developmentalism and the disaster preparedness discourses complicit in purposing authoritarian urban and spatial development.

In both chapters, extinction foregrounds the symbolic and material destruction of specific territories, which leaves behind deep wounds – most often beyond repair – as captured by the notion of 'rupture' in Murrani, Alobaydi and Merie's Chapter 9. This chapter delves into the profound socio-spatial ruptures caused by the US-led invasion of Iraq, which triggered massive displacement and destruction. While the invasion was a major event, the resulting displacement was also shaped by pre-existing policies of exclusion and segregation, now intersecting with climate and environmental crises to produce 'multiple temporal ruptures across material, geographical, and socio-spatial dimensions'. The chapter employs various lenses to examine the spatiality and continuity of violence and its traumatic legacies. Concepts such as 'geotrauma', 'place wounding', 'rupture', 'urbicide', and 'domicide' illuminate the ways in which war destruction, planning policies, and climate policies affect both the physical landscape and the psychological well-being of individuals and communities, overlapping ideas of place and space with violence, pain, and trauma.

Climate, environment, disasters, and the neoliberal-colonial discourse that surround them, is central to Eray Çaylı's chapter, which delves into the intersection of urban violence, place, and disaster preparedness politics, revealing how policies, ostensibly designed to protect communities, often serve to further marginalize and displace vulnerable populations. In Turkey, Çaylı argues, disaster preparedness is deployed through a neoliberal-colonial logic that frames certain populations and territories as 'undevelopable' – and thus disposable. In this framework, development prioritizes control and profit over social and environmental well-being, reinforcing cycles of displacement and exclusion. Çaylı characterizes this phenomenon as misdevelopment. Despite the systemic challenges it brings, the chapter foregrounds the resilience and agency of affected communities, which craft strategies not just to survive but to assert their right to the very promises – order, safety, and security – that state policies claim to uphold.

Centring community voices, the chapter also reveals how individualistic survival dynamics can edge towards extinction. As one fisherman reflects, 'If fish species are disappearing, that's because the Tigris River is dying. And if the river is dying, that's due to the dams ... The extensive damage they cause is not worth it – there's a different objective at work ... to not let anyone live except one's own, just like what the Prussian carp does.' It is precisely through this metaphor of selective survival that the chapter powerfully speaks to extinction.

Despite the grim landscapes portrayed in these two chapters, Murrani, Alobaydi and Merie offer a provocative idea: displacement as 'a process of housing'. While it uproots people and often forecloses return, it also compels them to adapt and reimagine home.

Part V: Endurance

This part builds on Part IV, inserting a glimpse of timid pragmatic hope into the otherwise stark realities of global displacement. Here, the condition of disposability, which intersects that of displaceability (the uninhabitable) becomes a form of endurance. Displaceability comes to refer less to a condition of being made disposable and more to a condition of living with the trouble. This part embraces current approaches that point to new politico-ethico-epistemologies to stay with the trouble of displacement, living the wound and confronting the negative as a commitment to the present, and scoping for other possibilities. It includes reflections on how refugees make lives outside camps in small and medium-sized cities in Uganda and in Northern France.

Chapter 11 by Peter Kasaija offers a reflection on modalities of endurance adopted by refugees who have moved from gazetted refugee settlements and self-settled in Arua City. Protracted displacement is at the centre of the narrative of the chapter. It is evident that self-settled refugees are caught up in complex socio-spatial transitions across time and place as they negotiate how to inhabit places outside formally established refugee settlements.

Chapter 12 by Kieran Tam and Irit Katz delves into the complex spaces of Calais, the cusp of the European continent and a place of many conflicting dualities: defence and reception, hospitality and hostility, development and decline. Reflecting on humanitarian and migratory imaginaries, the chapter seeks to reimagine the relationship Calais has with the border and the people who live in and pass through it. It offers a vision for alternative futures, where migrants are not excluded but rather embraced as part of the city's evolving identity.

In this part, but also in earlier parts, we see displacement intersecting the notion of un/inhabitability – how people can live in extreme spaces that frame them as sub-humans, as invisible, undeserving and unworthy. It is also a reminder of the importance of learning from the ways in which people themselves make sense of displacement or even live 'besides' the need to make sense. This means going beyond thinking that the world is as it is because we can think of it as such. Indeed, this part offers a triangulation of 'living with the trouble' conditions: on the one hand, a border territory (Calais) that is caught between multiple tensions of solidarity and rejection, care and violence, removal and refuge practices; on the other hand, an urban territory (Arua) that attracts people who end up in a condition of invisibility.

In Arua City, Kasaija explains how refugees find themselves invisible to policy and planning frameworks, unable to accessing basic services such as housing, healthcare, and education on their own. Left alone to fend for themselves in their struggle from destitution to self-reliance, this invisibility can lead to feelings of helplessness and despair, with some individuals resorting to suicide. Despite these challenges, solidarity exists within the community, with local leaders sometimes incorporating refugees into the provision of certain services – albeit informally and opaquely. 'Endurance in this context is conceptualized as the intersection of disposability and displaceability, two conditions that characterize the everyday lives of self-settled refugees who are differently positioned temporally in a context where their spatiality has been delegitimized by the prevailing policy, legal and institutional regime.' The existing policy and politics – or the lack of them – make individuals disposable, while endurance is a form of surviving within such disposability, alternating moments of political agency with helplessness. Kasaija unpacks the contradictions inherent in this condition, where refugees are simultaneously approached as out of place, and 'thus their presence or existence negated', while remaining visible members of society, 'their visibility exposing the irrationality and impracticality of these entrenched policy systems'.

Tam and Katz invite us to think of Calais otherwise, as a sanctuary rather than a hostile border, without romanticizing the idea and remaining cognizant of the fact that humanitarianism always comes with the risk of more bordering practices. Calais is an urban ruin where people on the move find temporary shelter, but also face scorched earth policies, to the point where, as the authors put it, 'humanitarian interventions are there to "hold off deaths"'. Yet, by 'reattempting Channel crossings, building and rebuilding shelters, and through protests, memorials, and squatting, migrants perform daily acts of citizenship and continuously claim to meaningful lives'. In response to the availability of ruins in the border territory, Tam and Katz provocatively suggest the concept of a Special Care Zone (SCZ) based on transit citizenship. This proposal challenges traditional notions of hospitality and citizenship, offering a novel framework for providing care and support to migrants in transit.

A note about the book's curation, methodologies, and positionalities

By engaging with the themes of extraction, expulsion, exhaustion, extinction, and endurance, each chapter in this book contributes to a broader conversation about the complex interplay between displacement, urban dynamics, and spatial practices. Each chapter can be taken in isolation, as a finite narrative of displacement and in conversation with the overall framework of displacement urbanism, but also, in conversation with other chapters, offering a complementary or opposite view of each theme, and even incorporating multiple themes. For example, Pasta's Chapter 5 focuses on expulsion, but by looking at urban decay, it also examines exhaustion as a form of extraction of all the possible value from building and spaces and peoples before their destruction; moreover, it discusses ways of staying with the trouble, enduring a protracted disposability. The same can be said for Mastromarino's Chapter 8, which examines spaces of holding existing as a form of endurance while acknowledging the continuous exhaustion and wearing down of Black and Brown bodies in the European hostile city.

The five themes of the book are not mutually exclusive; rather, they are interrelated and coexist within the diverse contexts of displacement urbanism. This approach reflects the complexity and contradictions of displacement, resisting linear or cyclical frameworks in favour of a multifaceted understanding. By acknowledging the intersecting factors – social, political, spatial, and temporal – this book offers a more nuanced reading of displacement urbanism. It invites readers to consider the contradictory, layered nature of displacement as it unfolds within urban life.

Methodologically, contexts, conditions, and effects of displacement are captured in a variety of ways, from drone flights to urban walks, discourse analysis, mapping, and territorial biographies. The authors' diverse backgrounds and positionalities further complexify the exploration of displacement urbanism. Some authors identify as displaced individuals; others offer insights from a variety of vantage points, such as scholars, activists, volunteers, humanitarian workers, and dwellers – across North and South, East and West. While providing an exhaustive account of the different politics of location across all 13 chapters is complex and difficult in the short span of an introduction, let be said that this diversity of perspectives allows for a comprehensive examination of displacement from various angles and contexts.

The chapters also highlight the importance of centring the voices and experiences of displaced individuals, with many chapters incorporating personal narratives and embedding the voices of others within the narrative. Most chapters show an interest in the messy, nuanced quotidian of displacement, rather than on its grand narratives. All, in different ways, question and deconstruct prevailing narratives around displacement. Whether examining dispossessory machines, the long durée of urban obsolescence, ambivalent spaces, or housing processes, the chapters centre the lived experiences, struggles, and agencies of displaced individuals and communities around the world.

The ruin, the camp, and the shelter-home: spatial figures, practices, and tensions across the chapters

The book also offers an engagement with a series of spatial figures, practices, and tensions, creating further connections beyond the five themes. The figures of the ruin, the camp, and the shelter-home in particular emerge in several chapters, offering a lens through which to examine the complex dynamics of space, territory, and socio-economic realities.

In both Fikirtepe, at the urban periphery of Istanbul, and in the outskirts of Castel Volturno, the figure of the ruin is a significant motif embodying various connotations. First, it symbolizes shelter and protection, providing a space of refuge for marginalized individuals such as migrants, refugees, and outcasts. Its accessibility and the inherent promise of a new beginning underscore its appeal as a haven for those in need. Moreover, the ruin represents a liminal space, existing at the end of one cycle yet holding the potential for a fresh start. In this sense, it embodies both decay and regeneration, offering a glimpse into the perpetual cycle of destruction and creation that affects buildings as much as territories and bodies. The contrasting treatments of the ruin in the two locations – Italy and Turkey – highlight its adaptability to different socio-economic contexts.

In Fikirtepe, the ruin is subject to care and repair, suggesting a practice of endurance amidst the constant threat of breakdown. This reflects a sense of attachment and investment in the space (although a minimal one), despite its dilapidated state. As Pasta puts it, the ruin is also 'always ready to be vacated with the lowest margin of loss', revealing how people make their calculations, knowing that they cannot capture the value and there is no point in putting in too much effort. By holding low expectations, ruins are more viable as a refuge. On the other hand, in Castel Volturno, the ruin is integrated into the infrastructure of excess, serving as a resource to be endlessly extracted in a process of endless vitalism. Here, the ruin embodies a sense of expendability, with little effort expended on its maintenance or preservation. This reflects a pragmatic approach to space, where the low expectations associated with the ruin make it a viable option for refuge.

The theme of ruin in the book transcends single physical structures to encompass neighbourhoods, territories, and even bodies. In Pellegrini and Chen's Chapter 4, ruins are intentionally produced – entire neighbourhoods are built with programmed obsolescence, whereby deterioration is embedded into the logic of development. Murrani, Alobaydi and Merie similarly explore rupture as a form of ruin in Chapter 9, noting that cities and architecture experience repeated breaks over time, often due to natural or structural ageing. This concept extends to the body in Prasse-Freeman's account of migrant workers in Myanmar in Chapter 2, where Pasta's idea of 'ruins maintained at the edge of liveability, but just enough to keep things going for the moment' resonates. Here, bodily ruin is manifest in the self-exploitation and pharmaceutical use that sustain workers just enough for them to keep functioning.

The camp, in its sociopolitical and philosophical reading of space and territory, emerges as a recurrent figure in the book. While displacement urbanism does not explicitly focus (solely) on the campization of cities or the urbanization of camps, it subtly integrates these themes. Moriconi's Chapter 3 touches on the concept of racialized territory and the existence of *zoé* (bare lives), connecting these ideas to the camp and extending them beyond it. In Chapter 8, Mastromarino further explores the camp as a threshold, analysing spaces that exist between the city and the camp, embodying characteristics of both yet fully belonging to neither. He also emphasizes that the concept of the camp is not confined to traditional camp boundaries, but has infiltrated urban spaces. Camp-like conditions are prevalent throughout the city, though they interact with and are influenced by other urban elements. In the context of Greater Paris, for example, interstitial spaces and networks of charitable solidarity provide a minimal infrastructure that allows for temporary survival. The notion of the camp emerges also in the biographical narratives of the

Kurdistan Region of Iraq in Zibar's Chapter 7, and the Calais migrant conditions in Tam and Katz's Chapter 12. While not always the central focus, the presence and influence of camp-like conditions permeate these accounts, demonstrating the pervasive impact of such spaces on both individual lives and broader sociopolitical landscapes.

The third spatial figure that permeates many reflections in the book is that of the shelter-home as a dynamic space – a relation, a way of being, and a promise. This concept is particularly prominent in Contreras Gatica's Chapter 6, where it is envisioned as a trajectory of struggle toward protection, refuge, and security. In Chapter 9, Murrani, Alobaydi and Merie discuss the idea of home in its processual form and in direct relation with displacement. The authors argue that 'displacement is a process of housing', referring to the way the pursuit of a home, its protection, and its stability in conditions of protracted displacement reshapes the social and spatial fabric of 'cities, villages and borders, meanwhile blurring the boundaries between instability and making that come with the stability of housing'.

A range of spatial practices emerge in this book – such as refuge-granting, protection-seeking, home- and place-making, repairing, and maintaining; these are intricately linked to the three spatial figures of the ruin, the camp, and the shelter-home. Refuge-granting involves offering shelter and safety, formally or informally, as seen in places such as the Kurdistan region or Greater Paris. Protection-seeking is the pursuit of safety, often through legal systems or support networks that guard against eviction or deportation. Home- and place-making refer to creating a sense of belonging – through routines, personalized spaces, or community ties – even in precarious conditions, such as in Istanbul. Repairing includes both fixing physical spaces and healing the social and emotional ruptures caused by displacement, such as women's labour in Chile, or recycling in Istanbul. Maintaining captures the everyday work of keeping spaces livable amid instability – resisting eviction, managing access, and holding together informal systems. Together, these embodied spatial practices shape how displacement is lived, negotiated, and resisted.

Many of these practices exist within ambivalent conditions – between hospitality and hostility, between being displaced and granting refuge. For instance, in Chapter 7, Zibar illustrates how refuge-granting practices shape territories as significantly as removals and resettlements, turning these areas into hosts for displaced populations. Similarly, in Chapter 8, Mastromarino explains how spaces designated for holding in Paris coexist with spaces of abjection, reflecting the dual nature of displacement as both exclusionary and relational. Here, displacement is depicted as simultaneously subtractive and projective, divisive yet capable of fostering relationships, as even negative interactions create a form of relationship.

Alongside these practices, the book brings to the forefront several tensions, especially between law and planning, development and modernity, violence and trauma. Dispossession – particularly violent dispossession – is frequently sanctioned by legal frameworks, regulations, and planning practices. In China, this relationship is explicit, but Myanmar and Turkey are also notable examples. Çaylı's Chapter 10 focuses extensively on how disaster laws in Turkey contribute to displacement, intersecting with colonial legacies and neoliberal agendas. In these countries, displacement is portrayed as a governmental tool, though the government is not the only actor involved. Building on Yiftachel, in Chapter 2 Prasse-Freeman illustrates how different 'dispossessionary machines' – as related to either the market or planning and policy – intersect. While Yiftachel's concept highlights differences in displacement processes between northern and southeastern regions (including in terms of actors and agencies), Prasse-Freeman shows us that they overlap in practice.

Several chapters underscore the tension between development and displacement, linked to specific notions of modernity and progress. This theme is particularly evident in China, the Kurdistan region of Iraq, Chile, and Turkey, as well as within humanitarian frameworks in Uganda. State rhetoric often equates urbanization with modernity, casting rural areas as antithetical to progress. This perspective, which combines economic growth with urbanization, is explored in Pellegrini and Chen's Chapter 4 and in Zibar's Chapter 7, with reference to the 'transformation of the village dweller into an urban dweller' (Pyla, 2006, quoted in Zibar's chapter). The relationship between modernity, development, and urbanity plays a critical role in driving displacement, removals, and resettlements in Chile, as well as erasures – even when projects fail or do not commence (as seen in Turkey and the Kurdistan region of Iraq). In Uganda, the shortcomings of the nexus between the humanitarian and development systems render those who move to cities invisible, highlighting a facet of this tension.

Many chapters reveal the intricate tension between displacement and violence, which emerges in both objective and subjective forms. Violence is not always overt; it can be perceived, normalized, and embedded within the very condition of displaceability. Migrant workers in countries such as Myanmar, Italy, and Chile, among others, often experience this violence – whether they are aware of it or not. This violence can stem from individual actors, such as landlords or border agents, or from broader structural systems such as housing and disaster policies, migration regimes, development agendas, and markets. Across contexts, the book shows how displacement often entails a continuum of violence – visible and invisible, direct and systemic – that shapes the everyday realities of those affected. It also intersects with personal stories and trajectories of emancipation, abolition, and liberation. Indeed, the book does not present the displaced as merely victims of violence; rather, within their precarity and suffering, they emerge as spatial agents. Across the chapters, there are multiple sociopolitical projects that reterritorialize and reposition people in history, cartographies, society, and the future, once more emphasizing such duality of displacement as both a violent condition and a force that reorganizes social and spatial structures.

This is not to downplay the trauma, pain, and suffering that accompany displacement – realities that permeate most chapters of the book. These experiences appear through personal testimonies, observations, and shared narratives. Trauma is embodied in the disabled, debilitated, and chemically sustained bodies in Prasse-Freeman's Chapter 2, and in the personal and collective territorial trauma explored by Zibar in Chapter 7. In Chapter 9, Murrani, Alobaydi and Merie centre concepts such as place-wounding and geotrauma, while in Chapter 6, Contreras Gatica recounts the emotional toll on migrant women. Kasaija shares stories of mental health struggles in Chapter 11, including a woman's suicide attempt. Intergenerational trauma also emerges in Zibar's discussion of the Kurdish experience, marked by cycles of eviction, genocide, and forced assimilation. These experiences of pain, suffering, and trauma, along with political and spatial agency and solidarity among people in situations of prolonged or recent displacement, form both the backdrop to and the foreground of all chapters.

Altogether, the 13 chapters offer a renewed engagement with a series of spatial figures, practices and tensions emerging from the complex interrelation of urbanization and displacement, life and death, and politics and space across a variety of contexts. They also provide a snapshot of the current state of discussion around biopolitics (multiple) as well as demonstrate how such an important and long-debated framework is still valid to better capture, visibilize, and historicize what we term displacement urbanism and its planetary diffusion. The value of the book, however, is in its continued efforts to interrogate the complex subjectivities and spatialities that are emerging under contemporary conditions of displacement beyond abstract, disembodied notions. Connecting different territories and research approaches, we hope to have foregrounded displacement urbanism as a project, an ontology, a relation, a lived experience of loss, pain, and liberation and, most often, just survival.

1

Framing Displacement Urbanism

Giovanna Astolfo and Camillo Boano

'The best reading is the uncertain reading', as Robert Glück (2009) reminds us. A reading that disorients us and leaves us bewildered. 'But what if the intention of the writing is to throw us into confusion, to provoke a state of wonder, and to unravel the fundamentals of our experience?' wonders Glück. Maybe this is the real question that introduces this book. Displacement urbanism disorients us and requires us to read uncertainly precisely because it undermines our awareness, certainty, and security about what regimes displacement and the form of urbanization it portends constitute an imaginary of territory and space.

It is curious that we stumbled upon Robert Glück's quotation while reading another book, Elvia Wilk's (2022) *Death by Landscape*, through an epigraph on p 239. Why curious? Not so much for the assonance of the two texts to unearth an alternative narrative and vocabulary for thinking about the future, or for the proximity to feminist and decolonial intellectual coordinates, or for a critique of colonial solutionism of conquest and domination, but rather for the title of Wilk's book. The intentionality of landscape – of its form, of its thought, to cause death – opens up assumptions of responsibility, which make its reading uncertain and recall a non-naturalness, a lack of innocence proper to modern thought in thinking the nature, the form, and the agency of displacement.

This chapter provides the intellectual scaffolding of the book and locates it in relation to current discourses in architecture and planning, geography, and forced migration, and across instances of feminist, decolonial, Southern, and critical urban theory. It examines displacement urbanism through its constituent terms – 'urban' and 'displacement' – and the in-between spaces created by these terms. It encompasses literature on urban displacement from a political economy to a biopolitical perspective, to highlight the co-constitutive nature of displacement and the urban. From the urbanization of refuge, through the camp-city, to frameworks of primitive accumulation and necropolitics, displacement emerges as immanent to the urban. The chapter continues by contextualizing displacement urbanism with regard to the current state of ruination, with an emphasis on the fragility of the human and non-human condition. In this context, acknowledging our precariousness and precarity brings renewed centrality to the meaning, role, and value of life. What is at stake when we speak of life? The chapter suggests that the importance of extinction is premised upon the fact that life has an inherent value, and this matters to displacement.

Taking life as a starting point, the chapter connects displacement urbanism more explicitly with the complex and rich developments of the biopolitical framework. The aim is to provide an account of how the politics of life (its management and protection) is imbricated in the production of the urban and as such structures what we have termed displacement urbanism. Here, displacement urbanism is framed as a political technology that controls, governs, constitutes, exposes, and ultimately disposes of life in, across, and beyond spaces, in the process taking seriously its productive and morphological agency over territories and ecologies. The chapter also attempts to go beyond the critical frame of biopolitics and necropolitics, towards an affirmative politics of more-than-human life, complicating, deepening, and enriching it by incorporating instances from (new) materialism and posthumanism, and providing a glimpse of hope within such a grim scenario.

The co-constitution of displacement and urbanism

From rural enclosures and mass population displacement of colonial conquest to socio-politico-environmental conflicts, military occupations, and uneven (neoliberal) development, from global land grabs to neo-apartheids, urban displacement is not an exceptional phenomenon, circumscribed to certain cities, epochs, or specific events. Instead, it is a persistent condition and a transnational practice that links across scales, times, and territories. Academic contributions point to how, globally, displacement cannot be viewed as a discrete time-framed phenomenon. Instead, displacement is a processual and unfolding moment that always overlaps with other forms of motions-mobilities (Fiddian-Qasmiyeh, 2020; Brun, 2015; Fiddian-Qasmiyeh and Qasmiyeh, 2016; Brun and Fabos, 2017; Pasquetti and Sanyal, 2020) and subalternity (Roy, 2011; Sanyal, 2012; Scott 1986) in increasingly prolonged exile-type contexts.

Beyond a singular incident – whether eviction, relocation, deportation, or regeneration – urban displacement is an ongoing state of being (Delaney, 2004), a situation of continuous displaceability (Yiftachel, 2020), a normality (Roast et al, 2022), and an 'accrual' that 'over time and through repetition ... solidifies as something enduring' (Strauss, 2022). Such permanent temporariness (Hilal and Petti, 2018; Isayev, 2021) calls for thinking 'less of endings and more of turning points that allow for a repositioning of the self in relation to the world' (Isayev, 2021, p 33). Seethaler-Wari et al (2022) further insist on the relationship of displacement with time, especially with how we become displaced *in* time, or outside the timeframe of modernity: 'By doing so, the project of modernity not only displaces space in/through time, making its colonization possible, it displaces itself in return. Thus, the modern subject is a displaced subject' (2022: 12).

The spatial and temporal ubiquity of displacement, its longitudinal scale of unfolding, and planetary diffusion suggest a closer examination of its relationship with the urban and its processes. Urbanization is a millennial trend that alters humanity's relationship with itself and with the planet, and that blurs the distinction between rural and urban (Brenner and Schmid, 2014; Brenner, 2018). In this sense, displacement and urbanization are not separate and independent processes. Rather, displacement concurs with the blurring of the urban–rural distinction by contributing to processes of *frontierization* (Schofield, 2020), *peripheralization* (Caldeira, 2017), and dislocation of urban populations. In this sense, displacement urbanizes urban edges, interstices, and rural areas as part of a capitalistic logic of continuous growth.

The urban/displacement relationship has been widely examined from different disciplinary, conceptual, and empirical angles, as well as from different geographies and even terminologies (Lees, 2012; Hirsh et al, 2020). Some literature looks at displacement and the urban as distinct phenomena that intersect, while others look at urban displacement, meaning the becoming urban of the phenomenon – for instance, how refugees end up in cities rather than in camps. However, the opposite has also been the object of extended study – that is, the fact that camps become cities as the result of the protraction of displacement. Some literature is more focused on what the urban characteristics of displacement are – for example, the presence of differentiated and distributed agencies and practices of place-making – and this has substantially changed the overall approach to displacement. In short, the examination of the urban/displacement relationship has taken different trajectories in recent literature. This book specifically engages with four strands: forced migration, camps, and border studies concerned with the urbanization of displacement and refuge; the political economy approach to urban processes of dispossession and production of surplus spaces; the biopolitical frame employed to examine displacement as a political technology of government; and those views that foreground the role of race and coloniality in relation to urban displacement.

Urbanizing the debate on displacement

As part of the so-called urban turn, studies on forced migration, camps, and borders are concerned with the urbanization of refuge (Grabska, 2006;

Sanyal, 2012; Darling, 2016; Herscher, 2017; Basu and Asci, 2020), with the integration of the camps into the urban (Fawaz, 2016; Katz et al, 2018; Mandic, 2018; Alkhalili, 2019), and more generally with the becoming urban of displacement (Malkki, 1995; Campbell, 2006; Crisp, 2010; Zetter, 2011; Darling, 2020) at the intersection with informality (Corsellis and Vitale, 2005; Roy, 2011; Sanyal, 2012; Huq and Miraftab, 2020) and with migrant agencies in urban settings (Brickell and Datta, 2011; Glick Schiller and Çağlar, 2011; Hall, 2015; Kreichauf et al, 2022).

The 'urbanity' of camps and resettlement sites, their contested nature (Agier, 2002; Albanski et al, 2021), and how camps urbanize into durable socio-spatial formations (Sanyal, 2012; Pasquetti and Picker, 2017) are also substantive parts of urbanizing the debate concerning displacement. The camp has also been linked to the city as a metaphor for segregation, destitution, and suspension (Diken and Laustsen, 2005), while in turn the urban has been used as an analytical frame to interrogate the camp (Martin and Taylor, 2020). Other literature traces the connections between the camp and the city (Qasmiyeh and Fiddian-Qasmieh, 2013) or attempts to dissolve the binary camp/city into the trope of inhabitation (Seethaler-Wari et al, 2022).

From a different angle, the co-constitutive nature of displacement and urbanism is pointed at by highlighting degrees of urban and spatial agency in displacement, widely documented forms and practices of de/re-territorialization (Raffestin, 2012; Rasmussen and Lund, 2017; Halvorsen et al, 2019; Lombard, 2021), spatial violations (Maqusi, 2019), squatting, occupation, and transformation (Simone, 2004; Sanyal, 2013; Vasudevan, 2017; Martin and Taylor, 2020), Southern encounters and hospitality (Fiddian-Qasmieh, 2016; Musmar, 2020, 2022) and, more generally, (re)inhabiting spaces and practices and negotiating the uninhabitability of displacement (Seethaler-Wari et al, 2022; Simone, 2016). They also indicate how making place and being displaced are not necessarily in contradiction/opposition, while displacement does not signal just a tempo-spatial rupture but also a re-spatialization across the spacetime.

Dispossessing spaces and producing surplus bodies

Influenced by the Marxist critique of space (Lefebvre, 1974; Massey, 1994), geographers and architects have examined the relationship between dispossession and the urban through value extraction and surplus production. Harvey's (2005) reformulation of primitive accumulation foregrounds how the occupation of urban space and land, as well as the exploitation of displaced groups, creates and captures value. Through this reading, the creation of surplus value within capitalist relations is premised upon the dispossession and displacement of previous occupiers (Harvey, 2005). Twenty years later, this framework has certainly not been exhausted. It has been complemented by the emergence of different trajectories, which reinforce how urban space is the product of (global) capitalist relations and thus displacement is functional to the commodification and financialization of the city (Swyngedouw et al, 2002; Li, 2010; Hall, 2013; Marcuse, 2013; Sassen, 2001, 2014; Lees et al, 2016; Shen and Wu, 2017; Tarazona Vento, 2017; Wang and Wu, 2019; Elliott-Cooper et al, 2020, among many others).

Primitive accumulation places violence front and centre in the discussion of urban displacement – whether violence is organized (Springer, 2013), spatial (Herscher and Siddiqi, 2019), planned (Boehmer and Davies, 2018), slow (Nixon, 2013), or systemic (Elliott-Cooper et al, 2020). In this light, displacement is a form and practice of extreme violence to the city and what it represents, a creative/destructive effort that dismantles a given urban order to create a new one, where the new is predicated upon the erasure of the old. Notions of territorialization and urban frontier spaces related to capitalism expansion clarify such a concept (Wade, 1959; Elden, 2010, 2013; Kelly and Peluso, 2015; Rasmussen and Lund, 2017; Bou Akhar, 2018; Blomley, 2019; Beverley, 2013; Cons, 2019).

Through this framework, the making of urban space is also imbricated in processes of production of subjects – in this case, the displaced. As part of the accumulative drive, bodies become valuable and tradeable through the same capitalistic logic. Although not related strictly to the urban context, Nail's (2016) *The Figure of the Migrant* and his kinopolitics play a central role in this line of thought. Kinopolitics is a political theory that focuses on the migrant instead of the citizen, moving beyond the nation-state and assuming migrancy as a permanent condition rather than an exception. What is relevant to the argument around displacement urbanism here is Nail's idea of 'expansion by expulsion', which radicalizes Marx's primitive accumulation and according to which the migrant is a product. Kinopolitics arises at certain specific moments when the expulsion of certain populations – such as the proletariat – becomes necessary for the consolidation of power. All societies, as Nail argues, have developed an ability for expansion premised upon forms of social expulsion where the migrant is the figure of such expulsion.

Intersections with bodies: biopolitical frames

Intersecting with the logic of value extraction but shifting the angle from the (politics of) space to the (politics of the) body, Foucauldian readings of the displacement–urban nexus abound. Most have been framed through a biopolitical lens according to which (urban) displacement is the spatial expression of the logic of 'making live and letting die', a formula that Foucault developed in his lectures at the College de France (1975–79) and that we will examine more closely below. Biopolitics has been used widely to explain how displacement operates as a technology of government to consolidate powers and a technique to produce kinds of subjects. In this light, displacement is seen as exogenous process that pushes around, expels, and removes unwanted and disqualified bodies. Operated by outside forces, the bodies of the displaced – 'the homeless, the refugees, the deportable aliens, the indefinitely detained asylum seekers, the removed indigenous peoples, and the vagrants' (Delaney, 2004: 849) – are objects in a process of de-subjectification.

As Minca et al (2022) remind us, after the translation of Agamben's *Homo Sacer*, biopolitical readings of the space of the camp have proliferated, spatializing Agamben's work, his ideas of bare life, the state of exception, and destituent and inoperative power (Hyndman, 2000; Diken et al, 2005; Ek, 2006; Elden, 2006; Minca, 2007; Ramadan, 2009; Hanafi et al, 2010; Sanyal 2012; Mastromarino and Boano, 2023; Minca et al, 2022). These have also included several critiques of the inherent limitations of such reading (Pratt, 2005; Comaroff and Comaroff, 2007; Owens, 2009; Sanyal, 2013; Martin, 2015; Sigona, 2015), particularly in terms of neglecting the kind of agency, identity, subjectivity, and intersectionality that refugees, migrants, and displaced individuals might have. The literature also distinguishes between bio and necropolitical views – with the latter to be found in postcolonial contexts (Mbembe, 2003), and/or integrating both (Davies et al, 2017).

Biopolitical approaches have also been used to understand the governmentality of migration in cities (Tazzioli, 2015; Darling, 2020). Using Esposito's dialectic of community/immunity, Darling makes a case for the urban application of the paradigm of immunity by comparing the dispersal and diffused housing/management of urban refugees (or UK urban governance of refugees) to the selective incorporation of threats as an immunitarian manoeuvre to keep the body of society/the state as healthy as possible. This differential inclusion of refugees and migrants in the city is widely examined by Mezzadra and Nielsen (2013). Beyond biopolitics and necropolitics, through Foucault, Agamben, Mbembe, and Esposito, the (biopolitical) framework has recently been extended to include Puar's (2017) 'right to maim' (see also Pallister-Wilkins, 2021; Tazzioli, 2021; Minca et al, 2022).

Biopolitics, necropolitics, and more recent developments – such as the concept of 'biogeopolitics' (Talocci et al, 2022) – have been widely employed to make sense of the trinity of space–planning–violence. Such frames enable us to build an argument around displacement urbanism being not only an analytical framework, but also a pervasive strategy and a political technology of planning that inscribes violence in institutions, policy, plans, and laws. Through various planning dispositions, the violence inherent to displacement becomes institutionalized and normalized – and hence undetectable – while its reproduction can hardly be challenged. In turn, planned violent displacement creates mass subjects whose presence in the city is either marginalized or normalized or invisibilized slaves, proletariat, aliens living in abject spaces (Isin and Rygiel, 2007), undeserving, economically unproductive homeless (Gillespie et al, 2021), colonial subjects, and so on.

Biopolitics also intersects theories on extraction in reading displacement. Through this reading, it is biological life rather than labour power that becomes the source of surplus value in what has been called bio and necroeconomy (Rose, 2007; Cooper, 2008). Connecting biopolitics and surplus production through a 'biopolitics of surplus', Gillespie et al (2021) highlight how displacement produces surplus populations and reinforces further their surplus status by separating them either from their homes, their land, or their employment. Thus, created surplus populations can then either be reincorporated into the needs of capital (make live) or not (let die) (Li, 2010). In this sense, the biopolitics of surplus creates a 'crisis of social reproduction' that 'concerns the reproduction of life itself' (Gillespie et al, 2021: 13).

Colonial, racial, and violent displacement

Stemming from necropolitical and biopolitical readings of displacement, another set of discourses points to the linkages between violence, urban contexts, race and coloniality (Mbembe, 2003; Gregory, 2004). Colonial and racial accumulation through dispossession is far too well accounted for (Fanon, 1963; Cesaire, 1972; Said, 1978). According to Black Marxism, cities are a mechanism through which capital produces racialized bodies and spaces (Gilmore, 2007; Kelley, 2015; Lowe, 2015). In this sense, capitalist relations are not universally homogeneous; rather, they distinguish between different kinds of exploitable subjects. The value of bringing race into discussion with political economy is precisely to remark that only some subjects are produced as surplus. Furthermore, looking at the racialized forms of expropriation, dispossession, and displacement that unfold alongside and intersect with the making of cities can help us to draw a parallel between current neoliberal urbanism and urbanization of empire (Turner, 2016; Danewid et al, 2021)

Sharma (2020) points to how the building of state-nations and consequent necropower and biopower are inherently based on a spatial demarcation of people of place and people out of place; such an important distinction will always be a colonial one. Displacement originates from the invasion, expulsion, and replacement of one group – Indigenous populations – by another – settlers (Johnson and Murton, 2007; Elliott-Cooper et al, 2020). The violent separation between these Indigenous and settler groups is 'a legacy of imperialism in both the colonies and in the metropoles and, thus, co-constitutive of the hegemony of nation-state power' (Sharma, 2020: 13, quoted in Seethaler-Wari et al, 2022: 9).

The making of cities globally goes hand in hand with racialized forms and practices of displacement and dispossession built on global dynamics of capital and planning, and colonial practices (Crawley and Skleparis, 2018; Rajaram, 2018; Danewid et al, 2021). From the mass deportations of millions of bodies in Africa to new formations of urban colonial regimes built on various forms of occupations and violences, urban displacement is the long durée of colonialism's exploitative and extractive project based on race and gender classifications, often accompanied by enduring violence and crafted to consolidate global powers. Over time, colonial capitalism has generated and benefited from displacement, making it central to its project of modernity based on a certain idea of development (Seethaler-Wari et al, 2022; Escobar, 2004) and through a dynamic of displacement and replacement. If the roots of displacement are colonial, we cannot discuss displacement urbanism without simultaneously querying everything that constitutes the foundation of the project of modernity (Hallaq, 2018, quoted in Seethaler-Wari et al, 2022).

Driven by the state's desire for economic growth and urban control, as well as by other forces of capture, such as control, privatization, and securitization – whether part of ethnonationalism or neoliberal urban governance – urbanisms of displacement traverse the political history of many urban spaces. While their origin is undoubtedly colonial, the forces that ensure their perpetuation are geopolitical. In this light, new urban regimes, such as those that have been called 'neo-apartheid' (Yacobi, 2015), depict variegated regimes of separation based on racial and ethnic discrimination and driven by consumer logic, privatization, and deregulation. These regimes intensify and deepen inequalities in urban settings. However, one of the characteristics and salient features of such neo-apartheid regimes is not only that they seclude and impoverish, divide and extract value, coerce and police, control and count bodies and movements, but also that they make inhabiting increasingly precarious.

Precariousness, colonial capitalism, and climate collapse

The acknowledgement that we live in a broken world started with Lovelock's 1970s book on Gaia, which furthered a 'new' ecological sensibility. Yet, as Povinelli (2011: 104) writes, 'For most natural scientists, life is that which can replicate itself. Gaia cannot. It can only provide the conditions of hospitality within which the life proper to it can flourish.' Reports from biodiversity expert panels (IPBES 2019) highlight the dramatic state of nature: a quarter of species are under threat of extinction, three-quarters of the terrestrial and marine environment is anthropized, one-third of all land is used for agriculture, and so on. The last Intergovernmental Panel

Climate Change (IPCC) report (2022) has recently sanctioned that we will not be able to keep the temperature below +1.5°C, which means we will hit a point of no return.

The sense of crisis has been there for a while – first as an ecological crisis, then as a climate emergency (Blanco, 2021). The preoccupation with a climate emergency has generated several interpretations and frameworks – from Crutzen's (2006) contested Anthropocene, to Moore's (2016) Capitalocene, Haraway's (2015), Plantatiocene and Tsing's (2015) damaged planet, to name a few. Displacement cuts across all of these 'cenes', as Carsten and Bozalek (2021) demonstrate. We all know only too well that extreme weather events increase the number of people who are displaced. Here, displacement is driven not just by climate, but also by broader forms of environmental change including biodiversity loss, changes to land and water resources, and the buildup of nuclear debris (Lunstrum and Bose, 2022). Root causes can be traced (back) to colonialism and capitalism, and more recently to neocolonialism – particularly carbon colonialism.

The act of tracing and narrating the uninterrupted process of destruction and construction that violently traverses the planet has been given different names, both prophetic and critical. The Capitalocene, and subsequently the Plantatiocene, are two alternative narratives with origins that are connected to capitalism and colonial capitalism. The first introduces a denaturalization of discourse, arguing that the present is not natural, but rather the result of historically determined power relations and forces, which can be overturned. The Capitalocene, on the other hand, focuses specifically on the role of capitalism as the primary driver of environmental degradation and ecological crises. Proponents of the Capitalocene argue that the current era should be understood as a product of capitalist modes of production, extraction, and consumption. They emphasize that the relentless pursuit of profit and the commodification of nature inherent to capitalist systems have led to widespread ecological destruction, climate change, resource depletion, and social inequalities.

Carsten and Bozalek (2021) examine in detail the relationship between colonial extraction, climate collapse, and displacement across different periods and definitions. They start from the Plantatiocene, the age of mass displacement of the African population from one continent to the other, which left behind vast colonized territories and masses of colonial subjects as disposable groups. During the Capitalocene, they continue, industrialization and financial capitalism have increased the scale and scope of displacement further and further. An example of this is the Amazonian region, where urban growth is a consequence of colonial and postcolonial extractive activities as well as rural and climate displacement. Extraction attracts migrant workers, displacing them from the jungle to the city; (rural) land grabbing pushes dispossessed groups to urban peripheries; and climate change removes people from riverine areas. In this context, the urban formation is the result of intersecting forms of imperial extractions, dispossessions, and climate change.

It is not only climate change and displacement that are related to colonial capitalism and extraction; many of the current climate solutions are also perpetuating colonialism through land grabs, extraction, and displacement. As Sultana (2022: 3) argues, 'climate coloniality reproduces the hauntings of colonialism and imperialism in the post-colony', laying 'bare the colonialism of not only the past but an ongoing coloniality that governs and structures our lives, which are co-constitutive of processes of capitalism, imperialism, and international development'. She further contends that the marginalization, death and devastation this brings about draws 'attention to continuities from the past and into the future', concluding that this is a form of slow wearing, or slow violence.

In this light, climate coloniality sheds light on how neocolonialism and racial capitalism are 'co-constitutive of climate impacts experienced by variously racialized populations who are disproportionately made vulnerable and disposable' (Sultana, 2022: 4). Gonzalez (2021) further articulates the strong bond between climate change-induced displacement, carbon capitalism, racism and environmental collapse, while Andreucci and Zografos (2022) argue that othering and racialization are central to the current governance of climate change, including the governing of climate migrants through interventions that are unwanted and often deadly. 'Climate apartheid' is the term used to describe the spatialization of racialized differences between Global South and Global North in terms of who pays more for the consequences of climate change and who is made more or less expendable (Tuana, 2019; Rice et al, 2021).

Anthropogenic climate change, global disasters, and conflicts embedded in colonial capitalist relations do not only affect new patterns of displacement of human beings alone, but also those of flora, fauna, and water. Within our damaged world, human and non-human lives are equally precarious, while displacement itself becomes a central element in the extraction and creation of value. In seeking to go beyond the limits of growth, greedy racial capitalist relations embedded in planetary urbanization invest themselves in the management of life. At the very core of the current neoliberal present is the transformation of life into surplus value – displacement. Within such a framework, displacement urbanism must continue to be discussed as part of a biopolitical and necropolitical framework. This is even more urgent now that a growing awareness of the deep crisis and the threat of mass extinctions have cast a dark shadow over everyone discussing urban (political) futures and what to leave to the next generations. The landscape emerging on the terrestrial planet is uninhabitable (Simone, 2016), not because the conditions are limiting people's ability to reside, to shelter, or to find a refuge, but rather because habitation is not only probable or possible, but just a matter of life – a life on the verge of dissipation. Displacement urbanism here shows the manifold and variegated tenacious struggle to resist the violent subtractions of future, of space, of possibilities, through creating space and forms of life.

Revisiting the biopolitics of displacement

Even if incomplete, the above review of the main literature sustains two arguments: the first is around the co-constituent nature of displacement and urbanization; the second is around the planetarization of displacement as a process and a condition. Cutting across these is a third argument, around how the production of planetary displacement – including current and past refugee and humanitarian crises, the complex geographies of encampments and resettlements, and the more or less visible forms of material and symbolic dispossession – is integral to urban capitalist relations and production, and as such is embedded into dynamics of value creation. Within global urban contexts, space, labour, and life are constantly drawn into (but also escape, as we will see below) circuits of value capture and creation; this happens in racialized ways. In this light, we suggest explicitly that displacement and the urban should be (re)centred around life and predicated upon (and beyond) the tension with death, following the original Foucauldian formula of 'making live letting die', and its unfolding into a biopolitics multiple (Aradau and Tazzioli, 2019).

We are cognizant of the limitations of such an approach, and in what follows we explore some of the main tenets, critiques and expansions of Foucault's thesis. The thinking of biopolitics has been widely questioned and criticized by several critical feminist and posthuman scholarship for being extraordinarily centred on human life overlooking other forms of life, or for being excessively negative or disembodied, portraying subjects without agency, affects, and emotions (Haraway, 1997; Gilroy, 2000; Braidotti, 2002; Barad, 2003: Butler, 2006; Povinelli, 2006). Braidotti (2016), for instance, argues that there are different lines of critique: first, biopolitics does not work for the advanced capitalist era; and second, biopolitics is excessively human-centric. The COVID-19 pandemic pointed to the limits of the classical biopolitical logic of analysis, calling for a new conceptual framework. Elsewhere, it has been pointed out how the extensive use of biopolitical frameworks might have been abused to the point of exhausting the meaning of the concept (van Wichelen, 2020). In this sense, Guyer et al (2016: 228) argue that 'we live and think in an era that is after biopolitics: one in which the idea of biopolitics will remain a part of meditations about life, but which will call for other frames for conceptualizing life'. Yet, we think that, even with its limitations, biopolitics is still a critical frame to engage with the question of life, especially in a context in which the survival of life – whether animal, human, Black, white, or queer – is at stake.

Foucault coined the term 'biopolitics' to signal a new political thinking and practice that targets life (Lemke, 2011), its management – including capture, control and so on – and its protection. In the meaning assigned by Foucault, biopolitics sanctions the inseparability between biological life and political life, and the politicization of life (Lemke, 2007; Vatter, 2009). This implies a separation between different lives: those that are worthy and those that are not. What marks the difference between biopolitics and other forms of power is that those lives that are not considered equal are not let die. This is encapsulated in the original Foucauldian distinction of 'making live and letting die' (Foucault, 2003, 2007) a flip of the medieval formula employed by the sovereign power. While sovereign power had a right of life and death over subjects (including, in extreme cases, disposing of the bodies of the subjects), biopower is instead directed to 'administer, secure, develop, and foster life' (Lemke, 2011: 35).

This resounds in Foucault's oft-quoted words, 'the ancient right to *take* life or *let* live was replaced by a power to *foster* life or *disallow* it' (Foucault, 2007: 138). According to Lemke (2011: 36), 'Foucault sees the particularity of this biopower in the fact that it fosters life or disallows it to the point of death, whereas the sovereign power takes life or lets live', and that is a substantial distinction. While the sovereign exercised power over life through killings and power over death through sparing lives, modern governments no longer use the threat of death to exercise their power. On the contrary, they promise to ensure the wealth of the population and stress the protection of life even when it implies an exposure to death. It is thus clear why biopolitics has traditionally been associated with many understandings and conditions of displacement.

The original Foucauldian distinction of fostering and disallowing life has been over the decades turned upside down and expanded to give life to many biopolitical turns. Various declinations of "affirmative", "negative" or of the tensions between "biopolitics and necropolitics" have marked extremely important debates in Foucault's literature with Agamben, Negri, Esposito, Mbembe (Minca et al, 2022) as well as Cooper, Rose, Haraway (Vatter, 2009; Tierney, 2016) and, more recently, Braidotti, Povinelli, Berlant, and Weheliye, to name a few. These encounters have highlighted the complicity of urbanism in the construction of political technologies and infrastructures that separate, constitute, capture, and expose life beyond the original binary opposition 'make live and let die', as originally expressed by Foucault, in the spirit of looking 'not at what he solved but at what remains open in his wake' (Povinelli, 2011: 453).

Between capture and excess

The reception of Foucault's biopolitics is divided into different lines. One is concerned with how the body, or part of it, becomes a commodity that circulates within the bioeconomy (Rose, 2007). Here, biopolitics is employed as a critique of the neoliberal city and focuses on surplus. Waldby coins the term 'biovalue' to describe the 'surplus value of vitality and instrumental knowledge which can be placed at the disposal of the human subject' (Waldby, 2000, quoted in Birch, 2012; see also Waldby and Mitchell, 2006), while Melinda Cooper (2008) brings about a Marxist-feminist critique to the neoliberal present, allegedly starting from where Foucault ends (Vatter, 2009; Tierney, 2016).

Precisely focusing on life as surplus, Vatter (2009) comparatively analyses Cooper's and Esposito's theories, arguing that they follow two distinct meanings of life, which are both present in the original texts by Foucault (see also Esposito, 2008: 32): a negative meaning, where life is referred to as capture of value (Cooper); and a positive one, where life is an excess that escapes capture (Esposito). To start with the first, Cooper (2008) examines how (biological) life, rather than labour, is the source of surplus value, thus bringing a biopolitical thinking inside Marx's primitive accumulation. This movement helps to collapse biopolitics and (Lemke's) political economy of life – instead of separating them, as Agamben does. Cooper merges the terms of a political economy equation: the value that is rooted in labour (production – political economy) and the value that is rooted in life (reproduction – biology) (Vatter, 2009). According to Cooper, neoliberal capitalism as a form of government has targeted biological life 'as the novel source of extraction of surplus value. In this sense, the neoliberal economy is essentially a bioeconomy' (Vatter, 2009: 4). To survive, capitalism must reach and exceed the limits of growth, so 'in the case of the bioeconomy, the extraction of surplus value from biological life requires that life be manipulated, controlled, and ultimately pushed beyond its "natural" limits to generate an excess or surplus of biological life' (Vatter, 2009: 4). 'Cooper's thesis is that all this creation of biological life in excess of its limits is paid at the price of a deepening devaluation of human lives: the second main sense in which life functions as surplus' (2009: 4).

According to Watson (2012), the idea that the protection of life requires the simultaneous negation of life – or, more specifically, of certain lives over others – and the simultaneous presence of affirmative and negative elements is common to Esposito as well as Butler. Contributing 'to the wider conversation on biopolitics from the perspective of suffering subjects marginalized and excluded by the current world order' (Watson 2012: 5), Butler (2006) developed a theory of precariousness that revolves around life and death to respond to the US-led 'war on terror'. Even though starting from the same idea of life as the central concern of modern political order, her notion of precarious life offers a reflection on suffering that is radically opposite to that of Agamben. According to her, precariousness and precarity are not the same: while the first is a universal condition, the latter is a differential element imposed on marginalized people. We are all equal, but some are more equal than others: 'some bodies are more protected and other more exposed' (Butler, 2016: 25). The only solution would be to be all equally precarious – this, in turn, implies that our future is predicated upon vulnerability. 'Vulnerability will serve as the basis for a new kind of community' (Butler, 2016: 25).

Debility, neither die nor live

Puar (2017) similarly reflects on the biopolitics of life with a focus on the human as more than biological life, and encompasses race, gender, and disability in her thesis. She advances the notion of debilitation (debility) in relation to disability: two interlocked terms that form part of a 'political economy of capacity' (Sheehi and Sheehi, 2020). Debilitation is a form of government that targets certain racialized, gendered, and capacity-differentiated bodies that are considered defective, unconforming, and dangerous to the neoliberal order. Debilitation as 'slow wearing down of populations instead of the event of becoming disabled' (Puar, 2017: xiii–xiv) does not fall entirely within either biopolitical or necropolitical frameworks because debility 'does not proceed through making live, making die, letting live, or letting die'. Here Puar adds an additional 'critical axis to these four quadrants', arguing that debilitation is 'a status unto itself that triangulates the hierarchies of living and dying that are standardly deployed in theorizations of biopolitics' (Puar, 2017: 137; Minca et al, 2022: 7). Thus, 'debilitated life is a different status produced through strategies where 'debilitation functions as "will not let die" or "will not make die"' (Puar, 2017: 8).

In this sense, debilitation is used to analyse and understand the management of migration in Europe, including hotpots that 'alter interrupt and capture migrant mobility' but 'do not make die either' (Puar, 2017: 8), or the forced hypermobility of migrants as a biopolitics of neither detained nor expelled (2017: 10). Following Puar, biopolitics does not ground in either of the terms of the formula make live let die; rather, it sits in between. As Minca et al (2022) point out:

> Indeed, the exhausting mobility that migrants are forced into, pushes us to find ways for registering modes of governing that consist of pestering and harassing migrants. As Jasbir Puar has observed in relation to the Palestinian context, 'alongside the "right to kill" I noted a complementary logic ... that of creating injuries and maintaining Palestinian populations as perpetually debilitated, and yet alive, in order to control them. (Minca et al, 2022: 11)

Puar's notion of debilitation, therefore, is different from Berlant's slow death, for instance. Berlant (2007: 754) reads biopolitics through the notion of slow death, as the 'physical wearing out of a population and the deterioration of people', which is linked to capitalism (the health of the body) and to sovereignty. She starts from Harvey's accumulation and from his reading of sickness related to labour (sickness as the inability to work), according to which health and wellbeing are subordinated to labour and production. Slow death, in her meaning, is not an exceptional event – such as genocide – but an absolutely ordinary one. The population 'wearing out' to which she refers happens in the space of ordinariness (2007: 761). In this domain, 'dying and the ordinary reproduction of life are coextensive' (2007: 762). It is a condition of living on in extended states of debility, suffering, and disease. Such debilitation manifests itself, for example, in the obesity epidemics that hit low-income populations, which are populations that are deemed 'dispensable' in the current neoliberal regime. Yet she also discusses agency as cruel optimism, which she defines as the desire of what obstacles our flourishing. Although they are extremely different theories, the key element that connects the thought of Puar and Berlant is that biopolitics does not necessarily comprise a clear-cut opposition of life and death, but it is better understood as an effort to differentially organize the grey area between them. They also constitute an important clarification of Foucault's original theory.

Albeit through an entirely different approach, the theme of suffering and trauma also becomes central to the work of French anthropologist, sociologist, and psychiatrist Didier Fassin (2009). He delves into the question of life, revisiting Foucault's concepts while departing from them to explore not only the issue of governance but also the meaning and value of life. Drawing on Foucault's notion of biopolitics, Fassin critiques humanitarianism and broader societal approaches to the 'unwanted' majority. He examines how their lives are shaped by dynamics of inclusion and exclusion, mediated through trauma.

Directly addressing the precarity, neglect, and dis-ability of life forces a new perspective on the relation between life and death that shapes most discussions of biopolitics. In particular, it helps with extending beyond conceptual frames, such as Agamben's naked life or Mbembe's (2003) necropolitics, which presume a clear opposition between living and non-living, or even organic and inorganic. This, in turn, allows the visibilization of processes of value extraction operated upon disposable and displaceable populations.

Abandonment and the ordinariness of suffering

Another complex elaboration of the original formula by Foucault is Povinelli's (2011) shift away from death to non-life. Povinelli starts from the notion of 'ordinary suffering' as the routine violence with which people live – a set of non-exceptional moments (a concept that is very similar to slow death). In this sense, biopolitical violence is not related to discrete events, but rather is diffused. According to Yusoff (2017), the problem of ordinary suffering emerges as a 'struggle for existence, rather than outright extinction, which constitutes biopolitics'. Povinelli's focus on perseverance, endurance, effort, and precarious survival, as opposed to biopolitically engineered elimination, is what really sets her work apart from much of what has been written about biopolitics, especially under the umbrella of state theory, which tends to focus on the hyper-intensification of what Foucault (2003: 170) called projects of 'making live and letting die'. Povinelli confirms the existence of Foucault's 'forms of life which persist, somewhere between life and death, despite them' (2003: 170), where there is no clear separation between life and death, but only in between conditions, where the body is debilitated. This is a form of survival and endurance (or 'living on', for Berlant).

Povinelli (2016) reformulates biopolitics as 'geontopower', an ensemble that is larger than biopolitics itself. It starts from a reinterpretation of death as nonlife, whereas nonlife is not that which had life and now does not, but rather the inanimate at large. While biopolitics is interested in life and death, geontopower is interested in life (*bios*) and nonlife (*geos*) (Yusoff, 2017: 171). Geontopower offers a new lens through which to understand and criticize the Anthropocene, a notion that has shed light on the precariousness of the relationship between bios and geos and the possibility of the dissolution of this relationship with the survival of the inanimate alone (Yusoff, 2017: 171). Povinelli makes another distinction – that biopolitics has been erroneously interpreted as the government of life and death, instead of the government *through* life and death.

Povinelli (2016) explains that geontopower is differentiated from biopower and it is meant to indicate and intensify the contrasting components of nonlife (*geos*) and being (ontology) currently in play in the late liberal governance of difference and markets (2016: 175). Geontopower is not only now emerging to replace biopolitics (2016: 173); biopower (governance through life and death) has long depended on a subtending geontopower (the difference between the lively and the inert). Like the function of necropolitics, which Mbembe showed openly operating in colonial Africa and only later revealing its shape in Europe, so geontopower has long operated openly in settler late liberalism and has been insinuated in the ordinary operations of its governance of difference and markets.

Povinelli (2011) explains how the relationship between biopolitics and posthumanism revolves around the notion(s) of (exhaustion and) endurance. She discusses the 1970s Project X, which was focused on recycling, to turn an exhausted object of capital (deep-fried oil used in restaurants) into motor fuel energy that could sustain the community. After being burnt, the oil produces waste, which in turn provides the material condition under which a new social product (project) can be built: new life starts from exhaustion. Povinelli adds that this dynamic includes human and non-human agencies and organisms. So, on the one hand, exhaustion is necessary for survival, but on the other hand, Povinelli asks, what has the right to exist, survive, and be killed? 'Deep ecology, posthumanism, and biopolitics would seem to converge around a central problem even as the issue of exhaustion raises, like a worm curled in the heart, the problem of endurance, of what endures and what can explain the fact of endurance' (2011: 123).

Povinelli (2011) continues to explain that capital produces both the oil (as a commodity) and the exhausted/burnt-out oil (as excess); furthermore,

> it also makes a different kind of excess, a difference beyond capital, outside the containment or definition of capital. This excess has at least two dimensions. It has the dimension of substance: forms of being that emerge from new biotic habitats. And it has the dimension of relationality: forms of relationality that can emerge from the striated possibilities of these new substances and habitats. (2011: 124)

To exemplify this, Project X was followed by several experiments in biofuels, which at some point became a profitable business, in turn leading the price of food to soar globally, thus making it inaccessible to people. It is all a tension between endurance and exhaustion. 'The exhaustions produced by and then reabsorbed into the system, such as waste oil, and the exhaustions produced when trying to create alternative ethical substances' (2011: 124), such as Project X did.

Life, death, and race: bodies that matter

Povinelli's instances have never been employed to examine displacement – at least not directly. However, this book wishes to connect her notion of exhaustion with Puar's debility, and her notion of endurance with ways in which people escape capture – the life in excess that is never completely reabsorbed by the system. Crucially, life in excess is Black. As Smith and Vasudevan (2017) point out, both Berlant and Povinelli foreground how 'the deaths of Black, brown, colonized, and other non-white subjects are infused with a sense of ordinariness, a wearing down of life towards slow and enduring death' (2017: 212). In this sense, 'race is fundamental to the rule of life and death' (2017: 212).

Foucault also touched upon racism. In the last lecture of 'Society Must Be Defended', Foucault (2003) argues that racism is 'a way of introducing a break into the domain of life taken over by power: the break between what must live and what must die' (2003: 254) and a precondition that makes killing acceptable. Foucault continues by saying that 'the distinction amongst races ... all this is a way of fragmenting the field of the biological that power controls. That is the first function of racism: to fragment, to create caesuras within the biological continuum ...' (2017: 212). Differences between those who are exposed to the risk of capture/death, and those who are not do indeed exist. Such differences are in terms of vulnerability as well as worthiness: some bodies matter, some do not; some count as human, others as not quite human, or not human at all (Weheliye, 2014). However, Foucault's idea of racism has also been widely questioned for offering a sanitized version of racism and its interplay with coloniality (Stoler and Cooper, 1997; Wynter, 2003; Bhambra, 2013; Mignolo, 2015), not only in its historical overview of biopower but also when analysing the present condition.

Filling Foucault's gaps, the most eminent elaboration of the intersection of power with race is Mbembe's (2003) necropolitical theory. Mbembe reformulates biopower into necropower to put race centre and front into a biopolitical reading of life. Necropolitics focuses primarily on colonial contexts and brutal forms of oppression in the plantations where entire populations were displaced, and where violence was/is in direct relation with the colonized body. Mbembe's focus is on 'death-in-life' (Mbembe, 2003: 21), not killing but harming and wounding. Suffering thus becomes a technology of power/control (Davies et al, 2017), through which bodies/subjects are 'kept alive but in a state of injury' (Mbembe, 2003: 21).

Necropolitical readings of spaces and bodies have often been integrated into literature related to border, refugees, and forced migration studies, as examined at the beginning of this chapter (see also Castro, 2015; Davies et al, 2017; Gebhardt, 2020). Among the abundant literature that analyses biopolitics and race (Amin, 2010; McIntyre and Nast, 2011; Richter-Montpetit and Howell 2019) and the critiques to such an approach, Weheliye (2014) in particular writes on how a certain reading of biopolitics commonly accepts a focus on the non-racialized being, as if subjects do not have race, as if all bodies were white, as if there was no difference, as if biopolitics did not operate on a racial basis. According to Nolan (2017: 2), 'For Weheliye, the deterministic submersion of race as an ontological signifier renders biopolitics unfit as an analytic for examining the correlations between constructions of humanity and what he calls "racializing assemblages".'

Weheliye (2014) coined a term, *Habeas Viscus*, to 'imagine a different modality of humanity through a material repopulation of critical discourse'. Nolan continues that, 'Of course, the project of "imagining humanity otherwise" is ongoing within Black studies. Black feminism has long been concerned with contesting liberal political formations by making visible the discursive and corporeal violence's enacted upon racialized, gendered, and sexualized bodies. *Habeas Viscus* is clearly indebted to this' (Nolan, 2017: 2). This is expanded further:

> Contesting ideas of suffering as somehow 'exceptional', as well as the notion that populations are equally at risk under Western modernity, the move toward a new relational model asks readers to interrogate the production of an ontological totality in order to perceive the authenticity of what Weheliye describes as the 'traditions of the oppressed': the production of new philosophical genealogies that take seriously the ongoing practices of freedom and new discursive spaces emerging out of, not despite, conditions of violence. (2017: 3)

This is but a humble, and partial, overview of the complex task of debating, criticizing, and expanding Foucault's complex, rich, and compelling work on biopolitics. The debate around biopolitics is ongoing, expansive, and continuous. Every work, in its own way, is an attempt to move beyond biopolitics as a condition of government of life and death, and to shift its margins. Biopolitics cannot be read as simply affirming the productivity of life, nor only considering its tanatopolitical returns and the manifold in-between spaces between life and death. It encompasses containments, control, and protection, as well as bans, exclusions, subtractions, violent inactions, forms of injury, debilitation, erosion, precarization – all imposed globally in a regime of what we term 'displacement urbanism', spanning from enclosures and uneven development to the government of refugees and migrants with the complicity of the humanitarian system.

The edited collection *The Black Mediterranean: Bodies, Borders and Citizenship* (Proglio et al, 2021) exemplifies this. Abandoning the consolatory, eurocentrist, neutral narrative of the Mediterranean as a space of connections and exchange, it provokes a 'crisis of representation' by inquiring when the Mediterranean became visible as Black. The reply may lie in Chambers's argument: when it started being scarred 'by slavery, drowning, brutality, and the wrecked lives of ferocious migration today' (Chambers, 2010: 681). The book makes a strong argument regarding the analogy between the Black Atlantic and the Black Mediterranean, in terms of 'new transnational affiliations, the diffusion of transnational capital, and diasporic Black existence ... addressing the response to the systemic and representational violence which affects Black people in Southern Europe' (Lombardi-Diop, 2021: 5) that is essentializing in the current epistemological construct and its conflation with political management. The book shows how the Black African migrant is framed either as a charitable subject or an uninvited guest within a narrative that portrays the Mediterranean as a single unitary space, neglecting its complex topography, while the infrastructure of support and rescue operations is reframed around the constant quest to the negation of ports – long, complex and violent detours that reposition sovereignty to a state legal decision.

Why is the centrality of the Mediterranean as invented violent geography today so important? And how could it be related to displacement urbanism? The move is to think of space and territory in terms of topological intersection of entanglements, trajectories, and infrastructures, and to refer to them as ambivalent spaces of conflict. In this sense, the Mediterranean is a paradigmatic epistemological construct for the complex network of intersected and intertwined narratives of displacement urbanism. Said otherwise, as both a precondition for modern racial capitalism and as a site for the ongoing reproduction of regimes of racialization and Black subjectivities (Danewid et al, 2021), the Mediterranean speaks to the many territories made of colour lines, forms of exclusion, and differential inclusion that spring to mind when we think of displacement urbanism.

The biopolitics of displacement urbanism

Both displacement and urbanism are a problem of population and its governance; moreover, they are an issue of politicization of life in its biological and more-than-biological meaning. Indeed, central to this book is an emphasis on the political economy of space and life in which urbanization processes linked to displacement – whether regarded as de/re-placement or emplacement – at the global margins are embedded. The kind of biopolitics we address is a biopolitics multiple, which includes and goes beyond the binary logic of 'make live let die' (Aradau and Tazzioli, 2020) to multiply the investigations into contemporary modes of protection and exclusion, of empowerment and impairment of every life, whether human or non-human. The book encompasses, problematizes, and connects instances of bioeconomy and necroeconomy that recall Cooper's logics of value capture; it includes views that are close to Mbembe's, Puar's, and Berlant's approaches to wounding and debility, as well as affirmative biopolitics that looks at life in excess, escaping capture.

Earlier in the chapter, we explained how the biopolitical frame has been employed to understand and describe a technology of government linked to displacement, violence, and coloniality. In this sense, displacement urbanism involves discursive and non-discursive practices, as well as the creation of knowledges and institutions – for eviction, for resettlement, and for the building of camps and humanitarian frameworks. Yet, taking a biopolitical lens to examine displacement urbanism does not only mean exploring the institutions' de facto governing bodies, the discourses constructing certain knowledge as true, and the modes that displacement takes (its legal basis). It is also important to recall the kinds of relationships and subjects that are produced, as well as the different powers, rationalities, and trajectories and how they intersect to create broader assemblages.

In this formulation, as a form of governmentality/political technology of government, displacement urbanism produces specific relations and subjects, premised on a distinction between worthy and less-worthy life. Through displacement, biopolitics creates the conditions for a life to become or to be not livable, expendable, or disposable, and for a body to be or not be displaced. Thus, displacement urbanism operates in the world by creating, classifying, and hierarchizing lives, which are considered the more precarious the less they fit certain criteria. This is rooted in a distinction based on race, as mentioned previously, but also on gender, ethnicity, ability, and sexuality, among others.

As such, displacement urbanism is simultaneously biopolitical and necropolitical at its core, as it implies the material destruction or wounding of certain bodies over others. A necropolitical reading of displacement urbanism allows us to understand how Black bodies are more exploitable, displaceable, and ultimately disposable than other bodies. A 'necrotic machine' – tied to capitalism, colonialism, extraction, and financialization – is deeply embedded into what we term displacement urbanism. The necrotic machine does not simply kill; rather, it throws lives into a condition of debility, of partial injury that is lived in the space of ordinariness, but where life and its negation are always tied to each other in manifold ways, as the book articulates.

We argue that displacement urbanism calls into question issues of devaluation, disposability, debility, and displaceability, to which some beings seem to be destined as they are coerced by a normalized system of exploitative inequality, dispossession, and violence that depends on the maintenance of naturalized hierarchies of difference. Yet, theorizing from the basis of embodied lived experience that is trapped in bio-political games that start from certain localized critical spatial practices signals the kind of agency bodies have in displacement. The representation of subjects as surplus can be illuminating, but it can reproduce a process of dehumanization, let alone the fact that it does not align with what one may think of themselves. As Wright (2006: 4) argues, few people 'identify themselves as the bearer of the abstract condition of disposability'.

While displaced subjects are the objects of manifold portrayals and representations – as exceptions, as bare lives, as racialized victims of colonial capital, as surplus population, and so on, life stories unsettle established scripts. The book is keen to provide an account of what 'falls away' from these accounts (Tadiar, 2009, 2013) to 'open up the possibility of other genealogies for understanding those remaindered ways of living in the world that move and generate that world in ways we would otherwise be unable to take into political account' (Tadiar, 2013: 43) beyond disposability.

The manifold dimensions of displacement urbanism

That displacement urbanism is underpinned by a (racialized) accumulation by dispossession logic, destruction through construction process, as well as biopolitics and necropolitics, is clear. However, it is also evident that there is more to it. Using the term 'displacement urbanism' in this sense has the advantage of naming the culprit, locating the spatial and temporal metaphor of displacement not merely related to one framework, one event, one regime, or one logic, but within the complex and interrelated processes of global-scale economic and political organization, with endless local variations, nuances, and outcomes. Displacement urbanism gathers and generalizes a range of what may otherwise be dissimilar events and lived experiences, highlighting shared elements. It interrogates displacement beyond a single moment, after it has happened and in between events. It offers the possibility to reflect on the tensions between permanence and temporariness, exception and normalization, politicization and depoliticization, and loss and home-making, in their role to shape and to be shaped.

The value of putting forward an argument on displacement being constitutive of the urban, and therefore assuming it both as an effect and as a form of urbanism, is to complicate the discussion, to get closer to the messy, subjective, perceived, and lived reality. Here, drawing on Delaney (2004), displacement urbanism is offered as an elastic framework that aims to expand understandings of displacement as violent accumulation from an exogenous force to a precondition of the urban that further connects space, bodies, planning, violence, life, erosion, death, and nonlife. It is both a process and a condition that holds together different tensions – difference/margin, vulnerability/agency, life/death, and *bios/geos*. Displacement urbanism indeed wishes to problematize and unsettle those binaries of urban thinking such as camp/city, migrant/citizen, formal/informal, and temporary/permanent, but also the biopolitical binary of life/death to capture all the in-betweenness. It stands for the interdependence of each of these categories. The overall effort is to put the universal and singular, the abstract and the concrete in a meaningful conversation – and necessarily stretch it over histories of colonialism, capitalism, racialization, and extraction (e.g. Zizek, 2016; Sharma, 2020; Carsten and Bozalek, 2021) and survival.

The term 'displacement urbanism' underpins an understanding of the 'urban' as both a presence and an absence – as it produces, through displacement, forms of erasure and abandonment, as well as new urban formations. As pointed out in several chapters in this book, urbanization processes trigger displacement, and in turn displacement is also a mode of urbanization on its own, as the dislocation of individuals within and around urban territories results in infilling and expansion and in transformations of the rural–urban landscape. While displacement is indeed integral to the urban, in turn urbanism is (always) inherent to displacement. In this sense, it is impossible to disassociate the urban from displacement. From the auto-constructed townships punctuating the peripheries of Asian cities, to the geographies of resettlement in Latin America, from the refugee camps in

Africa, the Middle East, and Europe, to the manifold interstitial humanitarian spaces of refuge worldwide, displacement is a mode of urban (re)production from the top and from below and through manifold territorial agents.

In this light, an urbanism of displacement is not only the result of coerced or restricted movement and dispossession, or of the biopolitics and necropolitics of managing and eroding life; it is also, and simultaneously, the result of individual and collective spatial practices *beyond capture* – often marginalized and invisibilized, or often too visible – that contribute to processes of (re)territorialization and 'constellations of home', as so many have pointed out (Ahmed et al, 2003; Feldman, 2006; Brun, 2012; Boccagni, 2017; Boccagni and Brighenti, 2017; Brun and Fabos, 2015; Dossa et al, 2019; Beeckmans et al, 2022; Seethaler-Wari et al, 2022) and this book further develops. This specific kind of urbanism drives a reorganization of public spaces, infrastructures and housing systems, in turn generating re-placements (Mezzadra and Neilsen, 2013; Seethaler-Wari et al, 2022), de-placements (Isayev, 2021) as well as new emplacements (Casey, 1993; Glick Schiller and Caglar, 2015) that allow temporary, precarious, improvised re-inhabitation of the urban.

Beyond the 'political economy of human deployment': making place in displacement

This chapter has foregrounded how urbanization and displacement are two complementary sides of the same capitalist logic of production and destruction: the urban in its carceral, fragmented, and exclusionary logic is co-produced by displacement, cancellation, and hypermobility where refuge is foreclosed, space is banned, and the unhoused remain banned. Yet, cities have also taken a central role for displacement, not only as oppressive machineries of coercion, control, and organization of population, but also as sanctuary, foregrounding narratives and imagination of inclusion and neo-cosmopolitanism. Cities are sites that receive displaced populations; they are magnets that attract migrants, refugees and displaced. In turn, migrants and refugees play a key role in the everyday constitution of urban space.

In what are termed the 'arrival cities' of Europe, the presence of refugees and migrants alters the city and its relations amidst urban regeneration, welfare decline, austerity urbanism, double standards, selective solidarity, and racism. Meanwhile, in the refugee camps, changes in the built spaces and a lack of them consolidate or erode the right to return, amidst political visibility and claims for recognition; and within the geographies of resettlement, the informalization of space is an expression of and a response to housing precarity. Beyond homelessness, loss, and passivity, these practices suggest a wide variety of transformative experiences embedded in urban places. Darling (2020: 895) has developed the concept of 'refugee urbanism' to precisely explore the intersection of agency and governance that shape how displaced subjects 'intersect with, are remade by, and themselves serve to constitute and rework, the urban'. In this sense, displaced people's movements, interactions, and transactions affect the urban realms, disturbing socio-material arrangements and calling for a constant re-theorization of the urban.

These engagements can even reposition the displaced as urban subjects (Sassen, 2014). In this sense, the urban emerges as a field of negotiation, as a place of encounter of subjects, agents, and voices where alternative subjectivities can be imagined. A growing body of work has focused on rethinking urban citizenship based on this approach (Holston and Appadurai, 1999; Delaney 2004; Isin and Nielsen, 2008; Bakewell, 2011; Ataç et al, 2016; Maestri and Hughes, 2017; Hirsh et al, 2020; Yiftachel, 2020; Wahab et al, 2022). When not taken as a universalizing framework, this approach holds the potential to understand subjective, intersectional, and more-than-human aspects of urban displacement (Doshi, 2013; Nail, 2016; Brickell et al, 2017; Isayev 2017; Tuitjer and Batréau, 2019; Fiddian-Qasmiyeh, 2020; Field et al, 2020; Montaser, 2020; Pasquetti and Sanyal, 2020; Carsten et al, 2021).

This book continues on this path by exploring different forms of survival, improvisation, and living with the trouble. It starts by thinking the city not as a well-defined container for processes of displacement and for displaced people, but rather as a relational configuration connected to other spaces and times, marked by local specificities. Here, the urban is not simply a physical space, an empty canvas on which processes take place, but also an assemblage of materialities, temporalities, and politics in constant flux (Star, 1999; Graham and Marvin, 2001; Larkin, 2013; Amin, 2014; Amin and Thrift, 2017, Simone, 2004, 2021).

Simone's (2004, 2021) concept of people as infrastructure captures this idea. Set against and responding to the 'political economies of human deployment', according to which 'urban populations become objects of increased extraction in systems of ensnarement' (Simone, 2021: 4), people as infrastructure encompasses 'manoeuvres' and 'antagonisms' revealing complex imbricacies of agency and power, a 'mathematics of multiple recompositions'. What Simone (2021: 4) terms 'the political economy of human deployment' is what we mean by displacement urbanism, where 'particular kinds of bodies are repositioned, moved around, left on their own, wasted'. Yet, within such a gloomy scenario, Simone reminds us that, despite eviction, displacement, and dispossession, people are capable of putting together forms of collective care – but 'they now often do so from locations where few are paying attention. For, physical displacement now most usually entails operating from the far hinterlands, or in territories intentionally made marginal or wasted from overuse or irrelevance' (2021: 5). This is life in excess, beyond capture.

As a line of inquiry into contested urban processes, displacement urbanism emerges precisely from the observation of spatial practices in those exhausted territories, and from the periphery of peripheries. Far from being a theory concept, as there is no theory of the margin, displacement urbanism is one of the plural urbanisms one might encounter in cities, marginal spaces, camps and peripheral territories. It is one of the heterogeneous articulations of temporality, materiality, and politics that form complex assemblages and that can be reiterated across different urban geographies.

References

Ahmed, S., Castaneda, C., Fortier, A. M., and Sheller, M. (2003) *Uprootings/Regroundings: Questions of Home and Migration*, Berg.

Agier, M. (2002) 'Between war and city: towards an urban anthropology of refugee camps', *Ethnography*, 3(3): 317–41.

Albanski, L. and Krywult-Albańska, M. (2021) 'Reinventing the refugee camp as the city: Theoretical considerations about unaccompanied minors', *Migration Studies – Review of Polish Diaspora*, 3(181): 253–65.

Andreucci, D. and Zografos, C. (2022) 'Between improvement and sacrifice: othering and the (bio)political ecology of climate change', *Political Geography*, 92. https://doi.org/10.1016/j.polgeo.2021.102512

Alkhalili, N. (2019) 'A forest of urbanisation': Camp Metropolis in the edge areas', *Settler Colonial Studies*, 9(2): 207–26.

Amin, A. (2010) The remainders of race. *Theory, Culture & Society*, 27(2–3): 285–98. https://doi.org/10.1177/0263276409350361

Amin, A. (2014) 'Lively infrastructure', *Theory, Culture & Society*, 31(7–8): 137–61.

Amin, A. and Thrift, N. (2017) 'Seeing like a city', *International Journal of Urban and Regional Research*, 42: 359–61.

Aradau, C. and Tazzioli, M. (2020) 'Biopolitics multiple: migration, extraction, subtraction', *Millennium*, 48(2): 198–220.

Ataç, I., Rygiel, K., and Stierl, M. (2016) 'The contentious politics of refugee and migrant protest and solidarity movements: remaking citizenship from the margins', *Citizenship Studies*, 20(5): 527–44.

Bakewell, O. (2011) 'Conceptualising displacement and migration: processes, conditions, and categories', in K. Koser and S. Martin (eds) *The Migration-Displacement Nexus: Patterns, Processes, and Policies*, Berghahn Books, pp 14–28.

Basu, R. and Asci, P (2020) 'Intermediary cities of refuge: from Istanbul to Kolkata', in R. Thakur, A. Dutt, S. Thakur and G. Pomeroy (eds) *Urban and Regional Planning and Development*, Springer.

Barad, K. (2003) 'Posthuman performativity: Toward an understanding of how matter comes to matter', *Signs Journal of Women in Culture and Society*, 28(3): 801–31.

Beeckmans, L., Gola, A. Singh, A. and Heynen, H. (eds) (2022) *Making Home(s) in Displacement: Critical Reflections on a Spatial Practice*, Leuven University Press, pp 11–42.

Berlant, L. (2007) 'Slow death', *Critical Inquiry*, 33(4): 754–80.

Beverley, E.L. (2013) 'Frontier as resource: law, crime, and sovereignty on the margins of empire', *Comparative Studies in Society and History*, 55(2): 241–72.

Bhambra, G.K. (2013) 'The possibilities of, and for, global sociology: A postcolonial perspective', *Political Power and Social Theory*, 24: 295–314.

Birch, K. (2012) 'Knowledge, place, and power: geographies of value in the bioeconomy', *New Genetics and Society*, 31(2): 183–201.

Blanco, A. (2021) 'Climate justice and the urban question: An introduction', Urban Studies, 58(1): 3–18.

Blomley, N. (2019) 'The territorialisation of property in land: space, power and practice', *Territory, Politics, Governance*, 7(2): 233–49.

Boccagni, P. (2017) *Migration and the Search for Home: Mapping Domestic Space in Migrants' Everyday Lives*, Palgrave Macmillan.

Boccagni, P. and Brighenti, A. (2017) 'Immigrants and home in the making: thresholds of domesticity, commonality and publicness', *Journal of Housing and the Built Environment*, 32(1): 1–11.

Boehmer, E. and Davies, D. (2018) 'Planned violence: post/colonial urban infrastructure, literature, and culture', *Journal of Postcolonial Writing*, 54(3): 320–37.

Bou Akar, H. (2018) *For the War Yet to Come: Planning Beirut's Frontiers*, Stanford University Press.

Braidotti, R. (2002) *Metamorphoses: Towards a Materialist Theory of Becoming*, Polity Press.

Braidotti, R. (2016) 'Critical posthumanism and planetary futures', in D. Banerji and M.R. Paranjape (eds) *Critical Posthumanism and Planetary Futures*, Springer, pp 1–10.

Brenner, N. (2018) 'Debating planetary urbanisation: for an engaged pluralism', *Environment and Planning D: Society and Space*, 36(3): 570–90.

Brenner, N. and Schmid, C. (2014) 'The "urban age" in question', *International Journal of Urban and Regional Research*, 38(3): 731–55.

Brickell, K. and Datta, A. (2011) *Translocal Geographies: Spaces, Places, Connections*, Ashgate.

Brickell, K., Dwyer, C., and Smith, T. (2017) *Translocal Geographies: Spaces, Places, Connections*, Ashgate.

Brun, C. (2012) 'Homes in limbo: Transformation of private housing in protracted displacement', *Journal of Refugee Studies*, 25(1): 2–52.

Brun, C. and Fabos, A. (2015) 'Making homes in limbo? A conceptual framework', *Refuge*, 31(1): 5–17.

Butler, J. (2006) *Precarious Life: The Powers of Mourning and Violence*. Verso.

Butler, J. (2016) 'Rethinking vulnerability and resistance', in J. Butler, Z. Gambetti and L. Savsay (eds) *Precarious Life: The Powers of Mourning and Violence*. Verso, pp 1–25.

Caldeira, T. (2017) 'Peripheral urbanisation: Autoconstruction, transversal logics, and politics in cities of the Global South', *Environment and Planning D: Society and Space*, 35(1): 3–20.

Campbell, E. (2006) 'Urban refugee camps and the politics of space', *Journal of Refugee Studies*, 19(3): 348–70.

Carsten, J. and Bozalek, V. (2021) *Reconceptualizing Displacement: Connections, Contestations and Coalitions*, Routledge.

Carsten, J., Cohen, A., and Davies, M. (2021) *Urban Displacement and Collective Action: New Approaches to Informal Settlement*, Policy Press.

Casey, E.S. (1993) *Getting Back into Place: Toward a Renewed Understanding of the Place-World*, Indiana University Press.

Castro, A.F.H. (2015) 'From the "bio" to the "necro"', in S.E. Wilmer and A. Žukauskaitė (eds) *Resisting Biopolitics: Philosophical, Political, and Performative Strategies*, Routledge, pp 237–53.

Césaire, A. (1972) *Discourse of Colonialism*, Monthly Review Press.

Chambers, I. (2010) *Mediterranean Crossings: The Politics of an Interrupted Modernity*, Duke University Press.

Comaroff, J. and Comaroff, J.L. (2007) *Ethnicity, Inc*, University of Chicago Press.

Cons, J. (2019) 'Geographies of displacement: the politics of mobility in South Asia', *Political Geography*, 73: 1–10.

Cooper, M. (2008) *Life as Surplus: Biotechnology and Capitalism in the Neoliberal Era*, University of Washington Press.

Corsellis, T. and Vitale, A. (2005) *Transitional Settlement: Displaced Populations*, Oxfam.

Crawley, H. and Skleparis, D. (2018) 'Refugees, migrants, neither, both: categorical fetishism and the politics of bounding in Europe's "migration crisis"', *Journal of Ethnic and Migration Studies*, 44(1): 48–64.

Crisp, J. (2010) 'Refugee camps as urban environments', *Forced Migration Review*, 34: 52–5.

Crutzen, P.J. (2006) 'The Anthropocene', in E. Ehlers and T. Krafft (eds) *Earth System Science in the Anthropocene*, Springer, pp 13–18.

Danewid, I., Proglio, A., Pesarini, A., Hawthorne, C., Raeymaekers, T., Saucier, K., Grechi, G., and Gerrand, V. (eds) (2021) 'Introduction', in G. Proglio, C. Hawthorne, I. Danewid, P.K. Saucier, G. Grimaldi, A. Pesarini, T. Raeymaekers, G. Grechi and V. Gerrand (eds) *The Black Mediterranean*, Palgrave Macmillan, pp 9–27.

Davies, T., Isakjee, A., and Dhesi, S. (2017) 'Violent inaction: the necropolitical experience of refugees in Europe', *Antipode*, 49(5): 1263–84.

Darling, J. (2016) 'The displaced city: urban regeneration, refugee camps, and urban refugees', *Urban Studies*, 57(5): 895–912.

Darling, J. (2020) 'Urban displacement and policy responses', *Geography Compass*, 14(1): e12476.

Delaney, D. (2004) *Territory: A Short Introduction*, Blackwell.

Diken, B. and Laustsen, C.B. (2005) *The Culture of Exception: Sociology Facing the Camp*, Routledge.

Doshi, S. (2013) 'The politics of the evicted: Redevelopment, subjectivity, and difference in Mumbai's slum frontier', *Antipode*, 45(4): 844–65.

Dossa, P., Carty, L., and Collins, P. (2019) *Displacement and Dispossession: Narratives of Belonging*, University of Toronto Press.

Ek, R. (2006) 'Governing homelessness: The disciplinary effects of the police and the welfare system', *Urban Studies*, 43(8): 1303–16.

Elden, S. (2006) *Spatial politics: essays for Doreen Massey*, Wiley-Blackwell.

Elden, S. (2010) 'Land, terrain, territory', *Progress in Human Geography*, 34(6): 799–817.

Elden, S. (2013) 'Secure the volume: vertical geopolitics and the depth of power', *Political Geography*, 34: 35–51.

Elliott-Cooper, A., Abdulah, S., and Scott, S. (2020) 'Climate change and displacement: a systematic review of the empirical literature', *Population and Environment*, 41: 1–23.

Escobar, A. (2004) *Development, Violence and the New Imperial Order*, Duke University Press.

Esposito, R. (2008) *Bios: Biopolitics and Philosophy*, University of Minnesota Press.

Fanon, F. (1963) *The Wretched of the Earth*. Grove Press.

Fawaz, M. (2016) 'Urban crisis and humanitarianism', *International Journal of Urban and Regional Research*, 40(3): 633–52.

Fassin, D. (2009) 'Another politics of life is possible', *Theory, Culture & Society*, 26(5): 44–60.

Feldman, I. (2006) 'Home as a refrain: remembering and living displacement in Gaza', *History and Memory*, 18(2): 10–36.

Fiddian-Qasmiyeh, E. (2020) *The Refugee-Jurist Nexus: A Socio-Legal Analysis*, Routledge.

Fiddian-Qasmiyeh, E. and Qasmiyeh, Y.M. (2016) 'Refugee neighbours and hospitality: exploring the complexities of refugee–refugee humanitarianism', *The Critique*. Available from: www.thecritique.com/articles/refugee-neighbours-hostipitality-2 [Accessed 12 June 2024].

Field, J., Cheek, J., and Lawson, V. (2020) *Urban Displacement: Rethinking Housing Policies for the 21st Century*, Policy Press.

Foucault, M. (2003) *Society Must Be Defended: Lectures at the Collège de France, 1975–1976*, Picador.

Foucault, M. (2007 [1978]) *Security, Territory, Population: Lectures at the Collège de France 1977–78*, Palgrave Macmillan.

Gillespie, A., Bennett, K., and Toole, M. (2021) 'Displacement, gender and mobility: Mapping new migrant experiences', *Gender, Place & Culture*, 28(10–12): 1420–38.

Gilmore, R.W. (2007) *Golden Gulag: Prisons, Surplus, Crisis, and Opposition in Globalizing California*, University of California Press.

Gilroy, P. (2000) *Against Race: Imagining Political Culture Beyond the Color Line*, Belknap Press of Harvard University Press.

Glick Schiller, N. and Çağlar, A. (2011) *Locating Migration: Rescaling Cities and Migrants*, Cornell University Press.

Glick Schiller, N. and Çağlar, A. (2015) *Displacement, Diaspora, and Geographies of Power: Small States in a Global Era*, Duke University Press.

Glück, R. (2009) 'Interview by *EOAGH: A Journal of the Arts*', *EOAGH: A Journal of the Arts*. Available from: https://eoagh.com/interview-with-robert-gluck/all/1 [Accessed 12 June 2024].

Gonzalez, R. (2021) 'Environmental justice and the politics of displacement in Latin America', Latin American Perspectives, 48(3): 52–69.

Grabska, K. (2006) 'Marginalization in urban spaces of the Global South: urban refugees in Cairo', *Journal of Refugee Studies*, 19(3): 287–307.

Graham, S. and Marvin, S. (2001) *Splintering Urbanism: Networked Infrastructures, Technological Mobilities and the Urban Condition*, Routledge.

Gregory, D. (2004) *The Colonial Present: Afghanistan, Palestine, Iraq*, Blackwell.

Guyer, S. and Keller, R.K. (2016) 'Life after biopolitics', *The South Atlantic Quarterly*, 115(2): 212–37.

Hall, S. (2013) 'The right to the city and social justice', *International Journal of Urban and Regional Research*, 37(4): 1509–19.

Hall, S. (2015) 'Urban geography and displacement', *Progress in Human Geography*, 39(3): 284–304.

Hanafi, S., Arar, R., and Kayyali, R. (2010) 'Refugees, forced displacement, and the politics of spatiality', *Journal of Refugee Studies*, 23(1): 16–33.

Haraway, D.J. (1997) 'The virtual speculum in the new world order', *Feminist Review*, 55(1): 22–72.

Haraway, D.J. (2015) *Staying with the Trouble: Making Kin in the Chthulucene*, Duke University Press.

Harvey, D. (2005) *A Brief History of Neoliberalism*, Oxford University Press.

Herscher, A. (2017) *Displacements: Architecture and Refugee*, Sternberg Press.

Herscher, A. and Siddiqi, A. (2019) 'Spatial violations and urban displacement', *Journal of Urban History*, 45(6): 1297–1315.

Hilal, S. and Petti, A. (2018) 'The politics of space in refugee camps', *Geoforum*, 96: 58–65.

Hirsh, E., Eizenberg, E., and Jabareen, Y. (2020) 'A new conceptual framework for understanding displacement: Bridging the gaps in displacement literature between the Global South and the Global North', *Journal of Planning Literature*, 35(4): 391–407.

Holston, J. and Appadurai, A. (1999) 'Cities and citizenship', *Public Culture*, 8(2): 187–204.

Huq, R. and Miraftab, F. (2020) 'Urban informality and displacement', *Environment and Urbanisation*, 32(1): 123–40.

Hyndman, J. (2000) *Managing Displacement: Refugees and the Politics of Humanitarianism*, University of Minnesota Press.

Intergovernmental Panel on Climate Change (IPCC). (2022) *Climate Change 2022: Impacts, Adaptation, and Vulnerability*, Cambridge University Press.

IPBES (2019) *Global Assessment Report on Biodiversity and Ecosystem Services of the Intergovernmental Science-Policy Platform on Biodiversity and Ecosystem Services*, E.S. Brondizio, J. Settele, S. Díaz and H.T. Ngo (eds) IPBES Secretariat. Available from: https://doi.org/10.5281/zenodo.3831673 [Accessed 12 June 2024].

Isayev, E. (2017) *Migration, Mobility, and Place in Ancient Italy*, Cambridge University Press.

Isayev, E. (2021) 'Displacement and the temporal turn', *Journal of Refugee Studies*, 34(2): 210–29.

Isin, E.F. and Nielsen, G.M. (2008) *Acts of Citizenship*, Palgrave Macmillan.

Isin, E.F. and Rygiel, K. (2007) 'Of other global cities: Frontiers, zones, camps', in B. Drieskens, F. Mermier, and H. Wimmen (eds) *Cities of the South: citizenship and exclusion in the 21st century*, Saqi, pp 170–220.

Johnson, C. and Murton, G. (2007) 'Re/placing trust: Indigenous perspectives on environmental monitoring in northern Canada', *The Geographical Journal*, 173(1): 39–51.

Katz, I., Parsloe, T., Poll, Z., and Scafe-Smith, A. (2018) 'Urbanisation and displacement in refugee camps', *Urban Studies*, 55(8): 1857–73.

Kelley, R.D.G. (2015) *Freedom Dreams: The Black Radical Imagination*, Beacon Press.

Kelly, A.B. and Peluso, N.L. (2015) 'Frontier spaces: territorialisation and resource control', *Journal of Peasant Studies*, 42(2): 205–21.

Kreichauf, R. (2022) 'Urban displacement in Europe', *European Urban and Regional Studies*, 29(2): 150–69.

Larkin, B. (2013) 'The politics and poetics of infrastructure', *Annual Review of Anthropology*, 42, 327–43.

Lees, L. (2012) 'Gentrification and social mixing: towards an inclusive urban renaissance?', *Urban Studies*, 49(7): 1379–1406.

Lees, L., Shin, H.B., and Lopez-Morales, E. (2016) *Planetary Gentrification*, Polity Press.

Lemke, T. (2007) 'An indigestible meal: Foucault, governmentality and state theory', *Distinktion: Journal of Social Theory*, 8: 43–64.

Lemke, T. (2011) Biopolitics: An Advanced Introduction, Trans. E.F. Trump, New York University Press.

Lefebvre, H. (1974) *The Production of Space*, Blackwell.

Li, T. (2010) 'To make live or let die?', *Antipode*, 42(5): 120–43.

Lombard, M. (2021) 'Urban displacement in the Global South', *City*, 25(1–2): 44–64.

Lowe, L.J. (2015) *The Intimacies of Four Continents*, Duke University Press.

Lunstrum, E. and Bose, P. (2022) 'Environmental displacement in the Anthropocene', *Annals of the American Association of Geographers*, 112(3): 644–53.

Maestri, G. and Hughes, S.M. (2017) 'Climate change, migration, and the crisis of humanism', in A. Baldwin (ed) *Climate Change, Migration, and the Crisis of Humanism*, Edward Elgar, pp 1–22.

Malkki, L.H. (1995) 'Refugees and exile: From "refugee studies" to the national order of things', *Annual Review of Anthropology*, 24: 495–523.

Mandic, D. (2017) 'Trafficking and Syrian refugee smuggling: evidence from the Balkan route', *Social Inclusion*, 5(2): 28–38.

Maqusi, S. (2021) 'Acts of spatial violation: the politics of space-making inside the Palestinian refugee camp', *ARENA Journal of Architectural Research*, 6(1). https://doi.org/10.5334/ajar.265

Marcuse, P. (2013) 'Gentrification, abandonment, and displacement: connections, causes, and policy responses in New York City', *Journal of Urban Affairs*, 35(3): 282–97.

Martin, A. and Taylor, L. (2020) 'Exclusion and inclusion in identification: regulation, displacement, and data justice', *Information Technology for Development*, 26(4): 755–73.

Martin, R. (2015) 'Forced migration and urban displacement: contested spaces in contemporary cities', *International Journal of Urban and Regional Research*, 39(1): 43–60.

Massey, D. (1994) *Space, Place, and Gender*, Polity Press.

Mastromarino, S. and Boano, C. (2023) 'Vallée de la Roya and its opaque infrastructures of transit. Inhabiting the border', *field*, 1. https://doi.org/10.62471/field.117

Mbembe, J.-A. (2003) *Necropolitics*, Duke University Press.

McIntyre, M. and Nast, H.J. (2011) 'Bio(necro)polis: Marx, surplus populations, and the spatial dialectics of reproduction and "Race"', *Antipode*, 43: 1465–88.

Mezzadra, S. and Neilson, B. (2013) *Border as Method, or, the Multiplication of Labor*, Duke University Press.

Mignolo, W.D. (2017) 'Coloniality is far from over, and so must be decoloniality', *Afterall Journal*, 43. www.afterall.org/articles/coloniality-is-far-from-over-and-so-must-be-decoloniality

Minca, C. (2007) 'Foucault and the governmentalization of geography', *Geography Compass*, 1(1): 84–99.

Minca, C., Rijke, A., Pallister-Wilkins, P., Tazzioli, M., Vigneswaran, D., van Houtum, H., and van Uden, A. (2022) 'Rethinking the biopolitical: Borders, refugees, mobilities', *Environment and Planning C: Politics and Space*, 40(1): 3–30.

Montaser, M.A. (2020) 'Environmental displacement and climate justice: The case of Middle Eastern migrants', *Journal of Refugee Studies*, 33(2): 365–86.

Moore, J. (2015) *Anthropocene or Capitalocene? Nature, History and the Crisis of Capitalism*, PM Press.

Musmar, A. (2020) Domestic Refugee Architecture in Jordan: A Socio-spatial Analysis of Chaotic Camps, master's thesis, the American University in Cairo.

Musmar, A. (2022) Out law yard: Reading traces of displacement as testimonial inscriptions, Unpublished manuscript, the American University in Cairo.

Nail, T. (2016) *The Figure of the Migrant*, Stanford University Press.

Nixon, R. (2013) *Slow Violence and the Environmentalism of the Poor*, Harvard University Press.

Nolan, R. (2017) 'The end of bare life?', *Journal of American Studies*, 51(3): E33.

Owens, P. (2009) 'The politics of displacement: urban redevelopment and racial segregation', *Urban Affairs Review*, 45(3): 367–93.

Pallister-Wilkins, P. (2021) 'The humanitarian politics of border control: migration and sovereignty in the Mediterranean', *Journal of Borderlands Studies*, 36(3): 371–85.

Pasquetti, S. and Picker, G. (2017) 'Confined informality: Global margins, statecraft, and urban life', *International Sociology*, 32(4): 532–44.

Pasquetti, S. and Sanyal, R. (2020) *Displacement: Global Conversations on Refuge*, Manchester University Press.

Povinelli, E. (2006) *The Empire of Love: Toward a Theory of Intimacy, Genealogy, and Carnality*, Duke University Press.

Povinelli, E. (2011) *Economies of Abandonment: Social Belonging and Endurance in Late Liberalism*, Duke University Press.

Povinelli, E. (2016) *Geontologies: A Requiem to Late Liberalism*, Duke University Press.

Pratt, G. (2005) *Working Feminism*, Temple University Press.

Proglio, G., Hawthorne, C., Danewid, I., Saucier, P.K., Grimaldi, G., Pesarini, A., Raeymaekers, T., Grechi, G. and Gerrand, V. (eds) (2021) *The Black Mediterranean: Bodies, Borders and Citizenship*, Palgrave Macmillan.

Puar, J.K. (2017) *The Right to Maim: Debility, Capacity, Disability*, Duke University Press.

Qasmiyeh, Y. M. and Fiddian-Qasmiyeh, E. (2013) 'Refugee camps and cities in conversation', in J. Garnett and A. Harris (eds) *Rescripting Religion in the city: Migration and religious identity in the modern metropolis*, Ashgate, pp 131–43.

Raffestin, C. (2012) 'Space, territory, and territoriality', *Environment and Planning D: Society and Space*, 30(1): 121–41.

Rajaram, P.K. (2018) 'Refugees as surplus population: race, migration and capitalist value regimes', *New Political Economy*, 23(5): 627–39.

Ramadan, A. (2009) 'Territorializing displacement: Urban refugees and the politics of space in Cairo', *International Journal of Urban and Regional Research*, 33(2): 489–508.

Rasmussen, M. and Lund, K. (2017) 'Spatial justice and displacement', *Antipode*, 49(2): 333–51.

Redclift, V. (2013) 'Displacement and dispossession: The social meanings of "home"', *International Migration*, 51(1): 154–67.

Rice, J., Long, J., and Levenda, A. (2021) 'Against climate apartheid: Confronting the persistent legacies of expendability for climate justice', *Environment and Planning E: Nature and Space*, 5(2): 625–45.

Richter-Montpetit, M. and Howell, A. (2019) 'Racism in Foucauldian security studies: biopolitics, liberal war, and the whitewashing of colonial and racial violence', *International Political Sociology*, 13(1): 2–19.

Roast, A., Conlon, D., Garelli, G., and Waite, L. (2022) 'The need for inter/subdisciplinary thinking in critical conceptualizations of displacement', *Annals of the American Association of Geographers*, 112(3): 626–35.

Rose, G. (2007) *Visual Methodologies: An Introduction to Researching with Visual Materials* (2nd ed), Sage.

Roy, A. (2011) 'Slumdog cities: Rethinking subaltern urbanism', *International Journal of Urban and Regional Research*, 35(2): 223–38.

Said, E. (1978) *Orientalism*, Pantheon Books.

Shen, Q. and Wu, J. (2017) 'Gentrification and displacement: an investigation of displacement pressures in Washington, DC', *Urban Studies*, 54(9): 2145–63.

Sanyal, R. (2012) 'Urbanizing refuge: Interrogating spaces of displacement', *International Journal of Urban and Regional Research*, 38(2): 558–72.

Sanyal, R. (2013) *Urbanizing Migrants: The Politics of Space and Displacement*, Wiley-Blackwell.

Sassen, S. (2001) *The Global City: New York, London, Tokyo*, Princeton University Press.

Sassen, S. (2014) *Expulsions: Brutality and Complexity in the Global Economy*, Harvard University Press.

Schofield, R. (2020) 'Borderland studies, frontierization, and the Middle East's in-between spaces', *Mediterranean Politics*, 25(2): 1–18.

Scott, J. (1986) *Weapons of the weak. Everyday Forms of Peasant Resistance*, Yale University Press.

Seethaler-Wari, S., Chitchian, S., and Momić, M. (2022) *Inhabiting Displacement: Architecture and Authorship*, Birkhäuser.

Sharma, A. (2020) *Biopolitics, Geopolitics, Life: Settler Colonialism and the Politics of Life*, Duke University Press.

Sheehi, S. and Sheehi, L. (2020) 'The settlers' town is a strongly built town: Fanon in Palestine', *International Journal of Applied Psychoanalytic Studies*, 17: 183–92.

Sigona, N. (2015) 'Campzenship: Reimagining the refugee camp as a social and political space', *Citizenship Studies*, 19(1): 1–15.

Simone, A. (2004) 'People as infrastructure: Intersecting fragments in Johannesburg', *Public Culture*, 16(3): 407–29.

Simone, A. (2016) 'The uninhabitable? In between collapsed yet still rigid distinctions', *Cultural Politics*, 12(2): 135–54.

Simone, A. (2021) 'Ritornello: "people as infrastructure"', *Urban Geography*, 42(9): 1341–8.

Smith, S. and Vasudevan, P. (2017) 'Race, biopolitics, and the future: introduction to the special section', *Environment and Planning D: Society and Space*, 35(2): 210–21.

Springer, S. (2013) 'Violent neoliberalism: development, dispossession, and the forgotten geography of violence', *Progress in Human Geography*, 37(5): 740–59.

Star, S.L. (1999) 'The ethnography of infrastructure', *American Behavioral Scientist*, 43(3): 377–91.

Stoler, A.L. and Cooper, F. (1997) 'Between metropole and colony: rethinking a research agenda', in F. Cooper and A.L. Stoler (eds) *Tensions of Empire: Colonial Cultures in a Bourgeois World*, University of California Press, pp 1–56.

Strauss, K. (2022) 'Introduction to displacements', *ARENA Journal of Architectural Research*, 7(1): 1–6.

Sultana, F. (2022) 'Water, climate change, and displacement: Vulnerability and resilience', *Geoforum*, 130: 225–35.

Swyngedouw, E., Moulaert, F., and Rodriguez, A. (2002) 'Neoliberal urbanization in Europe: large-scale urban development projects and the new urban policy', *Antipode*, 34(3): 542–77.

Talocci, G., Brown, D., and Yacobi, H. (2022) 'The biogeopolitics of cities: a critical enquiry across Jerusalem, Phnom Penh, Toronto', *Planning Perspectives*, 37(1): 169–89.

Tadiar, N.X.M. (2009) *Things Fall Away: Philippine Historical Experience and the Makings of Globalization*, Duke University Press.

Tadiar, N.X.M. (2013) 'Life-times of disposability within global neoliberalism', *Social Text*, 31(2): 19–48.

Tarazona Vento, A. (2017) 'Spatial justice and the politics of displacement in Latin America', *Journal of Latin American Geography*, 16(2): 23–42.

Tazzioli, M. (2015) *The Making of Migration: Refugees and Migrants at the Borders of Europe*, Routledge.

Tazzioli, M. (2021) *Liquid Politics: Border Dynamics, Refugee Politics and the Practices of Control*, Routledge.

Tierney, T.F. (2016) 'Roberto Esposito's "affirmative biopolitics" and the gift', *Theory, Culture & Society*, 33(2): 53–76.

Tsing, A.L. (2015) *The Mushroom at the End of the World: On the Possibility of Life in Capitalist Ruins*, Princeton University Press.

Tuana, N. (2019) 'Climate apartheid: The forgetting of race in the Anthropocene', *Critical Philosophy of Race*, 7(1): 1–31.

Tuitjer, L. and Batréau, Q. (2019) 'Urban refugees in a "non-Convention" city', *City*, 23(1): 1–16.

Turner, S. (2016) 'What is a refugee camp? Explorations of the limits and effects of the camp', *Journal of Refugee Studies*, 29(2): 139–48.

van Wichelen, S. (2020) 'More-than-human biopolitics', in S. Vint (ed) *After the Human: Culture, Theory and Criticism in the 21st Century*, Cambridge University Press, pp 161–76.

Vasudevan, A. (2017) *The Autonomous City: A History of Urban Squatting*, Verso.

Vatter, M. (2009) 'Biopolitics: From surplus value to surplus life', *Theory & Event* 12(2). https://doi.org/10.1353/tae.0.0062

Wade, R. (1959) 'The geography of human migration', *Geographical Review*, 49(4): 528–46.

Wahab, R.A., Kyaw, M.M., and Sueb, R. (2022) 'Post-migration stressors and educational coping mechanisms among adolescent refugees in Malaysia', *International Journal of Academic Research in Business and Social Sciences*, 12(7): 1199–1210.

Waldby, C. (2000) *The Visible Human Project*, Routledge.

Wang, Y. and Wu, F. (2019) 'Urban displacement and socio-spatial exclusion in China: the case of Beijing', *Urban Geography*, 40(7): 1020–43.

Watson, G. (2012) *The Politics of Life Itself: Biomedicine, Power and Subjectivity in the Twenty First Century*, Princeton University Press.

Weheliye, A.G. (2017) *Habeas Viscus: Racializing Assemblages, Biopolitics, and Black Feminist Theories of the Human*, Duke University Press.

Wilk, E. (2022) *Death by Landscape: Essays*, First Soft Skull.

Wright, M. (2006) *Disposable Women and Other Myths of Global Capitalism*, Routledge.

Wynter, S. (2003) 'Unsettling the coloniality of being/power/truth/freedom: towards the human, after man, its overrepresentation – an argument', *CR The New Centennial Review*, 3(3): 257–337.

Yacobi, H. (2015) 'Jerusalem: from a "divided" to a "contested" city – and next to a neo-apartheid city?', *Analysis of Urban Change, Theory, Action*, 19(4): 579–84.

Yiftachel, O. (2020) 'From displacement to displaceability', *City*, 24(1–2): 151–65.

Yusoff, K. (2017) 'Indeterminate subjects, irreducible worlds: two economies of indeterminacy', *Body & Society*, 23(3): 75–101.

Zetter, R. (2011) 'Unlocking the protracted displacement of refugees and internally displaced persons: an overview', *Refugee Survey Quarterly*, 30(4): 1–13.

PART I

Extraction

2

Displacement, Two Ways: Necroeconomic Navigations in the Peri-Urban Global Southeast

Elliott Prasse-Freeman

Introduction: Moments of displacement and conditions of displaceability

Urban geographer Oren Yiftachel (2020) encourages a break from the standard way of understanding displacement and dispossession. Critiquing the tendency in the displacement literature to focus 'almost solely on the impact of capitalism, neoliberalism, and gentrification in the global "northwest"' (2020: 151), Yiftachel argues that in the global 'southeast',[1] 'nationalism, statism, identity regimes and struggles for human and urban rights' (2020: 151) are just as important for how they spur and inflect displacement processes.[2] Or, as the Burmese scholar Than Than Nwe (1998: 89) put it when discussing Yangon more than a quarter of a century ago, 'in the preoccupation with economic conditions, insufficient attention is given to the influence of political change as a major factor in the urbanization process'.

Likewise, Yiftachel's delineation of the sources of displacement invites a schematization: of the northwestern space where dispossession applies primarily to individuals who are subjected to a 'single logic of capital accumulation through urban redevelopment' (Yiftachel, 2020: 157), versus a southeastern space defined by displaceability – 'a systemic condition through which spatial power is exerted by policy, legalities and violence' (2020: 161) and which operates on a collective actor – such that displaceability even acts as a 'new foundation of urban citizenship' (2020: 157). However, given that the former can be found in the latter – and vice versa (see Till, 2012; Roy, 2019) – the two forms of displacement can rather be thought together, imagined as separate but intercalating urbanization machines

(Simone, 2018: 25), often in tension (Boano, 2016), that produce a broader assemblage of dispossessionary forces that also build the built environment itself (Beeckmans et al, 2022) over different temporalities (Rokem and Boano, 2023). In this, the chapter echoes the work of Astolfo and Boano (2020: 430), who describe the city as 'the operative product of a constant conflict of rationalities and intentionalities, rather than the simple duality of intentions'.

In the following sketch of the dynamics introduced above, this chapter first clarifies the effects of the violence immanent to the intermixing of authoritarian state imperatives, desultory or absent biopolitical care, and capitalist extraction. The dual extrusive machines generated by market and non-market violence, respectively, produce effects that are adumbrated through the concept of the necroeconomy (Prasse-Freeman, 2022). This elaboration encompasses a history of displacements and mobility in Yangon, the country's dominant urban space, specifically, and in Myanmar more broadly. The chapter then turns to the interaction of the two machines described above, showing how they play out in Yangon, drawing on several years of ethnographic research conducted there. Finally, it reflects on the consequences for political action. This includes an exploration of how schisms and fragmentations in the displaced subject, perhaps Yiftachel's endorsement of a common subject position founded in displaceability, emerge in the wake of displacement.

Foundations of the necroeconomy

The necroeconomy, observable in spaces of the Global South but perhaps spreading globally, deviates in two critical ways from the political economy as it is classically conceived (Prasse-Freeman, 2022). First, it builds on emergent theories of extraction (Gago and Mezzadra, 2017; Mezzadra and Neilson, 2020), in which extractive capitalist operations harness or assemble for value extraction 'a social vitality and cooperation that they do not contribute to organizing' (Mezzadra and Neilson, 2020: 583). In the global southeast, this can mean that the necroeconomy treats human bodies not as labourers who must be directly cultivated and promoted (as in the way a biopolitical project would invest in the worker population), nor as disciplined and managed, but rather as an input that is affixed or inserted into a larger process (Tadiar, 2022: 170), an input that must articulate itself in between elements that constitute the critical and indispensable factors in production functions broadly conceived (particularly capital and infrastructure). Take 'putting out', for instance – where work that had previously been conducted under the watchful eye of the supervisor on the assembly line is removed from the workplace so labourers conduct small-scale tasks in their own homes. Stephen Campbell, who studied how Burmese migrants in the Thai–Burma border industrial zones conduct such putting-out work, argues that 'the return of putting-out work in Thailand's garment sector can be read as a capitalist response to the gains achieved by Thai and Myanmar workers in prior labor struggles and to the ongoing threat of such struggles in the present' (Campbell, 2016: 73). Yet, simultaneously, it seems that putting out is the ultimate neoliberal move – the labourer gets paid a fixed rate for each item they produce, and nothing more. Labourers in even more informal and violent environments (Campbell, 2022) – in Yangon's peri-urban zones, for instance – are not worth the investment of labour discipline. Campbell shows how they wander squatter settlements, picking up recyclables or harvesting worms in fields to sell to eel farmers. When such tasks lead to debility, the 'firm' (recycling plant owner, eel merchant, etc.) does not much care. While sometimes the relationship between merchant capitalist and labourer stabilizes into a pseudo boss–labourer arrangement (2022: 81), the boss is also not so concerned if that person gets stabbed in the gut (2022: 1), gets wounded, or falls into debt so deeply that they have to leave for even more dangerous work opportunities (Campbell, 2022: Prasse- Freeman, 2022). When such bodily destruction transpires, the boss simply makes it known that these kinds of commodities are valuable, and new labourers will likely emerge to provide them.

Consequently, the necroeconomy's second deviation from more standard labour relationships is that workers are subject to a particular form of value extraction in which operations are either apathetic to their death, cannot avoid producing some amount of death, or even function more efficiently with an acceptable amount of death. The necroeconomy hence describes the vanishing point where essential and surplus labourers converge: workers are necessary for capital until the moment when their lives also become objects of extraction. This creates a fraught subject position, in which labourers exist uncertain about whether they are relatively or absolutely unnecessary to the system. These features congeal into a political economic regime that coerces and incites participation of those who are necessary for that system's reproduction, even as those people are often killed or debilitated.

Displacement – forced or otherwise – is a useful key through which to reveal how this necroeconomic system has developed, at least in one specific southeastern context: Myanmar. The following summary uses a historical exploration of the different political economic motivations for, and consequences of, displacement in Myanmar as a way to outline how the specific contours of the two dispossessionary machines introduced above come into focus.[3] Specifically, while peasants working Burma's lands were historically necessary to generate the polity's wealth (and were lauded in its symbolic culture), the evolution of the global economy (which has substituted capital for labour in part as a by-product of technological advance), and the general transformation of land into a commodity (on which capital-intensive endeavours can be pursued), has meant that wealth is increasingly generated through means *less* involving labourers (workers or farmers). Bodies are excluded from the constellations of production inputs (land, capital, 'total factor productivity') in which wealth is generated, and forced into more parasitic positions where they arrange themselves in a way that enables them to eke out reproduction.

Forced displacement over the longue durée in Myanmar

In the precolonial era, displacement acted as the means by which Burma's lords agglomerated labourers to generate exploitable surpluses and make their political orders possible. Central to their functioning was the gathering of enslaved persons – a main objective of wars, for instance (Beemer, 2009). Such slave capture was necessary in the first place because self-displacement was also a protective technique through which peasants avoided dynastic state exploitation. Peasants either maneouvred between patronage systems within a given sovereign's broader remit, finding protection under elites competing with the sovereign (see Lieberman, 2010; Roberts, 2020: 423) or escaped its regulatory orbit entirely (as described by Scott, 2009).

In a second mode/era of displacement, state-capital assemblages deracinated bodies to then (re)deploy their labour power in productive spaces. The British colonial government induced massive population movements from the 1880s through the 1920s, then enacted unforgiving debt repayment laws that re-displaced Burmese peasants from newly settled land, forcing them to extend the rice-paddy frontier (Adas, 2011; Brown 2013). A mix of inducements and coercion under the British was replaced by violent compulsion under the post-colonial military regime, as the military state (1962–2011) attempted to forcibly resettle ethnic minority villagers into the equivalent of strategic hamlets in the country's upland areas (Bosson, 2007), moved hundreds of thousands of people in urban areas into what became manufacturing zones (particularly in 1990), and displaced farmers through forced land grabs and rice-procurement policies to often reterritorialize them as sharecroppers on their own lands (Prasse-Freeman, 2023). Across the postcolonial period, the military-state partially consolidated control of its territory and its margins, somewhat mitigating the availability of the self-displacement option for peasants. Considering both the colonial and postcolonial eras, while the state across this period deployed tactics for putting bodies down in space that diverged in the degrees and forms of violence it used, one common element was how reterritorialized bodies were made useful participants in the economy.

The third phase of displacement, dominant during the era of 'political transition' from 2011 to the military coup of February 2021, has significantly deviated from the previous eras. The reason for its deviation is that subjects' autonomy and their position of bargaining power in Myanmar's political economy have both eroded, prohibiting them from capturing the value they produce or consolidating their participation in production processes into stable lives. This is in part because political economic transformation wrought by Myanmar's liberalization processes made land productive for purposes that involve bodies to a vastly diminished degree – and sometimes not at all (i.e. when land has become a speculative asset). Indeed, Elizabeth Rhoads (2023: 143, n 4) describes this period in early 2010, locally referred to as 'the fire sale', where large pieces of public land were given away to well-connected individuals. This event marked a transition to a more intensively capitalist mode of land exploitation. Rhoads (2019) argues that before the 'transition', urban landowners had accrued a consistent, if small, income stream from their tenants: land investment was then a risk-management strategy.[4] Upon liberalization, however, land investment became a capital accumulation method: land is an asset that should generate significant and fairly immediate returns (Prasse-Freeman, 2022: 1478–79). On one hand, market liberalization has meant that speculators literally follow planning announcements, buying up land surrounding new project sites the day they are made public. On the other hand, liberalization has also made land valuable as a commodity, and hence desirable for theft by the military and military-connected elites (Rhoads, 2019).

In the cases where land still remains the site of production rather than the wealth generator itself, those production processes often do not rely on the same consistent labour-intensive operations: mechanized mineral extraction, agribusiness farming, and special economic zones mostly eschew labourers. Hence, displacement has become either a technique through which bodies are removed from physical locations more valuable to state-capital operations or a desperate tactic pursued by subjects who can no longer support themselves in their homes and must chase fleeting labour opportunities. From short-term on-farm work to peri-urban informal hustle (elaborated below), to agribusiness plantation or up-country jade, gold, or ruby mine extraction work, labourers have been put on the perpetual move, or remain in villages and slums eking out reproduction only through the support of remittances.

The next section closely explores the most recent era of displacement through an examination of Myanmar's largest urban space, Yangon, and the forms of social reproduction that are pursued there.

Yangon's dual displacement machine

From its effective beginning, Yangon's history has also been characterized by displacement, as outlined thoroughly by Rhoads (2018). Indeed, after the First Anglo- Burmese war, the British appropriated by fiat all the land that became what is now Yangon, then 'sold it to the highest bidder' (2018: 298). In order to avoid all public land being alienated to private hands, the British later leased lands to Burmese populations returning or settling in lands outside the city core (land they had cleared themselves, it should be added). When these lands in turn increased in value (in terms of lease at higher prices), the British evicted the Burmese populations and forced them to move to more marginal areas, which were provided with no sewerage system, water provision, roads, or affordable housing (2018: 284–7). Such patterns continued once the military took over in 1958, with 150,000 squatters displaced to the peripheries of the city between 1959 and 1960. As people perpetually returned to the city centre, in part seeking refuge from the ongoing civil war, the military-state continued with evictions, including 38,000 households in 1971 and then a mammoth expulsion, begun in 1990 after the 1988 mass uprisings, of half a million people, who were sent to what were at the time exurban lands with no infrastructure called the 'New Fields' (Skidmore, 2004; Cornish, 2020; Roberts, 2020).

Some of these workers eventually found reabsorption as labourers in industrial zones that were developed several years later (Lubeigt, 2007). Phyo Wai's research on communities relocated from Insein township (a suburb of Yangon) to Hlaingthaya (one of the 'New Fields' across the Panhlaing River 22 km northwest of the city center) notes that the absolute abjectness of the first five years (1990–95) of immured abandonment gave way to an improved standard of living as bodies (turned into captive labour pools) met capital on land deemed 'new'. To illustrate, Phyo Wai, whose own family was evicted to Hlaingthaya from Insein, highlights the irony that today those living in the transported communities are in general better off than those in Insein who were not forced to move (Wai, 2013). But formal sector employment has still been relatively scarce, meaning that most labouring opportunities emerged peripheral to the formal sector industrial jobs, in sectors such as services and construction.

While the advance of the political liberalization termed the 'transition' (2011–21) further increased employment opportunities, it also put further upward pressure on land values, not only displacing people from the countryside (Matelski and Sabrié, 2019; Campbell, 2022), but making squatting more difficult as legal ownership claims multiplied (Rhoads and Wittekind, 2018; Astolfo and Boano, 2020: 441). Yet, despite the ostensible dawning of democratic conditions, squatters were forcibly evicted with the same fervour (Kyed, 2019; Roberts, 2020). This history – how a rapidly neoliberalizing political economy combines with a state that has consistently policed and evicted citizens – now allows for an exploration of the dual urban displacement machines and their spatial consequences.

Disability, debility, debt: the daily displacement squeeze

While this history emphasizes evictions, it is important to consider how these evictions create a broader violent environment that influences more prosaic, non-episodic displacements. In the cases of expulsion described above (either from places in Yangon or from the rural countrysides), subjects thrown again 'into the breach to meet the changing needs of capital' (Wolf, 1982: 380) become more vulnerable to dangerous economies where death can be the end. Comparative analyses of displacement often feature those precise outcomes (McIntyre and Nast, 2011; Ortega, 2020). However, death is not always the reason why the ability to participate in these dangerous markets ceases; instead, exit from those specific markets – and hence their ultimate displacement from the particular urban spaces where they live – often derives from the way those bodies are altered by their engagements with the dangerous operations, such that they can no longer reproduce themselves – a phenomenon to which we now turn.

Drawing from accounts of life in peri-urban Yangon (Thawnghmung, 2019; Cornish, 2020; Campbell, 2022; Khine Zaw, 2022), and from my own ethnographic fieldwork in peri-urban Yangon and with a labour union operating in the Hlaingthaya industrial zone, I identify an affinity between peri-urban dwellers' '3D labour' (of the 'dirty, dangerous, and demeaning' variety) and another set of Ds: disability, debility, and debt – and, consequently, displacement.

While disability is highly culturally specific (Connell, 2011), the little research that has been done in the Myanmar context (Ware and Schuelka, 2019; Cole, 2020; Dan Seng Lawn et al, 2023) suggests that it is not conceived as a deviation from normative bodily capabilities, but rather adheres more closely to a Marxist sense of disability (Russell and Malhotra, 2002), in which it is defined as the inability to participate in livelihood labour. Debility, as defined by Jasbir Puar (2017: xiii), has much the same end: the 'slow wearing down of populations instead of the event of becoming disabled' if that 'wearing down' is defined as the inability to reproduce oneself.

The labour union with which I worked published a monthly periodical called *The Worker Journal* for two years (2014–15), and devoted significant discussion to both Myanmar's labour law and the need to navigate it precisely in order to achieve redress in the event of injury or disability (e.g. A Retired Employee, n.d.). Such stories cast an ironic tone, especially given that Ye Naing Win, the head of the union and journal editor, has been quoted in international press condemning the inefficacy of Burma's labour protection laws – e.g. in the case of the union advocating for a woman named Zin Mar Htwe, who lost her arm in a 2014 factory accident in Mandalay (see Turner, 2016). Ye Naing Win stressed how compensation, even with the union's advocacy, would never be sufficient to permit amputees, for instance, to survive economically in the labor market. As Yuzana Khine Zaw (2022: 139) puts it, workers are

> biopolitically abandoned ... by the factory who provides little to no occupational health service, abandoned by the social security clinic which functions to process sick leave requests more so than to provide adequate healthcare, abandoned by the industrial zone and the factory which continues to create exploitative working conditions, and last, abandoned by labour laws/regulations which fail to be properly enacted in practice.

Khine Zaw's (2022) research emphasizes how workers utilize over-the-counter pharmaceuticals as a method of self-medication, rehabilitating their broken bodies enough to participate again in the market. Given Myanmar's blunt biopolitical context (Prasse-Freeman, 2023), in which population groups are taken as an object of governance but neither promoted nor protected, populations are left to fend for themselves. Khine Zaw describes a process of debilitation in which medicine can only rehabilitate workers' bodies for a time, before sustained participation in labouring activities is undermined. Her work reveals the existence of what we might call, following Bernstein (1981), the 'daily displacement squeeze',[5] where health shocks or diminishing marginal returns for this kind of physically demanding work lead to the intensification of self-exploitation. Hence, in contrast to the land exhaustion that Bernstein described in rural areas, where peasants who cannot let their lands lie fallow ultimately initiate a perpetual spiral of decreasing yields, here labourers increasingly lack sufficient recovery time to stave off complete exhaustion of the body's very capacity to labour.[6] Finally, the formal workers in the industrial zone are predominantly young women aged 18 to 26 years, and Ye Naing Win reports that when they get 'too old', they are often fired. What these various cases have in common is the immediate or gradual erosion of the ability to participate in the necroeconomy.

This leads us to ask what spatial effects these processes produce. Campbell (2022), in his ethnography of a Yangon squatter settlement, features people engaged in factory work, small-scale vending, animal husbandry, recyclables collection, and material portering – occupations that often precipitate debility and disability as their byproduct.[7] Some of his interlocutors were directly forced into squatting because their bodies broke down; consider Aunty Cho and Uncle Hla Soe, a middle-aged couple both wounded by their labouring activities to the point of incapacity:

> When Aunty Cho, by then in her forties, was likewise unable to continue portering, the boss promptly evicted the couple and their two daughters without a single kyat in compensation paid to Uncle Hla

Soe for the foot injury he had incurred on the job, or to the couple for their years of hard labor. Husband and wife then moved down the road and into a rental shack at the Yadana [squatter] settlement. As a means of livelihood, they began collecting for resale waste that had been discarded along nearby roadsides. (Campbell, 2022: 40)

Moreover, to the extent that there was a wage differential between the couple's employment opportunities (from the wage of portering to that of waste collection) and a cost-of-living difference from the job's subsidized housing to that in the squatter settlement (which are often rented from longer-term resident 'owners'), such households may go into debt. While they can rely on community and kinship networks for a time, if repayment becomes impossible, they may end up fleeing lenders to whom they have defaulted or may be evicted by local landlords, such that they go further to the margins.

The social activist group members with whom I conducted fieldwork in peri-urban Yangon from 2014 relayed that most money lenders are rich people who live outside the peri-urban wards. Money lending itself is coordinated and managed within the wards by brokers (*pwesa*), who tend to receive only a small management fee. The rich lenders are also *pwesa* in a sense, as they help make land markets for money laundering pursued by 'drug smugglers, traders, two-digit and three-digit lottery owners', as the activists put it. Helen Kyed (2019: 4) also identifies similar processes, finding that moneylenders 'benefit from illegal land sales'. Hence, like real estate brokers the world over who benefit from churn, displacement is a money-making endeavour. As land prices increase, indebted landowners may be compelled to sell their lands to pay back a loan, their land having become a valuable commodity.[8]

Gillian Cornish (2020: 122) finds that all of her interlocutors 'had at some stage since [earlier forced] relocation, used their land title as collateral to get access to cash'. And while 'some had reclaimed [their land] documents', 'others have not because they defaulted on their loan, unable to afford the repayments'. Consequently, 'selling ... land has been a common action amongst the relocatees to manage debts' (2020: 122). As one of Cornish's interlocutors puts it: 'I have a [land] grant [certificate] but it is at the pawn shop. I have to get it back, but I don't have enough money to take it back right now. If we cannot take the grant back, we will lose it and will have to move from this place. I am afraid that I cannot take it back' (2020: 122). While informal microcredit groups can be more forgiving, Cornish's interlocutors relay that every six to 12 months in each ward a borrower 'runs away and the other members have to pay for it' (Cornish, 2020: 123). Cornish points out that the New Fields ward that she studied was occupied by newcomers who had displaced previous residents, 'families who were unable to stay ...

due to a lack of social and other supports' (2020: 138). Nyi Lin Maung et al's (2023: 7) large-scale quantitative survey on Yangon's squatter communities provides support for these qualitative conclusions regarding the displacement squeeze and concomitant spatial mobility. The study finds that the poorest squatter communities draw one-third of their residents from migrants born in wealthier Yangon townships. This evinces the vast amount of downward mobility in Yangon, and suggests that the compounding effect of debility, disability, and debt together constitute a machinic push, leading many to the perpetually expanding edge.[9]

Auto-construction or auto-eviction?

As these squatters exit their earlier neighbourhoods and find new spaces, they must make their homes anew. However, in contrast to other 'auto-construction' situations (Holston, 2008; Caldeira, 2016), Myanmar squatters may not capture the value they create.[10] Rather, by generating value in land they improve, squatters may inadvertently produce a rise in their own rents or spur a reassertion of ownership by absentees: in the end, they may end up experiencing a perverse corollary that might be named 'auto-eviction'. Maxime Boutry (2018) catalogues how labourers have in the last decade squatted on unclaimed or unused land near factories in ex-urban Yangon (in land at the margins of the New Fields which was still classified as farmland). Some of these areas of Yangon are simply inaccessible (due to flooding, for instance) for part of the year; all lack infrastructure (electricity, roads, water, and so on) that make them suitable for living (see also McPherson, 2016). Given the inculcated norm and need for self-reliance in Myanmar (McCarthy, 2023), many squatters devote labour and their savings to make these new spaces liveable (Astolfo and Boano, 2020). They build infrastructure such as roads and sewage solutions (rudimentary as they may be), and hence demonstrate to the authorities that the land is habitable and should and could be classified as an urban ward rather than as farmland. Yet, by so doing, they transform the spaces, making them simultaneously unviable as farmland and desirable as urban spaces.[11] Absentee landowners often reappear at this point, reasserting claims of ownership they burn through connections with coercive state authorities. This is the form of extraction that is emphasized by Mezzadra (2018), in which social cooperation (auto-construction) is pirated by those who did not play any role in creating that value (the evictors).

These data on auto-eviction dovetail with the larger trends in evictions manifesting in the last half-decade in Yangon. Eben Forbes' (2016) research on evictions shows that most evictees today are labelled 'squatters', and given little if any compensation before their housing is destroyed and they are forced to move. They are typically offered no resettlement opportunities. Forbes marks this change from the previous era and notes that it is because peripheral auto-construction 'is not sustainable'. Forbes attributes this unsustainability to 'government's inability to extend basic urban services to the extension areas and due to increasingly unbearable commute times' (2016: 234). But history itself has demonstrated the model's sustainability: evictees of previous eras generated their own services.

What has changed to prevent the state from using these evicted bodies to build the city out just as it did in the past? The marketization of land and the broader penetration of capitalism have provided more lucrative options for elites than using impoverished masses to haphazardly construct the city. Formalizing former squatters will allow them to capture the increased value of their land. Instead, development can be done by keeping contracts and tenders within the terrain of the elite economy, thereby concentrating land rent in the rising upper-middle class. This has seemed poised to happen on several occasions – as with the proposal of 'New Yangon City' in 2014 (Wittekind, 2024).

Conclusion: Subjective effects

The two machines – daily displacement squeeze and forcible relocation/ auto-eviction land grab – are not, however, the fate of everyone in Myanmar. Nyi Lin Maung et al (2023) show that some squatter areas have stabilized to the point where their residents are nearly middle class by Myanmar standards and enjoy relatively stable land tenure. Returning to Yiftachel, are these people displaceable in the same way that the squatters in the flood-submerged hyper margins are?

Let us return to the debt networks that help sustain those who have endured debility (or otherwise) shocks. While these may begin as mutual aid and support, they can morph into relationships of patronage and even exploitation that resemble a wage contract (Campbell, 2022: 81). People who arrive slightly earlier to a squat can leverage that felicity to become slum landlords, as Mike Davis (2006: 80–1) points out in comparative context. Here we can observe a secondary effect of the daily displacement squeeze – it enacts a splitting of the proletariat such that networks of care become mild class distinctions (Hall et al, 2011; Li, 2011).

As people move across the threshold, from proletarian to an owner of capital (in the form of debt holdings), what are the subjective effects? While the variegation of capital literature is concerned with the institutional regimes that inflect capitalism's expression, we might follow others who are interested in how those varied regimes create different subject positions (Read, 2003; Mezzadra, 2018). Danny Hoffman (2011: 106–8), for instance, in writing about violent labourers in Sierra Leone, identifies a subject who becomes 'completely subsumed' to capitalist dynamics, but we might suggest that there are variegations of subsumption – different ways in which subjectivity is re-formed and remade through interactions with capital. Being subsumed in the factory involves, as Tronti (1980) and the operaists show, a reworking of capital as well; by contrast, the forms of violence to which Hoffman's labourers are exposed, and which they react against, involve something different.

In other words, after being exposed to the brutalities of the necroeconomy, does moving into a position of relative strength and privilege encourage people to reach across the capital–proletarian divide to create a common politics of the displaceable? This is an open empirico-political question – we cannot assume a class politics, but instead must examine the forms of organizing that occur at the margins, both by organized crime syndicates or petit bourgeois capitalists undermining solidarities with the proletariat, and by activist groups encouraging people to see conditions and their interclass connections in new ways. The ways in which these political formations materialize may determine how cities take on their spatial form. Hence, this chapter has attempted to demonstrate how displacement urbanism operates to shape the city, but how movements against it may do so otherwise.

Notes

[1] South in 'southeast' for Yiftachel is economic while east indexes cultural difference.
[2] For some of the rich literature on forcible dispossession and relocation in the south, see Doshi (2013), Gillespie (2016), Ortega (2020), and Astolfo (2023).
[3] For an extended, if preliminary, version of this argument, see Prasse-Freeman (2016).
[4] See also MDRI and Mastercard (2015: 59, 68, 73).
[5] In this phraseology, I riff on Henry Bernstein's (1981) famous 'simple reproduction squeeze', which describes the constant pressures on small holders in the context of decreasing marginal returns to agriculture.
[6] See also Kramer (2022) and Meehan and Seng Lawn Dan (2024) for similar examples across Myanmar of attempts at bodily rehabilitation through drugs/medicines).
[7] Separate cases of debility, disability, or simple exhaustion can be found in Campbell (2022: 40, 42, 61, 103; see also Cornish (2020, 119, 120, 139).
[8] This is especially true if they lack alternative finance options and are subject to the leverage of their direct moneylender: see Green (2024) for comparative analysis in Cambodia.
[9] Harms (2011: 9) finds in Vietnam that edge zones are often re-designated, showing how parts of the edge get absorbed and resignified, with the unruly edge perpetually being pushed out.
[10] As Yiftachel (2020: 155) argues, while the lack of security of housing can go either way – it can solidify into durable claims (and even convert those spaces into capital) or can be eroded with the sweep of the bulldozer – such 'gray spaces' are 'increasingly associated with the rise of displaceability'.
[11] See also Chiu (2023) for the way a homologous situation plays out in Mandalay, Myanmar's second-largest city.

References

Adas, M. (2011) *The Burma Delta: Economic Development and Social Change on an Asian Rice Frontier, 1852–1941*, University of Wisconsin Press.

Astolfo, G. (2023) 'Yangon: Displacement urbanism, housing provisionality, and feminist spatial practices: an infrastructure of care at the urban margin', in R. Hu (ed), *Routledge Handbook of Asian Cities*, Routledge, pp 437–48.

Astolfo, G. and Boano, C. (2020) '"Unintended cities" and inoperative violence: housing resistance in Yangon', *Planning Theory & Practice*, 21(3): 426–49.

Beeckmans, L., Gola, A., Singh, A., and Heynen, H. (eds) (2022) *Making Home(s) in Displacement: Critical Reflections on a Spatial Practice*, Leuven University Press.

Beemer, B. (2009) 'Southeast Asian slavery and slave-gathering warfare as a vector for cultural transmission: the case of Burma and Thailand', *Historian* 71(3): 481–506.

Bernstein, H. (1981) 'Concepts for the analysis of contemporary peasantries', in R. Galli (ed), *The Political Economy of Rural Development: Peasants, International Capital, and the State*, SUNY Press, pp 3–24.

Boano, C. (2016) 'Jerusalem as a paradigm: Agamben's "whatever urbanism" to rescue urban exceptionalism', *City* 20(3): 455–71.

Bosson, A. (2007) 'Forced migration/internal displacement in Burma with an emphasis on government controlled areas', Internal Displacement Monitoring Center. Available from: www.refworld.org/reference/country rep/idmc/2007/en/41504 [Accessed 2 August 2025].

Boutry, M. (2018) 'Migrants seeking out and living with floods: A case study of Mingalar Kwat Thet settlement, Hlaing Tha Yar Township, Yangon, Myanmar', in C. Middleton, R. Elmhirst and S. Chantavanich (eds), *Living with Floods in a Mobile Southeast Asia: A Political Ecology of Vulnerability, Migration and Environmental Change*, Routledge, pp 42–62.

Brown, I. (2013) *Burma's Economy in the Twentieth Century*, Cambridge University Press.

Caldeira, T. (2016) 'Peripheral urbanisation: autoconstruction, transversal logics, and politics in cities of the Global South', *Environment and Planning D*, 35: 3–20.

Campbell, S. (2016) 'Putting-out's return: informalisation and differential subsumption in Thailand's garment sector', *Focaal*, 76: 71–84.

Campbell, S. (2022) *Along the Integral Margin: Uneven Development in a Myanmar Squatter Settlement*, Cornell University Press.

Chiu, F. (2023) Transforming the Outskirts: Planning, Property and People in Urban Myanmar, PhD thesis, University of East Anglia.

Cole, T. (2020) '"Power-hurt": the pains of kindness among disabled Karen refugees in Thailand', *Ethnos*, 85(2): 224–40.

Connell, R. (2011) 'Southern bodies and disability: re-thinking concepts', *Third World Quarterly*, 32(8): 1369–81.

Cornish, G. (2020) Settling into a New Place: Livelihood recovery and belongingness of households forced to relocate in Yangon, Myanmar, PhD thesis, University of Queensland.

Davis, M. (2006) *Planet of Slums*, Verso.

Doshi, S. (2013) 'The politics of the evicted: redevelopment, subjectivity, and difference in Mumbai's slum frontier', *Antipode*, 45(4): 844–65.

Forbes, E. (2016) 'On the frontier of urbanisation: informal settlements in Yangon, Myanmar', *Independent Journal of Burma Scholarship*, 1(1): 197–238.

Gago, V. and Mezzadra, S. (2017) 'A critique of the extractive operations of capital: toward an expanded concept of extractivism', *Rethinking Marxism*, 29(4): 574–91.

Gillespie, T. (2016) 'Accumulation by urban dispossession: Struggles over urban space in Accra, Ghana', *Transactions of the Institute of British Geographers* 41(1): 66–77.

Green, W.N. (2024) 'Agrarian financial ecologies: centering land and labor in geographies of debt', *Transactions of the Institute of British Geographers*, 49(3): e12664.

Hall, D., Hirsch, P., and Li, T. (2011) *Powers of Exclusion: Land Dilemmas in Southeast Asia*, NUS Press.

Harms, E. (2011) *Saigon's Edge: On the Margins of Ho Chi Minh City*, University of Minnesota Press.

Hoffman, D. (2011) *The War Machines: Young Men and Violence in Sierra Leone and Liberia*, Duke University Press.

Holston, J. (2008) *Insurgent Citizenship: Disjunctions of Democracy and Modernity in Brazil*, Princeton University Press.

Kramer, M. (2022) *Herbal Medicines, Motorcycles, and the Making of an Indigenous Resource Economy in the Myanmar Himalaya*. PhD dissertation. University of Chicago.

Kyed, H. (2019) 'Informal settlements and migrant challenges in Yangon', *Moussons* 33: 65–94.

Li, T. (2011) 'Centring labour in the land grab debate', *Journal of Peasant Studies*, 38(2): 281–98.

Lieberman, V. (2010) 'A zone of refuge in Southeast Asia? Reconceptualizing interior spaces', *Journal of Global History*, 5(2): 333–46.

Lubeigt, G. (2007) 'Industrial zones in Burma and Burmese labour in Thailand', in M. Skidmore and T. Wilson (eds), *Myanmar: The State, Community and the Environment*, ANU Press, pp 159–88.

Matelski, M. and Sabrié, M. (2019) 'Challenges and resilience in Myanmar's urbanisation: A special issue on Yangon', *Moussons*, 33: 11–31.

Maung, L.N., Kawasaki, A. and Amrith, S. (2023) 'Spatial and temporal impacts on socio-economic conditions in the Yangon slums', *Habitat International*, 134: 102768.

McCarthy, G. (2023) *Outsourcing the Polity: Non-state Welfare, Inequality, and Resistance in Myanmar*, Cornell University Press.

McIntyre, M. and Nast, H. (2011) 'Bio(necro)polis: Marx, surplus populations, and the spatial dialectics of reproduction and "race"', *Antipode*, 43(5): 1465–88.

McPherson, P. (2016) 'Evicting the residents of the 555', *Next City*. Available from: https://nextcity.org/features/yangon-myanmar-evictions-urban-cleanup-policies [Accessed 30 May 2023].

MDRI (Myanmar Development Research Institute) and Mastercard (2015) "Cash in context: uncovering financial services in Myanmar'. Available from: www.myanmar-responsiblebusiness.org/pdf/SWIA/Mining/07b-Community-Impacts-and-Development.pdf [Accessed 2 August 2025].

Meehan, P. and Seng Lawn D. (2024) 'Drugs and extractivism: opium cultivation and drug use in the Myanmar–China borderlands', *Journal of Peasant Studies*, 51(4): 922–59.

Mezzadra, S. (2018) *In the Marxian Workshops: Producing Subjects*, Rowman & Littlefield.

Mezzadra, S. and Neilson, B. (2013) *Border as Method, or, the Multiplication of Labor*, Duke University Press.

Nwe, T.T. (1998) 'Yangon: the emergence of a new spatial order in Myanmar's capital city', *Sojourn: Journal of Social Issues in Southeast Asia*, 13(1): 86–113.

Ortega, A. (2020) 'Exposing necroburbia: Suburban relocation, necropolitics, and violent geographies in Manila', *Antipode*, 52(4): 1175–95.

Prasse-Freeman, E. (2016) 'Sedentarised in motion: socio-political consequences of dispossession, displacement, deterritorialisation, and devalorisation of peasants and poor people in contemporary Myanmar', paper presented at Agrarian Studies Spring Colloquium, Yale University.

Prasse-Freeman, E. (2022) 'Necroeconomics: dispossession, extraction, and indispensable/expendable laborers in contemporary Myanmar', *Journal of Peasant Studies*, 49(7): 1466–96.

Prasse-Freeman, E. (2023) *Rights Refused: Grassroots Activism and State Violence in Myanmar*, Stanford University Press.

Puar, J. (2017) *Right to Maim: Debility, Capacity, Disability*, Duke University Press.

Read, J. (2003) *The Micro-politics of Capital: Marx and the Prehistory of the Present*, SUNY Press.

A Retired Employee (nd) 'Don't think about the small wounds', *Worker Journal*, 6.

Rhoads, E. (2018) 'Forced evictions as urban planning? Traces of colonial land control practices in Yangon, Myanmar', *State Crime Journal*, 7(2): 278–305.

Rhoads, E. (2019) Property in Transition: Uncertainty, Agency and Belonging in Yangon Myanmar, PhD thesis, Lund University.

Rhoads, E. (2023) 'Property, citizenship, and invisible dispossession in Myanmar's urban frontier', *Geopolitics* 28(1): 122–55.

Rhoads, E. and Wittekind, C. (2018) 'Rethinking land and property in a "transitioning" Myanmar: representations of isolation, neglect, and natural decline', *Journal of Burma Studies*, 22(2): 171–213.

Roberts, J. (2020) 'Displacement, encroachment and settlement: Interrogating Kyu in peri-urban Yangon', *City & Society*, 32(2): 421–35.

Rokem, J. and Boano, C. (2023) 'Towards a global urban geopolitics: inhabiting violence', *Geopolitics*, 28(5): 1667–80.

Roy, A. (2019) 'Racial banishment', in Antipode Editorial Collective, T. Jazeel, A. Kent, K. McKittrick, N. Theodore, S. Chari, P. Chatterton, V. Gidwani, N. Heynen, W. Larner, J. Peck, J. Pickerill, M. Werner and M.W. Wright (eds), *Keywords in Radical Geography: Antipode at 50*, John Wiley & Sons, pp 227–30.

Russell, M. and Malhotra, R. (2002) 'Capitalism and disability', *Socialist Register*, 38: 211–28.

Scott, J. (2009) *Art of Not Being Governed*, Yale University Press.

Seekins, D. (2005) 'The state and the city: 1988 and the transformation of Rangoon', *Pacific Affairs*, 78(2): 257–75.

Seng Lawn, D., Myrttinen, H., and Naujoks, J. (2023) 'Gender, disabilities and displacement in Kachin state', in J. Hedström and E. Olivius (eds), *Waves of Upheaval in Myanmar: Gendered Transformations and Political Transitions*, NIAS.

Simone, A. (2018) 'The urban majority and provisional recompositions in Yangon', *Antipode*, 50(1): 23–40.

Skidmore, M. (2004) *Karaoke Fascism: Burma and the Politics of Fear*, University of Pennsylvania Press.

Tadiar, N. (2022) *Remaindered Life*, Duke University Press.

Thawnghmung, A. (2019) *Everyday Economic Survival in Myanmar*, University of Wisconsin Press.

Till, K. (2012) 'Wounded cities: memory-work and a place-based ethics of care', *Political Geography*, 31(1): 3–14.

Tronti, M. (1980) 'The strategy of refusal', *Semiotext(e)*, 3(3): 28–34.

Turner, C. (2016) 'Myanmar: former prisoners fight for labour rights', *al Jazeera*, 16 November. Available from: www.aljazeera.com/features/2016/11/16/myanmar-former-prisoners-fight-for-labour-rights [Accessed 30 May 2023].

Wai, P. (2013) 'Drama of a town', *Pansodan Friday Journal*.

Ware, H. and Schuelka, M. (2019) 'Constructing "disability" in Myanmar: teachers, community stakeholders, and the complexity of disability models', *Disability & Society*, 34(6): 863–84.

Wittekind, C. (2024) '"Take our land": Fronts, fraud, and fake farmers in a city-to-come', *Cultural Anthropology*, 39(1): 91–117.

Wolf, E. (1982) *Europe and the People Without History*, University of California Press.

Yichtafel, O. (2020) 'From displacement to displaceability: A Southeastern perspective on the new metropolis', *City*, 24(1–2): 151–65.

Zaw, Y.K. (2022) An Ethnographic Study of Medicines, Care, and Antimicrobial Resistance Amidst Disorder and Decline in Yangon, Myanmar. PhD thesis, London School of Hygiene & Tropical Medicine.

3

Producing *Zoé*: The Camp as a Form of Extraction in Castel Volturno

Sofia Moriconi

Introduction

Urbanization under advanced capitalism has increased displacement and the reproduction of economic, racial, and citizenship inequalities. The case of Castel Volturno is paradigmatic of how the simultaneous presence of displaced populations and certain urban processes in a Southern European city can produce an extractive territory to cushion the crises of 'excess' capitalism. Through the capture of displaced and dispossessed bodies and their entanglement with discarded objects and exceptional norms, Castel Volturno represents a territory that makes 'survival at a low level of citizenship' possible. It serves as a readily accessible location for undocumented, racialized, and depoliticized individuals seeking employment due to the prevalence of informal economies and the availability of ruins that do not require maintenance and care to become shelters. Simultaneously, a diverse range of humanitarian actors, both formal and informal, engage in charitable activities, creating an infrastructure that entraps and enmeshes the surplus population within a network of surplus objects and spaces. In Castel Volturno, ruins offer low-expectation shelter options, and they are integrated into the humanitarian infrastructure of excess, functioning as an inexhaustible resource to be continually exploited in a cycle of perpetual vitality. Overall, this is a process that absorbs multiple excesses and feeds them back into value production. The result is an extraordinary spatial concentration of dispossessed population, and at the same time an extraordinary catchment of unskilled and cheap workers. Here, the excess population acts as a buffer for the production system by reducing the cost of the workforce. The workforce devaluation that allows excess capital to be absorbed operates primarily on a racial basis: the more the workforce differs from the 'white heterosexual male', the cheaper their work. Given that downward factors are mainly linked to race, the subjectification of the excess population becomes central to the functioning of the whole production chain.

In this chapter, I refer to a specific subjectivity, called *zoé*, in relation to the excess population. The term is derived from Greek and describes life in its biological and animal sense. Ancient Greeks used '*zoé*' to describe the life of a cow or a horse while reserving the term '*bios*' for human life, in light of its political participation. However, the life of some excluded human beings, who were not part of political life, was still identified as '*zoé*'.

The term informs different theories that are equally central to the development of the chapter. According to Braidotti (2013, p 60), *zoé* represents the 'vital force of life' and 'generative vitality'. She argues that we are currently living in the era of '*zoé*politics', where this form of life is becoming increasingly crucial to capitalistic dynamics, including accumulation, destruction, and extraction of capital. The mechanism according to which *zoé* is central to the production of capital does not just depend on its valorization (as in the case of biotechnology, intensive land exploitation, and data mining), but also on positioning *zoé* within systems of power whereby the territorial production system cyclically distances the production from its crisis – which, in this case, occurs through the subtraction of the political weight of human life. From the *zoé*, therefore, an extractive opportunity arises connected to the space to which this subjectivity is intertwined.

Agamben (1995) offers a different interpretation of *zoé* as 'bare life', or animal life that has been stripped of its political rights and belonging to the polis. In his work, bare life is associated with the production of dispositifs such as camps. Developing and expanding upon his theories, camp scholars (Gilroy, 2004; Agier, 2011; Boano, 2011; Ramadan, 2013; Minca, 2015) have examined the global diffusion of the camp as a territorial government device, whether within humanitarian frameworks or in its urban turn.[1] The evolution of camps over time has created new dynamics within capitalist urban processes in European territories, due to the presence of politically excluded populations. In this sense, the case of Castel Volturno is emblematic.

Through stories of material and immaterial encounters in Castel Volturno, and merging different lines of thought, the chapter focuses on how the dispositif of the camp (understood as a space of accumulation and retention of excess population) takes on a specific role in terms of cushioning the costs of work, life and bare life through its inclusion in urban production processes. First, the chapter describes the contextual elements and the accumulation characteristics that make it possible to catalyze and produce *zoé* in Castel Volturno. It then examines in detail the mechanisms of collection and distribution of the workforce through work exploitation and the existence of specific gathering and collection points for daily labourers. Finally, the chapter clarifies how capital extraction occurs through the complex concatenation of practices that racialize the workforce, through to its territorial implications.

Grounded in my doctoral research and previous years of humanitarian work in camps,[2] data for this chapter have been produced through an immersive ethnography. The first part of the fieldwork occurred in June and July 2019, and the second part in December 2019 and January 2020, as well as throughout 2020. I collected data through participant observation, a fieldwork diary, a focus group, and semi-structured interviews. In Castel Volturno, there is general distrust toward both journalists and researchers, but some individuals were willing to share their experiences to rewrite the narrative of the place. I conducted interviews with patients at the humanitarian clinic run by the NGO Emergency with Pentecostal pastors and community leaders. I visited and explored the area with Emergency's mediators, and I also accompanied vulnerable individuals. These explorations were complemented by a large number of informal conversations. I am deeply grateful to the humanitarian workers who warmly welcomed me into their work and the individuals I had the privilege of encountering and talking to for their openness and willingness to share their experiences with me.

Castel Volturno as a 'fertile land' for the capture and production of *zoé*

Castel Volturno is a small coastal town located about 40 minutes from Naples and Caserta (Figure 3.1). Known for its agricultural activities, it produces high-quality products such as Mozzarella di Bufala Campana and various tomatoes, which are exported across Europe. In the past, the town attracted tourists, particularly the Neapolitan middle class, during the summer. However, tourism declined by the late 1980s, leading many holiday homeowners to seek other vacation spots.

This resulted in numerous abandoned buildings (Figure 3.2), with prices dropping significantly. While some speculators rented these properties at low rates, others remained neglected. Consequently, many of these abandoned buildings became accessible to undocumented migrants, who became involved in local agricultural work. So, from the end of the 1980s onwards, the tourist population slowly faded away and was replaced by undocumented and low-cost workers. At first, it was mainly men from the Ivory Coast and Liberia who settled in the area. However, slowly but surely, the Ghanaians started to settle. Their peak presence was around the beginning of the new millennium, but now Castel Volturno boasts the largest estimated community of Nigerians in Europe.[3] The changes in the

Figure 3.1: Castel Volturno is situated on the coast, almost equidistant from two established urban areas

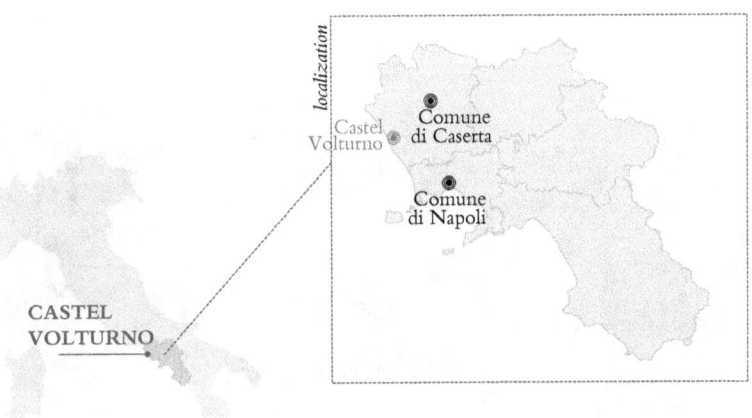

Source: Map illustration by Veronica Orlando, reproduced with permission

population triggered a process of racialization in labour (Mbembe, 2016) and the creation of *zoé* subjectivities. This, along with the proliferation of ruins and various material and immaterial operations aimed at capital reproduction (Mezzadra and Neilson, 2017), has effectively transformed the territory into a 'camp-like' environment.

This systematization of displacement simultaneously produces an attractive urban system of *zoé* life on a very large scale. Castel Volturno is a destination that many migrant communities have come to know very well. Indeed, it has become so well known that people often begin their journey with a Castel Volturno address in their pocket, recommended by friends or less-than-scrupulous brokers as a place to start building a life in Europe without papers. The area offers the bare minimum to ensure survival, and its economy relies heavily on the movement of individuals and other entities who have escaped from different 'systems' (such as the national reception system).

The production of a camp-like environment is also influenced by official or spontaneous humanitarianism that creates infrastructure and entangle a network of spaces. In Castel Volturno, newcomers often go to friends' homes or seek help from local churches and organizations such as Caritas. Sergio Serraino, the project manager of an international NGO (Emergency) since 2015, shared stories of young people arriving at reception centres in Cagliari or Roma Termini station looking for a clinic and assistance. Castel Volturno is preferred for its access to food, shelter, and job opportunities in agriculture and construction. A single name or contact can secure emergency housing

Figure 3.2: Buildings in Castel Volturno inhabited by day labourers

Source: Author

provided by individuals, Pentecostal churches, informal groups, associations, and NGOs. The availability of affordable beds for €50 to €100 per month ensures that Castel Volturno remains an extremely sustainable place to live. Additionally, the prevalence of Black communities and the extensive reach of humanitarian aid efforts ensures that there is ready access to food, with daily meals provided by organizations such as Caritas. This infrastructure seems to be guided by a moral law of brotherhood. P, a pastor and manager of a Pentecostal church, has been a resident of Castel Volturno for over a decade and has experienced Caritas's hospitality. Today, he champions the importance of the humanitarian network:

> The people recognize only Caritas, but, in a general sense, it's supposed not to be only Caritas. Today, my church also helps people who are in need. For instance, we don't do big things, but if we have the possibility, it could be €1,00, a drink for those thirsty … Caritas has the capacity to do it for hundreds of people, but if I can help and give to one soul, I would be like Caritas. (Interview with P, July 2019)

Work production platforms

The province of Caserta is known for its rich history and fertile land. Despite being affected by the phenomenon of dumping and spills known as the 'Terra dei Fuochi',[4] in recent years Caserta has continued to follow its agricultural vocation. The region has many farms that mainly produce and export tomatoes, vegetables, and fruit. Unfortunately, like others in the large-scale retail network, Campania's farms suffer from the prices imposed on them by the market. Unable to raise prices, they constantly look for ways to lower their spending. As Harvey (2001) points out, capitalism is inherently prone to crisis due to a surplus of capital – whether it be goods, money, or productive capacity. To avoid such crises, capitalism continuously seeks ways to absorb its surplus, often through 'spatial solutions' such as de-localization, as defined by the British geographer. This may take the form of transnational agriculture, which is organized in chains of transformation and distribution with specific power relationships, as outlined by Pedreño (2014). One means of absorbing excess capital is through exploiting the global centre–periphery or North–South tension, which has led many big companies to relocate production to regions with significantly lower labour costs in recent decades. What is taking place, especially following the migratory flows that have affected Europe since the new millennium, is the possibility of lowering the cost of labour on a racial basis, using new availability of migrant population and camp dispositives, avoiding delocalizing production chains. In Southern Europe and Southern Italy particularly, agribusiness has intertwined its production systems with humanitarian assistance (Dines, 2023) and the reproduction of a living workforce through the governance and regulation of migratory flows. Miguel Mellino (2012), speaking of 'postcolonial capitalism', explains how the hierarchization of the global workforce no longer corresponds with the classic international division of labour but is configured thanks to the subalternity of migrant people in the same European space. And, as argued by Reyneri (2001), in Italy, the occupational sectors able to absorb non-qualified and unorganized workforce are 'housekeeping, street selling, agriculture, construction, small manufacturing firms, catering and low-level urban services' (Reyneri, 2001, p 37). In Castel Volturno, the local agribusiness is one of the key employers of unskilled workers and is thriving thanks to the production of excellent food, including tomatoes, buffalo milk, and *mozzarella di bufala* (Di Salvo, 2018; SVIMEZ, 2019).[5] These products are typical of the Caserta region and are widely exported throughout a large-scale distribution network. Construction and small manufacturing also provide employment opportunities for displaced populations, with informal contacts and word of mouth being the primary modes of recruitment. The European workforce is increasingly characterized by its 'refugeezation' (Dines and Rigo, 2015) by hierarchies and 'grey' work relationships due to weakened forms of citizenship (Avallone, 2017). These forms of workforce devaluation allow excess capital to be absorbed primarily on a racial basis: the more the human differs from the 'white-heterosexual male', the more their work will be devalued.

Figure 3.3: Location of the main Kalifoo Grounds in the Castel Volturno area

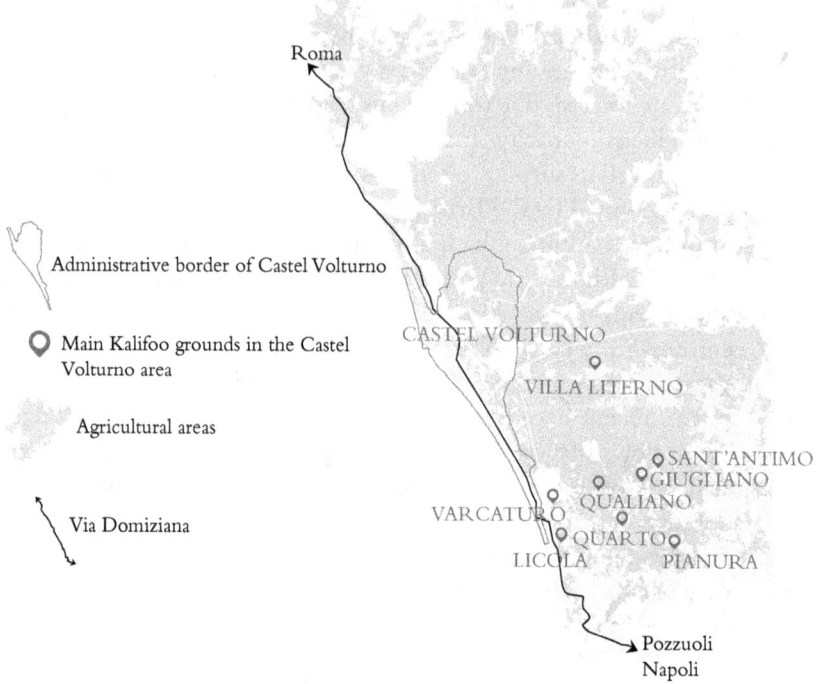

Source: Map illustration by Veronica Orlando, reproduced with permission

These relationships of racial devaluation are evident in Castel Volturno, especially in the places where those in the displaced population gather to offer their bodies to work: the Kalifoo Grounds roundabouts (Figure 3.3). For a poor and undocumented migrant who has just arrived in town, the fastest way to earn some money is by heading out at night and making your way there. Mainly located in areas like Licola, Pianura, Villa Literno, Quarto, Sant'Antimo, Qualiano, Giugliano and Varcaturo, the Kalifoo Grounds are where workers gather before dawn to get hired for the day. Despite this, many people still reside in Castel Volturno, living along a long road called the Domiziana.[6]

People are generally recruited in the Kalifoo grounds for daily labouring in different sectors or 'hired' for a full-time job and paid an average of €2 per hour in very hard-working conditions:

> As well as a labourer or bricklayer, you can be hired as a gardener, as a petrol station assistant, a porter, or a distributor of leaflets. If the boss is good, he pays you at the end of the day, and he must hope he tells you to come the next day too. If he likes you, he makes you work

with him for several days. If it goes wrong, the next day, it starts again.
(Interview with T, June 2019)

In Giugliano, Villaricca, Melito, Afragola, and Arzano, the demand for manual labour is for the shoe industry and sometimes for packaging and construction (Spagnuolo, 2005). In the nearest urban centres (Naples and Caserta), unskilled labour is highly requested for desultory and assorted activities: people work in the cities as factotums, porters, gardeners, cleaners, dishwashers, little peddlers (the so-called Mr Buongiorno), window cleaners, car park attendants, gas station attendants, warehouse workers (usually men) or babysitters or cleaners (usually women). The condition of subordination and disposability of this subjectivity, which nevertheless takes part in productive activities, tends to reduce the space for resistance to decisions about one's own body:

> I don't work in *campagna*[7] because it's too hard and it ruins your back. Often it happens that the boss does not pay or gives you very poor pay at the end of the day. At the roundabout, nobody tells you how much he will give you at the end of the day. They look at you and tell you to get in the car. But before, I always ask at least what kind of work it will be. If they tell me *'muratore'* [construction worker], it's okay, 'gardener' is okay, but if they tell me *'campagna'*, I won't go.
> (Interview with I, June 2019)

'At least' is the expression that outlines the claim of power over one's naked body. It is the only power allowed, because dead flesh no longer works for anyone. This is the mechanism through which capitalism extracts value through the racialization of bodies: synthesizing the political power of the *zoé* subjectivity to the exercise of sovereignty over one's naked, displaced and disposable body.

Exiting from the Kalifoo Grounds system happens occasionally. After a few weeks of work, gaining the boss's trust can lead to being called back, which is significant. At the start of the day, there is a general idea of where to go and what to expect, reducing the risk of unpaid wages and alleviating fear and tension. A regular relationship can create a small weekly income, allowing for short-term plans and sending money home. For young migrant men, this ability is crucial as it is tied to their family's esteem and their own sense of success or failure. Sometimes bosses talk about future contracts:

> The boss told me that now he can't get me the contract, but as soon as he gets the money, he'll do it for me. I hope soon. For now, it's okay because I'm not forced to get up at three in the morning like earlier, and I always go to the same place. I know the job. My brother and

I are the ones who go every day. He even gave him a scooter to get to work. (Interview with I, June 2019)

In these terms, the camp-space enters the city-space as a producer of *zoé* subjectivity, politicizing its body through inclusion in production processes, without ever recognizing its intrinsic political value. Some scholars note that new forms of citizenship and subjectivity are emerging in relation to economic productivity. According to Mezzadra and Neilson (2013), the traditional citizenship–labour nexus can no longer rely on the subject as a 'citizen-worker', nor can it depend on the gender-based division of labour that sustains it. The migrant profile – particularly if 'irregular' – also challenges the dichotomy of inclusion–exclusion: while it may be included in certain areas, such as productive activities, it is often excluded in others, such as legal recognition. This 'legal production of illegality' results in the provision of humanitarian services, infrastructures and performances that, while intended to protect human life, ultimately become essential and complicit to extractive economic and urban processes.

Extraction

The ways in which value extraction is referred to here are not traditionally understood as the literal extraction of raw materials or life forms from the earth – even if, as is evident, the type of life form involved – the *zoé* – is central to such a process. What is important to emphasize is how extractivity is achieved through the complete proximity between the production of a racialized subjectivity (*zoé*) and a space (the camp) within the urban space itself. Achille Mbembe explored the idea that individuals of African descent are transformed into 'living minerals from which metal is extracted' (Mbembe, 2017, p 40). This transformation is characterized by moving from 'homme-minerai to homme-métal and from homme-métal to homme-monnaie' (Mbembe, 2013, pp 67–68, cited in Mezzadra and Nielsen, 2017). In Southern Italy's agribusiness, migrant workers who are willing to move based on crop seasonality are highly sought after, as they provide the necessary flexibility for a global-scale distribution network. What pushes farms to employ a racialized workforce is their powerlessness to determine the amount of the final price of the product. They find themselves looking for ways to cut costs wherever possible, and eventually deciding to amortize costs by taking advantage of racial devaluation.

In Castel Volturno, there is a clear hierarchy of value among foreign workers, which is also spatially recognizable in the groupings of bodies at the Kalifoo Grounds, where workers are divided by skin colour and labour cost. Those from Romania are considered more valuable (and paid more) than those from Tunisia (they are white and European); a Tunisian more than an Indian and, above all, more than a Ghanaian. The division of labour is also often based on ethnicity. Most Nigerians work in the building sector or engage in small-scale commercial activities, while Indians and Pakistanis are usually requested for *mozzarella* production. Ghanaians are predominantly employed in the most arduous agricultural work, particularly during the tomato harvest. Tunisian and Romanian women are in high demand for fruit harvesting, particularly in the northern part of the 'Castel Volturno area'.[8] However, there is more to the instrumental use of dispossessed bodies than lowering the costs of the workforce.

In Southern Italy, the agri-business network is characterized by a clear definition of crop cycles and spatial organization (D'Ascenzo, 2014; Avallone, 2017). Castel Volturno plays a crucial role as a key node in this network. It sets itself apart from other tent cities in Apulia, Calabria, and Sicily due to its intersection with urban practices, economies, and housing availability. Interviews with workers and humanitarians revealed that Castel Volturno's population changes with the seasons, influenced by the harvest cycles. Summer sees the highest population due to the tomato harvest, while in winter many displaced individuals move south for the orange harvest. The city's ruins and humanitarian infrastructure also serve as recovery centres throughout the year, providing assistance to those in need and helping to re-catch some production systems (Figure 3.4). Mezzadra and Neilson (2017) state that the extraction processes are made of 'a proliferation of different operations that impinge upon its multiple outsides ... The heterogeneity of operations that surround and prepare the ground for extraction concatenate in ways that are constitutive of a particular fraction of capital that we might call extractive capital' (Mezzadra and Neilson, 2017, p 6).

In this sense, and in the case of Castel Volturno, the extractive operation of capitalist urban processes takes place through the production of a *territory* for a specific subjectivity. The many homes falling into ruins due to past economic disruptions have become a popular destination for people living in poverty who are looking for extra-affordable housing. Meanwhile, the institutional weakness of the municipality and the prevalence of informal practices and illegal work allow undocumented people to live with less fear. The humanitarian presence in the area provides a basic infrastructure for survival, with health services, emergency food, accommodation, and legal advice available. Ironically, raising a voice for the rights of migrants and refugees discloses the exceptional presence and legitimizes the concentration of an excess population. The Castel Volturno area is exceptional in terms of confluence and circulation of spaces, bodies, and objects overflowing from formal aggregates. They do not present critical issues in the functioning of flows and economies; on the contrary, they make this territory capable of putting excess back into circulation and generating a highly productive urban capacity through the *zoè* subjectivity. It is a territory ineluctably tangled

Figure 3.4: Gathering of people in one of the humanitarian spaces of Castel Volturno

Source: Author

with bare lives, ruined buildings, recycling economies, and charity systems. These ecosystems and infrastructures result from territorial dispositives of power and exist thanks to these bodies and to produce these displaced and disposable bodies. It is a specific piece of urban production that occurs through them. Several scholars have stressed reflections about the intertwined contemporary capitalism and race (Roediger, 2017; Vergès, 2017); however, as Mezzadra and Neilson (2021, p 64) clarify, 'the point is not ... to highlight the relationship between extraction, dispossession and racism ... but to keep an eye on the ways in which reproduction and transformations of race and racism intertwine with the contemporary capital operations' (translation by the author).

For this reason, I want to emphasize the role of racialized territories in fulfilling a distinct extractive function in western urban processes. By doing so, these territories prevent the global delocalization of labour in emerging economies and reintroduce excess, waste, and ruins into production cycles. Some workers (especially humanitarians) have brought to light during the interviews that in Southern Italy, there has been a concerning trend in which certain recruiters of day labourers approach migrants living in reception centres for job purposes to reduce the costs of board and lodging that workers must provide. These individuals primarily target those who have yet to pass into the second reception phase, which means they live in reception centres that do not provide training for job access. The Extraordinary Reception Centers (CAS)[9] offer basic services such as food, lodging, mediation, and legal guidance, and the average time spent in such a centre is around one year, even though it should only be the time necessary for the transfer of the person to the second reception centre. However, in some areas, such as Latina, Rome, Naples, and Caserta, entrepreneurs are seeking CASs' guest workers because they can pay them even less, as these workers have no living expenses to worry about. Asylum seekers make up a significant portion of these migrants (Omizzolo, 2019), and they often do not speak Italian and struggle to gain access to the labour market. Despite these challenges, the need to support their families financially makes them more susceptible to these recruitment tactics. This phenomenon highlights how the extraction takes place thanks to the existence of a humanitarian infrastructure – supporting a *zoè* subjectivity – distributed throughout the territory, which guarantees services to asylum seekers. Yet, reception centres are a meagre platform of recruitment compared to the current demand for low-wage labour. This is why recruitment takes place in territories that radically lower the cost of survival. It is important to emphasize how the 'extraction involves not only the appropriation and expropriation of natural resources but also, and in ever more pronounced ways, processes that cut through patterns of human cooperation and social activity' (Mezzadra and Neilson, 2017, p 10).

Castel Volturno is an emblematic place where different systems converge. Its singular morphology (the city extends along the coast for 17 km, and the numerous parallel streets closed by gates make some areas of the city an ideal place to hide), chronic lack of resources for services and controls, availability of bargain-priced accommodation, and humanitarian infrastructure make it an ideal place to live for a poor undocumented migrant. The agricultural production system in search of day labourers is intertwined with the humanitarian infrastructure. In turn, it allows labourers to access the work platform. Moreover, the accumulation of ruined buildings is resignified by the practice of brokers who, through appropriation, activate an economy at the service of bodies that the reception system is unable to contain.

This city functions as an urban area that reproduces itself together with dispossessed life and from which neighbouring cities benefit. It is not merely a place for labour where the workforce is extracted, but rather a place where *zoé* can survive even in the most difficult circumstances. The extraction takes place on racialized bodies entangled with humanitarian actions and infrastructures that offer free services, and on the ruins of houses that allow extremely marginalized groups to have a roof. It takes place on the deployment of sophisticated practices of resistance and knowledge of the territory, on the proliferation of continuous and heterogeneous micro-operations.

Conclusion

The chapter delves into the intricate dynamics of urbanization under advanced capitalism, using the city of Castel Volturno to illustrate how displaced/disposable populations become entangled in urban processes, resulting in the production of extractive territories and subjectivities that cushion the crises of capitalism. Castel Volturno emerges as a space where the convergence of dispossessed bodies, informal economies, and humanitarian infrastructure creates a complex ecosystem that sustains the production of an excess population while serving the needs of capitalist production.

Central to this discussion is the concept of *zoé*, representing a form of life stripped of political recognition and belonging, which has become increasingly important in capitalist dynamics. The chapter illustrates how the subjectification of the excess population – particularly migrants and refugees – is critical for the functioning of the production chain, especially in sectors such as agribusiness, where racialized hierarchies determine the value of labour.

The extractive operations in Castel Volturno involve not only the appropriation of natural resources but also the exploitation of the specific connections between human and non-human elements, practices, and activities. The city's unique morphology, chronic lack of resources, and availability of cheap accommodation create an ideal environment for the production and exploitation of dispossessed bodies.

Moreover, in this observation, the convergence of factors such as the availability of potential homes, the presence of humanitarian infrastructure, and a weakened municipal institution creates an environment conducive to the retention of a low-cost urban workforce. The camp, as a dispositive of retaining excess population, serves as a link between economic and territorial production, exploiting bodies within a state of exception.

While rooted in genuine feelings of charity, the humanitarian imperative to save lives inadvertently becomes an extractive opportunity within this context. The fatigue of local institutions and the complexity of governing rules further perpetuate the dependence on pain in the production of value.

In essence, Castel Volturno exemplifies how urban territories can become intertwined with racialized systems of labour exploitation and humanitarian assistance, resulting in the reproduction of dispossessed life while sustaining capitalist production. The chapter underscores the need to critically examine the intersection of race, capitalism, and urbanization to understand how displaced populations are incorporated into and exploited by the urban fabric.

Notes

[1] For example, during the Balkan War in the 1990s, the camp model was developed by liberal democracies, mostly with a passive dependence on assistance approach that made

its inhabitants controlled and addicted at the same time (Rahola, 2003). In the new millennium, the flows of Syrians fleeing the war have produced a different typology, whereby the camp has taken on urban traits.

2   I have been a humanitarian activist since 2003. During my degree thesis, I started engaging with refugee camps. Later, I got the opportunity to work as a humanitarian worker in a reception centre (CAS) in Italy for about a year and a half. I regarded this professional experience as my first long ethnographic fieldwork.

3   It is difficult to prove it with certainty since a large part of the population present is without documents or not registered at the registry office. However, according to several humanitarian operators interviewed, this figure appears to be sufficiently reliable. In particular, the project manager of the NGO Emergency tells an emblematic anecdote: 'In 2015, TB Joshua – a world-famous Nigerian Pentecostal pastor – went on a European tour. Two dates: Amsterdam, Castel Volturno.'

4   The term 'Terra dei Fuochi' (land of fires) was introduced for the first time in the 2003 Ecomafie Report, drawn up by Legambiente, the largest Italian association for environmental protection. it identifies an area located between the province of Caserta and the Metropolitan City of Naples (with a surface area of 1076 square kilometres and 57 municipalities, in which approximately 2.5 million inhabitants reside) where the Camorra dumped toxic waste in illegal landfills.

5   On the Consorzio di Tutela della Mozzarella di Bufala Campana [PDO Mozzarella Consortium] webpage, you can find a high concentration of buffalo mozzarella farms and dairies in the Castel Volturno area: www.mozzarelladop.it/mappasoci/

6   The origins of the name 'Kalifoo Grounds' are unknown. According to Sergio Serraino, the project manager of Emergency, some believe it may have originated from a linguistic distortion of the Libyan term '*califo*', which refers to the grouping posts for daily work in Libya. Others argue that the name 'Kalifoo' derives from how the expression 'carry you forward' is pronounced in Libya. The 'r' apparently becomes 'l' in the pronunciation, which may have led to the name 'Kalifoo.' However, Serraino himself thinks that the name may simply be a distortion of the French word '*carrefour*', which means 'intersection' (Interview with Sergio Serraino, June 2019).

7   The Italian word for 'farmland'.

8   Differently from the Castel Volturno administrative perimeter, the 'Castel Volturno area' is a larger region that encompasses productive parts of different municipalities where day labourers living in Castel Volturno usually go for work.

9   The Legislative Decree 142/2015 allowed the establishment of the CASs (Extraordinary Reception Centers) in cases where government centres were saturated. Hence, the system managed the surplus of asylum seekers by opening a large number of CASs, identified by the prefectures of regional capitals in collaboration with the local administration.

References

Agamben, G. (1995) *Homo sacer. Il potere sovrano e la nuda vita,* Einaudi.

Agier, M. (2011) *Managing the Undesirables: Refugee Camps and Humanitarian Government*, Polity Press.

Avallone, G. (2017) *Sfruttamento e resistenze. Migrazioni e agricoltura in Europa, Italia, Piana del Sele*, Ombre Corte.

Boano, C. (2011) 'Violent spaces': Production and reproduction of security and vulnerabilities, *The Journal of Architecture*, 16(1): 37–55.

Braidotti, R. (2013) *The Posthuman*, Polity Press.

D'Ascenzo, F. (2014) *Antimondi delle migrazioni. L'Africa a Castel Volturno*, Lupetti.

Dines, N., Rigo, E. (2015) 'Postcolonial citizenship and the "refugeeisation" of the workforce: Migrant agricultural labor in the Italian Mezzogiorno', in S. Ponzanesi and G. Colpani (eds) *Postcolonial Transitions in Europe: Contexts, Practices and Politics*, Rowman & Littlefield, pp 151–72.

Dines, N. (2023) 'After entry: Humanitarian exploitation and migrant labour in the fields of Southern Italy', *Environment and Planning D: Society and Space*, 41(1): 74–91.

Di Salvo, S. (2018) 'Raimondo, presidente del Consorzio: La mozzarella di bufala come la Ferrari'. Il Mattino. Available from: www.ilmattino.it/mangiaebevi/le_news/raimondo_presidente_consorzio_la_mozzarella_di_bufala_la_ferrari-3512542.html [Accessed 2 February 2024].

Gilroy, P. (2004) *Between Camps: Nations, Cultures and the Allure of Race*, Routledge.

Harvey, D. (2001) *Spaces of Capital: Towards a Critical Geography*, Routledge.

Mbembe, A. (2013) *Critique de la raison nègre*, La Découverte.

Mbembe, A. (2016) *Necropolitica*, Ombre Corte.

Mbembe, A. (2017) *Critique of Black Reason*, Duke University Press.

Mellino, M. A. (2012) *Cittadinanze postcoloniali. Appartenenze, razza e razzismo in Europa e in Italia*, Carocci Editore.

Mezzadra, S. and Nielson, B. (2013) *Border as Method, or, the Multiplication of Labor*, Duke University Press.

Mezzadra, S. and Neilson, B. (2017) 'On the multiple frontiers of extraction: Excavating contemporary capitalism', *Cultural Studies*, 31(2–3): 185–204.

Mezzadra, S. and Neilson, B. (2021) *Operazioni del capitale*, Manifestolibri.

Minca, C. (2015) 'Geographies of the camp', *Political Geography*, 49: 74–83.

Omizzolo, M. (2019) *Essere migranti in Italia: Per una sociologia dell'accoglienza*, Mimesis.

Pedreño, A. (ed) (2014) *De catenas, migrantes y jornaleros. Los territorios rurales en las cadenas globales agroalimentarias*, Talasa.

Rahola, F. (2003) *Zone definitivamente temporanee. I luoghi dell'umanità in eccesso*, Ombre Corte.

Ramadan, A. (2013) 'Spatializing the refugee camp', *Transactions of the Institute of British Geographers*, 38(1): 65–77.

Reyneri, E. (2001) *Migrants' Involvement in Irregular Employment in the Mediterranean Countries of the European Union*, International Labour Organization.

Roediger, D.R. (2017) *The Wages of Whiteness: Race and the Making of the American Working Class*, Verso.

Spagnuolo, D. (2005) *L'immigrato in Campania. Immagine distorta e percezione "di superficie". Una ricerca sui media e tra la popolazione*, Mira.

SVIMEZ (Associazione per lo Sviluppo dell'Industria nel Mezzogiorno) (2019) Rapporto Su Mozzarella Bufala DOP. Available from: http://lnx.svimez.info/svimez/bianchi-presenta- rapporto-su-mozzarella-bufala-dop [Accessed 26 July 2025].

Vergès, F. (2017) 'Racial Capitalocene', in G.T. Johnson (ed), *Futures of Black Radicalism*, Verso, pp 72–82.

PART II
Expulsion

4

Planning and Design of Rural-to-Urban Resettlements for Fast Urbanization in Suzhou, Yangtze River Delta

Paola Pellegrini and Jinliu Chen

Introduction

China was a rural country when the economic reform started at the end of the 1970s. It marked the so-called opening up of the economy to private enterprises and allowed foreign investment into selected Special Economic Zones (SEZs). Urbanization became one of the drivers of fast economic development, radically transforming physical and social landscapes (Hong et al, 2021; Liang et al, 2022). With land collectively owned in China – either by the state or by rural communities – local governments promoted urbanization through converting rural land into urban developments and resettling millions of people (Hsing, 2010; Xu et al, 2011; Li, Wang, 2013; Chen and Zhu, 2021). Within this context, Chinese urbanization can be described as a large-scale, government-driven process that supported industrialization and rendered land disposable and people displaceable.

Economic growth as public interest was sanctioned in government plans and national policies, and provided a rationale for rapid urbanization and the resettlement of China's rural population. One of the main documents guiding development, the Five Year Plan of the People's Republic of China, sets targets for increasing the urbanization rate (Lin, 2002; Wang, 2018; PRC, 2021) to meet both national economic and social development goals. Indeed, the government's promotion of urbanization was very efficient and happened in parallel with demographic growth. According to the World Bank, China's urban population increased from 18 per cent in 1978 to

34 per cent in 1998. Over the same period, and despite China's one-child policy of 1979, the population increased from 0.956 billion people to 1.24 billion in 1998. A combined effect was approximately 250 million new urban residents over two decades and a corresponding number of houses. Available data suggests that the urbanization process resulted in remarkable improvements in living conditions, as intended, with the percentage of the total population living on $2.15 a day or less dropping from 72 per cent in 1990 to 13.9 per cent in 2010 (Chen and Ravallion, 2020; World Bank, 2023).

The SEZs generated the development of entirely new cities, such as Shenzhen in the Pearl River Delta, or the extension of existing ones, such as Suzhou in the Yangtze River Delta. Within a few years, many urban environments and landscapes radically changed. While the same mode of urbanization was replicated and adapted to each new SEZ, urbanization was discursively construed as the synonym of modernization and 'well-off society', corresponding to the long-term goals indicated by the promoters of the reform (Hulshof and Roggeveen, 2010; Gu, 2021). In turn, the notion of rural was stigmatized and came to represent underdevelopment and backwardness (Cai et al, 2020; Rogers et al, 2020).

This chapter explores the phenomenon of displacement and resettlement, and its centrality to the modernization process in China after the economic reform, from an urban planning and design point of view and at the neighbourhood level. There is little systematic examination of this subject on which to draw, and even less that situates it beyond official discourses of modernization. The chapter offers a distinct perspective on the subject through looking at the planning and design process around the mass resettlement of China's rural populations and the position of the displaced people within the country. Here we provide a glimpse of the vast process and the societal effects of resettlement housing, and hope to encourage further investigation into the long-term impacts of this planning and design practice in the city and its contextualization within the broader academic landscape.

The chapter first details the strong relationship between economic growth and urbanization, and the constitutive role of rural-to-urban resettlement in the state-driven and efficiency-based urbanization process, to demonstrate the centrality of displacement to this process. It continues by explaining the regulations that informed the spatially homogeneous characteristics of the new residential areas and the planning model of the low-end re-settlements. The chapter then further investigates some early resettlement neighbourhoods in Suzhou in the Yangtze River Delta, an area that has greatly increased its Gross Domestic Product (GDP) since the reform. Finally, it concludes by reflecting on the future of resettlement in China and the associated challenges, including the obsolescence of existing resettlement buildings on the one hand, and the raising of a middle-class society on the other, highlighting the potential longer-term implications of this process.

From rural to urban land and society

In China's market-oriented economy with socialist characteristics, the expansion of cities serves both as a provision of public finances and as capital accumulation, and impacts the livelihood of the displaced in various ways (Wu, 2016). On the one hand, it is a major source of revenue for local governments, which auction and lease land to those who can urbanize it; on the other, it is a major source of wealth for those who are able to invest in real estate (Wang et al, 2017; Tang, 2018). In this way, a significant gap is created between those who enter the housing market and those who cannot do so. In fact, real estate values in China boomed until the recent crisis, but the displaced groups rarely captured the increased value of their land.

The very first version of the Urban Planning Regulation of China was issued by the State Council in 1984. It required each city plan to define, 'rationally and scientifically', economic and social development goals, the scale and layout of the city, and the areas to be developed. To promote urbanization, the 1984 Regulation allowed and favoured large-scale rural land expropriation. Article 33 specified that, 'If land is needed within the urban planning area, the government shall uniformly perform land requisition from rural communes and agricultural production cooperatives. The latter shall comply with the needs of the state's construction and shall not obstruct them' (State Council, 1984, translation by authors). Such regulations made dispossession a legal, planning-sanctioned approach; as a consequence, any form of resistance and obstruction became illegal and prosecutable.

Subsequent regulations confirmed this approach of collective-owned land expropriation for the public interest. Forced resettlements caused by the reclassification of rural land into urban areas were always initiated by the local authority and developed either by the same government or by real estate developers. The process unfolded over a few stages: the administrative department in charge announced the demolition and removal of properties, then explained the policies, and finally negotiated compensation and resettlement agreements with the local population (State Council, 2001; Shi et al, 2012). Public participation and consultation in decision-making was not contemplated.

The whole urbanization process was presented as a national political achievement, acclaimed for its speed, which is unprecedented and unparalleled globally (Chien and Woodworth, 2018). The rhetoric of speed, however, had little or no regard for the impact on the individual household, which ultimately had to bear the effects of such fast change – there were both losses and benefits. The reactions of farmers to resettlement were diverse, but given that dispossession was sanctioned by law, discursively construed as a nationwide modernization process, most of them did not engage in overt opposition or hostility. Some scholars reported land-related protests as frequent and widespread, but localized and not organized. There were also some rare episodes of resistance, such as the so-called 'nail houses' – homes where owners refused the compensation agreements and also refused to vacate (Taylor, 2015). The general consensus within the existing literature, however, is that only a few farmers fought against demolitions and resettlement because they were persuaded that protesting could not change the direction of the government (Hulshof and Roggeveen, 2010; Shi et al, 2012; Cai, 2016). The majority of farmers opted to adapt to the change, trying to get the most out of compensation agreements to make up for the loss of all or part of their farmland and houses, and to rebuild their livelihoods under completely different circumstances (Jiang et al, 2014; Zhang et al, 2018; Chen, Zhu, 2021).

The urbanization/resettlement model meant that, for the most part, the dispossessed farmers did not benefit from increases in the value of land they used to farm, nor from the revenues that urbanization produced: compensation did not take into account the increased market value of the land made available for real estate development (He et al, 2009; Hui et al, 2013). Yet, when resettlement was presented as a clear improvement of their living standards, farmers welcomed the change. There was a hope of capitalizing on general economic growth and acceptance of the prevailing narrative in China that urbanization was synonymous with progress and involved tenure security, employment opportunities, and access to services. This was particularly true of public and social services, access to which was only possible through changing a rural *Hukou* (the permanent registration as either a rural or urban dweller according to place of birth) into an urban one. Before 2014, those with a rural *Hukou* could not benefit from social services provided in urban areas (Wu et al, 2019; Hong et al, 2022).

Resettlement has impacted displaced people in very different ways, depending primarily on their economic conditions before displacement. In all cases, however, it required adaptation and resilience. Literature describes both the positive and negative aspects of resettlement and compensation, but there is general agreement that it involved detrimental financial deprivation, in particular from loss of livelihoods and employment. In principle, households were compensated based on the dwelling surface (up to a certain extent) and the housing conditions, as well as the possibility of annual income decrease as a result of the loss of employment causing vulnerability (Wu and Webster, 2010; Wilmsen et al, 2011; Smith, 2021). Indeed, relocated in an urban environment, farmers' labour skills and knowledge became redundant, and the abrupt change of lifestyle, combined with memories related to disappeared spaces, contributed to a decreased sense of belonging, community, and neighbourliness. In those cases where farmers were given more than one housing unit as compensation, they were able to rent one out, often to rural migrants, and made a new living out of it, but in all other cases they had no option other than to find a job, despite not being fit for the urban job market. Often, they ended up with government stipends or in low-skilled jobs (Chen et al, 2020; Qiu and Chen, 2023; Wang et al, 2023). Arguably, this income insecurity, resulting from embedding displacement within development planning, presents a fundamental flaw in the discourses of modernization, progress, and the public good.

The characteristics of the resettlement: *tabula rasa* and compact homogeneity

Typically, local authorities did not invest in the improvement of existing towns and villages around the expanding cities, but rather preferred to demolish them and move farmers to new neighbourhoods built in an *ad hoc* way. The reorganization of scattered villages into concentrated clusters was not new, as it had already been implemented in the 1950s (Wang and Cheng, 1959). Urbanization usually progressed by making a *tabula rasa* through the demolition of existing rural settlements, the realization of new infrastructures, the reorganization of the allotments and the water system, the change of the land use category from rural to urban, and the building of industrial districts and residential communities – usually including a school and a community centre, which served as a shopping centre.

The new neighbourhoods were intended to restore or surpass previous living standards because, in the first half of the 1990s, most rural settlements still did not have sewerage systems, clean water distribution, sanitary facilities, kitchens and water taps, paved roads, or parking lots. However, the lack of consultation or consideration of individual households, or the particular nature of settlement within the planning and design process, meant that settlements that reflected historic expression of centuries of socio-economic organization based on farming and agriculture were not distinguished from overpopulated shanty towns (Dowall, 1994) (see Figures 4.1 and 4.2).

The resettlement neighbourhoods targeted basic needs and produced comparable living conditions for every household. Desirable qualities were programmatically subordinated to what was feasible given the scarce resources available. Neighbourhood units were standardized and self-contained, with the same building layout, building types (four to six floors, single row, multi-storey), and repeated open spaces of the same size. The original land morphology and the traditional building types neither shaped nor inspired the design of the new urban communities. Farmers from several villages were concentrated into communities where neither the open space nor the buildings matched the spatial practices of the demolished villages.

There is little evidence of a disciplinary discourse in the 1980s and early 1990s in China on the urban planning and design of the resettlements. There are some academic articles about residential areas that discuss the

Figure 4.1: The transformation of the rural land east of the city of Suzhou, where the Suzhou Industrial Park was realized since 1994. The area in 1969 (top); the same area in 2022 (bottom).

Source: top, US USSG (1969); bottom, Google Earth Pro (2022)

Figure 4.2: The comparison of an ancient village south of Suzhou, Tongli, with the last large resettlement community built in the Suzhou Industrial Park (SIP), Lotus Village. The circle has a radius of 300 m.

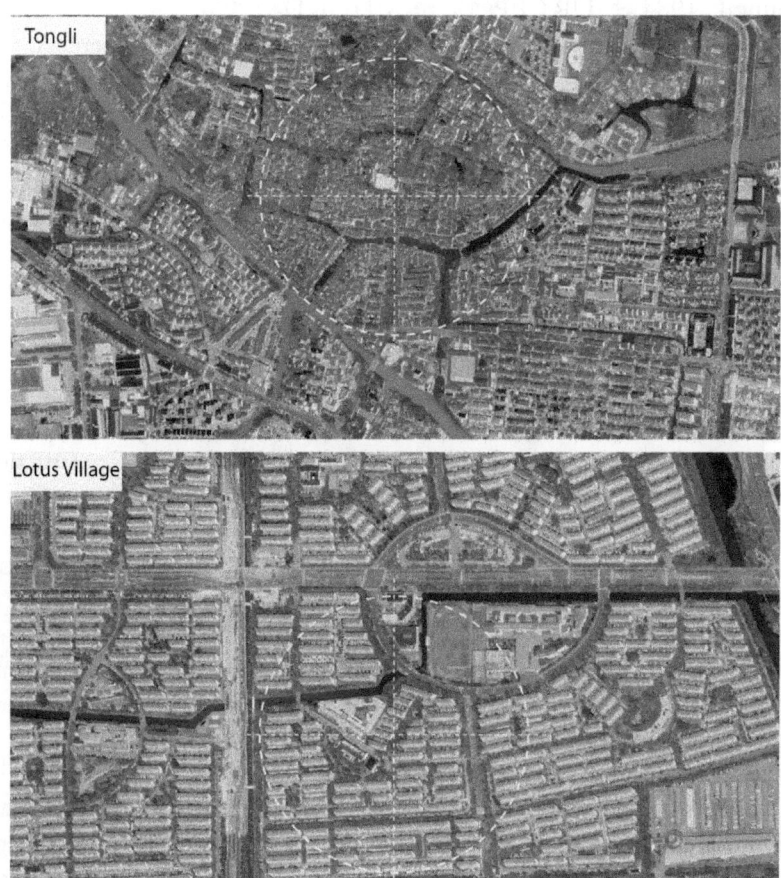

Source: Authors

design of high-density communities with particular attention to economic efficiency (Lu, 1991; Zhu, 1994), but there is no evidence of a disciplinary debate around new forms of community and living together. This is striking given the scale of the phenomenon and because these neighbourhoods were conceived of as a form of welfare, investing public resources, and impacting the farmland as well as urban residents. In fact, resettlement projects also affected the residents of buildings located in the old towns, which were deemed inadequate and demolished. The neighbourhoods for relocated urban residents had the same features as the new communities for dispossessed farmers.

Very few studies have investigated the reasons for the production of remarkably homogeneous urban forms for residential areas over the decades of the urbanization process. It was not required by urban planning codes, residential area regulations, and guidelines at the national level, nor were the building parameters of the regulations conceived to obtain it (State Council, 1984; MURCEP, 1986; MHURD, 1993). On the contrary, the 1984 code for residential areas recommended, over different points, that 'Standardization of architectural design should be combined with diversification' (Article 1.0.7); the layout should 'create the condition for diversification of building groups and spatial environments' (Article 1.0.5.6); and the design should 'adopt a variety of apartment types and a variety of area standards' (Article 5.0.4) (MURCEP, 1984). In other words, the resettlement neighbourhoods could, and should, have offered diversified spaces and residential units. Failing to do so produced a homogeneous urban environment of compounds and no variation in the residential buildings/housing units offered.

There is also no evidence of specific studies or consultations conducted to define what kind of settlement would best suit the relocated farmers in the reformed China. However, the State Administration of Urban Construction commissioned the Urban Planning and Design Research Institute of China to conduct research on residential areas in 1980, during the initial phase of the urbanization process. This research defined the layout of residential neighbourhoods in homogeneous rows as the most common arrangement in the country since the 1960s and criticized it as 'very dull and barracks-style'. The research insisted on combining standardization and diversification, and this recommendation was included – albeit superficially – in the subsequent national regulation (UPDRIC, 1985).

Three reasons can be given to explain the lack of diversification and the homogeneous character of this large-scale, state-sponsored, and technocrat-administered resettlement and planning process. The first is the perduring influence of the Soviet Union and its version of the Modern Movement, which strongly influenced the Chinese urban planning system in the 1950s. The planners who first dealt with the reform plans were trained in the Soviet Union; they were also the last generation of city planners before the Cultural Revolution, during which planning teaching and activities were stopped (Duan and Liu, 2022; Li, 2022). The model was repeated over and over (Lu, 2006; Dreyer, 2014; Takamura and Shao, 2021).

The second reason can be traced back to the planning guidelines issued by the State Council in the 1950s, which were in essence repeated in planning codes until the 1990s: every residential development must be functional and economic, and aesthetically pleasant if possible (State Council, 1956; MHURD, 1993; Wu, 2001). Accordingly, resettlement and planning projects reduced costs to the minimum, and made the most cost-effective use of land and labour resources. This translated into compact settlements, with little variations in design, and cheap solutions for the structural elements, finishings, and the open spaces. Common elements across settlements were the separation of land uses, the east–west alignment of the buildings, which guaranteed equal access to sunlight and cross-ventilation, and the presence of facilities and common areas within the neighbourhood (Xue et al, 2021). The Code for Planning and Design of Urban Residential Areas of the 1980s codified the building type of resettlement neighbourhoods as multi-storey, and defined the maximum index of net density, the green space ratio, and a set of basic public facilities (MURCEP, 1984).

A third argument can be proposed: the top-down technocratic approach and the speed of the operations produced a one-size-fits-all model, while people's consultation could have supported a more nuanced modernization.

The urban development of the Suzhou Industrial Park and its new villages

The case of Suzhou provides an insight into the planning and design of the large-scale urbanization and displacement process after the reform. Suzhou (苏州市) is an ancient city in the Yangtze River Delta region. Following the establishment of the Suzhou Wuzhong Economic Development Zone in 1993, it was transformed into the third-largest manufacturing city in China. Here, urban population growth accompanied economic growth (Wang et al, 2021). In fact, in 1990 the GDP of Suzhou was US$4.23 billion and by 2019 it had reached US$290 billion with a registered foreign capital of US$99.9 billion and per capita GDP of US$25,900. In 1990, the permanent resident population in the metropolitan area was 1,067,000, increasing to 7,070,000 in 2019 (SSY, 2020). It should be noted that the rapid population increase was also due to the fact that over the years the metropolitan areas incorporated some adjacent municipalities.

To achieve economic growth, the city expanded onto surrounding farmland and became a manufacturing hub. Suzhou Industrial Park (SIP) – a 27,800 ha New Town based on the Singaporean development model – became one of the main industrial areas of the city. Its establishment involved the reclassification of 12,000 ha of farmland to urban land and the displacement of almost 55,000 households from around 70 villages. The development started in 1994 and was completed by 2017; displaced people were mostly housed in four resettlement areas at the edges of the SIP perimeter (Shi et al, 2012; Choi and Reeve, 2018; He and Chang, 2020) (see Figures 4.3 and 4.4).

The Local Chronicles of SIP, issued by the SIP government, tell the story of the first stages of the Park's development, and of the transformation of Loufeng Township (娄葑分区) into an urban area. The Master Plan of SIP started to be implemented in the township on 1530 ha of land close to Suzhou old town (SIP, 2006). Prior to development, the area mostly

Figure 4.3: Aerial view facing south from the roof of a high-rise in Nanhuan New Community, Gusu District, Suzhou

Source: Drone flight, June 2021 by the authors

Figure 4.4: Aerial view facing north of Xujiabang neighbourhood, SIP, Suzhou

Source: Drone flight, March 2023 by the authors

comprised low-lying rice fields and fish ponds, with villages situated along canals, scattered on average by 20 minutes' walking distance. The capillary water network and country roads located primarily on the field ridges allowed for the mobility of people and goods (Fei, 1939). The rural population relied on the fertility of the agricultural land and, although improvements such as in situ rebuilding had been carried out during the 1970s and 1980s, the land use and landscape was not very different to that in 1969 when a US flight took aerial photos of the city (see Figure 4.5).

Figure 4.5: The first resettlement neighbourhoods built at the western edge of SIP (the large dashed line). Xujiabang and Xiayuan are within the dashed outline between two main roads, the Eastern Ring Road and the Suzhou-Hangzhou Expressway. Satellite view capturing the situation in 1969, with the perimeter of the main rural resettled villages (top); the same area in 2022 (bottom).

Source: top, US USSG (1969), dashed area marked by authors; bottom, Google Earth Pro (2022)

Suzhou City leased the land required for development to a Sino-Singapore joint venture. The first task for urbanization was land acquisition and the relocation of everything: farmers, enterprises, and institutions. The Chronicles report that from 1994 to 1997 in Loufeng Township, a total of 4,467 rural households were relocated, and 1.2 million m² of houses, 67 village-run enterprises, and eight schools were demolished.

It was decided that farmers should be resettled near to their original villages, so the new neighbourhoods for those displaced by the first wave of demolitions were built in Loufeng Township, in the 500 m-wide strip of land between two main arteries: the Eastern Ring Road and the Suzhou-Hangzhou Expressway. Among these resettlements, the adjacent neighbourhoods of Xiayuan New Village and Xujiabang Second Village were built from 1995 in around 51 ha. The term 'village' is a reference to the original rural community (see Figure 4.6).

Xiayuan New Village (夏园新村) occupies an area of 97,600 m² and has a floor area ratio of 1:02. There are 30 six-storey buildings, with an average area of 72.6 m² per unit. Xujiabang Second Village (徐家浜二村) occupies an area of 85,000 m² and has a floor area ratio of 1:18. There are 28 six-storey buildings, with an average area of 70 m² per unit. The buildings in both of these new villages have brick-and-concrete structures and contain units of one, two, or three bedrooms, with a living room. The per capita resettlement housing area is almost 35 m², nearly four times the per capita housing area of urban residents in Suzhou in 1997, but less than the farmers' original rural houses, which were between 200 and 400 m² hosting extended

Figure 4.6: The remaining houses along the canal of a rural village included in Nanhuan resettlement community

Source: Drone flight, June 2021 by the authors

families (SIP, 2006; Ke, 2023; Lianjia, 2023). In other words, and on average, the displaced rural population experienced a reduction in their living space.

Each village in the resettlement area houses approximately 5,000–6,000 residents, plus a floating population of migrants. When the villages were built, they had basic public facilities: a primary school, a kindergarten, and a medical station; they often included restaurants, a food store, a vegetable market, a barber shop, and a bank. Each village was designed as a system of urban governance built to be self-sufficient and self-contained (Zeng et al, 2016). In this way, at the urban level, the assemblage of gated resettlement compounds, each containing basic facilities or connected to a neighbourhood centre, dismembers the urban tissue both spatially and socially. As a result, the residents do not experience a city, but rather a polished and zoned version of a village.

The open space was designed for a population without cars: the main roads were 6 m wide, while the distribution roads were 3–4 m wide and the footpaths, when present, were 1.2–2 m wide. There were green buffers along the roads, a green lawn in-between parallel buildings, and sometimes a small park in the centre of the neighbourhood. When the households started to acquire cars, the green spaces were often transformed into paved parking areas and the inner circulation area became congested.

The description and data of the SIP development indicates clearly how extensive, forceful, and determinate domestic land expropriation was. Yet, there is little record of people's reactions and resistance, and few studies have examined the long-term effects of displacement on rural populations. For example, little literature addresses the risk of decline of the second generations, or the resettled farmers' failed attempts to reshape the imposed space to support their adaptation (Yang and Qian, 2022). However, avant-garde art expressed the disturbance and distress of the impact of this violent change and one of the main subjects of Chinese artists of the 1980s and 1990s was the reappropriation of space (Gao, 2011). From a planning and design perspective, further questions are raised by the assessment of the longer-term durability and functionality of resettlement neighbourhoods.

The condition of the resettlements

When the SIP was built, the Chinese economy was booming, but governance methods, planning practices, and technical standards to produce an internationally attractive New Town had yet to be acquired. With the support of the Singaporean government, international standards and know-how were applied to the industrial areas and business districts of SIP, but not to the planning and design of resettlement housing (Wong and Liang, 2020). The new neighbourhoods for dispossessed farmers were built cheaply and quickly in order to provide decent housing in compliance with local regulations (Jiangsu Provincial Government and SIP Government 1996; Pellegrini and Chen, 2020). The resettlement, however, did not provide a general improvement in living conditions for all those who had been displaced. Because the Suzhou region is a fairly rich agricultural area. The compensation received in a lump sum or/and as apartment(s) provided a new structure and basic comfort, but could not replace the livelihood, the community links, the generous living spaces, and the well-known environment. In addition, the decay of the structures opens up uncertain perspectives.

Twenty to 30 years after their realization, the authors carried out qualitative research direct observation and fieldwork on the current conditions of the resettlement communities that had been built in the 1990s and 2000s in Suzhou. The research confirmed the presence of highly repetitive standardized layouts and buildings, as discussed in the previous section. The main characteristics of the buildings (type, number of floors, depth, number of units) and their layout in the neighbourhood (east–west orientation, symmetrical alignment, minimum distances between buildings) came with little variation and design quality. The residential mono-functionality of the resettlement neighbourhoods and the dimensions and features of the open space were repeated as well.

A close inspection of the physical and spatial features of the resettlement villages highlighted three kinds of obsolescence, which disclose the intention of their promoter to realize short-duration buildings. The first is the obsolescence of the building structure itself. Some of the buildings we observed have structural issues and outdated equipment and appliances. Sewerage, plumbing, heating and cooling systems, electricity and water supplies and access, and soundproofing installations were all found to require updating. Thermal insulation is needed to increase sustainability and comfort. This decay is rooted in the regulation, because standards concerning the durability of structures were only introduced in 2001. The Unified Standard for Reliability Design of Building Structures (GB50068) introduced the concept of a planned service life – that is, that the service life of building structures and structural components must be no less than 30 years (more recently, service life was increased to 50 years) (Cimillo et al, 2019).

The second is the obsolescence of the living standards inside the units and in the open space. Units were designed according to the Residential Building Design Code (MURCEP, 1986), so every unit has a kitchen and one bathroom, but the buildings have no elevator, no heating, and not enough parking space. Indeed, often the neighbourhoods were designed without parking areas, which were added later, occupying the limited green areas as discussed previously. While some units are very small – the smallest are 35–42 m^2 gross surface area – in general they are not particularly small, with an average minimum gross surface of 65 m² and a maximum of 125 m². However, no unit has a kitchen large and comfortable enough to accommodate a dishwasher (according to the Design Code the minimum dimension was between 4 and 5.5 m²), nor a bathroom large enough for a washing machine (according to the law, the minimum dimension was between 1.8 and 2 m²), and none has two bathrooms.

The national government acknowledged this obsolescence in the five-year National Plan 2021–25, which sets out requirements for the renovation of neighbourhoods built before 2000 (PRC, 2021). In 2019, Suzhou was listed as one of the pilot cities for renovation by the Ministry of Housing and Urban–Rural Development and the 'Old Community Renovation Plan' was launched, which targets 79 communities (PRC, 2021). The goal is to improve accessibility, parking spaces, open spaces, water pipes, power supply, lighting, roof waterproofing, to solve structural problems, and to demolish illegal buildings (Ding, 2022). It also aims to improve the current image of the communities, which the Loufeng sub-district government described as 'dirty, chaotic, and poor'. The renovation of Xujiabang Second Village is included in the program and in March 2023 the first elevator in the community was added to a six-storey house. Among the renovations, around 200 parking spaces for residents of Xiayuan New Village and Xujiabang Second Village were added in an adjacent plot of land (SIP, 2022).

The third obsolescence is that of the design. In the resettlement villages, generic design was imposed across different sites – that is, the same materials, technology, and façade design were used, offering approximately the same condition and visual image to everyone. Similar characteristics can be found in over 170 residential communities in Suzhou built by the local government (Chen et al, 2022) (see Figures 4.7 and 4.8).

The image and the obsolescence of buildings and public space impact the residents of the resettlement, and its real estate value. The villages are stigmatized as poor and uncivilized (Zhang et al, 2021), partly because they constantly provide low-cost housing to low-skilled workers migrating from rural areas into the city (He and Chang, 2020). This prejudice towards the agricultural labourer that persists in Chinese society combines to obsolescence and produces enclaves and housing depreciation.

Future resettlements

Asynchronous economic growth was programmed at the very beginning of the economic reform, enabling some areas of the country to grow more quickly while others followed in a more gradual process (Wang, 1994). The narrative was that national economic growth would benefit the whole society in the long term – which it did, but not in equal ways. A diversified

Figure 4.7: Photo of Xujiabang neighbourhood

Source: Authors

Figure 4.8: Example of a neighbourhood with the same characteristics in Suzhou, view from the road

Source: Authors

growth happened on different scales: at the scale of the whole country only the SEZs had the opportunity to increase their GDP, while at the local scale, the dispossession of those living or working in areas planned for industrial and real estate development was the first step in producing a new built environment. Certainly, little capital accumulation from real estate development would have been possible if rural land had not been transformed and farmers removed. The 'success' of this model of rapid economic development means urbanization is still a major goal and large-scale resettlements are normal in China's top-down and efficiency-based strategy of state entrepreneurialism. Urban expansions or redevelopments through dispossession and resettlement keep occurring in Suzhou, as shown by the official announcements of the Suzhou Office of Housing and Urban-Rural Development (SOHURD, 2023) and all over China.[1] The development of recent resettlement neighbourhoods repeats the planning and design model of the past; plans, infrastructure, constructions, and facilities follow a programmatic uniformity and no informality is allowed (Ma et al, 2006).

If, on the one hand, the economic reform created different rates of development, on the other it offered similar basic living conditions to the resettled (Yu, 2014; Gomersall, 2018). However, uniformity does not fit an increasingly diversified Chinese society and the challenge posed by the design obsolescence of the old resettlement sites, even if renovated, lies in whether they appeal to an increasingly middle-class society and to the moderately prosperous society that is the goal of the national government. In fact, there are increasing demands for better-quality housing (Guanghua, 2018), and several years after displacement many resettled households are financially better off and absorbed into the market logics. The stock in decay is very large because it includes not only the resettlements but also, in general, the residential structures: in Suzhou alone there are 1,273 urban communities with almost 600,000 residences built before 2000 (Wang, 2021). Will better-off households keep appreciating these compact and homogeneous conditions? Will diversified housing types and neighbourhoods be required for diversified lifestyles and households? If so, will this trigger future redevelopments and more displacement from rural land, or even from old resettlement areas?

For now, the practice of resettlement continues. In 2016, the National Development and Reform Commission promoted a new round of rural resettlements – the Resettlement Plan for Poverty Alleviation – to accelerate the urbanization of millions of farmers in villages with insufficient employment opportunities or that lacked infrastructure and public services (NDRC, 2016; Rogers et al, 2020). Similarly, the Rural Revitalization Program 2018–22 worked to urbanize rural land and rationalize agricultural production. In all these initiatives, the narrative of progress through urbanization normalizes the idea of resettlement as a state development project (Rogers et al, 2020; Yang et al, 2020). When urbanization is proposed as a strategy to reduce poverty, the outcome can be a territorial reorganization without the social and cultural assets of a city, as demonstrated in the case of Suzhou. Not only is this less attractive for its inhabitants, but also for investments and enterprises, requiring the government to continue supporting the local economy. While resettlement policies have been promoted to support marginalized groups and reduce social and economic differences between urban and rural populations, they have lacked consultation with those affected.

In more recent years, there has been some degree of change. On the urban side, the Ministry of Housing and Urban–Rural Development determined that from 2021 large-scale demolitions and relocations should gradually be stopped in cities with high housing prices and a shortage of stock. In line with this, the last five-year plan supported urban–rural integration, which often means the improvement of rural settlements with public facilities, in lieu of their demolition and redevelopment. On the rural side, instead of expropriation, governments have moved towards supporting the commodification of rural land by villagers. This can be described as a shift from accumulation by dispossession to the accumulation by rental revenues (Kan, 2019). At the same time, the approach to resettlement is gradually evolving towards a more participatory approach. Significantly, the Rural Revitalization Strategic Plan states the importance of considering the conditions of every household in the urban transformation process, and clearly states that farmers shall not be forcibly relocated to and concentrated in apartments (Li, 2004). It also states that expropriation must consider the will of the expropriated (Shi et al, 2022).

While recent policy changes certainly mark a move away from imposed dispossession and displacement as central pillars of modernization and development, it is only in the coming years that it will be possible to assess whether this new approach – the reduction of demolitions, the consideration of the household, the shift to accumulation by rents – will bring about actual change, especially considering the recent real estate crisis, which could reduce new urbanization and land grabbing. Likewise, it remains to be seen what the future holds for residents of existing resettlement neighborhoods that display forms of obsolescence, especially in wealthy areas such as Suzhou. On an extended scale, further questions should be raised about the position of rural land and lifestyles within China's development goals.

Note

[1] Shanghai government (2023) Administrative Measures for Expropriation and Resettlement of Housing. Available from: https://fgj.sh.gov.cn/gfxwj/20200622/457b0b378f2d4986afce318ffa80d1ed.html; Hunan Province (2023), Details of Compensation and Resettlement Standards for Rural House Demolition and Resettlement in Hengdong County. Available from: www.163.com/dy/article/I3B1095U055635E0.html; 'How do

I know in advance that my house will be demolished? Here are 10 signs it's coming' (2022). Available from: https://zhuanlan.zhihu.com/p/85735403; 'The 40 relocated residents of Tiancizhuang completed the lottery for the sequence number of resettlement housing selection' (2024). Available from: www.gusu.gov.cn/gsq/zwyw/201701/38a3f9c4fb5546b3bcde9a9b144979bd.shtml

References

Cai, M. (2016) 'Land for welfare in China', *Land Use Policy*, 55: 1–12.

Cai, M., Liu, P., and Wang, H. (2020) 'Land commodification and *hukou* policy innovation in China: evidence from a survey experiment', *Journal of Chinese Governance*, 5(4): 419–38.

Chen, J., Pellegrini, P., Xu, Y., and Ma, G. (2022) 'Evaluating residents' satisfaction before and after regeneration: the case of a high-density resettlement neighbourhood in Suzhou', *Cogent Social Sciences*, 8(1).

Chen, J., Yue, C., Ren, L. and Yan, J. (2020) 'Determinants of urban identity in urbanizing China: findings from a survey experiment', *Chinese Sociological Review* 52(3): 295–318.

Chen S. and Ravallion M. (2020) *Reconciling the Conflicting Narratives on Poverty in China*, NBER. Available from: www.nber.org/papers/w28147 [Accessed 2 August 2025].

Chen, Y. and Zhu, Q. (2021) 'Resettlement with Chinese characteristics: the distinctive political-economic context, (in)voluntary urbanites, and three types of mismatches', *International Journal of Urban Sustainable Development*, 13(3): 496–515.

Chien, S. and Woodworth, M. (2018) 'China's urban speed machine', *International Journal of Urban and Regional Research*, 42(4): 723–37.

Choi, H.S. and Reeve, A. (2018) 'Understanding the impact of economic migrants and landless farmers on mass-produced housing and community space in China, using the case of Zhangjing, Suzhou', *International Journal of Urban Sustainable Development*, 10(1): 60–78.

Cimillo, M., Calcerano, F., Chen, X., Chow, D., and Gigliarelli, E. (2019) 'Energy modelling and retrofit of the residential building stock of Jiangsu province', *KnE Social Sciences*, 3(27): 546–58.

Ding, Y. (2022) 'China advances renovation of old urban residential communities to improve people's quality of life', *China Daily*, 25 November.

Dowall, D.E. (1994) 'Urban residential redevelopment in the People's Republic of China', *Urban Studies*, 31(9): 1497–1516.

Dreyer, J. (2014) '(Re)made in China: The Soviet-era planning projects shaping China's cities', *ArchDaily*, 27 July. Available from: www.archdaily.com/530434/re-made-in-china-the-soviet-era-planning-projects-shaping-china-s-cities [Accessed 3 April 2023].

Duan, J. and Liu, J. (2022) *Contemporary Urban Design Thoughts in China*, Springer.

Fei, X. (1939) *The Life of Chinese Peasants*, Kegan Paul.

Gao, M. (2011) *Total Modernity and the Avant-Garde in Twentieth-Century Chinese Art*, MIT Press.

Gomersall, K. (2018) 'Resettlement practice and the pathway to the urban ideal', *Geoforum*, 96: 51–60.

Gu, H. (2021) 'The century-old splendour of the Communist Party of China and China's modernisation', *China Economic Transition*, 4(3): 12–21.

Guanghua School of Management (2018) Guanghua Dialogues: how property developers are shaping urbanisation in China. Available from: www.youtube.com/watch?v=zpeNHOALD5U [Accessed 10 January 2024].

He, S., Liu, Y., and Webster, C., Wu, F. (2009) 'Property rights redistribution, entitlement failure and the impoverishment of landless farmers in China', *Urban Studies*, 46(9): 1925–49.

He, S. and Chang, Y. (2020) 'A zone of exception? Interrogating the hybrid housing regime and nested enclaves in China-Singapore Suzhou-Industrial-Park', *Housing Studies*, 36(4): 592–616.

Hong, R., Tseng, Y., and Lin, T. (2022) 'Guarding a new Great Wall: the politics of household registration reforms and public provision in China', *China Quarterly*, 251: 776–97.

Hong, T., Yu, N., Mao, Z., and Zhang, S. (2021) 'Government-driven urbanisation and its impact on regional economic growth in China', *Cities*, 117 (2): 103299.

Hsing, Y. (2010) *The Great Urban Transformation. Politics of Land and Property in China*, Oxford University Press.

Hui, C., Bao H., and Zhang, X. (2013) The policy and praxis of compensation for land expropriations in China: an appraisal from the perspective of social exclusion, *Land Use Policy*, 32: 309–16.

Hulshof, M. and Roggeveen, D. (2010) *How the City Moved to Mr Sun*, Sun.

Jiang, Y., Waley, P., and Gonzalez, S. (2014) 'Nice apartments, no jobs: how former villagers experienced displacement and resettlement in the western suburbs of Shanghai', *Urban Studies*, 55(14): 3202–17.

Jiangsu Provincial Government and SIP Government (1996) 'Sunshine impact analysis rules. Technical regulations for planning and design of residential areas in Suzhou Industrial Park'. Available from: http://sfj.suzhou.gov.cn/sfj/basc/201801/ede1838bdbf842bfb978995511642409.shtml [Accessed 3 April 2023].

Kan, K. (2019) 'Accumulation without dispossession? Land commodification and rent extraction in peri-urban China', *International Journal of Urban and Regional Research*, 43(4): 633–48.

Ke Real Estate Agency (2023) 'Xiayuan New Village'. Available from: https://su.ke.com/xiaoqu/2311055041969 [Accessed 10 September 2023].

Li, H. (2022) Soviet specialists' urban planning technical assistance to China 1949–1959, *Planning Perspectives*, 37(4): 815–39.

Li, P. and Wang, X. (2013) *Legal Review of China's Property Rights Regime*, World Bank. Available from: www.worldbank.org/content/dam/Worldbank/document/EAP/China/Urban-China-SRs4-7.pdf [Accessed 2 August 2025].

Li, Z. (2004) 'Forced from home: Property rights, civic activism and the politics of relocation in China', *Urban Anthropology* 33: 247–81.

Liang, L., Chen, M., and Lu, D. (2022) 'Revisiting the relationship between urbanisation and economic development in China since the reform and opening-up', *Chinese Geographical Science*, 32: 1–15.

Lianjia Real Estate Agency (2023) 'Xujiabang Second Village'. Available from: https://su.lianjia.com/xiaoqu/2311055093306 [Accessed 10 September 2024].

Lin, G. (2002) 'The growth and structural change of Chinese cities: a contextual and geographic analysis', *Cities*, 19(5): 299–316.

Lu, D. (2006) 'Travelling urban form: the neighbourhood unit in China', *Planning Perspectives*, 21(4): 369–92.

Lu, W. (1991) 'Several problems in residential area planning', *Urban Planning*, 4: 11–13.

Ma, C., Shao, A., and Hu, X. (2006) 'About several issues related to the resettlement of rural settlements in the construction of new urban areas', *Small Town Construction*, 8: 87–89.

MHURD – Ministry of Housing and Urban-Rural Development of the People's Republic of China (1993) *Code of Urban Residential Areas Planning and Design GB 50180–93* (2002 version). Available from: www.codeofchina.com/standard/GB50180-2018.html [Accessed 2 August 2025].

MURCEP – Ministry of Urban and Rural Construction and Environmental Protection of the People's Republic of China (1984) *Code of urban Residential Areas Planning and Design GBJ50180*.

MURCEP – Ministry of Urban and Rural Construction and Environmental Protection of the People's Republic of China (1986) *National Standard Code for the Design of Residential Buildings GBJ96–86*.

NDRC – National Development and Reform Commission (2016) *National Poverty Resettlement Plan*. Available from: www.cpad.gov.cn/module/download/downfile.jsp?classid=0&filename=170124 1019276682501.pdf [Accessed 3 April 2023].

Pellegrini, P. and Chen, J. (2020) 'Hypothesis of densification for a sustainable urbanisation in a wealthy Chinese city', *IOP Conference Series: Earth and Environmental Science*, 588(1.15–1.19): 052029.

PRC – People's Republic of China (2021) *14th Five-Year Plan 2021–2025 for National Economic and Social Development and Long-Range Objectives for 2035*. Available from: https://cset.georgetown.edu/publication/china-14th-five-year-plan [Accessed 8 January 2023].

Qiu, F. and Chen, G. (2023) 'The impact of housing demolition on residents' happiness: empirical evidence from China Social Indicators', *Journal for Quality-of-Life Measurement*, 170(1): 137–59.

Rogers, S., Li, J., Lo, K., Guo, H., and Li, C. (2020) 'China's rapidly evolving practice of poverty resettlement: moving millions to eliminate poverty', *Development Policy Review*, 38(5): 541–54.

Shi, G., Zhou, J., and Yu, Q. (2012) 'Resettlement in China, in C. Tortajada, D. Altinbilek and A. Biswas (eds), *Impacts of Large Dams: A Global Assessment*, Springer, pp 219–42.

Shi, G., Tianhe, J., and Sun, Z. (2022) 'Evolution of land and resettlement laws in China: Setting new standards', in M. Zaman, R. Nair and G. Shi (eds), *Resettlement in Asian Countries: Legislation, Administration and Struggles for Rights*, Routledge, pp 56–70.

Shi, K., Liu, H., and Lin, Z. (2012) *The Making of a Chinese Model New Town: Planning and Development of Suzhou Industrial Park*, Architecture & Building Press.

Smith N.R. (2021) *The End of the Village: Planning the Urbanisation of Rural China*, University of Minnesota Press.

State Council (1956) *On the Decision of Enhancing Planning*.

State Council (1984) *Town Planning Regulation*. Available from: www.npc.gov.cn [Accessed 2 February 2023].

State Council (2001) 'Regulation on the Administration of Urban Housing Demolition and Relocation', *Chinese Law and Government*, 44(1): 10–16SIP.

SIP – Suzhou Industrial Park government (2022) Xujiabang Community Old Community Reconstruction Project. Available from: www.suzhou.gov.cn [Accessed 2 August 2025].

SOHURD – Suzhou Office of Housing and Urban-Rural Development (2023) Available from: www.suzhou.gov.cn/search4/s? [Accessed 2 August 2025].

SSY – Suzhou Statistical Yearbook (2020) Available from: www.suzhou.gov.cn/szsrmzf/tjnj/nav_list.shtml [Accessed 2 August 2025].

Takamura, M. and Shao, S. (2021) 'Impact of Soviet worker residential district design on Beijing no. 2 Textile Factory: research of worker residential planning during the First Five-Year Plan', *Journal of Architecture and Planning*, 86(787): 2378.

Tang, B. (2018) *China's Housing Middle Class: Changing Urban Life in Gated Communities*, Routledge.

Taylor A. (2015) 'And then there was one', *The Atlantic*, 14 April. Available from: www.theatlantic.com/photo/2015/04/and-then-there-was- one/390501/?utm_medium=website&utm_source=archdaily.com [Accessed 2 August 2025].

UPDRIC – Urban Planning and Design Research Institute of China (1985) *Detailed Planning and Design of Residential Areas*, China Architecture and Construction Press.

Wang, H. (1994) *The Gradual Revolution*, Rand.

Wang, K. (2021) 'Suzhou makes best use of ancient and modern', *China Daily*, 13 May.

Wang, L. (2018) *Changing Spatial Elements in Chinese Socio-economic Five-Year Plan: From Project Layout to Spatial Planning*, Springer.

Wang, S. and Cheng, J. (1959) 'Research on the distribution of residential clusters', *Architectural Journal*, 1: 10–14.

Wang, X., Hui, E., and Sun, J. (2017) 'Population migration, urbanisation and housing prices: evidence from the cities in China', *Habitat International*, 66: 49–56.

Wang, Y., Wu, W., and Boelens, L. (2021) 'City profile: Suzhou, China – the interaction of water and city', *Cities*, 112.

Wang, Z., Shen, J., Luo, X. (2023) 'Can residents regain their community relations after resettlement? Insights from Shanghai', *Urban Studies*, 60(5): 962–80.

Wilmsen, B., Webber, M. and Duan, Y. (2011) 'Development for whom? Rural to urban resettlement at the Three Gorges Dam', *Asian Studies Review*, 35(1): 21–42.

Wong, J. and Liang F. (2020) *Suzhou Industrial Park: Achievements, Challenges and Prospects*, World Scientific Publishing Co.

World Bank (2023) 'Data'. Available from: https://data.worldbank.org/indicator/SP.URB.TOTL.IN.ZS?locations=CN https://data.worldbank.org/topic/poverty?locations=CN [Accessed 2 August 2025].

Wu, F. (2016) 'State dominance in urban redevelopment: beyond gentrification in urban China', *Urban Affairs Review*, 52(5): 631–58.

Wu, F. and Webster, C. (eds) (2010) *Marginalisation in Urban China: Comparative Perspectives*, Palgrave Macmillan.

Wu, L. (2001) 'Basic ideas, regional culture, time models: the exploration of the development path of Chinese architecture', *China Construction Information*, 36: 35–39.

Wu, W., Zhang, M., Qing, Y. and Li, Y. (2019) 'Village resettlement and social relations in transition: the case of Suzhou', *International Development Planning Review*, 41(3): 269–91.

Xu, Y., Tang, B., and Chan, E.H.W. (2011) 'State-led land requisition and transformation of rural villages in transitional China', *Habitat International*, 35: 57–65.

Xue, Y., Mao, K., Weeks, N., and Xiao, J. (2021) 'Rural reform in contemporary China: development, efficiency, and fairness', *Journal of Contemporary China*, 30(128): 266–82.

Yang, C. and Qian, Z. (2022) 'Urbanisation through resettlement and the production of space in Hangzhou's concentrated resettlement communities', *Cities*, 129: 103846.

Yang, Y., de Sherbinin, A., and Liu, Y. (2020) 'China's poverty alleviation resettlement: progress, problems and solutions', *Habitat International*, 98: 102135.

Yu, J. (2014) 'The "urbanisation" of peasants is fundamental', *Contemporary Chinese Thought*, 46(1): 37–40.

Zeng, W., Wang, H., You, J., and Wang, L. (2016) 'A study on planning strategies for urban housing block development', *China City Planning Review*, 25(4): 44–54.

Zhang, M., Wu, W., and Zhong, W. (2018) 'Agency and social construction of space under top-down planning: Resettled rural residents in China', *Urban Studies*, 55(7): 15–41.

Zhang, M., Qiao, S., and Gar-On Yeh, A. (2021) 'Blemish of place: territorial stigmatisation and the depreciation of displaced villagers' resettlement houses in Chengdu, China', *Cities*, 117: 103330.

Zhu, X. (1994) 'Planning of residential area for the new century', *Journal of Tongji University*, 2: 229.

5

Between Augmented Disposability and Deferred Disposal: A View from Istanbul

Francesco Pasta

Amidst escalating inequalities and housing insecurity (MacLeod and McFarlane, 2014; Brickell et al, 2017), development-induced displacement is today commonplace across globalizing cities. Many low- and mixed-income urban areas, where an 'urban majority' has established a terrain of sustenance and liveability (Benjamin et al, 2022), are invested by policies of curated disinvestment, underservicing, and social disentanglement (Simone, 2018). These policies concur to magnify conditions of socio-material deterioration that urban redevelopment will eventually fix – or at least erase from view. Financialized urbanization, entrepreneurial governance, and top-down planning narratives often frame such neighbourhoods as disposable, feeding into urban interventions premised upon logics of 'rule by aesthetics' (Ghertner, 2011), 'resiliency revanchism' (Alvarez and Cardenas, 2019) 'hygienization' (Garmany and Richmond, 2020), or 'punitive containment' (Wacquant, 2008). 'Popular quarters', and the lifeworld nested therein, are recast by the dominant discourse as the 'constitutive other' of development (Roy, 2011), while their embeddedness within urban metabolism is systematically overlooked (Amin, 2013) and are thus made expendable: they may yield value through their destruction.

Urban disposability, in this sense, is a multi-layered and pervasive condition that speaks to the spatial overlap of 'remaindered lives' (Tadiar, 2022), expendable bodies, devalued labour, and 'exhausted territories' (see Chapter 1). In the current era characterized by the continuous production of 'wasted people and wasted places', urban disposability thus emerges as a spatial manifestation of the 'wasting relationships' that separate value from waste and, crucially, render disposable communities that are framed as such (Armiero, 2021; see also Bauman, 2004). It is a lens through which to observe the territorialization of processes of 'structural violence' that distinguish between worthy and worthless, categorize and hierarchize lives, stratify citizenship rights, and unevenly distribute displacement (Bayırbağ et al, 2023; Yiftachel, 2015; see also Chapter 1). Urban disposability is part and parcel of regimes of socio-spatial ordering that are sustained by manifold technologies of disenfranchisement, such as labour precarization, differential inclusion (Mezzadra and Neilson, 2013), and territorial stigmatization (Wacquant, 2007). Manufactured, reproduced, and circulated by hegemonic coalitions, urban disposability is a discursive-material construct that lays the ground for socio-spatial restructuring, enabling and legitimizing acts of displacement and dispossession that are often confronted with splintered and ineffective opposition.

Extractivist projects premised on the narrative of urban disposability, however, are intrinsically prone to unexpected setbacks and prolonged crises. Although unflinchingly sustained by governments and the private sector, aspirations of overnight transformation frequently get stranded into the complexities of urban politics, face open or covert local counteractions and legal and institutional obstacles, and teeter on the brink of failure amid unstable economic conjunctures. I emphasize the erratic unfolding of large-scale urban development plans not as an oddity in itself (Gupta et al, 2015; Carse and Kneas, 2019), but because the drawn-out temporality of redevelopment exposes the disposability–restructuring nexus. From the planning stage through implementation and onto the aftermath of completion (sequential stages that in fact are often not clearly discernible), profit-oriented redevelopment schemes may extend over decades and generally concur to magnify local conditions of precariousness, deterioration, and marginalization. They induce an 'augmented disposability' that not only fuels urban transformation projects further – at least discursively – but is also partly an outcome of their non-linear and contested unfolding. We can conceptualize urban disposability and redevelopment as mutually constitutive, always in tension.

Yet, life between disposability and redevelopment exceeds the dialectic tension between the two. In the stretched-out transitional timespan of urban change muddling through cycles of boom and bust, urban disposability is more than a moment between the exhaustion of the life-cycle of an urban environment, with its interwoven forms of sociability and productivity, and its eventual elimination. The array of arrangements, transactions, and collaborations undertaken by those inhabiting the time and space of prolonged expendability and potential displacement defy reductive readings of this conjuncture as a static interlude where passive subjects await absorption or expulsion by the urban growth machine. In this 'ordinary emergency', where moving on happens through unstable practices that blur 'the clear delineation of who extracts what' (Lancione and Simone, 2021: 1), residents 'stay with breakdown' (Thieme, 2021) by dwelling, connecting, making do, and advancing their own individual or collective trajectories in the face of increasing economic and political pressure, socio-technical disentanglement, and environmental degradation. Inhabitants may participate in reproducing disposability, mobilizing and redeploying it, and reworking it to their own ends. They do so through practices of maintenance, repair, recycling, and adjustment that unfold alongside, and intertwine with, processes of exclusion, expulsion, extraction, and estrangement. Urban disposability thus emerges as a dynamic, generative, and stratified condition that is continuously remade, both as a driver of urban change and as a context for everyday living: a space of endurance, of 'living with the trouble' (see Chapter 1).

This chapter reflects on these issues from Fikirtepe, a 'popular neighbourhood' in Istanbul that has been undergoing a botched redevelopment scheme for more than 15 years. In this inhabited 'demolition area', as we shall see, precarious socio-material assemblages unfold between populations that are deemed expellable, discarded material waste, and leftover spaces. The case of Istanbul and Fikirtepe adds substance to the concept of urban disposability and complicates it, shedding light on its contested and incoherent genealogy, its inherent ambivalence and contradictions, and its manifold, unforeseeable effects. In this chapter, I provide an overview of urban transformation in Istanbul, followed by an exploration of the ongoing dynamics in Fikirtepe. The four field notes are supported by 'fragments' of personal stories of residents navigating life under conditions of augmented disposability.

The crisis of urban transformation, urban transformation as a crisis

Over two decades of uninterrupted rule by the Justice and Development Party (Adalet ve Kalkınma Partisi, or AKP)[1] in Turkey, extractivist urban transformation was streamlined as a key mechanism for socio-spatial restructuring and resources redistribution. From the early 2000s, as concerted efforts to turn Istanbul into a global city regained momentum, informally originated neighbourhoods turned into a frontier for profit accumulation through redevelopment. Originally resembling 'rural villages' on the urban fringe, such *gecekondu* ('landed at night') areas had gone through subsequent cycles of densification, commodification, and regularization, providing pathways for upward mobility to more established residents (Işık and Pınarcıoğlu, 2008). With relentless urban expansion and infrastructural development, many of these neighbourhoods came to sit on prime land with a considerable rent gap (Karaman, 2008), and within the framework of profit-oriented urban development, they had to get out of the way for a further cycle of capital accumulation.

The mainstream discourse legitimizing this large-scale clearance, turning 'squatter settlements into slums' (Mercan and Sen, 2020: 2), had been in the making for decades. Although the variegated development trajectories of Istanbul's informal settlements make generalizations impossible, it is relevant to notice how rendering *gecekondu* areas 'dispensable' (Karaman, 2008) occurred in parallel to, and arguably also as a backlash against, sustained upgrading processes and socio-economic and political advancement for a segment of residents alongside the rise of neoliberal urban governance after the 1980 military coup. While, on one hand, free-market reforms and a sustained influx of migrants with narrower opportunities for upward mobility generated new forms of poverty and socio-economic vulnerability (Işık and Pınarcıoğlu, 2008), a large segment of *gecekondu* dwellers advanced their socio-political position. Precisely to cushion the social impacts of neoliberal restructuring, the government formalized property ownership in squatter areas and allowed for higher construction volumes, turning long-term residents into formal stakeholders in the rent-based urban economy, and engendering a construction boom (Esen, 2008). Local authorities, in parallel, were providing services and infrastructural upgrading to these rapidly verticalizing 'apart-kondus' (Karaman, 2013). Moreover, following the post-coup crushing of unions and leftist organizations, conservative and religious networks deployed clientelist support systems, which won them widespread consent in several lower-income areas (Karaman, 2013). The rise of neoliberal Islamism to a hegemonic position (Tuğal, 2016) is arguably grounded, in part, in *gecekondu* neighbourhoods.

It is against this backdrop that the designation of *varoş* (suburb, slum) emerged in popular parlance as a class-based derogatory term to describe popular neighbourhoods, where 'probably a majority of Istanbulites live' (Öktem, 2008: 407), and their residents, reframed as petty profiteers, scroungers, criminals, and terrorists (Aslan and Erman, 2014).[2] Especially after the 1999 Marmara earthquake, this rhetoric was complemented by a disaster risk-reduction discourse, invoking the demolition of informal areas with their shoddy structures, unlicensed buildings, and tightly packed tissue. Former *gecekondu* districts, alongside run-down inner-city areas, were depicted by the Istanbul Metropolitan Municipality in 2005 as 'eyesores that actively undercut Istanbul's global city bid' (Karaman, 2008), and a set of legislation was designed to expedite the wholesale remaking of areas defined as 'at risk' or 'dilapidated'.

Throughout the AKP era, public authorities in partnership with private investors embarked on a massive program of demolitions, resettlement, and redevelopment targeting numerous mixed and low-income urban areas in Istanbul. Extensive research has analysed how such top-down wholesale urban transformation projects often disrupt livelihoods, displace residents, deepen existing cleavages, erode social cohesion, and incur various additional overt or hidden costs (e.g. see Lovering and Türkmen; 2011; Karaman, 2013; Mercan and Sen, 2020). However, this financialized urban growth machine is not the relentless juggernaut it is often depicted as being. In a context of economic and geopolitical instability, urban transformation is prone to contestations, miscalculations, and setbacks. Many ambitious megaprojects in Istanbul advanced sluggishly and reached gridlock as an ill-designed policy framework, intra-institutional conflict, and coordinated opposition and effective legal mobilization by civil society groups (Kuyucu, 2022) collided with the worsening macroeconomic conditions, particularly from 2016 onwards. While the remaking of individual plots, the urbanization of unbuilt land, and the reconversion of idle sites have proceeded apace, wholesale redevelopment of rundown historic neighbourhoods and informally developed areas has proven to be more challenging. In many instances across the city, redevelopment projects are currently on hold, postponed, abandoned, or possibly just around the corner.

Under such conditions, urban transformation tends to be indefinitely prolonged, dependent on political backup, and highly unpredictable, resulting in a condition of open-ended displaceability for residents in the city's popular neighbourhoods (Yiftachel, 2020). Long before the first stone is even laid, redevelopment schemes produce significant effects on the socio-material makeup of targeted urban areas (Sakızlıoğlu, 2014), often triggering dynamics of material deterioration and social disentanglement. Where urban transformation does get underway, it often creates hybrid urbanscapes in which residents uneasily adjust to the gap between the purported 'inevitability' of completion and displacement, and the factual condition of 'suspension' of the project (Arican, 2023). The present-day crisis of urban transformation in Istanbul may thus be better interpreted through the lens of urban transformation *as a crisis*: a controversial and contested process that often entails prolonged disruption of livelihoods, multiple displacements of residents, escalating uncertainty, and gradual erosion of the city's socio-spatial fabric, amidst recurring setbacks and intermittent leaps forward. The case of Fikirtepe, which I will now discuss, encapsulates these dynamics and illustrates how people continue to inhabit this crisis in ways that exceed simple binaries.

Augmented disposability, deferred disposal in Fikirtepe

The five-month eviction notice has expired. It's getting dark as we talk. Electricity and water have been cut off in the street and most buildings have already been vacated. Mehmet's rental house, in the sector slated for demolition, has been for years both his dwelling and a storage space for his scrap-dealing activity. Since relocating from central Anatolia to Fikirtepe in the 1970s, he has worked as a mobile *hurdacı* (scrap dealer) from this base, combing with his pushcart more affluent coastal neighbourhoods where he had cultivated an invaluable network of contacts among the apartment-keepers, who would notify him when valuable pieces were thrown away. With the impending demolition, Mehmet has moved to Istanbul's eastern outskirts, where his daughters reside, but keeps returning almost daily to work, clinging to the very end to the two-storey *gecekondu* where his goods are stored. Uncertain about how to continue his activity in the new location, he ponders the possibility of returning to his village: 'It's not safe here now, after sunset – we better go.' One month later, he calls to inform me that his house has been demolished.

The wave of evictions, relocations, and demolitions affecting Mehmet in 2021 was only the most recent sprint in an extensive renewal project that, nearly two decades in the making and with no end in sight, lay waste to the area's socio-spatial fabric but failed to concretize its vision. Since the mid-2000s, the authorities have attempted to redevelop the neighbourhood, which provided viable accommodation and income-generation opportunities for a heterogeneous, mostly lower-income population within a middle-class district in Istanbul's Asian area. Offering hefty incentives for land assembly and increased development rights (Parmaksızoğlu, 2014), the master plan aimed to reassemble Fikirtepe's composite urbanscape into a few dozen high-rise mega blocks developed by contractors, which would supposedly agree with property owners in a competitive market with minimal planning and design guidelines. With a favourable macroeconomic conjuncture, the scheme prospected high yields to both developers and right-holders within a few years.

The name of Fikirtepe,[3] however, resonates nowadays as a byword for urban redevelopment failure. The project kicked off in 2012, but various criticalities coalesced to turn the vision of instant makeover into a protracted standstill. Amid legal and planning shortcomings, lack of trust and cooperation among stakeholders, intra-institutional conflicts, and lengthy legal disputes (Parmaksızoğlu, 2014; Soytemel, 2017), redevelopment unfolded intermittently and unevenly across the vast site, eventually coming up against a worsening macro-economic conjuncture from 2016 onwards. Many contractors went bankrupt, and thousands of residents were displaced as homes were vacated, and in many sectors razed, while new units were not realized. With many construction sites grinding to a halt and flattened blocks turning into wastelands, completed high-rises and idle skeletons stood beside still-inhabited streets and deserted buildings. Uncontrolled demolitions and endless construction created a toxic environment (MAD, 2021). Rising crime and a sense of insecurity strained community relations and socio-economic vulnerability escalated, prompting the remaining residents to leave the neighbourhood. Stuck between a condition of augmented disposability and stalled disposal, Fikirtepe seemed to slip below the threshold of liveability.

Eventually, in 2021, the government took over from non-compliant developers to implement first hand a revised project over 60 per cent of the originally envisioned perimeter, with the remaining parts scheduled to be rebuilt in two further stages. The northern flank of the neighbourhood's high street – where Mehmet had his home and depot – now overlooks a massive construction site where the previously completed condos coexist with cranes and concrete skeletons. The 'New Fikirtepe' master plan aims to deliver 11.295 housing units in the next few years (Ministry of Environment, Urbanisation and Climate Change, 2021).

One month before the elections in 2023, attending a ceremony to hand out keys for units still under construction, President Erdoğan employed Fikirtepe as a metaphor: 'We took Istanbul's most problematic area and turned it into the most prestigious one. You see, we also took Turkey 21 years ago in the same conditions as' (Ministry of Communication, 2023). From the outset, the project was narrated as spearheading a model whose relevance exceeded the site: the 'New Turkey' contrived by the ruling coalition would be concretized in Fikirtepe,[4] its vertical ascension also symbolizing a temporal acceleration into the future (see Gupta et al, 2015). The hegemonic vision of future circulated by the authorities and real estate sector recast Fikirtepe, with most of its residents, built stock, and livelihoods, as remainders to be wiped out for the country's advancement.

In this chrono-political battleground, a lingering past on the brink of obliteration is materially entwined with an impending future which continuously recedes. Yet in what remains of Fikirtepe (Figures 5.1 and 5.2), conditions of uncertainty and provisionality persist. As disposability intensifies, urban transformation recedes further away into the future. But disposal has only been deferred.

Precarious balance

'Once they finish that side, they'll come to this side.' For decades, Şeref had operated an *eskici* (old-stuffer) business in Teker street, a scrap-dealing hub razed during the recent dash of demolitions. He managed to remain in Fikirtepe by renting an abandoned real estate office in the not-yet-redeveloped sector. The bird's eye view of Manhattan printed over the storefront doesn't suggest this is a second-hand depot. Open for shopping only on Mondays – also to avoid retail taxes – the place is mainly used as a storage facility. The bulk of the business consists of salvaging recyclable goods from local scrapyards and reselling them to more upmarket secondhand shops in Kadıköy. Şeref also eats and sleeps in the space, which is not the most comfortable arrangement, but it's doable, since he runs the activity in

Figure 5.1: Fikirtepe, 2023: 'The right time, the right man': Erdoğan's electoral poster in the area scheduled to be redeveloped in Phase 3

Source: Author

Figure 5.2: Fikirtepe, 2022: the existing texture in Fikirtepe in the area that will be redeveloped in Phase 2

Source: Author

Figure 5.3: Fikirtepe, 2023: a closed-down real estate office turned into a second-hand shop

Source: Author

turns of a couple of months with his brother. He spends the rest of his time in his village, in the Kurdish South-East, where he maintains a house and family, although living off agriculture is no longer viable. Already displaced from their homeland, and then within Fikirtepe, they are now awaiting a possible further eviction, holding on to two precarious terrains.

At least a dozen evicted scrap-dealers, such as Şeref, managed to remain in Fikirtepe by repurposing busted real-estate offices, carving out a space between the exclusionary effects of redevelopment and its momentary 'failure' (Figure 5.3). As durable settlement is beyond the range of possibility, many residents hold on in Fikirtepe just for the time being, while actively organizing a future elsewhere: combing nearby districts for housing solutions, like Şeref; contemplating returning to their family village, like Mehmet; sending money 'back home' to build a house; or organizing an onward migration, like many of the migrants who have come to reside in the area over the past decade.

The prospect of redevelopment from scratch, its continuous postponement, and the intrinsic unpredictability led to disinvestment from authorities and neglect from residents, resulting in deteriorating conditions in the remaindered areas. As the local community unravels, the neighbourhood's material fabric is affected by a lack of maintenance. Impending relocation hinders the remaining residents' will and capacity to invest, as expenditures on material improvements might be wasted, while resources should be preserved for an anticipated 'new start' elsewhere.

Interestingly enough, obsolescence in Fikirtepe oversteps the boundaries of the remaining *gecekondu* areas: it also haunts the newly completed projects, which were hastily designed, poorly built and managed, and rushed into planning approval.[5] News and rumours about electricity cuts, dirty water, or malfunctioning elevators in the 'luxury' high-rises are rife (Hürriyet, 2020), while circulating claims assert that the density increase has not been matched by an upgrade in infrastructural provision. Most retail spaces in the mall-like street-level slabs already lie in ruins, between stuck escalators, missing tiles, and vacant units. In October 2022, Fikirtepe once again hit the headlines as an explosion and ensuing fire destroyed a *gecekondu* building, and only a few days later flames engulfed a 24-storey skyscraper nearby.

Furthermore, after the devastating effects of two major earthquakes in the country's Southeast in 2023 revealed the scale of corruption and mismanagement in the construction industry, the perception of safety wobbled in Fikirtepe too. Residents voiced concerns about the stability of the high-rises completed by private contractors, and some opted for the units that are being built by the government instead, because of their alleged higher quality (Interviews and informal talks, 2023) – which is paradoxical considering that seismic hazard was weaponized by authorities to expedite the project. Urban disposability in Fikirtepe thus seems to be hovering over the 'shanties' and 'elite residences' alike: it seeps from the doomed remnants of the past into the built concretization of the future, which observed closeup already looks prematurely wasted.

Such decay, however, is not a linear process, nor a uniform one. There are scattered examples of small-scale care, material improvements, and service provision carried out both by local authorities and inhabitants. One may still find a newly refurbished house, its shiny painted windows standing out in an alley where most properties are in a state of disrepair, or the odd well-kept vegetable garden appears amidst empty lots overtaken by weeds and rubbish. Practices of homemaking in limbo (Brun and Fábos, 2015) surface in the neat arrangement of shared rooms within a waste-collection centre inhabited by Afghan youngsters, or in the unkempt emptied flats rented and refurbished by Uzbek migrants. There are also cases of small-scale entrepreneurial ventures, from the central Asian eatery on the main road, catering to the Uzbek and Turkmen diaspora, to the pet shop set up in a bricked-up building targeting the incoming middle-class condo residents. Furthermore, once past the moment when the demolition looked imminent and justified a general abandonment, the local administration resumed its provision of some maintenance, filling potholes, unclogging water drains, and laying fibre cables.

Rather than a constant slide towards erasure, in Fikirtepe urban disposability looks more like a precarious balancing to steer clear of breakdown, vacillating between neglect and repair – only just enough to keep going for now, or just keep going later, somewhere else. Both dwellers and authorities strive to strike a balance between all-out forsaking and restrained investment, based on fluctuating prospects. While the authorities work to hold the neighbourhood 'on the thin edge between working and abject poverty' (Amin, 2013: 479), some residents sparingly invest resources to keep living conditions acceptable, adjust to contingencies, and maintain the place inhabitable for the time being – yet always ready to be vacated with the lowest margin of loss. For some, Fikirtepe's in-between state matches their transient permanency, and this precarious balance allows them specific affordances to advance their own life trajectory.

A twofold condition

The four-storey building on the ring-road lies empty, its main entrance bricked over. Writings in Dari on the bare inner walls point to its recent past as a waste-collection centre employing dozens of Afghan youngsters. Originally a factory, it was vacated and gutted in 2015, when demolition seemed imminent, but as redevelopment stalled its barebone structure was repurposed. The entrance was widened in size and height, cutting through the upper floor to accommodate trucks, with waste-sorting and loading taking place with all-night shifts. Undocumented migrant workers were sheltered upstairs, in rooms hosting five to ten people. I was there in 2019 with Mohammad, a young man who had lived in the building for two years, alongside dozens of other Afghans, many of them aiming to reach Europe. Conditions were harsh, but this was also a space of mutual support, conviviality, and relative safety in their overland journey. With no rent or bills to pay, they could save money for their onward journey. Fikirtepe's in-between state matched their transient permanency. By the time police raided and shut down the centre in 2020, detaining undocumented migrants, Mohammad had already managed to cross into Bulgaria.

The combination of Fikirtepe's state of decay, substandard built stock, urban location, provisional status, and its flexible arrangements makes it a fertile ground for all sorts of 'last-minute economies' through which many of its inhabitants – who were not framed in the vision of development – maintain a temporary foothold in the metropolis. The area's deterioration – be it material or discursive – opens up a space of opportunity for disadvantaged (and less disadvantaged) populations, such as Mohammad and his fellows (Pasta, 2022).

This open-ended standstill indirectly facilitates the provision of homes for transient populations in need of temporary accommodation. The prospect of impending displacement frees up units, as live-in owners and tenants who can afford it move out, which combined with the deteriorating housing stock keeps rental prices relatively affordable. As one former resident, now renting out two flats to foreigners, puts it: 'Look at our street, look at the houses: who would come to live here? Only Afghans and Syrians would.' Inexact as it is, this statement speaks to how disadvantaged profiles may access housing in otherwise unaffordable well-located districts – often with no need for official contract – within this window of opportunity. Such an affordance is only possible, in the words of one resident, 'since this is a demolition area' (Interview, 2022). The influx of new inhabitants provides a lifeline to struggling neighbourhood businesses and homeowners whose properties would remain idle, in many cases thus supporting their own relocation (Interviews, 2022).

On the other hand, induced decay reframes redevelopment as the only viable way out of this dead-end. As the 'utopia of development' is interrupted (Roy, 2011), but never called off, degeneration emerges as the 'demonic other' of regeneration (Watt, 2022). By exacerbating blight and widening the state-induced rent gap, curated disinvestment feeds into the narrative of disposability, portraying Fikirtepe as an unlivable terrain in need of wholesale overhaul. Film crews periodically blow in to represent the area as a dangerous slum or war-torn city, while news outlets sensationalize it as a space of illegality, where anything from drug trade to torture is allowed to happen (Haber Türk, 2017; T24, 2017). This externally manufactured discourse is reiterated by long-time residents who voice their anxiety about their neighbourhood's derangement and nostalgically evoke the good old days, sometimes drawing on exclusionary rhetoric on foreign newcomers (Interviews, 2018–19, 2021–22). Rather than contesting the redevelopment itself, residents' associations, primarily representing homeowners (including absentee ones), critique its implementation and call for a swift extension of works to the still-not-redeveloped areas. With Fikirtepe seemingly beyond repair, alternative pathways to development are by now foreclosed: in the words of many dwellers, it's too late (Interviews, 2018–19 and 2021–22).

In this twofold condition, different local actors, by urgent necessity or out of entrepreneurial instinct, engage in disparate transactions to squeeze out value from the built environment for as long as it is possible, deploying a vast array of adaptive reuse practices. Though hardly quantifiable, it is possible to argue that a large share of the population in Fikirtepe gets by through such interstitial economic circuits. While for most this may just be enough to make ends meet, some are making hefty profits in this last-minute economy centred on urban disposability.[6]

Upcycling the leftovers

'Everyone here lives off scrap dealing. Well, not everyone, but almost,' Erkut remarks as we sit on the pavement, sipping tea while passers-by inquire about the prices of assorted pieces arranged across his rented shop, an early *gecekondu*. Many of them are Uzbeks and Turkmens who settled recently in the area, such as Shoira, Erkut's wife and work partner, who arrived in Fikirtepe from Termez in 2018 following a neighbour's advice. Erkut describes how wasted objects can be recycled, upcycled, or may yield value through their destruction – not unlike Fikirtepe's abandoned buildings. A secondhand sofa beyond repair can be chopped down for firewood, while an unusable mattress can be disassembled for its metal springs. Erkut also purchases broken items to resell their components separately – for instance, a broken vacuum cleaner may cost 20 tl, but its copper interior fetches 140 tl per kilo and the bolts 90 tl. While we talk, functionaries from the Ministry of Environment, Urbanisation and Climate Change, with their distinctive vests, are busy in the street, taking pictures of buildings and filling in forms. In the Phase 2 sector, redevelopment is scheduled to start within a few months and eviction notices are expected anytime: 'Once this place is razed, we'll be done with this job.'

In this remaindered built environment, an entire scrap economy has developed around the gathering, sorting, repairing, upcycling, or destroying of discarded materials within leftover spaces that are themselves adapted, repurposed, and reactivated (Figure 5.4). In 2022, more than 80 such

Figure 5.4: Municipal and informal waste collectors compete for access to the rubbish bins

Source: Author

Figure 5.5: Fikirtepe, 2022: Mandıra caddesi, Fikirtepe's high-street, had its entire northern flank razed

Source: Author

activities[7] in the not-yet-redeveloped sectors were operating as different links of a value chain that includes sorting and recycling materials (metal, plastic, paper), junk up-cycling and trading (anything from clothes and knick-knacks to technological devices and home fittings), second-hand furniture and repaired home appliances reselling.

Scrap dealing was a source of income for many prior to the transformation project. Geographical and topographical features make Fikirtepe a good base: it is close to middle-class areas that produce 'valuable waste', as well as to the huge secondhand Friday market, and comprises low-lying sectors (a key point considering Istanbul's rugged terrain and the fact that most garbage pickers work with hand-pull carts). But as redevelopment was interrupted in many sectors – with thousands of buildings evacuated, gutted, and partly demolished – plenty of space was freed up to collect and sort materials, as well as to accommodate labourers, turning Fikirtepe into an informal scrap-dealing hub on the city's Asian side. The pre- and post-demolition phases, furthermore, generate economic circuits of their own: buildings slated for demolition are stripped off anything resaleable – pipes, wires, taps, sinks, doors, windows, light switches, radiators – before being razed (Figure 5.5), while in the post-demolition wasteland, people comb through the debris in search of potentially valuable leftovers.

In myriad site-specific variations, spaces are recycled to accommodate recycling activities. Vacant buildings and plots have been reconverted into depots and live-in informal rubbish collection centres, such as the one where Mohammad used to live, where workers are sheltered and materials are conferred, sorted, and shipped to treatment plants. Ephemeral real-estate offices that sprouted at the height of the redevelopment frenzy and went bust amidst the ensuing downturn have been repurposed as secondhand shops – such as Şeref's live-in depot. An idle beerhouse was split with plywood partitions, a new entrance cut into its side wall, to host multiple scrap-dealing units. The *hamam* (bathhouse) lay idle for a while after its furnace broke down, and repair appeared pointless given the impending demolition, but it was eventually rented out as a secondhand shop and depot for the nearby flea market. Such practices point to ways in which residents harness disposability and contribute to its concrete articulation.

As a labour-intensive sector, informal scrap dealing provides sustenance to many of the most marginalized social groups, including Roma, seasonal Kurdish workers, and unregularized foreign migrants, who are often undocumented and deportable. Their livelihoods are currently under attack, as intensifying competition from local municipalities, which attempt to control the sector, coalesces with an intensifying anti-migrant clampdown. In 2020, amid the COVID-19 pandemic, Istanbul governorate raided several irregular waste-collection centres across the city, detaining hundreds of undocumented migrants and destroying or blocking the access to the waste collection structures where they used to reside. In Fikirtepe, some collection centres have been forcefully vacated and bricked over – such as the one where Mohammad used to live – but some are still open and fully operational, and others popped up in the aftermath of the crackdown.

The room available for making a living out of waste in the city's wasted spaces seems to be getting narrower by the day, yet there is room for tentative headways. Half a year later, while redevelopment has not kicked off yet, Erkut and Shoira's business has expanded into the shopfront of the building next door. The new shop is much cleaner and better ordered, while the old one is now used as a depot. 'It was an occasion – I said let's take it,' explained Erkut. 'Anything could happen anytime.'

Conclusion

Framed as expendable, Fikirtepe was then rendered so. Representing the area as a leftover to be liquidated, the alliance between political power and big capital initiated restructuring policies that ravaged the neighbourhood's social and spatial fabric. Amid recurrent setbacks, however, the projected redevelopment became mired into a dragged-out impasse. As disposal was indefinitely deferred in large sectors of the neighbourhood, a state of augmented disposability was induced that renewed the urgency of total makeover, while also testifying to the unpredictable ways in which such vision misfired. Here, the mutually constitutive relationship between urban disposability and redevelopment stands out manifestly. This terrain also complicates readings of urban disposability.

By looking at the everyday experience of life in this spatio-temporal conjuncture, we observe how Fikirtepe, rather than sliding irreparably towards erasure, is uneasily maintained on the edge of liveability – but just enough to keep things going for the moment. Intensifying decay seemingly forecloses pathways to development other than urban transformation from scratch, while also preventing the emergence of a locally grounded polity that could formulate, and advocate for, any alternative imagination. Meanwhile, deterioration seems to blemish the materialization of development from within. If, a decade ago, architectural renders promised to turn Fikirtepe's shanties into a Turkish 'Manhattan' within a few years, nowadays the recently completed high-rises appear to be slipping into accelerated decay, while uncompleted skeletons look like ruins from the future.

In parallel, Fikirtepe emerged throughout this protracted deadlock as a temporal and spatial interstice, where those who were not envisaged in the prospect of redevelopment managed to establish a temporary foothold in the city. Over more than 15 years of botched redevelopment, the widening gap between augmented disposability and deferred disposal offered old and new residents disparate affordances to navigate urban transformation on the brink of breakdown, attempting to stand up to the impact of exclusionary redevelopment.

As disparate trajectories of displacement and dispossession converge in Fikirtepe, discriminated citizens, dispossessed residents, and deportable migrants put up improvised systems of temporary endurance. Precarious economic circuits developed among individuals rendered displaceable, spaces framed as expendable, and discarded materials. Structures that were stripped of any use beyond demolition were recycled into spaces of last-minute value production, momentary socialization, and fleeting home-making. Yet, in this unsettled context, where the forces of 'thrownapartness' (Gawlewicz and Yiftachel, 2022) strain relations between residents in differing conditions of precariousness, the purported inevitability of redevelopment hinders the local emergence of an alternative imagination of the future.

Skewed and uneven as they are, these transactions reveal forms of affordability and sustenance that emerge as a side-product of Fikirtepe's disposable condition. Arguably, these forms of making-do allow residents to momentarily withstand the negative impacts of redevelopment and broader structural forms of injustice. Yet they are hardly enough to overcome the exclusionary effects of top-down restructuring in the long term. None of these practices – 'neither just troublesome nor hopeful, but rather a fragile oscillation between the two' (Thieme, 2021) – contests the inner logic of disposability upfront. What emerges is the idea that urban disposability is reproduced and mobilized – if not openly challenged – by those individuals depicted as expendable, remaindered, or superfluous.

Notes

[1] Justice and Development Party, the Islamist-Neoliberal party led by Recep Tayyip Erdoğan in power at the national level since 2002.

[2] For instance, in 2007 the head of the Mass Housing Administration (TOKI) declared at a real estate fair: 'Today, the *gecekondu* is one of the most important two or three problems that Turkey faces. It is well known that such things as terror, drugs, psychological negativity, health problems and oppositional views all come out of *gecekondu* zones and irregular areas' (Quoted in Lovering and Türkmen, 2011).

[3] The toponym Fikirtepe refers to a vast area, spanning four different administrative neighbourhoods; it is currently being transformed by the urban transformation project.

[4] A Ministry of Urbanisation undersecretary addressed Fikirtepe residents in 2015: 'With this project, which will set an example for Turkey, you are bringing great and important value to our country. As some of you say from time to time, Turkey's Manhattan will rise in Fikirtepe' (quoted in Eyidoğan, 2021).

[5] As Honsa (2014) maintains, present-day large-scale 'formal' developments in Istanbul are hardly more carefully planned and thought through than the unauthorized 'informal' settlements they replace: 'Projects are still "built overnight", the only difference is scale.'

[6] For instance, locals with some capital to invest are buying properties from their neighbours, speculating on their value increasing before the transformation.

[7] The activities were surveyed in 2022. They vary in size and deal with scrap in various combinations – from waste-collection centres employing dozens of workers to family-run secondhand shops.

References

Alvarez, M.K. and Cardenas, K. (2019) 'Evicting slums, "building back better": resiliency revanchism and disaster risk management in Manila', *International Journal of Urban and Regional Research*, 43(2): 227–49.

Amin, A. (2013) 'Telescopic urbanism and the poor', *City*, 17(4): 476–92.

Arıcan, A. (2023) 'Counterfactual future-thinking', *Environment and Planning D: Society and Space*, 41(4): 637–55.

Armiero, M. (2021) *Wasteocene: Stories from the Global Dump*. Cambridge University Press.

Aslan, Ş. and Erman, E. (2014) 'The transformation of the urban periphery: once upon a time there were *gecekondus* in Istanbul', in D.Ö. Koçak and O.K. Koçak (eds), *Whose City is That? Culture, Design, Spectacle and Capital in Istanbul*. Cambridge Scholars Publishing, pp 95–156.

Bauman, Z. (2004) *Wasted Lives: Modernity and its Outcasts*. Polity Press.

Bayırbağ, M.K., Schindler, S., and Penpecioğlu, M. (2023) 'Structural violence and the urban politics of hope in Ankara, Turkey', *City*, 27(3–4): 464–82.

Benjamin, S., Castronovo, A., Cavallero, L., Cielo, C., Gago, V., Guma, P., Gupte, R., Habermehl, V., Salman, L., Shetty, P., Simone, A., Smith, C., and Tonucci, J. (2022) 'Urban popular economies', *Public Culture*, 34(3): 333–57.

Brickell, K., Arrigoitia, M.F., and Vasudevan, A. (2017) 'Geographies of forced eviction: Dispossession, violence, resistance', in K. Brickell, M.F. Arrigoitia, and A. Vasudevan (eds), *Geographies of Forced Eviction*. Palgrave Macmillan, pp 1–23.

Brun, C. and Fábos, A. (2015) 'Making homes in limbo? A conceptual framework', *Refuge: Canada's Journal on Refugees*, 31(1): 5–17.

Carse, A. and Kneas, D. (2019) 'Unbuilt and unfinished', *Environment and Society*, 10(1): 9–28.

Esen, O. (2008) 'Post-*gecekondu*', in P. Derviş, B. Tanju, and U. Tanyeli (eds), *Becoming Istanbul: An Encyclopedia*. Garanti Gallery & Deutsches Architekturmuseum, n.p.

Eyidoğan, H. (2021) 'On beş yıldır bitmeyen bir kentsel dönüşümün hikâyesi: Fikirtepe'. *T24*. Available from: https://t24.com.tr/yazarlar/haluk-eyidogan/on-bes-yildir-bitmeyen-bir-kentsel-donusumun-hikayesi-fikirtepe,30099 [Accessed 15 June 2023].

Garmany, J. and Richmond, M.A. (2020) 'Hygienisation, gentrification, and urban displacement in Brazil', *Antipode*, 52(1): 124–44.

Gawlewicz, A. and Yiftachel, O. (2022) 'Throwntogetherness in hostile environments: Migration and the remaking of urban citizenship', *City*, 26(2–3): 346–58.

Ghertner, D.A. (2011) 'Rule by aesthetics: world-class city making in Delhi', in A. Roy and A. Ong (eds), *Worlding Cities: Asian Experiments and the Art of Being Global*, Wiley-Blackwell.

Gupta, J., Pfeffer, K., Verrest, H., and Ros-Tonen, M.A.F. (eds) (2015) *Geographies of Urban Governance: Advanced Theories, Methods and Practices*, Springer.

Haber Türk (2017) 'Kadıköy Fikirtepe'de uyuşturucu gerginliği' (7 May). Available from: www.haberturk.com/gundem/haber/1486287-kadikoy-fikirtepede-uyusturucu-gerginligi [Accessed 15 June 2023].

Honsa, J. (2014) 'Istanbul's fading metabolism: failed architecture'. Available from: https://failedarchitecture.com/istanbuls-fading-metabolism [Accessed 15 June 2023].

Hürriyet (2020) 'İstanbul'da lüks sitede elektrik kesintisi çilesi!' (2020). Available from: www.hurriyet.com.tr/gundem/istanbulda-luks-sitede-elektrik-kesintisi-cilesi-41558802 [Accessed 15 June 2023].

Karaman, O. (2008) 'Urban pulse: (re)making space for globalisation in Istanbul', *Urban Geography*, 29(6): 518–25.

Karaman, O. (2013) 'Urban neoliberalism with Islamic characteristics', *Urban Studies*, 50(16): 3412–27.

Kuyucu, T. (2022) 'The great failure: The roles of institutional conflict and social movements in the failure of regeneration initiatives in Istanbul', *Urban Affairs Review*, 58(1): 129–63.

Lancione, M. and Simone, A. (2021) 'Dwelling in liminalities, Thinking beyond inhabitation', *Environment and Planning D: Society and Space*, 39(6): 969–75.

Lovering, J. and Türkmen, H. (2011) 'Bulldozer neo-liberalism in Istanbul: The state-led construction of property markets, and the displacement of the urban poor', *International Planning Studies*, 16(1): 73–96.

MacLeod, G. and McFarlane, C. (2014) 'Introduction: Grammars of urban injustice', *Antipode*, 46(4): 857–73.

Mekanda Adalet Derneği (2021) 'İstanbul'da Kentsel Dönüşüm Ve İyilik Hâli'. Available from: https://mekandaadalet.org/wp-content/uploads/2020/09/MADrapor_01_20211015_cift-1.pdf [Accessed 5 June 2023].

Mercan, B.A. and Sen, M. (2020) 'Advanced marginality and criminalization: The case of Altındağ', *Turkish Studies*, 22(4): 1–23.

Mezzadra, S. and Neilson, B. (2013) *Border as Method, or, the Multiplication of Labor*, Duke University Press.

Ministry of Communication of the Republic of Turkey (2023) 'Cumhurbaşkanı Erdoğan, Fikirtepe Kentsel Dönüşüm Projesi 1. Etap Anahtar Teslimi ile 2. Ve 3. Etaplarda Kentsel Dönüşüm Başlangıç Töreni'ne katıldı' (18 April). Available from: www.iletisim.gov.tr/turkce/yerel_basin/detay/cumhurbaskani-erdogan-fikirtepe-kentsel- donusum-projesi-1-etap-anahtar-teslimi-ile-2-ve-3-etaplarda-kentsel-donusum-baslangic-torenine-katildi [Accessed 7 June 2023].

Ministry of Environment, Urbanisation and Climate Change of the Republic of Turkey (2021) 'Yeni Fikirtepe—Anasayfa'. Available from: www.yenifikirtepe.com [Accessed 7 June 2023].

Öktem, K. (2008) 'Varoş (I)', in P. Derviş, B. Tanju, and U. Tanyeli (eds), *Becoming Istanbul: An Encyclopedia*, Garanti Gallery & Deutsches Architekturmuseum, n.p.

Parmaksızoğlu, D. (2014) 'From home to real estate: Urban redevelopment on the axis of speculation in Istanbul', *Jadaliyya*. Available from: www.jadaliyya.com/Details/31310/From-Home-to-Real-Estate-Urban-Redevelopment- on-the-Axis-of-Speculation-in-Istanbul [Accessed 15 June 2023].

Pasta, F. (2022) 'Fikirtepe in limbo: urban transformation, cross-border migration, and re-peripheralization in Istanbul', in Forte, G. and Hwa, G.K. (eds), *Embodying Peripheries*, UC Berkeley Global Urban Humanities Initiative, Florence University Press.

Pinarcioğlu, M. and Işik, O. (2008) 'Not only helpless but also hopeless: Changing dynamics of urban poverty in Turkey: the case of Sultanbeyli, Istanbul', *European Planning Studies*, 16(10): 1353–70.

Roy, A. (2011) 'The agonism of Utopia: dialectics at a standstill', *Traditional Dwellings and Settlements Review*, 23(1): 15–24.

Sakizlioğlu, B. (2014) 'Inserting temporality into the analysis of displacement: living under the threat of displacement', *Tijdschrift Voor Economische En Sociale Geografie*, 105(2): 206–20.

Simone, A.M. (2018) *Improvised Lives: Rhythms of Endurance in an Urban South*, Polity Press.

Soytemel, E. (2017) 'Urban rent speculation, uncertainty and unknowns as strategy and resistance in Istanbul's housing market', in G. Erdi and Y. Şentürk (eds), *Identity, Justice and Resistance in the Neoliberal City*, Palgrave Macmillan, pp 85–115.

T24. (2017) 'Dehşet evi: İstanbul'da kaçırılan 3 İranlı 37 gün işkence gördü!' (July 29). Available from: https://t24.com.tr/haber/dehset-evi-istanbulda-kacirilan-3-iranli-37-gun-iskence- gordu,416911 [Accessed 15 June 2023].

Tadiar, N.X.M. (2022) *Remaindered Life*, Duke University Press.

Thieme, T.A. (2021) 'Beyond repair: Staying with breakdown at the interstices', *Environment and Planning D: Society and Space*, 39(6): 1092–1110.

Tuğal, C. (2016) *The Fall of the Turkish Model: How the Arab Uprisings Brought Down Islamic Liberalism*, Verso.

Wacquant, L. (2007) *Urban Outcasts: A Comparative Sociology of Advanced Marginality*, Polity Press.

Wacquant, L. (2008) 'The militarisation of urban marginality: lessons from the Brazilian metropolis', *International Political Sociology*, 2(1): 56–74.

Watt, P. (2022) 'The dialectics of regeneration and degeneration: taking a long view perspective on incomplete social housing estate regeneration in London', presentation at the RC21 Conference, Ordinary City in Exceptional Times, Athens.

Yiftachel, O. (2015) 'Epilogue: from "gray space" to equal "metrozenship"? Reflections on urban citizenship', *International Journal of Urban and Regional Research*, 39(4): 726–37.

Yiftachel, O. (2020) 'From displacement to displaceability: a southeastern perspective on the new metropolis', *City*, 24(1–2): 151–65.

PART III

Exhaustion

6

Displaced and Evicted Migrant Women: Informal Settlement as a Mechanism of Resistance and Territorial Self-Management

Yasna Contreras Gatica

Introduction

This chapter examines the causes and effects of displacement and eviction of migrant women living across two forms of urban spaces: in deteriorated housing in central urban spaces, or *tugurios*; and in self-managed informal settlements, or *campamentos*, on the peripheries.[1] Through examining the displacement trajectories and mobilities of women, the chapter sheds light on the processes and drivers of, and agency within, displacement and informal settlement in Chile. In particular, it analyses and focuses on the experiences of migrant women resident in the Iquique and Alto Hospicio metropolitan area, located about 1,800 km from the capital city of Santiago, to demonstrate how their experience of displacement, their priorities, and their decision-making have given rise to particular forms of distinctions between displacement and eviction and to agencies and urbanisms that resist them both.

The findings and reflections derive from two consecutive research projects financed by the National Research and Development Agency, dependent on the Ministry of Sciences of Chile (ANID).[2] The projects explored residential trajectories of migrants and their mechanisms of accessing housing while living in the Norte Grande of Chile – a region known for its extractive economic system. With the purpose of investigating a female perspective, or exclusively focusing on women's experiences in the face of displacement and eviction, methodologically the discussion emerges from the analysis of 15 in-depth interviews conducted between 2017 and 2023.[3] The research period, however, was longer: having started with a study on self-managed informal settlements in 2014, we broadened the research in 2017 when we obtained the second research grant.

This chapter situates the debate on displacement within the experiences and voices of marginalized immigrant women and their encounters with housing insecurity, precarious living conditions, and informality of inhabitation. The case and arguments presented here incorporate a feminist perspective that centres the roles played by women who reside in self-managed informal settlements, whether in leading settlement or relocation processes or in negotiating with the authorities to demand that housing policies incorporate solutions that take into consideration the multiple roles fulfilled by these women. The aim is to provide nuance to discussions of displacement, evidencing its exhaustive nature, but also highlighting the agency of women experiencing and resisting it within their housing trajectories. Accordingly, the discussion is structured in three sections. First, the general characteristics of the cities of Iquique and Alto Hospicio are presented and a socio-demographic comparison between them is provided. The housing description and demographic data situate the research in the particular urban landscape within which the interviewees struggle to build safe homes. The chapter then examines the drivers of migrant women's residential mobility within these urban areas, to understand the underlying forces of displacement and eviction, before analysing how and why self-management in informal settlements shapes place-based resistance and the construction of safe spaces, new urbanities, and communities organized around housing rights.

The case study offers an example of the multiplicity of factors causing displacement and producing what could be characterized as a condition of latent displacement, or of displaceability (Yiftachel, 2020), as these women become trapped within exhausting cycles of informality and distance from rights associated with urban citizenship. Yet, beyond common association and experience of displacement with violence (slow or rapid), rupture and with un-homing (e.g. Nixon, 2011; Elliott-Cooper et al, 2020; Atkinson, 2015), by focusing on the roles, agency, and paths of women, an alternative conceptual reading of displacement emerges, in which it is also central to generative processes of building home, community, and refuge. The case examined here demonstrates the complexity of displacement as, on the one hand, exhausting, rupturing, and pervasive, and on the other, productive of resistance activities and negotiations that generate new urban spaces and dwelling strategies that repair and generate connections between people and place.

Iquique and Alto Hospicio: uneven urban development in a Chilean metropolitan area

The metropolitan area of Iquique and Alto Hospicio constitutes a single urban and residential system (Figure 6.1), consisting of an agglomeration of almost 353,000 inhabitants. The two cities are highly dependent on each other for labour. Much of the region's formal employment is concentrated in the city of Iquique, within the service and commercial sectors. In Alto Hospicio, on the other hand, informal employment is more common. Iquique and Alto Hospicio are located in the administrative region of Tarapacá, the metropolitan area has been influenced by the regional transformations related to the lucrative copper mining industry. In 2015, the mining industry produced 42.2 per cent of the regional gross domestic product (GDP), accounting for 2.3 per cent of the national GDP (Lardé et al, 2008). The largest mine in the region is the Collahuasi mine, which began its operations in 1999. Its extraction centre is located 175 km from Iquique, at an elevation of 4,500 m. This large mine generates revenues that significantly impact the cities in the region and their communities.

Chile's mining and extractive cities, especially those located in the regions of Tarapacá and Antofagasta, have a significant impact on the housing market, in terms of both property purchase prices and rental costs. Families that access rental housing spend more than 45 per cent of their family income on housing payments, since the housing market is preferentially oriented to workers in the mining industries or within services related to mining. The lower-middle and low-income population cannot access new housing developed for purchase. Rather, they are relegated to renting properties under conditions that can be described as undignified and unsafe due to poor housing quality and high housing costs (Contreras et al, 2015). The high average value of housing prices and rents partly explains the increase in the number of families living in informal settlements. Although it is not the only cause, it is key to how the creation of a real estate market for workers and professionals around the extractive industry has impacted on the housing market, both formal and informal. At the same time, the increase in the number of families living in close quarters, the increase in households waiting more than ten years to obtain a housing subsidy, and the effects of the economic crises in Chile's extractive cities are at the heart of the increase in both native and immigrant households residing in informal settlements.

Within the Tarapacá region, there are 62 self-managed informal settlements, referred to in Chile as *campamentos*, characterized by precarious housing, self-built with waste materials, with informal and self-managed connections to electricity, drinking water, and sanitary services. Informal settlements occupy vacant land owned by the state or by private owners. Almost 9,000 families inhabit these self-managed informal settlements throughout the region,

Figure 6.1: Metropolitan area of Iquique-Alto Hospicio

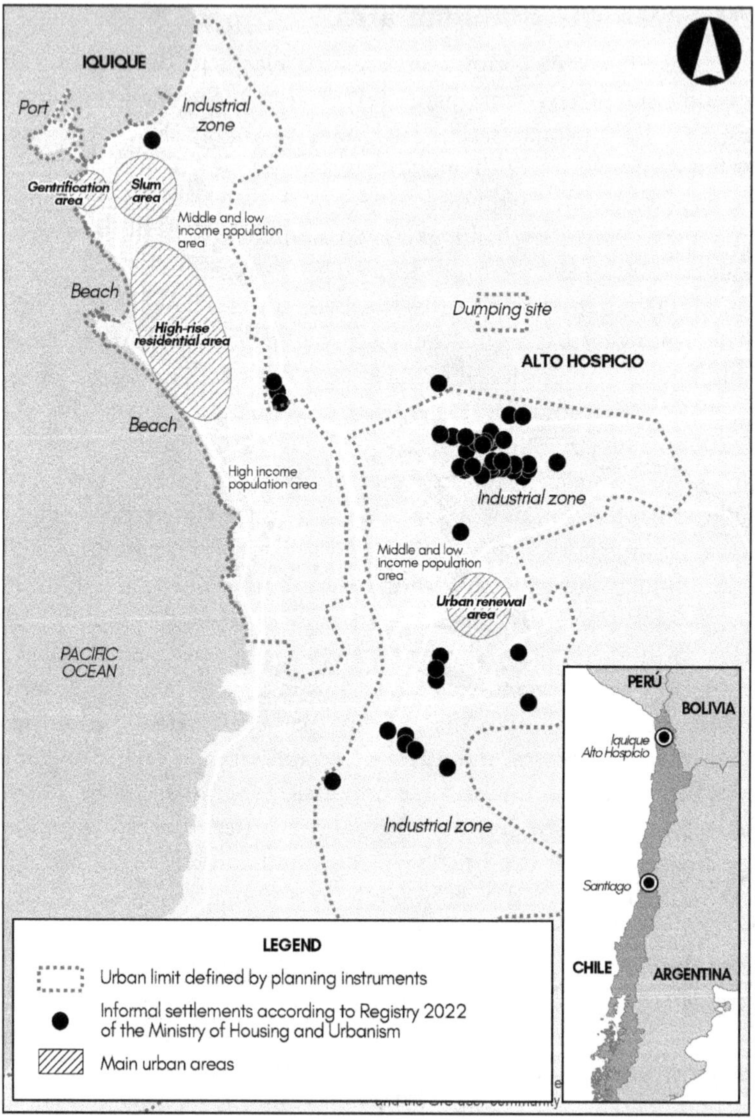

Source: Author from Google Earth, 2023

accounting for 7 per cent of all families that reside in this type of housing in Chile (115,000 families) (Techo Chile, 2023). This trend of peripheralization and urban informality affects the non-migrant Chilean population as well as the majority of migrants. Indeed, it is important to mention that more than 60 per cent of the increase in informal settlements in Chile has been produced by native families and not exclusively by migrant families. Data from the 2022–23 Catastro of the NGO Techo para Chile show that almost 35 per cent of the households living in informal settlements are immigrants (approximately 40,000 immigrant families). This represents an increase of almost 15,000 households with respect to the 2020–21 Catastro.

Beyond the figures, qualitative research conducted in cities in the extractive north shows that Afro-descendant migrants are the households and individuals who most question the restrictions on access to housing. Some interviewees feel that being Black and stereotyped by nationality relegates them to an abusive and disenfranchised housing market. Many of those interviewed pay more than 55 per cent of their salaries to rent rooms in the centre of Iquique or Alto Hospicio. Such rooms are, on average, 20 m^2, without a right to privacy, tranquility, or security. The ubiquity of such cramped conditions is at the heart of the increase of immigrants in informal settlements.

In this context, the patterns of socio-spatial distribution and types of housing exhibit an unequal relationship between Iquique and Alto Hospicio, with the majority of informal settlements concentrated within Alto Hospicio and the primary urban and commercial areas located in Iquique. The production of this inequality can be ascribed directly to the extractive mining industry.

Iquique and Alto Hospicio present evident differences. The city of Iquique has a demographic and housing situation characteristic of a regional administrative capital and a commercial hub. It has a population of 223,462 inhabitants, of which 20 per cent are immigrants from Latin America and the Caribbean (44,555 inhabitants). Despite being a city that guarantees a high monthly income to its residents (close to US$770), the housing deficit is also high (10,120 units). Likewise, problems with housing conditions are recorded, with many (8,373 people) living in deteriorating housing in central spaces (Servicio Nacional de Migraciones, 2023), representing a significant number within the city and the region. The unequal and limited access to housing in Iquique is also reflected in the fact that families in the city use more than 55.8 per cent of their monthly income for rent and subleases.

Iquique sits within a privileged location, not only for the use of its amenities and housing along the coastline, but also because it has developed as an international commercial port in relation to the Free Trade Zone (*Zona Franca de Iquique*) [ZOFRI] located in the northern district of the city. This has fostered the expansion of housing for the middle class, especially in the southern and south-central areas of Iquique, creating a highly polarized city. Since the 1970s, the low-income population has resided in social housing or self-managed housing in the northern and western districts of Iquique. The self-managed informal settlements are located in the southwestern part, and consist of eight *campamentos* that house 1,785 families (Techo Chile, 2023).

The largest informal settlement is named Laguna Verde; it is located in the southern area of the city, close to amenities, public transportation, and food stores. In south Iquique, another group of peripheral settlements exists, which primarily house Venezuelan immigrants who have arrived since 2020.

Compared with Iquique, the city of Alto Hospicio has a smaller population (129,999 inhabitants), of which 14 per cent are migrants from Latin America and the Caribbean (18,516 people). The arrival of immigrants to Alto Hospicio resulted in a population increase of 1.7 per cent between 2002 and 2020. Inhabitants of Alto Hospicio have lower average income levels (close to US$493). While the city has a lower housing deficit (7,025 homes) and fewer people living in deteriorated housing in central spaces (2,878 inhabitants), Alto Hospicio also has a larger number of self-managed informal settlements. In 2020, 10,079 people were living in 49 informal settlements located throughout the city – quite a different housing environment from that observed in Iquique. This uneven concentration of self-managed informal settlements in Alto Hospicio can be explained by the comparatively higher land and housing values in Iquique, the development of social housing projects for low-income populations in Alto Hospicio, and the large movement to the area of vulnerable populations, domestic migrants, and immigrants who consider Alto Hospicio to be a more affordable housing market. However, most formal employment opportunities, health centres and education facilities remain located in the city of Iquique, as explained above.

The housing history of Alto Hospicio is connected to the lack of available land to build social housing (Vivienda de Interés Social, or VIS) and affordable units in Iquique. In response to such a lack, the local government and the Chilean state proposed the development of Alto Hospicio as a residential satellite city in 2004. Its urban space comprises 1,822 ha and is one of the areas in Chile with the highest concentration of low-income families living in social housing (Figure 6.1). Since the 1990s, the Chilean government has had difficulty building low-income housing for the lowest income groups, especially in cities in the extractive north. There are multiple reasons for this. One significant cause relates to the increase in the value of land available for the construction of low-income housing. Second, land tenure in Chile is mostly private, and there is even less public land available in extractive mining cities that could be used for the construction of such housing. Third, cities such as Iquique and Alto Hospicio are in the process of updating their urban regulations, which is essential for the liberalization of land for public purposes.

Displacement and high residential mobility within central urban areas

The mining boom associated with the intensification of extractive activities in diverse Chilean territories has projected an image of economic and financial stability within Latin America and the Caribbean. In this context, migration to Chile began to increase in the 1990s, a decade characterized by the establishment of a post-dictatorship ideology based on continual economic growth. As an incentive, these economic factors partly explain the influx of migrants from neighbouring countries such as Peru, Bolivia, Colombia, and to a lesser extent the Dominican Republic (Contreras and Seguel, 2022). However, the women interviewed in this research also noted that, in addition to prospects for better work opportunities, the constructed image of Chile was also one that offered tenure security, access to housing or land, and social rights.

The Tarapacá region has historically been the centre of international migration processes. Since the end of the nineteenth century, there has been a record of Andean migrants – especially Bolivians and Peruvians – who occupied central spaces in cities such as Arica, Iquique, and Antofagasta (Tapia Ladino et al, 2021). More recently, immigration to the northern hemisphere has diversified regional migration flows, although cross-border migration remains representative of these shifts. According to data from the National Institute of Statistics of Chile (INE) and the National Migration Service, approximately 1.6 million migrants were living in Chile in 2022. Of these, 47,000 resided in the city of Iquique, with the most represented nationalities being Bolivian citizens (46 per cent), Peruvians (23.9 per cent), Colombians (7.9 per cent), and Venezuelan citizens (6.8 per cent). The rest (13 per cent) consisted of various nationalities (Servicio Nacional de Migraciones, 2023).

In this context, the migrant women interviewed are in the first stages of migration in Chile; they may or may not have social or family networks in the country, and they have been living in centrally located, squalid, and deteriorated housing. In Latin America, such housing is referred to as *tugurios*, and describes formal or informal precarious buildings subdivided by landlords or owners for rent purposes and to obtain larger profit margins, or even overcrowded housing to satisfy families' housing needs. In Chile, this *tugurization* process is produced within the buildings, especially in older housing. Over the last 15 years, this process has been consolidated and has generated an informal housing market within legalized spaces. In turn, this has increased the cost of rent for families, especially Peruvian, Bolivian, Dominican, Colombian, and Venezuelan migrants, among others.

Within the formal city, regulations govern rental contracts, including the rights and responsibilities of both landlords and tenants. The *tugurios* rental market is, by contrast, totally unregulated. The absence of formal housing contracts denies many families the rights and security associated with such leases. This affects Chilean citizens, documented migrants, and people in the process of establishing permanency, but it particularly affects undocumented migrants and migrants of Afro-descent. With few municipalities in Chile

Figures 6.2 and 6.3: *Tugurios*: overcrowded central housing

Source: Author, October 2020

concerned with guaranteeing access to decent housing, prices and conditions of habitability are imposed by landlords. Figures 6.2 and 6.3 show two rental properties studied for this research. In both spaces, families – especially migrants – report that they lack adequate bathrooms, privacy, and kitchen facilities. In this area, no local authority monitors the conditions under which the rental market operates, despite the existence of formal regulations.

Within *tugurios* housing, additional controls and conditions are exercised by owners or landlords over migrant groups, such as curfews on tenants, visitor restrictions, shared use of bathrooms, and a lack of cleaning and maintenance. These create conditions of insecurity, discomfort, and subordination that go some way towards explaining the high rate of residential movement within central spaces, and between them and peripheral informal settlements. This type of housing not only fails to ensure basic rights, but also forces residents to abide by the arbitrary rules characteristic of the informal housing market.

Data collected during fieldwork, and about rental and real estate housing prices, reveal that the traditional housing market that has taken over in the centre of Iquique is not the only mechanism that captures rents. Administrators and/or long-standing middle-class property owners of old, deteriorated buildings, or the impoverished, once middle-class individuals view immigration as an opportunity to extract income through informal renting and subletting rooms at monthly prices over US$319. As explained already, this deregulation of the rental housing market within the regulated city leaves tenants subject to the arbitrary rules imposed by each owner or intermediary. There are no local standards that control the price and conditions of habitability inside old buildings in central areas. Although there are norms in Chile that regulate rentals, in practice municipalities such as Iquique and Alto Hospicio do not have offices or supervisors to guarantee compliance within the formal rental market, let alone the informal market.

The accounts of the migrant women interviewed speak not only about the problems of accessing housing but also about the complexity they face when they need to access visa documentation for themselves and their children, which remains a barrier that hinders integration within the country. It took each of the 15 women almost three years to obtain identification documents, or *Cédula de identidad*. Even after securing these documents, they do not guarantee them access to formal job opportunities or to health services, nor the possibility of residing in more comfortable homes with better living conditions. Whether related to the infringement upon or the denial of basic rights, all their stories demonstrated the rupture of the migration illusion, paralleling the abovementioned criticism towards the construction of certain imaginaries of development (Carsolio, 2014). Within the region, Chile markets its progressivism through promoting the presence of work opportunities in the mines, but these do not result in equal access within this area and community. Rather, the result is the exposure of vulnerablized and racialized migrants to exploitation from informal rent extraction and in employment:

> I arrived to Iquique, this, it is hard to come, to leave ... come here, sometimes the people are discriminated in housing, as well as in work ... Housing is very difficult for us if we're migrants and don't have work contracts because they require work contracts, payroll stubs, this ... lots of requirements. (Bolivian woman, one year's residence in Chile)

This excerpt is an example of the multiple barriers facing the women. Without documents or an identification number, they cannot apply for state subsidies or participate in formal application processes to access welfare benefits from the local government or state-based institutions. Under such conditions, social and family networks are the main form of support, and it is through Facebook or housing committee networks that they negotiate permanent residency or avoid eviction, especially when they live in informal settlements. Residing in deteriorated housing in central spaces is challenging and exhausting. There, they have no rights, and they cannot file a lawsuit against landlords, nor can they access official institutions that might protect them, such as the National Migration Service, Ministry of Housing and Urban Development, Municipality of Iquique and Alto Hospicio.

> I live here because I don't have a choice even though I'm a doctor. I pay a lot of money monthly, but I can't file a lawsuit or ask anyone for help. The only support comes from some acquaintances or from my partner. Here, you feel naked, unprotected. (Cuban woman, a *tugurio* resident in Iquique)

Tugurios are spaces where strangers cohabit in small spaces with shared bathrooms. They are controlled by administrators, property owners, or intermediaries between the property owner and the landlord. In Chile, these spaces attract public attention primarily when structural fires cause fatalities, or when a fire uncovers a building's lack of maintenance, high levels of overcrowding or shared beds, and the property owner's or administrator's irresponsibility in ensuring the well-being of their residents. *Tugurios* are becoming increasingly common in Iquique and Alto Hospicio. There is neither urban regulation that enforces maintenance of these buildings, nor state subsidies that enable the property owners to renovate and make repairs. There are not even any local ordinances that protect the living conditions of the families that rent and sublet. Consequently, occupants – primarily migrants, with few recourses to secure housing or rights – are exposed to increased insecurity and risk of harm from unsafe, overcrowded, and dilapidated housing.

> When we didn't have a place to live there [she laughs], we slept on cardboard, but we slept like that for a week. (Colombian woman, resident in Chile for four years)

The accounts of these women demonstrate an institutional lack of concern for city centre life and emphasize the commodification of migrant housing, especially when building owners fail to comply with their responsibility. Despite the prevalence of such properties, to date there no policies and regulations have been put in place in Chile to allow local governments to sanction those who profit from *tugurios*. Although each municipality could impose some regulations, the fact that *tugurios* are developed within private property prevents more effective sanctions, perversely incentivizing the informalization of the housing market in central areas. In the same way, vulnerable families who rent and sublease housing in the city centre, whether in an old house or even inside a flat or a room in an apartment building, do not sue their landlords out of fear of being sanctioned, or because they understand the immense difficulties of accessing housing in central areas with migrant or low-income status.

Tugurization is a problem at the national level, but in the last 15 years, public policy discussion on the revaluation of old housing in central areas and historic centres has ceased. Since the 2000s, policy has focused on urban expansion, with less or no concern for the recovery of deteriorated central areas. It is a phenomenon common throughout most of the Norte Grande of Chile where densification occurs, not only in old and deteriorated housing but also, in parallel, within new high-rise buildings. In both processes, and in Iquique as well as in the centre of Alto Hospicio, property subdivision is a mechanism to capture rent (Smith, 2012). The transformation of these buildings into sublet accommodation is largely invisible, except when there is a fire.

In addition to processes of densification and increasing number of subletters, much of the housing in central Iquique and Alto Hospicio is used for commercial as well as residential purposes, to enable working from home. This is an important resource, especially for migrant women whose residency applications are in process or who cannot access formal employment, but it means that informal insecure living spaces also become spaces of informal employment, extending and facilitating the extractive capacity of these spaces. Buildings, both old and new, are turned into spaces of speculation and extraction – extending even to peripheral informal settlements, where migrant families typically resort to escape the control, racism, and abuse that occurs in central neighbourhoods.

> When we arrived at the terminal, we went searching for a place to rent, and we found a room … with bad and horrible structural conditions. It had 10 rooms … actually, a section was made of wood, a number of rooms, more or less 35 … imagine that many rooms and just one bathroom … or having two bathrooms, is not enough. With poor hygiene … many times they turn off the water at night so that the owners can save water, sometimes five days pass without using the bathroom. (Cuban woman, *tugurio* resident in Iquique)

This quote testifies to the difficulties that women migrants face when renting or subletting central housing. Migrant women navigate many layers of insecurities, from accessing identification documents, to accessing housing and land, to making decisions about who to live and share housing with, to the difficulties of accessing jobs without documents, which in turn submerge them in a spiralling infringement of their rights (Stefoni, 2004). As a result, women are often caught in multiple processes of diverse changes in residence across central areas of the city, driven by the hope of finding a more secure space to live, or of constructing their own secure place – both physically and socially – for themselves and their children.

To represent the embodied overlap of insecurities and the relationship between a life in deteriorated housing in central spaces and a life in informal settlements, the residential trajectories of two women are mapped out in Figures 6.4 and 6.5. The maps trace all the housing changes and choices

Figure 6.4: Residential trajectories. Woman A: Colombian migrant from Buenaventura

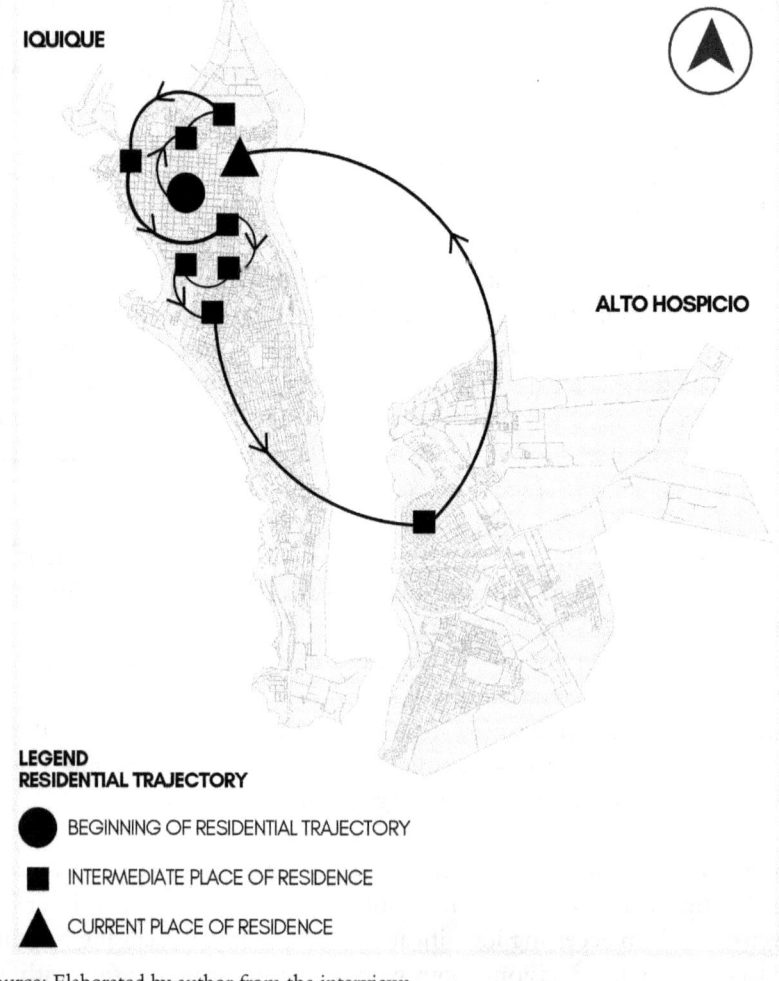

Source: Elaborated by author from the interviews

Figure 6.5: Residential trajectories. Woman B: Bolivian migrant from Sucre

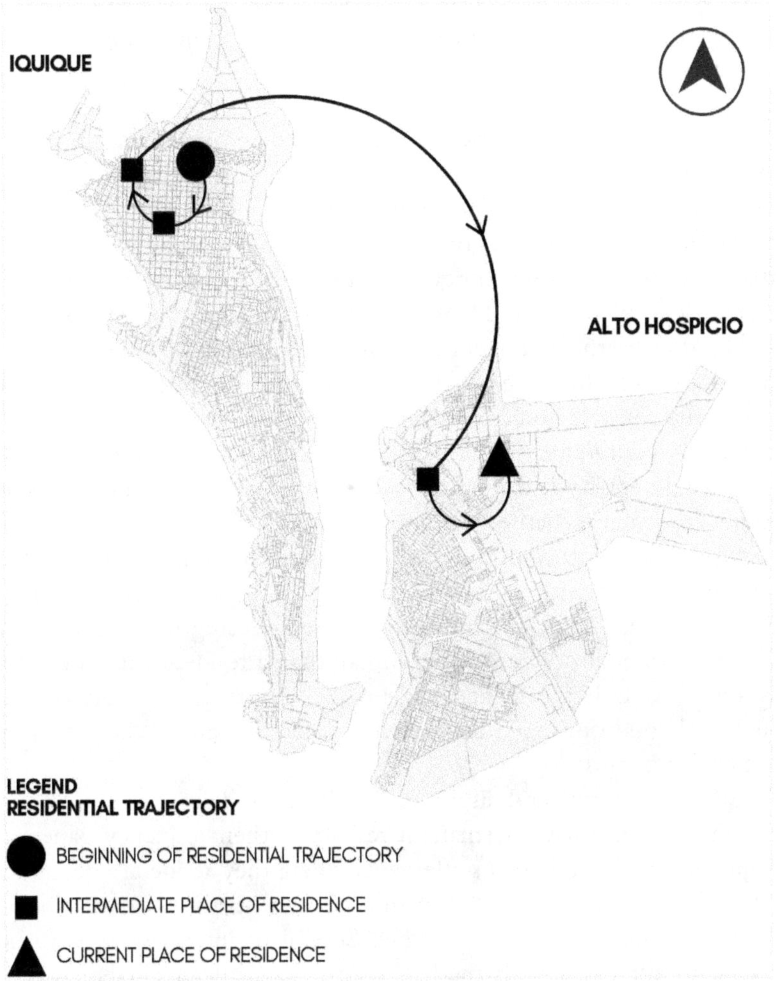

LEGEND
RESIDENTIAL TRAJECTORY

● BEGINNING OF RESIDENTIAL TRAJECTORY

■ INTERMEDIATE PLACE OF RESIDENCE

▲ CURRENT PLACE OF RESIDENCE

Source: Elaborated by author from the interviews

within the cities (renting a house, renting a room, living in an informal settlement). Woman A was born in Buenaventura, Colombia and arrived in Iquique, her first city of residence, on her own. She has two children who arrived two years after she established herself in Iquique. Her migrant trajectory was driven by the lack of life opportunities in her home country due to the armed conflict and the continuous political displacements that affected her entire family. In Iquique, she rented a room that had restrictions on cooking, inviting friends or using other spaces within the building. While living in Iquique, she moved ten times, all in response to infringements of her rights, her fear of having to share space with others, the inability to file lawsuits against abusive rent prices, and a lack of privacy, among other factors. She rented multiple houses in the city centre, but the living conditions were not adequate: the housing was poorly maintained, at high risk of fire, and any repair work had to come out of her own pocket in addition to the monthly cost. With the support of social and work networks, she decided to move to Alto Hospicio in order to find housing at a lower cost than that available within the Iquique housing market.

The residential trajectories of Woman A, contextualized by the housing market and its conditions underscore how immigrant women are latent subjects of displacement. Displacement is an omnipresent condition, whether due to the negligence of the state and local governments to maintain the old housing stock or because of neoliberal policies that promote the construction of new buildings in deteriorated neighborhoods. The local governments of cities such as Iquique encourage the arrival of larger land payers, both around the coastline and in the central city. In this context, informal settlements emerge as an alternative to central rented housing – their high rent and cost of living, the demands and controls placed on tenants without access to rights and the constant latency of being displaced, directly or indirectly. Older housing in the central area today tends to be less secure for a woman than a residence in an informal settlement. It is less safe because no one controls its habitability or contractual conditions, and because tenant families are left helpless in the event of fire hazards.

Precarity, insecurity, and displacement occur also because, in some cases, the women do not have permanent residence, their residency paperwork is in process or the informal settlements where they reside are beyond the reach of the regulated city. Uncertain residential status, however, does not adequately explain displacement here. Several of interviewees who have permanent residence confirmed that being a Chilean citizen does not guarantee equal access to state subsidies, except for the financial support and benefits they received during the pandemic. The latency of displacement, their displaceability, is a consequence of the women's lack of protection, regardless of their migration status.

The interviews with the 15 migrant women show that displacement, particularly within central spaces, operates in at least three different ways: as direct/indirect displacement due to the increase in renting prices or uncontrolled monthly increases; as forced displacement when migrant women demand that their rights are safeguarded, in terms of improving old and deteriorated buildings, overcrowding, and a high risk of fire; and/or as forced, voluntary, or involuntary displacement when their lives are in danger and the central deteriorated building, or *tugurios*, infringes upon multiple rights.

The residential trajectory and experience of Woman B (see Figure 6.5) highlights how opting to reside in informal settlements is a method of managing the forces of displacement. Woman B was born in Sucre, Bolivia, and arrived in Chile in 2013 for work-related reasons since she could not find work as a nurse in Sucre. With time, she married a Peruvian migrant who worked in construction, who supported her economically and in day-to-day care for her children. She arrived thinking that she would have a better salary and job; however, she faced many obstacles upon entering the Chilean job market and now she makes a living selling clothes and accessories at a commercial market in Alto Hospicio. She has had diverse formal and informal employment, including cleaning houses and working at Bolivian commercial stores. In the early stages, she lived in the Bolivian neighbourhood, located in Iquique's city centre. As is common among the Bolivian community, she rented a room from Bolivian property owners and merchants. She shared a bathroom with men and women, all of whom were strangers, and her room only had one bed and a small chair, with no place to store clothes.

> The rented room, although the room was even smaller than a hotel room, only fit my small single bed and a chair ... the thing is that you had like a bag that you had to put on top of the bed. One time I moved because there was a man who lived next door that would fight and drink a lot. (Bolivian woman, current resident of Alto Hospicio)

The case of Woman B demonstrates a common housing trajectory among the women interviewed. That is, for Woman B and all the women who were interviewed, moving to the self-managed informal settlement in Alto Hospicio represented a residential strategy and an opportunity that allowed them to not only escape the abusive real estate market, but also to find childcare and have husbands, partners, and jobs in close proximity.

> We lived there in Villa Frei, and my husband said to me, if everyone obtains housing in the *toma* [land occupation], why don't we talk to the [Housing] Committee. The committee accepted us, since my husband had something, he had wood posts, and there was a large plot of land that they were giving all the *tomas* from here. They took us there and later it was a scam. We had to return. They evicted us by force, because it was state-owned land, we couldn't be living there. We went to the San Lorenzo *toma* via a contact of my husband. Over time, we built the house, because my husband worked in construction, but we had to set up a local store because my husband got sick. My plot is 10 m long and 8 m wide, and it is my house, I have a bathroom. (Bolivian woman, self-managed informal settlement resident in Alto Hospicio)

All the stories shared by the women demonstrated how the form of displacement that they experienced was prompted by deteriorated conditions and lack of maintenance as an unequal mechanism to capture rents and to invest in the face of gentrification or to capture rents from subletting. However, for the women, moving to informal settlements was an attempt to mitigate at least some of the negative forces of displacement, and their experiences and conversations about their housing situations revealed nuanced understandings of displacement and eviction and attempts to practically navigate these forces within the condition of displaceability.

Table 6.1 presents the conceptual differences between displacement and forced eviction as extrapolated from the accounts of the 15 women interviewed.

Forced evictions experienced by the women consisted of abrupt exits with police involvement, exclusively from self-managed informal settlements. Interviews revealed, however, that despite the risks of eviction, the autonomy offered within informal settlements better mitigated some of the underlying forces of displacement. Among them, one resident of Laguna Verde *campamento*, located in the centre of Iquique, stated that she was forcibly evicted from the informal settlement at least eight times, and after each occasion she returned to organize and rebuild her home:

> The police evicted us many times from Laguna Verde. I first made my house of cardboard and things that the neighbours gave me. Each time that I came back, I rebuilt my house once again. Now here you see, it's beautiful, and I'm not worried any more if the police will come, because there are a lot of us now. (Dominican woman, Laguna Verde resident in *tugurio* of Iquique for more than five years)

Contextualizing the analysis of in-depth interviews within the relevant literature (e.g. Marcuse, 1985; Lees et al, 2008), displacement emerges as a continuous or discontinuous, involuntary or voluntary, direct or indirect movement over time, and it can be explained by different and overlapping causes, among them gentrification resulting from the renovation of central spaces, the construction of new buildings, and/or the reuse of real estate for commercial means. Forced eviction, on the other hand, is generally associated with the act of occupying buildings or public and/or private land. It is also related to the low purchasing/spending power of migrant households within the exclusionary land market, not only in Iquique, but also in Alto Hospicio.[4]

> The Governor came and evicted us. They beat us. We had to disassemble the house. I built my house, and I've built like five houses since I've lived here, and lady, I am going to rebuild every time it is necessary

because I cannot go back to renting, where you can't complain to anyone. (Colombian woman, resident in Chile for four years)

Table 6.1 contextualizes the motivations that prompted migrant women to transition from a condition of voluntary and involuntary displacement (renting rooms in the city centre) to the perpetual risk of forced evictions (occupying state-owned or private land). The main cause of forced eviction is associated with the fact that informal houses were constructed underneath high-voltage towers. All 15 women interviewed had been forcedly evicted at least once. However, the Colombian migrant women told us that they had experienced even more forced evictions, both in their home country related to narcotrafficking and then in Chile due to racism, especially in the northern region of the country. They did not speak of their experience of displacement while renting rooms in the city centre as a particularly traumatic experience because it did not involve any use of physical force or the presence of the police. The multiple changes of residency, however, are

Table 6.1: Differences between displacement and forced eviction for women migrants

	Displacement	**Forced eviction**
Definition	Continuous/discontinuous movement associated with social mobility processes in contexts of urban renovation, densification, rehabilitation, and/or gentrification Immediate, prospective, slow, direct, indirect, voluntary, and/or involuntary movement	Practice that involves physical force or intimidation of vulnerable groups, mainly occurring or visible in peripheral informal settlements (*campamentos*)
Factors	Abusive monthly costs of rent or sublet; inadequate living conditions; renting without lease contracts Housing fires due to lack of maintenance Looking for larger spaces to live with children	When private and/or state-owned land is being inhabited When housing in informal settlements are around high-voltage towers When the state builds social interest housing on state-owned land
Actors that produce	Real estate agents, contractors, local governments, small- and medium-scale property owners	Chilean state institutions, courts of law, private institutions and/or police forces, regional government
The situation	Unlicensed landlords, unlicensed intermediaries, long-standing owners or former middle-class people looking for additional income	

Source: Author's own elaboration based on Marcuse (1985), Lees et al (2008), and analysis of in-depth interviews.

indeed a violent practice, since they are related to symbolic and normalized acts of (everyday) violence perpetuated through abusive and deregulated housing market conditions.

Self-managed informal settlement as a mechanism of care and construction of safe spaces

Over the past decade, Chile has faced a deep housing crisis related to the increasing housing deficit, rising mortgage loan interest rates, and uncontrolled increases in housing and rental prices, which have resulted in a corresponding rise in the number of families living in *campamentos* or informal settlements. Self-managed informal settlements are built as part of a search for just spaces – that is, spaces that allow people to feel secure and protected, be at ease, where they can find jobs and childcare. However, being part of a deregulated informal housing market, migrant families are subject to the risk of eviction and they are stigmatized and blamed for the development of these peripheral urban spaces. Such informal housing also exposes them to additional risks, including environmental factors, such as close proximity to dumping grounds and sinkholes, or exposure to pest infestations.

Factors that force urban dwellers and migrants to settle and build informal housing include those drivers of displacement already explained in the chapter: the high rents of central housing; overcrowding; restrictions on access for mothers and caretakers to central housing; and a perceived lack of protection in central areas where social capital is minimal, given the residential conditions. In addition, over time, many of the women interviewed brought their families to Chile from Colombia, Peru, and Bolivia, among other countries, and therefore required additional space, or conditions more favourable to family life than were available in central areas. Family reunion is thus a deciding factor in occupying lands and in negotiations for permanent settlement.

Self-management for many of those interviewed is an alternative to the abuses of the central housing market. It is paradoxical that, within the regulated city, families are helpless and have no recourse against landlords, or local and regional authorities. Although informal settlements expose them to eviction and multiple disaster risks, for many of those interviewed, informal settlements have offered the best means to become registered and to become beneficiaries of a social housing property, or to participate in urbanization projects that the current government is developing in some Chilean cities, such as Alto Hospicio. Likewise, for many interviewees, the informal settlement is a safe territory, especially when they suffer domestic violence or when their rights are violated. Many of them argue that rights can be mobilized in a more agile way from informal settlements.

> We are in the process of 'building your city'. We are developing the plans, trying to see if the state will allow us to stay here, because we have invested. We have built a playing field. We are organized among the neighbours. We hold workshops. (Colombian woman, resident in Chile for ten years, lives in Alto Hospicio)

As a result, informal settlements involve and represent the re-signification of place – a process and a project to reduce the risk of forced evictions and foster greater security in more spacious housing suitable for the size of the households. Some interviewees live in informal settlements, hoping to access home ownership in the same city or in other cities in the same region. For others, the main struggle is settling in their current place of residence since they have invested time and money to building a house that fits their family's size and needs. For many, territorial self-management is an alternative political housing project to the traditional Chilean single-family housing model, located far from the central areas and with small housing size. Several interviewees have worked in partnership with NGOs to propose a territorial housing project that would give them access to land ownership.

The leading role of women within informal settlements and their mechanisms of territorial struggle in the context of racialization, especially for Afro-descendant migrant women, speaks to how displacement is a violent condition. In this context, displacement also emerges as a mechanism of socio-political action that generates a new territoriality, to re-signify their migratory trajectories, to reclaim the time and material investment for the family, or because being part of a territorial settlement project is a tool that gives meaning to their lives. Many of the women interviewed have managed to rebuild social capital with other women who have had similar displacement experiences in their birthplaces and/or throughout their migratory trajectories.

Many of the women leaders of informal settlements across Chile, especially in the extractive mining areas in the north of the country, have both challenged and influenced the role and character of research on informal settlements. Seeking reciprocity, they have required researchers to follow ethical frameworks that support their collective projects and transmit experiences that enrich their leadership. Most of the interviewees have demanded the co-construction of leadership schools aimed at building knowledge and capacity, especially about land prices, how to access and manage public and/ or private land in Chile, and the existing rights framework – especially for women, mothers, migrant women and Afro-descendants.

The interviewees revealed a form of resistance to displacement and an attempt to manage the risks of eviction and precariousness. Most residents of informal settlements are negotiating with the state regarding the possibility of settling in their current places of residence or moving to other places within the Tarapacá region, although Alto Hospicio is the territory that provides the greatest availability of land for the construction of low-income housing. Likewise, the interviews point out the paradox that exists regarding the behavior of the rental market in the central city. All cases warn of a greater violation of rights within the regulated city than in informal settlements. Given the scale of the phenomenon, this is an issue that requires further debate about how to protect families who rent in central housing, especially when they are old houses and even have declared historical heritage.

Conclusion

This chapter has focused on eviction, displacement, and migrant women's quest for shelter security and agency. Their stories entail multiple movements, a state of hypermobility, and the production of informal settlements and resistance self-managed by migrant women. Most of the informal settlements are produced within the traditional city, on the edges of the city limits, and even in its peri-urban and rural spaces. These factors lead us to question the origin and or starting point of displacement: what are the roles of place and geographical position in this debate and how does displacement intersect with housing choices, trajectories, mobilities, and informalities?

The women interviewed have experienced multiple displacements, whether in the territories where they were born or along their migratory trajectories, and a pervading housing insecurity linked to this displacement background. They related specific narratives of multiple displacements and insecurity shaped by denial of rights, stigma, and racialization stemming from their migrant background. This required looking at displacement across scales, as an overlapping and protracted, exhausting condition. It also begged the question: at what point and under what conditions can women – especially migrants – demand a human right such as access to decent housing?

While the state regularly uses eviction to prevent the occupation of public or private land, or the construction of informal houses under high-voltage pylons, it does little to challenge the drivers of informality. The *tugurization* of central spaces and the production of direct and indirect displacements by the extractive mining industry through its (de)regulation of the market, raising land cost, or making rents unaffordable for vulnerable or middle-class families remain unchecked. The consequent precarization, exhaustion, impoverishment, and hypermobility of women migrants, produced through displacement and displaceability within central areas, leaves few other options or strategies other than to occupy land in informal settlements.

The impacts of extractivism, or the imaginary that it creates in relation to the northern region of Chile, is controversial, not only because it creates false expectations for migrant families, but also because the institutionalized approach to migration focuses on border control and the biometric screening of migrants without ensuring basic human rights to those individuals who wish to be integrated into society. The women interviewed had been bombarded for at least five years with racist institutional discourses that depicted them as criminals, freeloaders, and creators of the informal housing sector – a stigmatization and wearing out that subjugates them and renders them devoid of rights, reliant on informal housing and employment, vulnerable and disposable. They came with dreams of a progressive society that turned out to be hostile to them. In all the stories, they explained that the imaginary of Chile as an attractive country to live in was a false construction. They all ended up working in the informal labor market, in insecure work without contracts, and with no connection to the mining activities of the Tarapacá region. They faced barriers that prevented them from accessing basic rights and it took a long time for many of them to obtain permanent residence in the country.

Evidence collected through the stories of 15 migrant women, and within workshops held between 2017 and the time of writing, shows how life in *tugurios* or deteriorated housing pushed migrant families towards self-managed spaces and informal settlements. Their narratives not only brought to the fore how the housing crisis affects migrant women and produces displacement, but also its intersection with several other crises and structural forces, such as extraction, migration governance, racialization, exploitation, and environmental risks. The place and housing in which migrant women live are determined by what they can afford for rent/sublets, and the way they live is grounded in prior life experience. They all spent time living in central districts, and many were later able to construct their own housing or obtain a plot of land in informal settlements in the periphery. While this offered some forms of security and freedoms, informal housing also exposed them to other disillusions and evictions related to environmental disaster risk and injustices. Nevertheless, such informal settlements provide them with greater autonomy than living in a centrally rented *tugurios* and mitigate to some degree the immediate risks of perpetual urban displacement and high residential mobility associated with those central spaces.

Although rendered displaceable subjects through exhaustive structural forces, including market pressures, state negligence, conflict, and profit-seeking by small landowners, the reclaimed agency of women within the space of informal settlements has fostered engagement in individual and organized struggle and place-based resistance. In the face of such structural adversity, the practices of the women interviewed in securing and making homes manifests as a form of resistance, constructing safer spaces, new urbanities, and communities organized around housing rights and access to land.

Notes

1. This chapter was funded by ANID Fondecyt Regular 1231116 and ANID FONDAP COES 15130009.
2. The findings of this chapter were obtained from two research projects: ANID FONDECYT Regular N°1231116 (2023- 2026) and N° 1171722 (2017 to 2020).
3. Among the 15 interviewees are immigrant women from Latin America and the Caribbean, including one Afro-Cuban woman, three Afro-Dominican women, five Afro-Colombian women, four Bolivian women, and two Peruvian women. Their profile includes women who are mothers or do not have children, and they could be married, divorced, or single. Most are experiencing downward social mobility in Chile, either as a result of precarious living conditions or because, despite having university degrees, the country's policies make it difficult for them to validate their degrees and work properly. With regard to their visa status, only 11 women have permanent residency and, in each case, obtaining this visa was complex and arbitrary. Currently, all the women live in informal settlements on the periphery of Alto Hospicio.
4. In this sense, it is important to note that the state in Chile can construct social housing, provided that the average cost of land is less than US\$85/m^2.

References

Atkinson, R. (2015) 'Losing one's place: narratives of neighbourhood change, market injustice and symbolic displacement', *Housing, Theory and Society*, 32(4): 373–88.

Carsolio, V. (2014) 'Extractivismo minero: saqueo y resistencia social en la Sierra Norte de Puebla, México', *Liminales. Escritos Sobre La Psicología y Sociedad*, 16: 129–47.

Contreras, Y., Ala-Louko, V., and Labbé, G. (2015) 'Acceso exclusionario y racista a la vivienda formal e informal en las áreas centrales de Santiago e Iquique', *Polis*, 14(42): 53–78.

Contreras, Y. and Seguel, B. (2022) 'Territorio informal. Una nueva lectura del acceso a la vivienda y al suelo en Chile', *Revista de Geografía Norte Grande*, 136(81): 113–36.

Elliott-Cooper, A., Hubbard, P., and Lees, L. (2020) 'Moving beyond Marcuse: gentrification, displacement and the violence of un-homing', *Progress in Human Geography*, 44(3): 492–509.

Lardé, J., Chaparro, E., and Parra, C. (2008) *El aporte del sector minero al desarrollo humano en Chile: el caso de la región de Antofagasta*, United Nations. Economic Commission for Latin America and the Caribbean. División de Recursos Naturales e Infraestructura.

Lees, L., Slater, T., and Wyly, E. (2008) *Gentrification*, Routledge.

Marcuse, P. (1985) 'Gentrification, abandonment and displacement: connections, causes and policy responses in New York City', *Journal of Urban and Contemporary Law*, 28: 195–240.

Nixon, R. (2011) *Slow Violence and the Environmentalism of the Poor*, Harvard University Press.

Servicio Nacional de Migraciones, C. (2023) *Reporte 1. Estadísticas generales registro administrative*, Servicio Nacional de Migraciones.

Smith, N. (2012) *La nueva frontera urbana*, Traficantes de Sueños.

Stefoni, C. (2004) 'Inmigración y ciudadanía: la formación de comunidades peruanas en Santiago y la emergencia de nuevos ciudadanos', *Revista de Ciencia Política*, 43: 319–36.

Tapia, M., Contreras, Y., and Stefoni, C. (2021) 'Movilidad fronteriza, sujetos móviles y multianclados en el acceso de la vivienda. Los casos: Iquique, Alto Hospicio y Antofagasta', *Anales de Geografía de La Universidad Complutense*, 41(1): 265–91.

Techo Chile and Centro de Estudios Territoriales (2023) *Catastro Nacional de Campamentos 2022–23*.

Yiftachel, O. (2020) 'From displacement to displaceability: a southeastern perspective on the new metropolis', *City*, 24(1–2): 151–65.

7

Shifting Geographies of Presence: Territorial Biographies and Forced Displacements Entanglements Within the Kurdistan Region of Iraq

Layla Zibar

Introduction

In a conversation with a friend, the elusive nature of Kurdistan's location on a printed world map became apparent. Despite being aware of my research on the Kurdistan region of Iraq (KR-I), my friend embarrassingly confessed her inability to locate Kurdistan, as its borders still remain opaque on a world map. Her cursory online research only revealed a plethora of historical maps that barely align, along with images of displacements, misery, and makeshift structures. Instead, what maps highlight are territories and pockets inhabited by Kurds, with vast territories covering parts of the national state borders of Turkey, Syria, Iraq, and Iran, and even appearing within various European ones. Her research reflects the complexity of tracing Kurds' presence, trapped between borders' absence in the realm of maps and demographic concentration that exists across (and transcends) multiple political borders (O'Shea, 2004). Without political recognition, Kurdistan's borders remain in flux and only mark inhabited geographies. 'Is this Kurdistan?' she asked, pointing to Kurdistan Federal Region dotted lines on Iraq's map.

Borders and forced displacements coincide with geopolitical shifts that legitimize power to inhabit certain geographies. Given its size, geopolitical sensitivity, ecological diversity, and socio-political complexity, in the case of Kurdistan, geography matters. A wealth of studies exist on the contested political legitimization, and on oppression and resistance forms related to the Kurdish question and the Kurds' right to their land. Amidst clashes and conflicts over resources and (re)asserting presence, these territories have been particularly exhausted by periodic political shifts, violent events, and chronic instabilities. Conflicts and involuntary displacements come forward as a lived reality in the territories inhabited by the Kurds, entwined with refuge-seeking-granting practices and shifting power spheres. These spheres profoundly restructure the (il)legitimization of presence, granting protection mechanisms and, consequently, how these territories are (re)inhabited and collective memories are transmitted (Tejel, 2009). The Kurdistan Region of Iraq (KR-I) stands as a poignant example of what Chapter 1 refers to as 'exhaustion' in the context of displacement urbanism. This chapter reframes the territorial biographies of the KR-I through the lens of exhaustion, highlighting how continuous cycles of displacement, slow and infrastructural violence, and geopolitical shifts have worn down both the land and its people, reproducing fragile landscapes of perpetual instability and resilience.

This work began with my personal displacement trajectory, having a Syrian nationality with Kurdish roots, and the inherited question of a legitimized presence while testing borders and temporary presence in every country in which I resided. To pinpoint a home on a geographical map, I ended up with many dots on locations in Syria, Egypt, Germany, KR-I, and Belgium, all carrying expiration dates. But are homes like mine just forgotten even though they are ever-present in personal memory packages? Does the land somehow hold traces of our former presence? These questions led to an exploration journey through a doctoral dissertation and fieldwork, where I used (visual) ethnography, mapping, and hanging out methods.

Narrating displacement continuums: territorial biographies, violence, and 'exhaustion'

During ethnographic fieldwork in 2018 in KR-I, visiting Arbat refugee camp in Sulaymaniyah governorate required crossing various security checkpoints. Despite its UNHCR official name, locals referred to it as Barkia camp. Examination of satellite maps crossed with historical texts revealed multiple settlements aggregations, formed and repurposed to house displaced groups from 1976–2020. Arbat's strip constitutes an archipelago of settlements shaped by displacement waves consisting of two main typologies: humanitarian and former purpose-built towns (Figure 7.1). Involuntary displacement patterns in the KR-I contributed to aggregating similar strips, as subsequent paragraphs show, and were linked periodically to fluctuating and overlapping power dynamics. The (fading) map lines submerge, leaving these territories as timeless witnesses for stories untold.

Figure 7.1: Arbat strip

Source: Author, 2023 based on Google Maps image

According to the *Cambridge Dictionary*, a biography is the life story of a person told and written by someone else. The power of telling a story lies in the reconstructions of reality as 'existential imperatives', which hold a 'restorative praxis' of identifying the turning points, 'sharing a common ground', and 'restoring one's place in the public sphere' (Jackson, 2013, p 23). Telling a story is thus an 'action of meaning-making': it subverts the unanchored presence and political absence 'deprived of the reality that comes from being seen and heard by others' (Arendt, 1958, p 58). This chapter embraces this power and reasserts territories and its spatial agency role as storytellers, where territorial biographies become living records and active companions.

To comprehend KR-I complexities and to contextually trace its territorial biographies, the chapter first combines Corboz's (1983) urban landscape as a palimpsest and Gregotti's (2009) form of the territory into the main framework. Second, to frame displacement continuums due to violence within these territorial biographies, the chapter focuses on two temporal frames of violence: acute and slow. Acute and annihilating violence exercised over the land to discipline, punish, and/or disfigure inhabitation patterns has been extensively discussed in various academic discourses. For this research, the chapter employs the concept of 'urbicide' (Coward, 2008; Abujidi, 2014) to frame how acute violence leading to destruction irrevocably exhausts and deforms habitats. Urbicidal practices deliberately strive to kill and reassert power by targeting and then reordering the socio-material fabrications, hence partially or completely eroding the systems and life-worlds ingrained within them.

Last but not least, the work on slow violence. Nixon (2011) provides a valuable framework for tuning the territorial biography lens to underpin the 'slow' tempo of depletion over time. Slow violence refers to the gradual, often invisible forms of harm that unfold over extended periods, making them less perceptible but no less exhausting or devastating. Infrastructural violence as discussed by Otsuki (2024), which builds on slow violence, serves to uncover the long-term impacts of displacement continuum in the KR-I. Infrastructural violence is 'exclusionary and selective' (Otsuki, 2024), and is also operated to accentuate geographical control zones and the 'infrastructural power' of the state within them over its dwellers (Mann, 1984, 2008). It has the power to exclude or include and stigmatize particular groups, to make society spatially 'legible' and a target for social and economic engineering (Scott, 1998). As such, infrastructural violence brings forward the process whereby material depletion, destruction, and displacement cycles slowly wear down communities and sever their (generational) connection to their habitat.

By incorporating concepts such as slow violence and infrastructural violence, the territorial biographies approach allows for an examination of forced displacement patterns and the historical (re)construction of the territorial logic of shifting powers, deeply entwined with refuge-seeking-granting practices, in the interplay of steadfastness, resistance, interdependencies, and home-making. This examination in the KR-I (proper) reveals how delineating presence through a spatial apparatus categorizes, legitimizes, and constructs the self and the other in a multi-scalar and territorial-based way. Therefore, the territorial biographies methodological approach questions the authentication of the (il)legitimized presence within and beyond temporal and spatial frames of (shifting) political agendas, legal permits, and (un) anchored homes, and paves the way for resisting and (re)claiming presence.

'Since at least the second millennium BC and the emergence of the first empires of the Akkadians and Assyrians ... massive deportations, involuntary dislocations and relocations constituted the norm in inhabited Kurdish territories' (Izady, 2015). These mass forced movements were part and parcel of sovereign powers' disciplinary strategies towards their unruly and non-loyal subjects (King, 2014; Izady, 2015). These strategies covered a wide spectrum of violence, annihilations, and scorched earth policies, including burning pasture/agricultural lands, killing domesticated animals, destroying villages and towns, dispersing and relocating those who survived hundreds of miles away from their former habitat, and finally filling the resulting vacant spaces with their loyal subjects (Izady, 2015; McDowall, 2020). By rendering territories uninhabitable, the goal was to assert, maintain, and expand their control over territories and boundaries.

Forced displacement and refuge-seeking vectors varied depending on the conflict/destruction acuteness, power spheres' ability to grant protection, and opportunities concentrated in receiving territories. Similar to the region's societies, refuge practices were entangled with Islamic customs (Shoukri, 2010) and articulated as a form of patron–client contract of reciprocal relations, and attachments rooted in kinship ideology. In pre-WWI period, (local) power spheres that granted refuge were sustained through power reassertion by conquest and conflict resolution, subjected to shifting dynamics between tribal laws, religious jurisprudence and feudal practices (Izady, 2015; King, 2014; McDowall, 2020; van Bruinessen, 1992). Legitimized presence, as such, was also measured in controlling powers over resources accumulated in territorial rights, land ownerships, and number of loyal subjects. Thus, the ability to grant asylum, extend protection to the vulnerable and host guests in the pre-modern Kurdish communities qualified, (as) 'an index of power and greatness' (Loescher, 2021), and increased the loyal subjects ready to battle and resources under control. Whether villages or hamlets, settlements localities convey historical overlaps between two local power spheres: tribal and religious.

Traditional power and protection spheres Prior to World War I

Within KR-I's proper territories, the Kurdish tribe represented a durable territorial socio-political unit of patrilineages and kinship networks headed by chiefs and Aghas (van Bruinessen, 1992). Villages, along with surrounding agricultural and pasture lands, acted as primary territorial units, where tribes anchored their presence and exerted control over resources. Thus, the power of granting user rights and access spatiotemporally conditioned the presence and incorporation of 'foreigners', including passers-by, pastors, and refuge-seekers. Resource scarcity, due to population growth fed by consecutive waves of 'foreigners', resulted in process of socio-spatial emanations due to splits in clan segments, forming new villages within the territory, and thus territorially welding tribal power sphere and land rights.

Between the sixteenth and nineteenth centuries, many tribes unified, forming territorial meshes of semi-independent Kurdish emirates, who 'carve[d] out high levels of autonomy' (Owtram, 2019) and acted as de facto sovereigns, resulting in further shifts in legitimacies and presence. Gaining the loyalty of these emirates was essential for the Safavids and the Ottomans to assert their ultimate sovereignty over the mountainous borders. However, Ottoman/Persian empires' disciplinary campaigns painted them as 'rebels' and violently fragmented their territorial tribal control, resulting in mass displacements.

Displaced groups sought refuge within growing Sufism religious spheres that undermined traditional authority (Anjum, 2006). The Qadiriyya and Naqshbandiyya orders' networks constituted these spheres, which provided the 'organizational framework' that was ideally perceived as independent from both the tribe and the state (van Bruinessen, 1992, 2011). Joining an order meant following and owing absolute obedience to the authority ladder of Sheikhs or Mullas, composing networks chains (*silsila*) of allegiances that would 'act like a family' (Anjum, 2006). In this period, Sufi locations were bound to religious status, so they withdrew legitimacy to act as sanctuaries, attracting the vulnerable. Refugees' arrival and incorporation among their followers fed their networks, which (re)rooted territorially by establishing buildings close to or within settlements, mainly located close to or on the boundaries of two or three tribal territories. Such strategic positioning of the Sufi socio-spatial nodes,[1] connected across tribal boundaries, ensured that the order's power and continuity were sustained (van Bruinessen, 1992). Being the powerful protectors and conflict resolvers, and having power over resources, Sheikhs and Mullas of notable bloodlines[2] remained the 'leaders of Kurdistan and the obvious focal point for the nationalist sentiment' (van Bruinessen, 1992). One concrete example is the Barzani Naqshbandiyya sheikhs, whose influence expanded over areas in northeast Erbil; they are the ancestors of many of today's KR-I national leaders.

In the nineteenth century, Ottoman Kurdistan witnessed administrative (re)structurations through the 1839 Tanzimat Acts' reformations and (shifting) land regimes, aimed mainly at asserting centralization, abolishing local governance, and punishing disloyal subjects (Bozarslan, 2019). These Acts segmented territorially enmeshed traditional authorities into a more fragmented individualistic structure. Whole villages were registered as 'personal possessions of local notables', whether Aghas or Sheikhs,[3] hence creating distinct groups of landowners and tenants. With constant power hunger, exploitation, and threat of displacement, even in periods of relative stability, the population experienced exhaustion, with the very notion of belonging becoming tenuous and fraught. Consequently, exhaustion slowly deepened mistrust and resentment between traditional power structures and their subjects (McDowall, 2020).

Between the World Wars: erasing Kurds from world maps

The disorder, displacement, and destruction ensuing from the World War I period and the fall of the Ottoman Empire were exacerbated by the 1916 Sykes-Picot Agreement. Despite various (international) attempts to weave a de facto autonomy of a demarcated 'Kurdistan', this agreement, followed by the Treaty of Lausanne in 1923, omitted any reference to a Kurdish homeland (Owtram, 2019), disregarded population ethnic composition, and effectively trapped the Kurds within state borders known today as Iraq, Syria, Turkey, and Iran (O'Shea, 2004). These borders ruptured generationally woven Kurdish networks, significantly obstructed former spatial fluidities, and dissolved former modalities of local governance to be gradually substituted by the containing states (Figure 7.2).

The post-World War I collateral damage further aggravated internal and ethnic conflicts in the short-lived British mandate (1920–32). Before its end, the British delegated their power by appointing King Fasil as the King of Iraq under their supervision. This appointment aimed at disengaging with internal unrest, yet ensured prolonged access to oil-rich locations in KR-I proper (Owtram, 2019). This power delegation, and finalizing the 'Brussels line' in 1926, which fixed administrative states' borders (Lloyd,1926), accentuated the legitimized non-Kurdish authority over territorial resources and consolidated it into lived realities. By 1932, the Kurds had gradually become a minority under an Arab administration (McDowall, 2020), surrounded by a climate of suspicion and uncertainty for decades to come. Within these shifting realities, the growing authority of non-Kurds over the Kurds incited nationalist sentiments, leading to political awakenings fuelled by distrust, economic crises, and intensifying dismissal of Kurds' cultural rights by nation-state practices. Consequently, former tribal and sheikh spheres adapted to the changing political landscape by restructuring themselves as political parties, which were distributed as branches in Kurdish-inhabited territories.

Rewriting presence: 1950–91

Modernization aspirations: 1950–70

In the early 1950s, Iraq was experiencing a period of modernization aspirations, which continued after the 1958 revolution and the shifting from monarchy to republic (Pyla, 2006). Coupled with tripled oil revenues, these

Figure 7.2: Shifting Kurdish borders

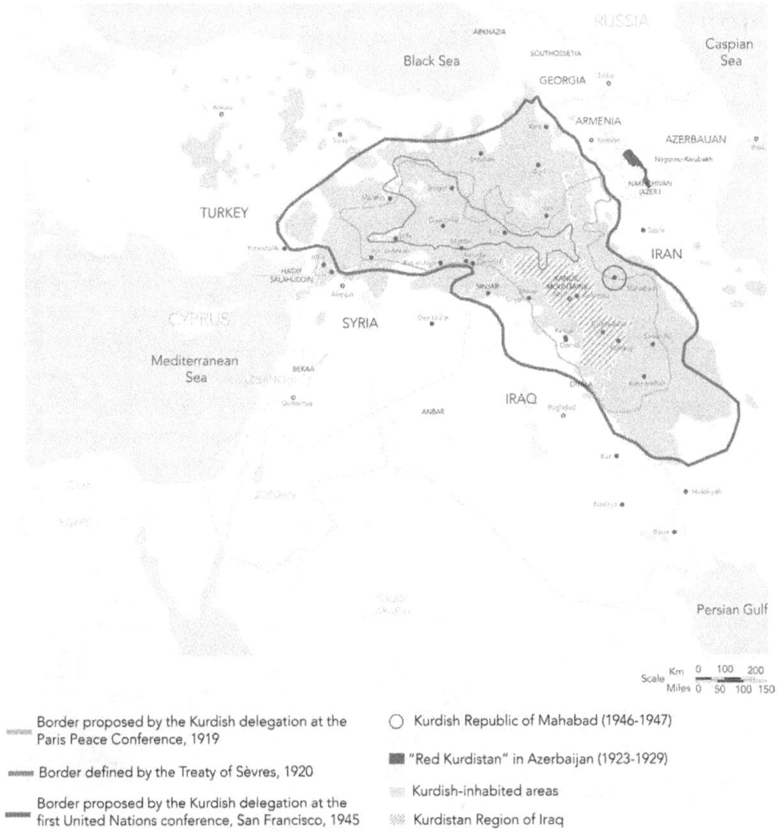
RUSSIA
Black Sea
GEORGIA
Caspian Sea
ARMENIA
AZERBAIJAN
TURKEY
IRAN
SYRIA
CYPRUS
Mediterranean Sea
IRAQ
ANBAR
SINJAR
Persian Gulf
Scale Km 0 100 200
Miles 0 50 100 150
Border proposed by the Kurdish delegation at the Paris Peace Conference, 1919
Border defined by the Treaty of Sèvres, 1920
Border proposed by the Kurdish delegation at the first United Nations conference, San Francisco, 1945
Kurdish Republic of Mahabad (1946-1947)
"Red Kurdistan" in Azerbaijan (1923-1929)
Kurdish-inhabited areas
Kurdistan Region of Iraq

Source: Maps reproduced by author (2022), based on Kurdish Institute of Paris and Izady (1998)

aspirations resulted in expanding the state's infrastructural power of cross-territorial projects, ranging from dams and highways to regional master plans. These projects contributed to advancing faster connections and modes of production, thereby modernizing and upgrading rural areas and the agricultural sector. All these projects served to facilitate the 1958 Agrarian Reform Law, with Soviet-influenced social justice ideologies, through the redistribution of half of Iraq's cultivated land to peasants (McDowall, 2020).

Modernization included residential schemes developed as part of the Iraq National Housing Programme (1955–61) by international architectural companies such as Doxiadis Associates (Doxiadis Associates & DBoGI, 1963). They included modern collectives (*mojamma't assrya*), cooperative farming projects, and peasants' housing villages (Figure 7.3). To facilitate the modernization of rural Iraq, 250 locations were constructed and subsidized with credits and loans for self-help schemes and skills upgrade programmes.

Figure 7.3: Iraq National Housing Programme

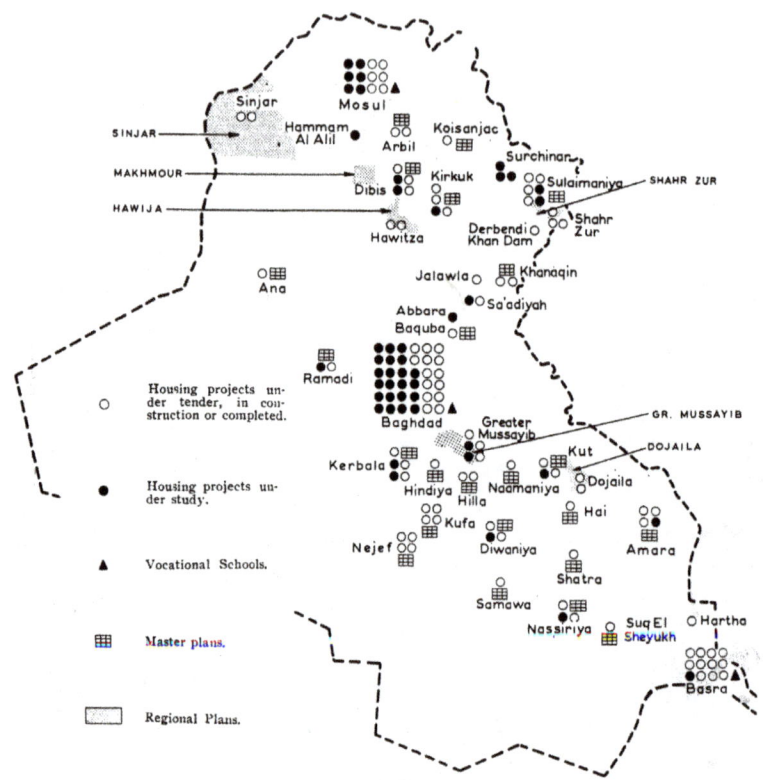

Source: Doxiadis Associates & DBoGI, 1963. © Constantinos and Emma Doxiadis Foundation. This image is sourced from the archives of Doxiadis Associates in collaboration with the Department of Building and General Infrastructure (DBoGI), dated 1963. It was originally published in Constantinos A. Doxiadis's article 'The National Housing Programme of Iraq', *Ekistics* 16(94) (1963).

Compared with the 'primitive situation in the unserved villages' (Recchia, 2014), these sites had modern iron-grid layouts, connections to public infrastructures (electricity, water) and recreational areas. In addition, all housing schemes were coupled with vocational schools and supporting communal services, all to facilitate the 'transformation of the village dweller into an urban dweller' (Pyla, 2006).

Nonetheless, these projects were primarily halted in the Kurdish inhabited areas due to chronic instabilities and (counter-)insurgency wars that broke out after the short-lived alliance between Mulla Mustafa Barzani and the Iraqi state. The Iraqi state declined Barzani's demands for Kurdish autonomy to reassert a unified Iraq and its state's ultimate power, and labelled him and his followers 'plotters against the republic'. This legitimized Iraqi military and air-force brutal operations and their use of napalm and chemical weapons in the northern parts, where 'Kurdish rebels' resided. Contrary to expectations, the Kurdish front became more fragmented under nationalism banners between the Barzani group in north and the Ahmad-Talabani group in the south, with more than 4,000 people who feared retaliation fleeing to Iran. Additionally, this mayhem steered small peasant uprisings against their landlords, who feared losing their lands due to agrarian reforms. Clashes, urbicidal practices, and forced displacement movements continued in an assault–halt situation, only to end with the 1968 Ba'ath Party's coup and its rise to power.

Around 750 Kurdish villages were destroyed, and 200,000 villagers were forcibly displaced, massively disfiguring the territories and their enmeshed networks. Coupled with drought seasons and economic hardship, Kurds fatigued by cycles of violence were converted into economically fragile subjects, and hence 'better objects of political control' (Scott, 1998).

Under mirages of peace: 1971–74

The Iraqi and Kurdish fronts needed a breather to heal and rearrange their cards. Consequently, the Ba'athist regime and the Kurds joined the negotiation table, reaching the Peace Accord on 11 March 1970, which granted Kurds conditional autonomy.[4] Behind the scenes, however, both players were re-evaluating their strategies, widening their national influence and assessing their international allies' powers; the latter, in turn, exploited the conflict to ensure access to oil fields. The peace accord included a development fund dedicated to strategies addressing the needs of war-affected villages and the displaced, and to improve 'the specific conditions of underdevelopment in the Kurdish region' (Genat, 2017). Thus, the aforementioned modernization schemes reached the region as a remedy to heal war scars, including areas set aside for landless and refugee peasants, new settlements, housing, schools, vocational centres, accompanying infrastructures, financial compensations, and self-help subsidies (Genat, 2017).

The peace curtain fell quickly, revealing the new regime's counter-insurgency strategy. This strategy utilized modern reconstruction remedies and agrarian reforms to spread infrastructural power over arable areas and oil facilities. The Ba'athist government also orchestrated a vast Arabization movement (*ta'rib*) of demographic (re)engineering, using collective towns as spatial tools to shift the Kurds' presence and create state-dependent communities (Talabany, 1999). By 1974, around 64 Kurdish villages were Arabized, while others were either evacuated or bulldozed, not to mention around 50,000 Shi'a Fayli Kurds being denied citizenship and expelled from Iraq (Human Rights Watch, 2004; McDowall, 2020). These urbicidal practices, coinciding with displacements, placements, and replacements, deepened fissures within remnants of territorially enmeshed networks. Unsurprisingly, the 'temporary stability' mirage crumbled by 1974, leading to another Kurdish revolt that collapsed shortly afterwards. This revolt was led by Mullah Barzani, backed by Iranian and US support, against the Iraqi army backed by the Soviets.

These power shifts restructured how refuge was sought, and where future vectors were directed. The sudden and continuous refugee waves evacuating clash areas were unprecedented. Those who backed the revolt headed outwards, first seeking temporary refuge in their alliance networks' villages supporting Kurdish forces in the north, then taking mountainous routes, seeking refuge in newly formed international protection spheres that mushroomed along Iraqi–Iranian mountainous borders. UN-set camps (such as Nelliwan and Ziwa) accommodated over 100,000 Kurdish refugees who suffered confinement, isolation, and harsh environmental conditions.

The short-lived peace accord, the 1974 Autonomy decree, and the Kurdish revolt were foundational to KR-I's (partial) autonomy and political reformation, which marks its presence as a federal region on Iraq's map today. Nonetheless, despite the declared right to autonomy, the conflict's aftermath deepened the split within the Kurdish front, both ideologically and geographically: the Kurdistan Democratic Party (KDP), led by Mulla Barzani, concentrated in the north covering Duhok and Erbil governorates; the Patriotic Union of Kurdistan (PUK), formed by Jalal Talabani, was based in the southern parts of the Sulaymaniyah governorate. This split's conflict infrastructures, including checkpoints and security gates, fractures the region to this day.

Cordon sanitaire: 1975–79

The signing of the 1975 Algerian Accord between Iraq and Iran included agreeing on 'ending any intervention in the other's territory', which meant cutting off the official Iranian backup for Kurds. This accord served Iraq's state goals at this stage of reasserting its ultimate power within its borders, eliminating local and cross-border support feeding the rebels and crushing the revolution once and for all. Thus, the counter-insurgency strategy was devised to eradicate the generationally rooted networks bridging from the mountains to the plains, by rendering the territories uninhabitable. As such, they followed a scorched earth policy in the *cordon sanitaire* created along stretches of the Iran and Turkey borders some 12 miles deep and 500 miles long (Farouk-Sluglett et al, 1984). This creation involved

> 'military force and intimidation: entire Kurdish villages were completely depopulated and bulldozed ... followed up the brutality

with legal decrees aimed at consolidating the displacement ... property deeds of the displaced Kurds were invalidated by legal decree, most frequently without compensation or with nominal compensation. The Iraqi government nationalized the agricultural lands, making them the property of the Iraqi state ... [and] embarked on a massive campaign to resettle the formerly Kurdish areas with Arab farmers and their families, thus completing the Arabization process. (HRW, 2004)

The state's urbicidal practices resulted in 1400 Kurdish villages being evacuated and razed, coupled with economic embargoes, increasing violence and insecurities, all steering additional massive displacement waves. Those trapped within the territory, away from their ancestors, were accommodated within newly 'purpose-built towns' by the Iraqi military within their controlled boundaries (McDowall, 2020). Newly constructed highways and 'modern village' schemes served the counter-insurgency strategies in facilitating large-scale relocation processes (Figure 7.4). These sites were

Figure 7.4: 1970s collectives built for relocation purposes

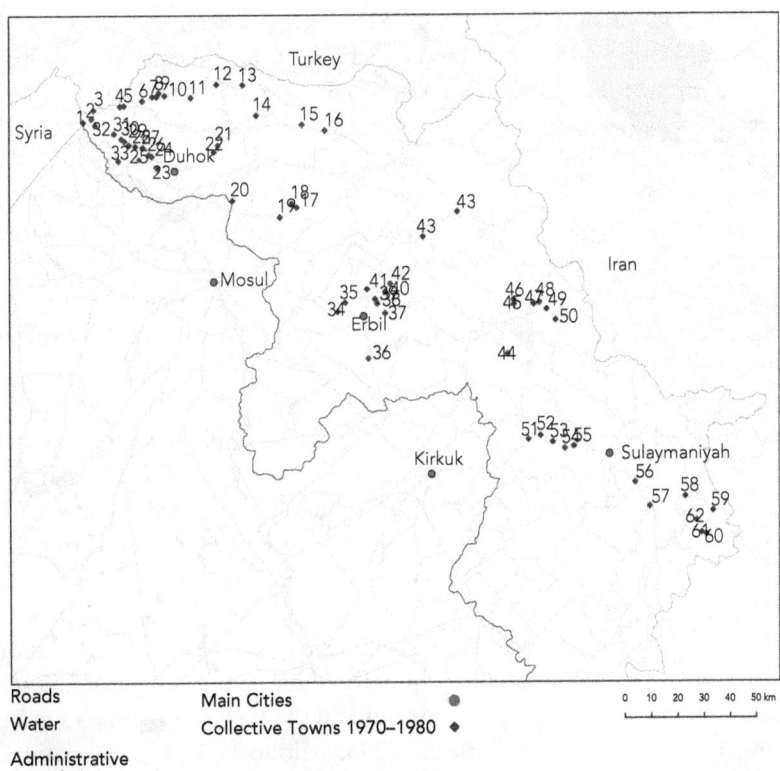

Source: Made by author based on Stansfield (2003)

set along the main highways, accessible by Iraqi military, juxtaposed near either large towns, farmlands, factories or workshops for economic purposes (Human Rights Watch & Black, 1993; Mlodoch, 2017). Within these infrastructures, food rations were provided for those following the national assimilation programme: all male members were forced to undertake military training to join the army, while women had to attend compulsory Arabic courses (Leezenberg, 2000). Hence, acute and slow violence remoulded the displaced into survival needs-dependent subjects conforming to the Ba'ath ideology.

Genocides and eradicating presence: 1980–91

As the Iraq–Iran war (1980–88) broke out, the internal tensions between the PUK and KDP groups eased, leading to a Kurdish Front formation backed by Iran. By 1987, their control had expanded north and south, covering almost all Kurdish-claimed territories. These shifts and alliances threatened Ba'athist regime power in this war, leading to an acceleration of violence. Among this mayhem, many tribal and religious leaders found opportunities to renew their patronage roles and (re)create their power spheres of (sub) territorial pockets of protection inside the Iraqi borders.

The Kurdish population suffered collateral damage. Depending on their alliances with the regime and local leaders, they were treated either as friends or foes. Driven by uncertainties, many juggled their loyalties: some joined the Peshmerga, others joined the Kurdish paramilitary Iraqi forces (*jash*), while the rest suffered. Those who lived within clash areas experienced urbicide through a series of evictions, destructions, executions, and depopulation, which coincided with the Arabization and placement of pro-government groups. Tribes were fragmented into smaller entities; each of which was juxtaposed with segments from different tribes (Stansfield, 2001). Displaced individuals clogged the territories, with additional returnees who repatriated from Iranian refugees camps after the 1979 general amnesty. In response, the Iraqi military forcibly relocated and confined 'suspicious groups' within incomplete infrastructures and vacant parcels of collectives built between 1977 and 1983 (Human Rights Watch and Black, 1993) (Figure 7.5). As such, what was once planned as modern schemes was subverted into coercive ones, perpetuating infrastructural violence materially in wide roads facilitating military machinery movements and symbolically in permanent surveillance (Recchia, 2014). Unlike the former models, there was nothing but tents, surrounded by the Iraqi military control apparatus (gates, fences, posts), decorated with Saddam's portraits and the Ba'athist regime's symbols (Human Rights Watch and Black, 1993; Mlodoch, 2017). To maintain survival dependency, the displaced still received a piece of land, a budget for housing, and monthly distributed food rations.

Figure 7.5: 1980–87 collectives: confinement model

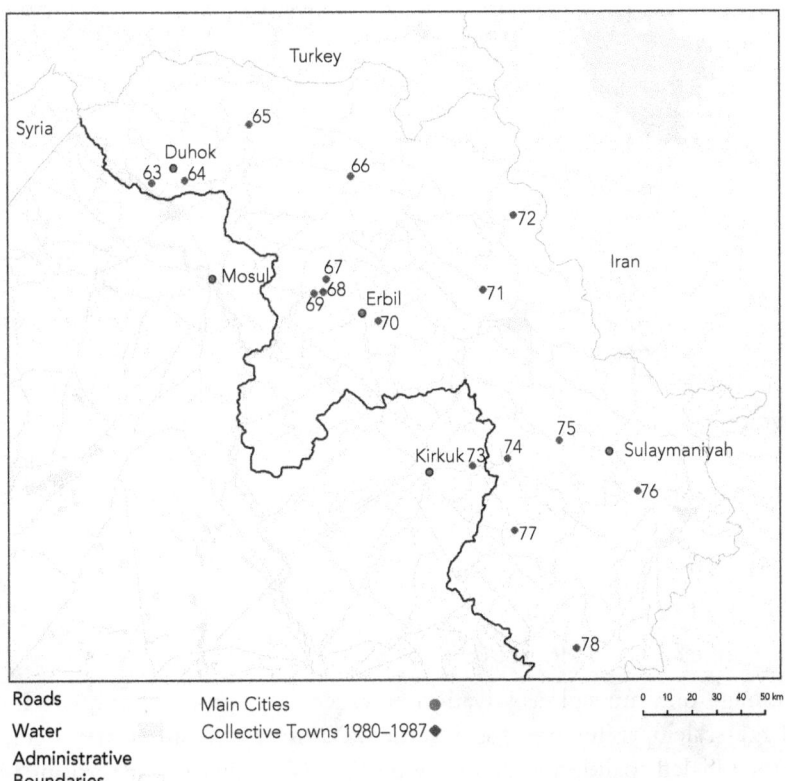

Source: Made by author based on Stansfield (2003)

The Kurdish–Iranian front expansion became alarming to the Ba'athist army, which in response implemented the 'solution': eradicating forever the sociospatial bonds supporting this front, actualizing the solution using a mix of conventional and chemical weaponry. Hence, violence reached its climax during the Anfal campaign (February to September 1988). The Iraqi military's urbicidal and genocidal practices involved annihilating around 4,050 Kurdish villages and towns, including inhabitants, livestock, and agricultural fields, violently displacing hundreds of thousands to the mountainous borders of Iran and Turkey (Leezenberg, 2004). The Iraqi military persecuted and performed executions on 'Iranian collaborators', and relocated hundreds of thousands of women and children in crafted punitive collectives (Human Rights Watch and Black, 1993) that amplified violence through the exclusion from basic life-sustaining running water, sewerage networks, and electricity. Infrastructural violence proliferated in degrading situations: shelters were lines on the ground, demarcated by war rubble gathered by women and children, who were also denied food rations or access to livelihood activities (Leezenberg, 2004; Mlodoch, 2017).

In 1988, following the 1988 Iraq–Iran peace agreement, the Iraqi military cleared 75,000 km² of Kurdish inhabited territories, extensively laying them with minefields (McDowall, 2020), where return was forbidden and punishable by immediate execution (Human Rights Watch and Black, 1993). Executions and imprisonment carried on, and survivors were 'simply dumped on relocation sites near the main roads to the region's major cities surrounded by barbed-wire fences' (Leezenberg, 2004). Roughly, 32 army-guarded confinement towns were constructed with a capacity of 10,000–15,000 persons, who were denied housing, construction materials, food, medicine, and financial compensation, and were left to their own devices (Human Rights Watch, 2004).

Urbicidal and genocidal practices, and the devastation to social networks enmeshed geographically led to territorial exhaustion, where the physical landscape itself bears the scars of violent displacement cycles. This erosion rewrote the Kurds' presence beyond the physical entrapment: fragmentation, psychological tolls, and survival needs drained the displaced, who never returned to their hometowns (Human Rights Watch and Black, 1993; Zibar, 2023).

(Re)calibrating presence with the rise of the humanitarian sphere

Relief under siege: 1991–2003

A mirage of a miraculous salvation emerged for repressed groups in Iraq. A large-scale uprising spread against the Ba'athist regime after its 1991 defeat by the US-led coalition in the first Gulf War. Nonetheless, the uprising was easily crushed. The Ba'athist regime brutally retaliated against the rebels, creating mass panic that resulted in another displacement cycle, this time with two million people crossing the mountainous borders seeking refuge. Along the Turkish and Iranian borders, new makeshift and emergency camps mushroomed within the rocky landscapes, adding to the pre-existing fatigue (Leezenberg, 2000; Human Rights Watch, 2004). Kurdish refugees in Iranian camps suffered dire conditions, while those within the Turkish borders were denied official relief (Brown, 1995).

Inhumane conditions and hosting governments' pressures overshadowed the Gulf War victory. Shortly afterwards, the UN Security Council passed Resolution 688, establishing a 'no-fly zone' and 'safe haven' in northern Iraq (UNSC, 1991). This establishment translated logistically into signing unilateral agreements between humanitarian agencies and the central government of Iraq (CGoI), legitimizing its presence and activities. Relief programmes, coinciding with the sudden influx of international actors and refugees' repatriation, marked the region as an intensified humanitarian arena (Yildiz, 2004), adding a new 'humanitarian' power sphere to the existing ones.

In the early stages, relief practices were initiated by the military, spatially establishing 'protected enclaves' (Figure 7.6). A relief network of safe routes

Figure 7.6: 'Protected enclave' set by the allied forces in 1991 (top); leaflets used during operation Provide Comfort, 1991 (left); and safe routes within protected enclaves (right)

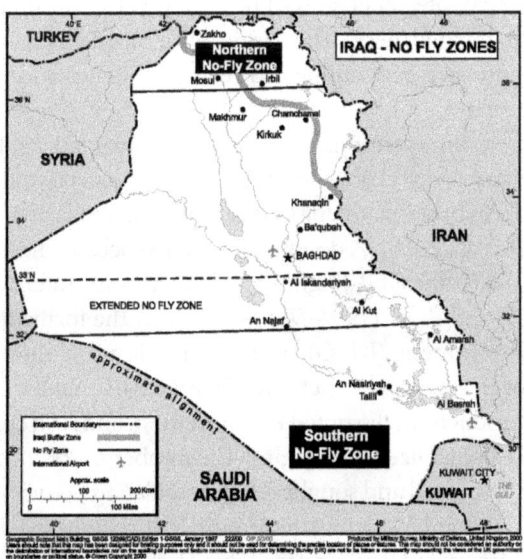

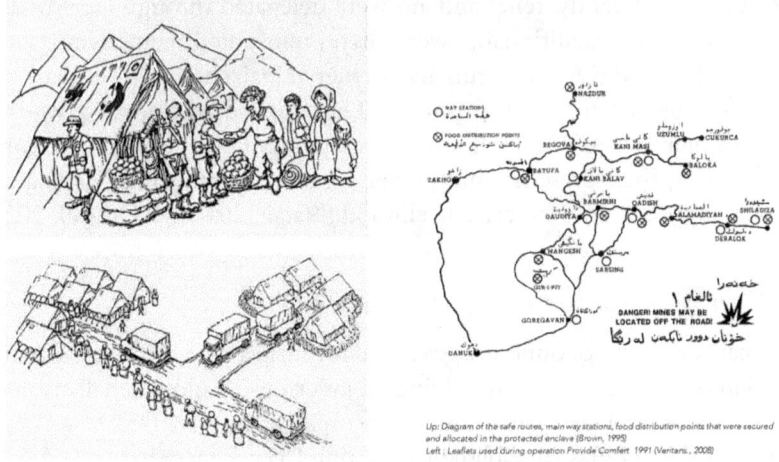

Source: top: No-fly zone map. Military Survey, Ministry of Defence (UK). (2000). Iraq – No fly zones [Map]. Geographic Support Map Building, GSGS 1229B(CAD) Edition 1-GSGS, January 1997. Institute Kurde De Paris, 1992. Bulletin de Liaison et d'information, 83-84, Fevrier-Mars 1992, Institut Kurde de Paris, 17-18, www.institutkurde.org/publications/bulletins/pdf/8384.pdf; left: Humanitarian Operations in Northern Iraq, 1991: With Marines in Operation Provide Comfort (Brown, 1995); right: Safe routes within protected enclaves diagram (Brown, 1995). HathiTrust, https://catalog.hathitrust.org/Record/003031238

and nodes stretched from the Turkish borders into northern territories (Brown, 1995). This establishment incorporated the partial rehabilitation of collective towns and setting up more than ten resettlement camps to act as temporary safe relief sites. The scarce yet consistent relief and post-displacement-formed networks, along with shared everyday steadfastness, subverted oppressive geographies, fostering resilience and endurance amidst extreme precarity.

Despite these interventions, the situation remained far from stable. The Peshmerga–Iraqi army clashes resumed, causing extensive destruction, while eviction and Arabization operations continued, displacing another 200,000 people (McDowall, 2020). A double economic blockade and the power vacuum exacerbated war-inherited fragilities. Furthermore, internal war broke out between KDP and PUK (1994–98) shortly after the formation of the Kurdish Regional Government (KRG) in 1992, resulting in the official territorial delineation of areas under their control (Natali, 2010; Yildiz, 2004). Declines in agricultural production, disrupted transportation, and land confiscation further depleted and destabilized the region (Leezenberg, 2000). Around 200,000 people were evacuated and sought refuge, oscillating between patronage zones and again demographically restructuring KR-I regions (McDowall, 2020).

By 1995, foreign aid was hindered due to the CGoI obstacles and funding scarcity. Consequently, relief and aid were delegated through local bodies, where the former traditional power spheres reinvented themselves (Natali, 2010). Many NGOs were run by former tribal chieftains, Aghas, and Sheikhs, attached to political parties. This allowed traditional powers to reinvent themselves, through business expanding their patronage networks, recalibrating their presence and power spheres, accumulating capital and offering opportunities to earn a livelihood (Natali, 2010; McDowall, 2020).

UN surrogacy and the OFFP: 1995–2003

Internal conflict, economic struggles, and favouritism led the KR-I situation to fall into chaos again, causing additional suffering. To address civilians' needs without allowing Iraq to boost its military capabilities, the 1995 Oil-for-Food Programme (OFFP) was established, allocating 13 per cent of Iraqi oil proceeds to the KR-I (UNSC, 1995). These goals undoubtedly laid the ground for a humanitarian presence linked to development and stability in the KR-I and gave UN bodies legitimacy to act as a 'surrogate state', filling the institutional vacuum of the CGoI and stipulating the de facto KRG (Kagan, 2011).

Under the OFFP, UN-Habitat's Settlements Rehabilitation Programme (SRP) targeted vulnerable and displaced groups through spatial recovery and socio-economic empowerment projects (Figure 7.7). Initially, intervention strategies included dismantling collective towns, which represented oppression apparatuses, and rehabilitating Kurdish villages in areas heavily

Figure 7.7: Location of UN Habitat SRP interventions, 1995–2003

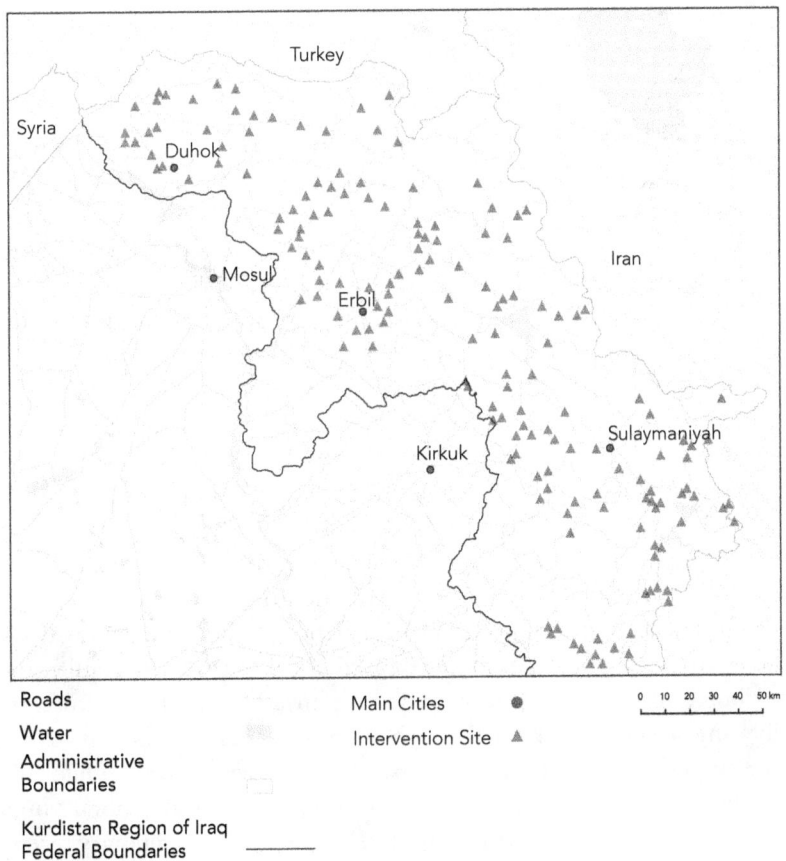

Source: UN Habitat, 2001, reproduced by author

destroyed during the 1980s (UN Habitat, 2001). However, around 55 per cent of the surveyed population, reluctant to repatriate, remained in collective towns despite the prolonged violence of crippling conditions and depleting infrastructures (UN Habitat, 2001). Therefore, the SRP incorporated 52 former collective towns, and their improvement projects attracted unemployed (displaced) Kurds to participate in the reconstruction process (Mlodoch, 2017). These crippled infrastructures became a canvas for humanitarian intervention, subverting their former oppressive notion into prosperity promises.

Despite all efforts, the OFFP 2003 termination due to corruption, political instabilities, and scarce funding intervals retriggered infrastructural violence in the form of uneven and unfinished territorial improvements, compounding into high dependency and illiteracy rates (Mahzouni, 2013). Paradoxically, relief efforts perpetuated cycles of violence and exhaustion, institutionalizing displacement and creating new forms of dependency and precarity while providing aid.

(Re)structuring political presence in the KR-I: 2003–11

After the Iraq War and Saddam's overthrow in 2003, the balance of power notably shifted towards the Kurds. While southern Iraq was engulfed in protracted conflict, the KRG gained legitimacy as a distinct political entity following the 2005 Iraqi constitution reform. The KR-I thus appeared as an island of safety amidst turbulence and chaos (Leezenberg, 2017). This legitimacy included the KRG's control of its federal borders, its own police and security forces, and budget and resources. Oil revenues fuelled private sector development, large infrastructure, and housing projects, thereby attracting regional and international investor groups. This enabled the humanitarian sphere to restructure, integrate with KRG institutional frameworks, relocate its headquarters to Erbil, and thus root itself deeper within KR-I territories (Natali, 2010; McDowall, 2020).

These geopolitical shifts transformed the spatiality and meaning of former collective towns as they benefited from the KRG's overall investments. Various projects focused on the reconstruction of housing, coupled with socio-economic privileges dedicated to Anfal survivors, significantly contributed to the rehabilitation and modernization of infrastructure, thus facilitating access to capital through income-generating activities. This sparked significant urbanization processes: nearby towns merged, while others were absorbed by expanding cities, becoming economically vibrant hubs.

Furthermore, vacant spaces in collective towns became temporary receptor infrastructures for Arab IDPs, converting suppression apparatuses into hospitality and prosperity sites (Mlodoch, 2017). Nonetheless, the arrival of Arab IDPs ignited anxiety towards 'a new style of Arabization', echoed in pushing for setting up temporary camps as 'the most efficient way to control the displaced Arabs while providing them with assistance' (Younès, 2007). Humanitarian actors relocated the undesirable groups outside the KR-I's borders, either to camps or to safe urban enclaves. Controversially, three gridded settings appeared near former collective towns within the KR-I territories to accommodate the displaced Kurds in 2006 (UNHCR, 2007). Barika and Kawa refugee settlements accommodated approximately 4000 Iranian Kurdish refugees from the 1980s transferred from central Iraq, and Makhmour refugee camp accommodated 12,000 Kurdish refugees from Turkey. Such spatial allocation and differentiation became the strategy for hosting (un)desirable displaced groups.

Development and progression temporarily glossed over crisis-inherited fragilities and exhaustion. The region's poorest parts, remote from vibrant urban cores, and outside of patronage networks, lacked services and were excluded from development schemes. Similarly, former collectives – which were neither dismantled nor abandoned – deteriorated gradually, further entrenching inequality and violence in their dwellers' fragile presence (Mahzouni, 2013).

A fragile safe pocket amidst chronic geopolitical instability

The Arab Spring and the rise of the Islamic State of Iraq and Syria (ISIS)
Following the 2003 Iraq war, the Middle East and North Africa (MENA) region underwent significant socio-political changes, while political instability and sectarian divisions plagued the CGoI. These changes culminated in the 2011 Arab Spring uprisings, shaking political scenes in various countries. Despite the initial peaceful intentions calling for reforms, the uprisings hardly ended as hoped. The Syrian trajectory transformed dramatically by 2012 into a (civil) war with multiple ideologies, fronts, regional and international players (Fares, 2016). In 2013, Iraq and Syria's trajectories overlapped as ISIS brutally carved out and expanded its presence within their geographies (Leezenberg, 2017; McDowall, 2020) (Figure 7.8) The acute violence was unprecedented, echoing former urbicidal and genocidal practices of destruction, bombarding, and mass killings among other atrocities, and extending to enslaving women and children. Such a violent turn of events generated what scholars believe to be the second-largest forced displacement movement since World War II, thus again changing the territorial structures of presence, power, and refuge practices.

Despite the war-inherited fragilities, the KR-I emerged as an enclave of stability amidst intensified instabilities. By sheltering the vulnerable, the KRG aspired to enhance its progressive image internationally. Accordingly, the KR-I acted as a refuge hub and as an aid arena for humanitarian collaboration, functioning as a localized humanitarian regime (LHR).

Protection enclaves: collective towns, newly set camps, and typologies

The KRG and hosting communities perceived Syrian refugee flows (mainly Kurds) as 'brothers and sisters', and collaborated to make a home for them (RUDAW, 2019). Cross-border kinship and patronage networks, maintained generationally despite cycles of violence, greatly facilitated hosting the early arrivals (UNHCR Iraq, 2012), while others had access through jobs or financial means. Peripheral spaces, situated on the fringes of major KR-I cities rich with socio-economic opportunities and networks, served as receptor infrastructures for the newly arrived. Early refuge spaces also included former collectives, which were abundant with vacant and affordable housing units. Others later found a place in the newly constructed Domiz1 refugee camp.

Figure 7.8: The expansion of ISIS control and the concentration of ethnic groups in both Syria and Iraq

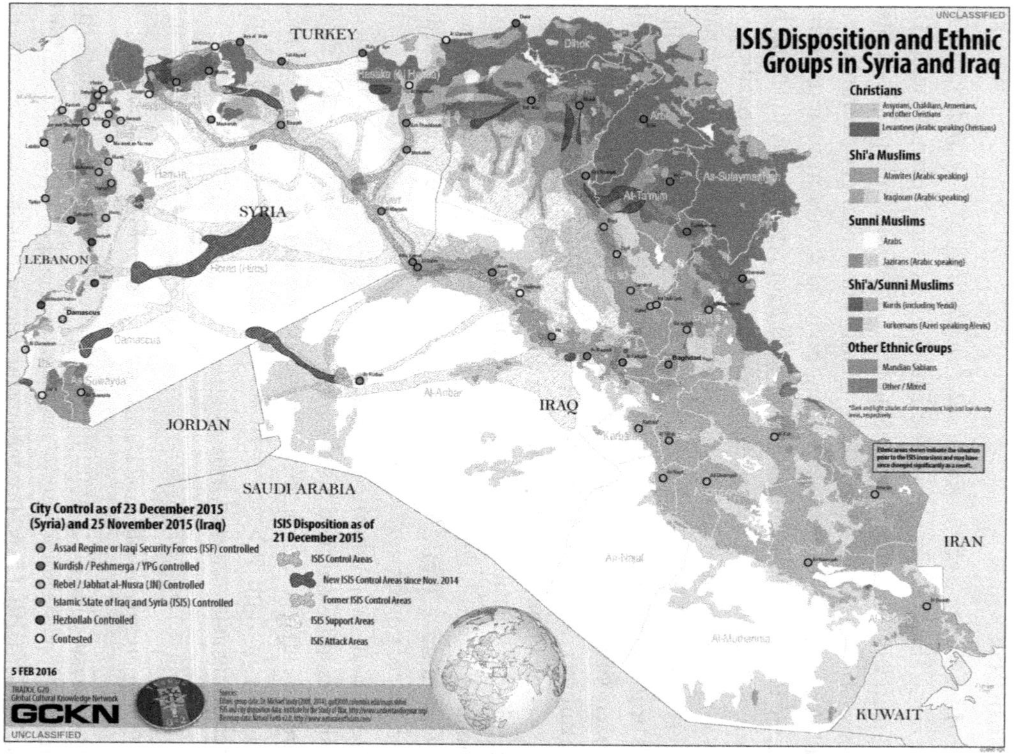

Source: US Army Maps, 2016, https://publicintelligence.net/us-army-ethnic-groups-isis

Sequential IDP and refugee flows increased with in 2013, as the Syrian conflict intensified and the impending ISIS war loomed. Domiz1 exceeded its capacity fourfold in less than a year (UNHCR Iraq, 2013). The urgent need for housing spiked rental prices, exhausted national resources, and strained fragile infrastructures (World Bank, 2015). Irregular transit areas with emergency shelters furnished the outskirts of urban cores and former collectives, while their public buildings (schools, mosques) became temporary bedrooms for the Iraqi IDPs. Consequently, the long list of people needing housing and humanitarian aid became difficult to manage. To reduce these pressures, the LHR and its partners relocated many of the displaced to wait in 'transit spaces', while they appropriated, planned, and constructed separate purpose-built camps to be operational soon (DRC, 2013).

Initially, all camps were temporary solutions, allocated with direct access to main roads and highways, ensuring the presence of basic communal services (schools, health units, administration) to facilitate day-to-day humanitarian operations and needs. These spatial interventions also spurred regional institutional and infrastructural upgrades in the broader KR-I, covering highways and roads, centralized sanitation and electricity, and more area-specific skill upgrading programmes serving both towns and camps.

Nevertheless, 'temporariness', space-time frames, spatial articulation, and geographical fixity varied based on occupational categories, translated into transit, temporary, and permanent camps (Figure 7.9). Decades of mistrust, geopolitical shifts, and former refuge-granting traditional practices have spatially influenced power disputes between the KRG and CGoI over territorial authority and, consequently, rights within their borders. Categorization of brothers and (un)desirable guests in the KR-I was influenced by ethnicity, origin, conflicting interests, fear of Arabization, and ISIS infiltration. Essentially, transit camps temporarily served as interim holding areas before transferring displaced groups to other camps.

For IDP camps primarily hosting Arab displacees, it appears that the KRG implemented its 2006 idea of using transit camps as a defence mechanism. IDP camps are (re)located in disputed areas under KRG's control and/or outside federal borders. The transit nature is materially present in using basic tents/caravans and communal facilities, directly laid on the soil, with minimal (if any) infrastructure. The CGoI has been pushing to decommission these camps, despite the uninhabitability of former areas of residence. The number of operational camps numbers decreased from 43 in 2016 to 25 by 2022 (OCHA, 2022). Conversely, operational humanitarian camps hosting desirable brothers and guests of Syrian refugees and Yazidi IDPs (included in population count as Kurds) are located within KR-I official borders (Figure 7.10). These camps are mostly juxtaposed and/or annexed to 1970s and 1980s former collective towns, resulting in a broader humanitarian intervention that extended from camps to host communities.

Figure 7.9: Ashti IDP Camp

Source: Author, 2018

Figure 7.10: Kawergosk Refugee Camp, KR-I

Source: Author, 2018

Nonetheless, desirable camps also differed materially. For refugee camps, on the one hand, temporariness is glossed with more-permanent materialization, ranging from brick-walled shelter typologies to individualized facilities, evolving infrastructures, and developed public and communal services. These camps are being handed over to the KRG, which now is bridging spatial gaps with host communities through the creation of communal services shared with hosting populations (UNHCR Iraq, 2022).

For Yazidi IDP camps, on the other hand, a temporary, yet welcoming nature is materially present: using basic caravans, enhanced communal facilities, and basic infrastructure. Maintaining their temporary aspect seems to be a strategy to ensure these groups return to their areas of origin outside KR-I's federal borders. This strategy reflects former traditions of expanding power spheres and wielding the KRG's presence through expansion of networks of clientelism outside its official borders.

Conclusion

The chapter has contributed to existing scholarship on displacement urbanism by seeking to illustrate how displacement has been an integral of the Kurds' collective memory, legitimate presence, and inhabitation modalities (Figure 7.11). It introduced 'territorial biographies' as a methodological approach to storytelling that encapsulates 'being' and 'presence' as spatial phenomena. This biographical account focusing on the KR-I's territory's history of urbicidal and genocidal practices, violence cycles, displacement continuums, and humanitarian interventions has created a landscape where exhaustion is not just a temporary condition but a defining feature of spatial and social relations.

By chronologically tracing the settlement allocation for the forcibly displaced, the chapter delved into the geopolitical complexities of the Kurdish region amidst periodic clashes and conflicts over resources and borders to (re)assert a legitimized presence. It highlighted how map lines, drawn, changed, and sustained through violence, reflect the contested Kurdish claims to land and territorial presence, which remain in flux and lack political recognition.

The palimpsest of displacement in the KRI, where each layer of forced movement adds to the region's exhaustion, illustrates the temporal dimension of acute and protracted violence. From the pre-World War I era to the present, the Kurdish people have faced relentless cycles of acute urbicidal and genocidal practices, evictions, forced relocations, and resettlements. This ongoing process resembles the slow, structural violence that Nixon (2011) describes, aligning with Otsuki's (2024) observation that infrastructural violence can unfold over time. Furthermore, humanitarian interventions, much like those described in Chapter 1's examples from Paris and the Franco-Italian border, have created 'infrastructures of holding' that, while offering

Figure 7.11: 1975–2022 documented forced displacement receiving sites in the Kurdistan region of Iraq

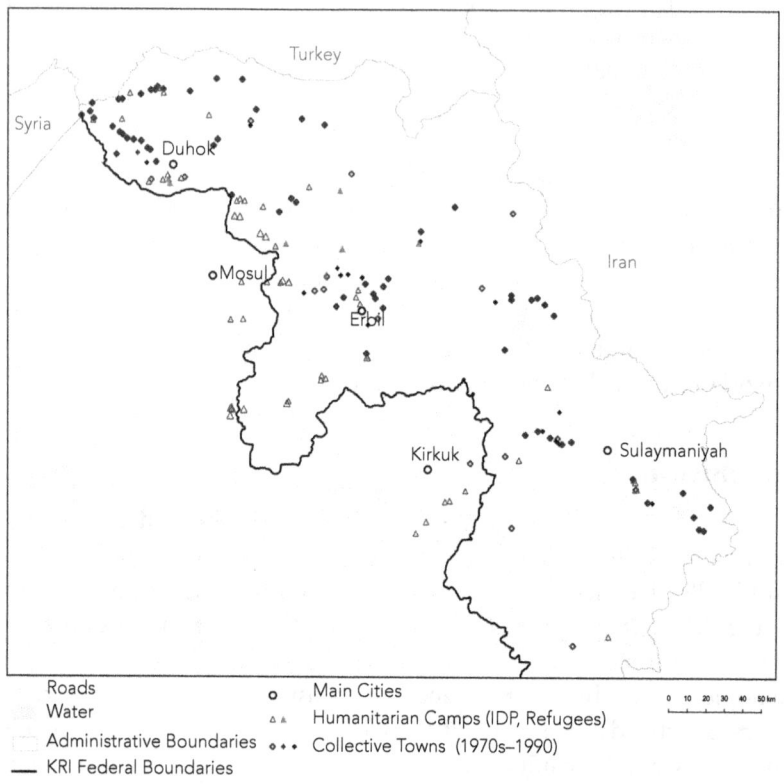

Source: Author, 2022

temporary respite, also perpetuate cycles of displacement and exhaustion. The chapter's analysis of how these spaces of oppression and refuge have evolved and subverted over time illustrates the complex interplay between (violent) spatial practices, resilience, and endurance within conditions of extreme precarity, and the (re)production of exhausted territories.

Ultimately, this analysis of the KR-I through the lens of exhaustion contributes to a deeper understanding of displacement urbanism as a global phenomenon, highlighting the need for approaches that recognize the cumulative, erosive effects of repeated displacement while also acknowledging the persistent efforts to 'make life in displacement' despite the ongoing precarity.

Notes

[1] They vary in size and degree of isolation in relation to the function, followers and head of their master: *ribat* (isolated dwelling for meditation and prayer), *zawiya* (small circles'

residences), *khanaqa* (larger dwellings/mosques that act as meeting places), *tekiyahs* (lodges) to host the disciples, and *madrasah* (teaching institution).
2   They were not necessarily from a notable bloodline; nevertheless, they gained status recognition by marrying into a tribe's notable families.
3   Sheikhs gained additional access to resources of the *waqf* (endowment treasury) at their disposal, further feeding their power.
4   As long as Baghdad retained control over oil-rich zones based on the population census.

References

Abujidi, N. (2014) *Urbicide in Palestine: Spaces of Oppression and Resilience*, Routledge.

Anjum, T. (2006) 'Sufism in history and its relationship with power', *Islamic Studies*, 45(2): 221–268.

Arendt, H. (1958) *The Human Condition*, 2nd ed, University of Chicago Press.

Bozarslan, H. (2019) 'An overview of Kurdistan of the 19th century', in M.M. Gunter (ed), *Routledge Handbook on the Kurds*, Routledge, pp 48–61.

Brown, R.J. (1995) *Humanitarian Operations in Northern Iraq, 1991 with Marines in Operation Provide Comfort*, US Marine Corps.

Corboz, A. (1983) 'The land as palimpsest', *Diogenes*, 31(121): 12–34.

Coward, M. (2008) *Urbicide: The Politics of Urban Destruction*, Routledge.

Doxiadis Associates, DBoGI (1963) 'Five year basic foundations programme: IRAQ Housing – Development Board of the Government of Iraq (DBoGI)', *Ekistics*, 16(94): 157–8.

DRC (2013) 'Iraqi Kurdistan opens new camps for Syrian refugees', media release. Available from: https://reliefweb.int/report/iraq/iraqi-kurdistan-opens-new-camps-syrian-refugees [Accessed 2 June 2024].

Fares, O. (2016) 'The Arab Spring comes to Syria: Internal Mobilisation for Democratic Change, Militarisation and Internationalisation', in L. Sadiki (ed), *Routledge Handbook of the Arab Spring: Rethinking Democratisation*, Routledge, pp 183–97.

Farouk-Sluglett, M., Sluglett, P., and Stork, J. (1984) 'Not quite Armageddon: Impact of the war on Iraq', *MERIP Reports*, 125/126: 22–37.

Genat, M. (2017) 'From agrarian experiments to population displacement: Iraqi Kurdish collective towns in the context of socialist villagisation in the 1970s', in A. Fischer-Tahir and S. Wagenhofer (eds), *Disciplinary Spaces: Spatial Control, Forced Assimilation and Narratives of Progress Since the 19th Century*, Transcript Verlag, pp 137–64.

Gregotti, V. (2009) 'The form of the territory: on Territories', *OASE*, 80: 7–22.

Human Rights Watch (2004) 'Claims in conflict: reversing ethnic cleansing in Northern Iraq'. Available from: www.hrw.org/report/2004/08/02/claims-conflict/reversing-ethnic-cleansing-northern-iraq [Accessed 5 December 2020].

Human Rights Watch and Black, G. (1993) *Genocide in Iraq: The Anfal Campaign Against the Kurds*, Human Rights Watch.

Izady, M. (2015) *Kurds: A Concise Handbook*, Routledge.

Jackson, M. (2013) *The Politics of Storytelling: Variations on a Theme by Hannah Arendt*, 2nd ed, Museum Musculanum Press.

Kagan, M. (2011) '"We live in a country of UNHCR": The UN surrogate state and refugee policy in the Middle East'. Available from: www.unhcr.org/research/working/4d5a8cde9/live-country-unhcr-un-surrogate-state-refugee-policy-middle-east-michael.html [Accessed 5 December 2020].

King, D.E. (2014) *Kurdistan on the Global Stage: Kinship, Land, and Community in Iraq*, Rutgers University Press.

Leezenberg, M. (2000) 'Humanitarian Aid in Iraqi Kurdistan', *CEMOTI, Cahiers d'Études sur la Méditerranée Orientale et le monde Turco-Iranien*, 31–49. Available from: www.persee.fr/doc/cemot_0764-9878_2000_num_29_1_1517 [Accessed 5 December 2020].

Leezenberg, M. (2004) 'The Anfal operations in Iraqi Kurdistan', in S. Totten, W.S. Parsons and I.W. Charny (eds), *Century of Genocide: Critical Essays and Eyewitness Accounts*, Routledge, pp 395–419.

Leezenberg, M. (2017) 'Iraqi Kurdistan: a porous political space', *Anatoli*, 8(8): 107–31.

Lloyd, H.I. (1926) 'The geography of the Mosul boundary', *The Geographical Journal*, 68(2): 104–13.

Loescher, G. (2021) *Refugees: A Very Short Introduction*, Oxford University Press.

Mahzouni, A. (2013) 'The missing link between urban and rural development: lessons from Iraqi Kurdistan region', in A. Fischer-Tahir and M. Naumann (eds), *Peripheralisation*. Springer Fachmedien Wiesbaden, pp 121–44.

Mann, M. (1984) 'The autonomous power of the state: its origins, mechanisms and results', *European Journal of Sociology*, 25(2): 185–213.

Mann, M. (2008) 'Infrastructural power revisited', *Studies in Comparative International Development*, 43(3–4): 355–65.

McDowall, D. (2020) *A Modern History of the Kurds*, 4th ed., I.B. Tauris.

Mlodoch, K. (2017) 'Appropriating and transforming a space of violence and destruction into one of social reconstruction: survivors of the Anfal campaign (1988) in the collective towns of Kurdistan', in A. Fischerp-Tahir and S. Wagenhofer (eds), *Disciplinary Spaces: Spatial Control: Forced Assimilation and Narratives of Progress since the 19th Century*, Transcript Verlag, pp 263–86.

Natali, D. (2010) *The Kurdish Quasi-State: Development and Dependency in Post-Gulf War Iraq*, Syracuse University Press.

Nixon, R. (2011) *Slow Violence and the Environmentalism of the Poor*, Harvard University Press.

O'Shea, M.T. (2004) *Trapped Between the Map and Reality: Geography and Perceptions of Kurdistan*, Routledge.

OCHA (2022) *Humanitarian Response Plan Iraq*. Available from: www.unocha.org/publications/report/iraq/iraq-humanitarian-response-plan-2022-march-2022 [Accessed 2 August 2025].

Otsuki, K. (2024) 'Infrastructural violence and its temporalities', in O. Coutard and D. Florentin (eds), *Handbook of Infrastructures and Cities*, Edward Elgar, pp 240–54.

Owtram, F. (2019) 'The state we're in: postcolonial sequestration and the Kurdish quest for independence since the First World War', in M.M. Gunter (ed), *Routledge Handbook on the Kurds*, Routledge, pp 299–318.

Pyla, P. (2006) 'Rebuilding Iraq 1955–58: modernist housing, national aspirations, and global ambitions', International Working-Party for Documentation & Conservation of Buildings, Sites & Neighbourhoods of the Modern Movement (Docomomo).

Recchia, F. (2014) 'Devices for political actions: the collective towns in Iraqi Kurdistan. Available from: https://architexturez.net/doc/az-cf-123984 [Accessed 2 June 2024].

RUDAW (2019) '"This is your home": PM Barzani to northeast Syria refugees after camp visit', *Rudaw*, 11 November. Available from: www.rudaw.net/english/kurdistan/09112019 [Accessed 2 June 2024].

Shoukri, A.M. (2010) *Refugee Status in Islam: Concepts of Protection in Islamic Tradition and International Law*, Bloomsbury.

Scott, J.C. (1998) *Seeing Like a State: How Certain Schemes to Improve the Human Condition Have Failed*, Yale University Press.

Stansfield, G.R.V. (2001) 'Iraqi Kurdistan: An analysis and assessment of the development and operation of the political system', doctoral thesis, Durham University. Available from: http://etheses.dur.ac.uk/1205 [Accessed 2 August 2025].

Stansfield, G.R.V. (2003) *Iraqi Kurdistan: Political Development and Emergent Democracy*, Routledge.

Talabany, N. (1999) 'Iraq's policy of ethnic cleansing: onslaught to change national/demographic characteristics of the Kirkuk region. Available from: www.kurdipedia.org/files/books/2013/87924.PDF?ver=130286343280814632 [Accessed 2 August 2025].

Tejel, J. (2009) *Syria's Kurds: History, Politics and Society*, Routledge.

UN Habitat (2001) *Settlement and Household Survey Report*. Available from: https://mirror.unhabitat.org/list.asp?typeid=3&catid=203 [Accessed 2 August 2025].

UNHCR (2007) *UNHCR's Eligibility Guidelines for Assessing the International Protection Needs of Iraqi Asylum-Seekers*. Available from: www.refworld.org/policy/countrypos/unhcr/2007/en/91922 [Accessed 2 August 2025].

UNHCR Iraq (2012) *UNHCR Iraq Syria Situation Update Number: 11*. Available from: https://reliefweb.int/report/iraq/unhcr-iraq-syria-situation-update-number-11 [Accessed 2 August 2025].

UNHCR Iraq (2013) *Syria Situation Bi-Weekly Update No. 43 15–28 May*. Available from: https://peace-winds.org/en/wp-content/uploads/2013/07/UNHCRIraq- SyriaBiMonthlyUpdate15-28May13.pdf [Accessed 2 August 2025].

UNHCR Iraq (2022) *Area-Based Programming for Protection and Solutions (A2PS)*. Available from: https://reliefweb.int/report/iraq/area-based-programming-protection-and-solutions-a2ps[Accessed 2 August 2025].

UNSC (1991) *Security Council Resolution 688 (1991) [Iraq], 5 April 1991, S/RES/688*. Available from: www.refworld.org/docid/3b00f1598.html [Accessed 2 August 2025].

van Bruinessen, M. (1992) *Agha, Shaikh and State: The Social and Political Structures of Kurdistan*, Bloomsbury.

van Bruinessen, M. (2011) *Mullas, Sufis, and Heretics: The Role of Religion in Kurdish Society: Collected Articles*, Gorgias Press.

World Bank (2015) *The Kurdistan Region of Iraq: Assessing the Economic and Social Impact of the Syrian Conflict and ISIS*, World Bank.

Yildiz, K. (2004) *The Kurds in Iraq: The Past, Present and Future*, Pluto Press.

Younès, K. (2007) *The World's Fastest Growing Refugee Crisis*. Available from: www.refworld.org/pdfid/47a6ebaf0.pdf [Accessed 2 August 2025].

Zibar, L. (2023) Forced Displacement Urbanisms: Territorial Biographies and Contemporary Narratives in the Syrian Refugee Camps in the Kurdistan Region of Iraq. PhD thesis, KU Leuven.

8

Beyond Shelter: Makeshift Inhabitation in Displacement in Greater Paris

Stefano Mastromarino

Introduction

Over the past ten years, France has become one of the largest EU nations hosting people seeking asylum, with an average of 109,700 applications annually from 2015 to 2019. Data from the French Office for the Protection of Refugees and Stateless Persons (OFPRA) revealed that of 121,554 applicants in 2021, only 21,340 were granted refugee status, resulting in a rejection rate of 72.3 per cent (OFPRA, 2022). Nevertheless, France's Home Office reported that only 16,819 so-called 'irregular immigrants' left the national territory in 2021 (Ministère de l'Intérieur, 2022), indicating a significant number of people who lacked access to essential living facilities and accommodation, yet needed places to inhabit throughout the country. In response, various institutions, NGOs, associations, and collectives have set up different infrastructures to provide aid and shelter to people on the move. Assisting in the urban context has become increasingly challenging for both humanitarian organizations and the government, resulting in individuals on the move settling in informal accommodation, squats, and makeshift camps, or simply occupying public spaces. These camp-like settings are primarily makeshift, made up of people in transit to the United Kingdom or those intending to seek asylum in France. Greater Paris has been particularly critical in this regard, as settlements and subsequent evictions at multiple camps have occurred regularly throughout the year. The lack of government aid has led to a substantial increase in various forms of resistance from independent associations and collectives, which offer private forms of shelter, outreach, and daily material distributions.

Urban areas have appeared as references to study these ongoing processes of managing people seeking asylum and people on the move as a spatial dispositif to 'stop, make stranded populations in their attempt to cross borders', but also to keep 'them on the move and forced to remain in motion across convoluted geographies' (De Genova et al, 2022: 817). At the same time, such means of imperfect inhabitation on the move have testified to the power of the invisible and oppressed, the strategies elaborated by refugees and people on the move to imagine and inhabit the uninhabitable (Simone, 2016). This chapter is grounded in a series of empirical, participatory observations focusing on the ambivalent relations between control (Aradau and Tazzioli, 2020; Tazzioli, 2020) and care (Coutant, 2018; Agier and Le Courant, 2022; Ramakrishnan and Thieme, 2022), drawing through the notion of the makeshift (Minca, 2015; Minca and Collins, 2021) and articulating what previously referred to as the architectural embodiment of some form of hold[1] (Mastromarino and Boano, 2023a). Here, practices of rejection and reception enact inevitable and ambivalent dispositifs of control and care on a phenomenon distinguished by its constant displacement and opacification. It represents the state and architectonics of capture of the less-than-human beings (Sharpe, 2016) but also institutional forms of 'hostipitality' (Derrida, 2000) on edge. Containment, dispossession, and protracted displacement are consequently coexisting with the production of dynamics of collective resistance and solidarity. These legacies necessarily generate a series of ambiguous, ambivalent spaces in urban environments – spaces marked by the concurrent embodiment of mobility and immobility, the visible and the opaque, support and hostility; spaces between the camp and the city. Drawing from the work of Simone (2016), Sharpe (2016), Boano and Astolfo (2020), and Rendell (2022), these spaces are termed 'spaces of holding' in order to figure out the ambivalent gesture represented by acts of solidarity and control.

The chapter presents very peculiar yet contiguous scenarios in which people's displaced presence in the territory forges new categories of urbanity, in its architectural, social, and political connotations. The Greater Paris area and its varied representation of assistance and abandonment across borders and urban interstices provide an interesting sequence of the infrastructure of holding. However, the intention is not to provide an exhaustive spatialization of the phenomena of migration in the country or to comment on the sociopolitical implication of displacement; rather, it is to show, through a patchwork of different focalized observations and methodologies, new patterns of space production generated by violence, pushbacks, and evictions on one hand, and resistance, vulnerability, and transit on the other. It aims to unveil models of support emerging from informal networks that assist people on the move to challenge dominant paradigms by blurring boundaries through acts of solidarity.

Porte de la Chapelle, Delphine Seyrig, and Soixante AdaDa are shelters and makeshift refuges built, managed, or supported by this peripheral humanitarianism (Ramakrishnan and Thieme, 2022). These different modes of inhabitation in the archipelago of underdetermined and temporary dwellings allow us to draw attention to the limits and potentials of practices that alternate between emergency and endurance. In other words, such spaces recount the different conformations that spaces of displacement take in both their materiality and the collective imagination. In this respect, this brief catalogue of spaces of displacement in Paris made it possible to study displacement urbanism not in its exceptional characters, but through different axialities central to the ongoing reproduction of urban dynamics extremely characterized by displacement's mobility and opacity: they provide a framework for looking at such spaces through practices, fears, and necessities generated by the act of displacing itself.

The observations included in this chapter emerge from a year's research between Greater Paris and the French–Italian border as part of an MSc Architecture and Urban Planning dissertation at Politecnico di Torino, Italy and the École Nationale Superieure d'Architecture (ENSA) de Paris Belleville (Mastromarino, 2022). The research was accomplished through collaboration with various local collectives and associations supporting people on the move in the two territories. Ultimately, the findings and outcomes of the study culminated in a series of peer-reviewed papers (Mastromarino and Boano, 2023a, 2023b, 2024) and collaboration with the IPRAUS Lab at ENSA Paris Belleville. At the time of writing, the research has taken the form of a PhD at the Development Planning Unit, UCL, investigating the relationship between migrants' shelters and migrants' politics of movement in both humanitarian praxis and urban theory. The information included in this chapter will only refer to the observations of the Parisian case. Exploring three makeshift inhabitations in the Great Parisian area, this chapter aims to provide a non-exhaustive spatialization of the different temporary spaces and axialities of resistance generated by displacement in urban environments. Thus, looking at the different ecologies that situations of displacement produce in the urban sphere allows us to raise questions about the interdependency between the capital and dominant relations that are the basis of the contemporary spatial production and the establishment of makeshift resistances and necessities to subvert the uninhabitability of certain spaces of the city.

The chapter begins by summarizing the main theoretical and methodological references for the research, specifying the methods and engagement with the sites analysed. Therefore, a brief explanation of the territory of Greater Paris introduces Porte de la Chapelle, Delphine Seyrig, and Soixante AdaDa, three 'spaces of holding' on the northeastern periphery of Paris. Here, some forms of makeshift inhabitation and resistance emerge or are provided; thus, they serve to epitomize the questions raised in the research and develop the arguments. The chapter concludes by analysing the three fields as border topologies where migrants' differential governmentality is performed yet lifelines beyond the shelter and the institutional refuge proliferate, creating some form of inhabitation 'on hold'.

A makeshift urbanism

Over the past decades, a growing number of scholars reflected on the development of camps and the analysis of their architecture of confinement (Sanyal, 2012). The camp has been a main topic of discussion in different forms, from its biopolitical dimension (Arendt, 1951; Agamben, 1998) to the formation of zones of violence and detention (Minca, 2005; Katz et al, 2018) and its precarious temporality as constantly at the limit of evictions and reconstruction (Sanyal, 2011; Martin et al, 2020). Based on that, migrants' camps and other spaces of migrants' carcerality have begun to be looked at as city-like (Malkki, 2002), as a scenography of complex social management, economic activities, and humanitarian assistance. In other words, camps have been included as forms of urbanity increasingly becoming cities themselves (Agier, 2002). Various scholars have studied these processes in a variety of camps worldwide, showing the proliferation of different work and commercial activities established among inhabitants of camps, as well as the settlement of institutional or makeshift infrastructures in the camp, such as places of worship, education, health facilities and shops (Sanyal, 2014; Martin, 2015; Jordan and Minca, 2023). Therefore, these discourses combined have brought research to consider camps not merely as spaces of exception, violence, and control, but also as generators of practices of solidarity and resistance, places where new politics articulate (Sanyal, 2014) and where the autonomous power of the oppressed and marginalized become visible. Following this framework, observing the dynamics and spatial logic that characterize makeshift camps helps to shed light on the intricate relationship between displacement and urbanization, from the diasporic identities and localities that emerge. These places reconstruct new identities (Hilal and Petti, 2018) and forms of citizenship within the camp, within the host territory (Sanyal, 2014) and across transnational borders.

Reversing this discourse on the neoliberal twenty-first century European city, French makeshift camps and shelters, as well as their supportive network of solidarity, provide an opportunity to enquire about cities becoming some sort of encampments, in the way displaced people inhabit public spaces and wastelands and the consequent reaction of public hostility and humanitarian assistance. Associating the camp and the city follows the assumption that most refugees and displaced people in Europe are inhabiting urban liminal spaces, at the margin between the legal and the illegal, constantly reshaping functions, forms and accessibility of the spaces they inhabit, including public areas and wastelands. From a broader perspective, makeshift practices and appropriation of public spaces have been emerging in big cities and across international borders in recent years, as new features of the urban, reframing set identities and belongings by informal dynamics of resistance (Altin, 2020; Amigoni et al, 2021; Ramakrishnan and Thieme, 2022; Katz, 2023). Typically, makeshift camps consist of rudimentary tents and fragile shelters constructed from locally available materials, such as cardboard sheets, blankets, sleeping bags, nylon, and timber studs or branches (Martin et al, 2020). Such settlements are usually supported by local charities and associations through recurrent distributions and other forms of assistance, while in cases where these camps expand and persist over time, international humanitarian agencies and municipalities may intervene to supply water tanks, portable toilets and other infrastructures. According to Martin et al (2020), makeshift camps are temporary and ephemeral dwellings made by people 'on the move', which reflect the precarious essence of their condition and need for shelter. In most cases, they are made by people who are stuck in the limbo of ongoing revaluation of their asylum claim or those wishing to continue their route somewhere else, which contributes greatly to their proliferation in big urban centres and across borders. The people who inhabit them are therefore on the move and on the margins: such condition questions the fundamental ambivalence of both the framework of inclusion and hospitality and that of integration and settlement, but constitute an opportunity to rethink the shelter and spaces of reception by embracing the assumption that displacement itself is a new pattern of urbanity.

In 2021, in Greater Paris, this was reflected in Porte de la Chapelle, Delphine Seyrig, Cheval Noir, Soixante AdaDa, La Marseillaise, l'Ambassade des Immigrées, and many more. Engaging with and studying such places was challenging in practice and in terms of ethics. Preliminary observations were carried out through various individual inspections from the very beginning of the settlement of the makeshift camps and squats, and they were consolidated and continuously renegotiated by participant observations and both formal and informal interviews that occurred in concurrence with militant and volunteering activities. The collaboration with the local collective Solidarité Migrants Wilson on the north-eastern periphery of Paris included outreach, food distribution, emotional support, and information-sharing. The weekly involvement contributed to coming into contact with various other associations and spaces of refuge – either autonomously settled, as in the case of Porte de la Chapelle and Delphine Seyrig, or supported by the informal network of squatters and solidarity, as with Soixante AdaDa. However, situating the involvement and research in my conflictual positionalities as a researcher, activist, volunteer, and citizen was challenging as it shaped my perceptions as somehow concurrently 'outsider' and 'insider' in the process. At the same time, the weekly involvement allowed me to gain information about evictions and settlements quickly, strengthening a broadened understanding of the evolvement and implications of the ambivalent practices of support and hostility towards people on the move in Greater Paris. Moreover, it contributed to reconstructing a longitudinal analysis of the territory observed throughout the year. In fact, these camps do not just witness the constant possibility of being suddenly evicted by municipalities and law enforcement; they are also transient by nature, with new people constantly arriving and others leaving (Minca, 2022), as well as new people and associations supporting them. As a consequence, studying these places means incorporating their precariousness and analysing left legacies and memories of post-eviction or voluntary transits.

Greater Paris

The state of emergency and mediatization around migratory arrivals into the European Union from 2015 have commonly depicted this situation as one of 'crisis'. However, not only are the conditions and modes of displacement far from being new and exceptional but so is the inclination to welcome and protect the marginalized and oppressed in the European neoliberal city. In this regard, Greater Paris represents emblematic examples of spatial inequality, where conflictual bodies and spaces have long coexisted due to differential accessibilities and legitimacies driven by aggressive capital forces. The eighteenth-century Haussmanian zoning[2] was already spatially strategical, by overcoming sanitarian and production crises through the recodification of zones and connections between dynamic centres of activity to systematically generate capital (Harvey, 2005). However, while on one hand the city was moved by the intention to recreate a new image of social order under the pressure of progress and innovation in the nineteenth and twentieth centuries, on the other a variety of dynamics of resistance and support towards vulnerable classes proliferated. This conflictual coexistence shows how urban capital forces are equally generative of spatial separations and dynamics of exclusion and central to the reproduction of collective opposition and support, as well as the elaboration of new forms of self-organization and dwelling in spaces and practices of refuge.

Multiple experiences have followed this ambivalence throughout the years, such as the development of La Zone, the area of slums and informal dwellings that occupied the voids left by the deconstruction of the Enceinte de Thiers; the *bidonvilles* of the industrial areas around Nanterre or Saint-Denis, responding to the urge of housing for the labour force;[3] the porous system of squats and shelters; and nowadays, the makeshift camps of people seeking asylum and people on the move of the northeastern arrondissements of the city and in neighbouring municipalities. All these are crucial examples of such simultaneous practices of reception and rejection in the urban development of Paris. They show displacement as a crucial element of the ongoing reconstruction of the city, as a form of self- and collective care against the negligence of institutions and public policies. Drawing from the analyses on the makeshift and the social-historical context presented here, the next section will introduce field observations and findings. As outlined in what follows, Porte de la Chapelle, Delphine Seyrig, and SoiXante AdaDa are three territories manifesting both the very similar dynamics that characterize the establishment of makeshift camps and the different infrastructures that displacements create in the urban sphere, thus blurring the conventional distance between the limits of the camp and the city.

Porte de la Chapelle

Porte de la Chapelle is a neighbourhood situated in the 18th arrondissement of Paris, bordering the department of Seine-Saint-Denis.[4] It is one of the 17 gates enclosing the French capital, along the old Enceinte de Thiers replaced by the current Boulevards Périphérique. The area is connoted by the extensive presence of transports, as the intersection of the rue de la Chapelle, the avenue de la Porte-de-la-Chapelle, and the Boulevard Ney, as well as the A1 highway. Due to its peripheral location, the presence of significant infrastructure, and the historical existence of informal settlements, Porte de la Chapelle holds a distinctive urban and social character in the minds of its residents, closely associated with issues of immigration, clandestine activity, precariousness, and insecurity. The uniqueness that defines its boundaries gives rise to a territory consisting of a variety of transitional spaces with unclear purposes or suspended waiting for development. These indeterminate spaces create a mosaic of areas that challenge the distinction between public and private realms, accessible and inaccessible, visible and opaque. In this context, Porte de la Chapelle emerges as a privileged place for migration and a kind of sanctuary within the urban landscape, offering opaque zones that provide opportunities for settlement and semi-invisible dwellings for bodies in search of a place to reside, dwell, or simply stop for a while.

Since 2015, with the increased number of people transiting through Paris to reach the United Kingdom–France borderland following the gradual dismantling of the Calais camp, makeshift settlements have emerged on the northeastern outskirts of Paris, particularly in the district of La Chapelle (Katz, 2019). The increasing displacement of people from La Chapelle and the surrounding areas has resulted in a persistent push outside the city, into a continuous limbo of undefined reception responsibilities between municipalities, and state and non-state actors. This has transformed the urban border into a densely populated place of refuge, yet one that leaves its inhabitants in a constant state of 'placelessness', confined to the opacity of their living spaces and somehow abandoned. The presence of this vulnerable population has further exacerbated the neighbourhood's connotation as a stage for various precarious lives, including prostitution, trafficking, and other forms of criminality. A renowned example is the high-profile case of the Colline du Crack, a camp occupied by crack dealers and users that has been regularly evacuated and re-established since 2005 in and around the area. Local associations have repeatedly voiced concerns about the coexistence of different forms of precarity, particularly the proximity of institutional refugee and makeshift camps, and drug-related activities. However, institutional efforts have focused primarily on maintaining boundaries between formal residents and inhabitants in the camps, with police balancing constant evacuations and displacements with the need to safeguard public safety and protect urban decorum, while keeping camp inhabitants in a continuous and convulsive state of placelessness and increased exposed vulnerability.

Despite this, Porte de la Chapelle was also home to one of the main reception centres established by the Paris municipality in 2016. The Centre Humanitaire de Porte de la Chapelle – also known as 'the Bubble' for its extravagant architecture – was designed by architect Julien Beller to provide temporary housing for first-time arrivals for five to ten days before relocating them to other reception centres. Its main objective was to curb the situation of people living in the streets and makeshift camps and to provide emergency assistance to people transiting in the city. However, due to limited places to accommodate the large numbers of arrivals in the city and the ambivalent procedures of accommodation through biometric assessment, the centre was indeed largely insufficient, temporary, and exclusionary. It was also largely criticized for promoting a new place of categorization and concentration, an ambiguous dispositif to spectacularize the humanitarian efforts of the city through its distinctive design (Katz, 2022). Moreover, other authors have also argued that there was a lack of municipality engagement with the local associative network of support in the area (Bouagga, 2017), as with the collective Utopia 56 – which, despite an initial commitment, withdrew its participation because of the differential administrative treatment of the people hosted in the camp. Because of the insufficient places in the centre, the differential procedures of reception and the presence of solidarity, cultural and personal networks around the camp, a variety of new dispersed makeshift camps proliferated across its proximity.

More than 7,000 people have been evacuated from makeshift camps in Porte de la Chapelle since 2015 and more than 10,000 in the whole 18th arrondissement, comprising the evacuations of the camps in La Chapelle, Stalingrad, and the Jardins d'Eole. Recent inspections carried out from December 2021 to July 2022, through weekly involvement in food distributions and outreach in the area, revealed a less-dense presence of people on the move and people seeking asylum, with makeshift camps appearing as an archipelago of tents distributed diffusely within and across public infrastructures and parks. Nevertheless, the presence of solidarity actions and a multicultural community willing to provide support maintains Porte de la Chapelle as a fundamental place of care and assistance for refugees, people seeking asylum, and people on the move in the capital, as a place of encounters and solidarity, somewhere to find food, shelter, and a supportive community, despite the violent evacuations and institutional hostility. It remains a frequent destination for unhoused people seeking shelter or temporary refuge before continuing their journey. Such a continuous overlap between the construction of makeshift settlements, evacuations, and convulsive displacement in the area remains an ongoing feature of this Parisian landscape. As a consequence of the intertwining of different precarious situations, stories of differential inclusion, and its very marginalized and opaque infrastructurability, Porte de la Chapelle has indeed become one of the main spaces of displacement in the capital since 2015, where the state of holding people as a concurrent act of control and care is manifested on people's bodies and place legitimacy as an unsolved and ambivalent consequence of the encounter between displacement and urban instability.

Delphine Seyrig

In early October 2021, a small camp comprising around 15 tents began to be established along the Ourcq Canal, in an area called Delphine Seyrig, situated between the 19th arrondissement of Paris and the municipality of Pantin. The makeshift camp appeared to be somewhat haphazardly organized, with tents being set up under the bridges of the Boulevard Périphérique or the Pont du Canal de l'Ourcq. Throughout the different stages of settlement, tents of various sizes, mostly accommodating up to three individuals, were observed. However, the exact number of inhabitants present in the area remained largely unknown.[5] Despite being situated between two municipalities and comprising a series of urban interstices, the Delphine Seyrig area benefits from its proximity to leisure areas and its excellent accessibility to public transport, making it a bustling and lively location. However, proximities and coexistence of displaced and marginalized communities and the vibrant neighbourhood activated by the park and the canal result in ambivalent practices of reception and rejection by residents and public forces. Such ambiguity prompted progressive hostility, police controls, and evacuations, and at the same time acts of resistive support by the involvement of the associative network.

Between October 2021 and January 2022, Delphine Seyrig makeshift camp underwent several stages of settlement. The initial arrivals occurred in early October, with several tents gathering under the Boulevard Périphérique bridge. Yet, settlement conditions remained rather mild, and no evacuation was planned. However, from October to December 2021, the number of tents and people in the makeshift camp grew, with approximately 40 tents between the Boulevard Périphérique bridge, Boulevard Sérurier bridge, and the Pont du Canal de l'Ourcq. On 17 December 2021, at 6 am, police evicted the inhabitants of the camp, relocating the 105 people identified to reception centres within the Ile de France region and neighbouring areas. During this process, an administrative assessment of their situation was carried out, including biometric recognition and provision of medical assistance. The local collective Solidarité Migrants Wilson intervened during the evacuation to ensure it was violence free and that individuals were provided with proper protection. The collective raised concerns about the lack of transparency on the part of authorities regarding accommodation facilities and effective status evaluation methods for people. They claimed that, in most cases, reception was not only extremely temporary but also highly selective, which only accelerated the need for further displacement. In fact, evacuations, identification, and receptions by police authorities pose significant obstacles to the migratory routes of people transiting in France to reach other countries, which contribute to the hesitation to accept accommodation and opt to move somewhere else, to avoid biometric checks and the fear of repatriation or administrative detention.

Following the initial evacuation, the makeshift camp was left vacant for nearly two weeks, returning to its previous function as a canal walkway. In early January 2022, new individuals began to repopulate the area, settling in the sheltered walkways under the bridges and expanding to the Pont de la Mairie in Pantin, and a playground located midway between the two main bridges in the area. The new settlement was visibly larger than the previous one, with a significant number of tents, chairs, electric stoves, and thermal blankets provided by local associations. Despite a general hostility reported by residents in the area during interviews and observations, the increasing size of the camp and the vulnerable conditions of its inhabitants also prompted a great commitment from local citizens and associations. The aforementioned collective Solidarité Migrants Wilson visited the camp at least three times per week to provide support, distribute food and drinks, and share information, masks and blankets. Utopia56 and Les Restos du Cœur were other organizations that not only distributed food and beverages but also supplied tents, blankets, and general assistance. Their frequent presence enabled them to gain a better understanding of the specific needs of the individuals in the camp and to compile continual responsive reports on the situation. However, the camp was subjected to a second evacuation by the police of the prefecture of Seine-Saint-Denis on 26 January. The 180 individuals in the camp – mainly single men and small families from Afghanistan – were again subjected to administrative and health evaluations before being housed in temporary reception centres located throughout the region.

Soixante AdaDa

Soixante AdaDa, situated on 60 rue Gabriel Péri in the city centre of Saint-Denis, is an artistic laboratory that operates with the support of the municipality. Through workshops and exhibitions, the association self-manages a publicly owned space for creative and social experimentation. Beginning in January 2021, the association, in alignment with its strong social vocation and the pressing need to address the 'refugee reception crisis', opened up the space to temporarily house a group of 20 unaccompanied asylum-seeking young people and young refugees in collaboration with Les Midi du Mie, a solidarity collective dedicated to supporting unaccompanied young people seeking asylum and young unhoused people in the Parisian region. The space, comprising two distinct rooms, was equipped with basic installations and could accommodate people for one to two months. While Soixante AdaDa managed the artistic ateliers with hosts, exhibitions, and other public events to raise awareness and get the young people involved in leisure activities with the community, Les Midi du Mie was responsible for addressing their fundamental needs, including food supply, managing sanitary and hygiene necessities, and eventual administrative works. The temporary shelter was housed in the main space of the facility, normally dedicated to artistic practice and exhibitions. This included a small dining room, a kitchenette, a large central table with food supplies and necessities, and a large space where ateliers took place and where the minors stayed overnight with volunteers. On this occasion, several mattresses were provided by the association to young people. The walls and surfaces of the shelter were adorned with artwork created by the young people during their stays, and other cultural and personal decorations such as flags and postcards, to make the space feel more home-like. While Les Midi du Mie oversaw the shelter's organization, it also collaborated with other associations and volunteers to ensure that the hosted people received all essential necessities. To provide water, sanitation, and hygiene facilities, the shelter had a toilet with a sink, but no shower was available. To address this need, a network of neighbouring houses offered their showers weekly, while the association managed a timetable to ensure that every minor had access to a shower with a reasonable frequency. As Soixante AdaDa was a temporary yet recurrent reception, Les Midi du Mie was able to establish connections with local residents in its proximity, who contributed to the wellbeing of the young people hosted, not only in terms of hygienic assistance, but also food supplies and general support.

In addition to managing temporary shelters, Les Midi du Mie is also still actively engaged in food distribution in the Jardins Pali-Kalo in the neighbourhood of Belleville in Paris every weekend. This involvement enables them to continuously monitor the situation of unsheltered young refugees and maintain communication with the support network in the capital, including Utopia56, Solidarité Migrants Wilson, and Emmaus Solidarité. Despite the effectiveness of Soixante AdaDa in providing temporary shelter and fundamental necessities, the volunteers acknowledge the inherent temporariness of such informal shelters and the constant search for new solutions. Like makeshift camps, the shelter was established in response to the lack of adequate and equitable housing access and proper attention by municipalities to young people on the move or seeking refuge. However, not quite differently from the inhabitants of camps, who are subject to police evacuations and harassment, the informal network of shelters copes with the temporary nature of housing young people seeking refuge for a few months, weeks, or even days.

Conclusion

Forced migration across borders and within cities is not an isolated phenomenon, but rather an integral part of broader global policies and planning agendas shaped by the intersecting dynamics of global capitalism. The production of forced migration is therefore equally linked to capitalist urbanization and global/local governance, (de)colonialization and socio-economic inequalities across the globe, contributing to peculiar stories and trajectories of dispossession and displacement that are far from unique, new, or over (Squire, 2020). In this context, what is commonly described as a 'refugee/migration crisis' can instead be argued to be the ongoing effect of intersectional battles impacted by the capitalist order through a series of 'multicrisis' events (Crawley and Sklepafis, 2018): the housing, food, climate, refugee crises that find spatialization in what many have described as a 'crisis of reception' (Hanappe, 2018; Lendaro et al, 2019). Although refugee studies and related disciplines have recognized the urban dimension of forced migration and settlement processes, there is still a lack of understanding in urban studies regarding the material and socio-spatial aspects of forced migration and asylum at the urban level. Research into the interrelation between urban theory and forced migration is still relatively sparse in terms of how displaced individuals contribute to the ongoing reproduction of urban spaces in opposition to contemporary neoliberal policies of gentrification and urban renewal.

Just as refugee camps can be referred as potential cities (Katz et al, 2018), where the urban becomes an analytical framework to interrogate refugeeness and its spatialities (Martin et al, 2020), they also reframe city developments, urban economies, and community-building (Agier, 2002; Sanyal, 2012) in urban environments. Based on this, studying the ambivalent yet close relation between displacement and urbanism does not just crucially shed light on the conditions, logic, and practices of urban developments in their responses to transit migration and arrivals, but also reveals counter-narratives of reception and assistance that are often kept opaque by public institutions. Drawing on encounters between the lack of institutional refuge and the proliferation of solidaristic movements (Della Porta, 2018), the territories analysed in this chapter serve to shed light on the ambivalently welcoming gesture operated by spaces and practices of holding people on the move in cities, as a concurrent and ambiguous act of solidarity and control. Through the spatial ethnography and participant observation of the spaces and rituals of displacement in the Greater Paris area, I have attempted to explain how the temporariness, exclusion, and differential management that shape displacement and solidarity strongly contribute to the production of ambivalent border topologies (Awan, 2016) in the neoliberal European contemporary city.

Thinking through practices of rejection and reception as unique concurrent dynamics, rather than a sequence of dependent actions, permits highlighting the unpredictable and conflictual relation between vulnerability and resistance (Butler et al, 2016). Enhancing this bond, the analysis of spaces of holding as roofs of 'sheltered exclusions' represents an image of the city through patterns of neglected, yet inhabited spaces. The spatialization of the resistive practices to evictions and harassment provides knowledge about what is left of migrants' spaces (Tazzioli, 2020), both in terms of legacies and what has been voluntarily or consequently forgotten. In this regard, the experiences of Porte de la Chapelle, Delphine Seyrig, and Soixante AdaDa have been reported as the material representation of gatherings that establish sedimented practices within the city, with the potential for everlasting reproducibility (Butler, 2015). At the same time, the same places have been identified as the oppressive response of the state's power, in managing differential spatial inclusivity, in opacifying migrants' experiences, and in the ongoing reproduction of a violent and hegemonic infrastructure of waiting (Agier, 2008). Porte de la Chapelle, Delphine Seyrig, and Soixante AdaDa raise questions about the rooted attachments and genealogies generated by displacement in urban spaces by showing the strong relationship between the placeless condition of people seeking asylum, refugees, and people on the move, and the spaces they are forced to inhabit. Infrastructures, opaque liminalities, and undefined wastelands, as well as spaces of displacement's marginality, testify to the very blurred threshold between accessible and legal, private and public, and they are all spatial reflections of the ever-lasting status of holding embodied by displaced persons.

On this basis, such spaces emphasize how different conditions of settlement, assistance, and eviction have shaped the space both in its materiality and its collective imagination. In this context, new urban and architectural conceptions of space production are present, supporting practices of informal managing of the public space. The actions of Solidarité Migrants Wilson, Les Midis du Mies and all the other associations not included in this chapter have the power to respond to necessities, re-establish identities, and delocalize functions into the mentioned spaces of the city through an approach that is exquisitely non-differential, non-colonial, non-extractive, non-singular. These spaces show how displacement defines new patterns of space production in an entrenched transnational urban system, through sociocultural and political processes by which actors forge connections between localities across national frontiers. These dynamics coexist, on the one hand, with the uncertain and opaque marginalization of the displaced people and, on the other, with a system created and regulated by boundaries and geopolitical liminalities.

To conclude, Porte de la Chapelle, Delphine Seyrig and Soixante AdaDa are simultaneously spaces of difference (Di Campli and Bianchetti, 2019) and fragile infrastructures of livability (Boano and Bianchetti, 2022), where bridges, infrastructures, and wastelands are turned from public areas into shelters, in some ways subverting what right to space entitles, deconstructing the monist criteria that classify spaces and practices as legal and illegal, mobile and immobile, accessible and inaccessible, or 'us' and 'them', both in urban environments and collective imaginaries. They show how ambivalent practices of control, care, emergency, and endurance enact such forms of displaced urbanity, reacting to the differential exclusion that public spaces embody in the neoliberal European city. Hence, through different practices of reappropriation of space across borders and wastelands, inhabitants and their network of support are building the public space, subverting its norms and limitations, and reshaping the apparent selective uninhabitability of the city. By reshaping the marginal, these ecologies testify to the power of the invisible and oppressed, the strategies elaborated by refugees and people on the move to 'live with their trouble' (Haraway, 2016). Beyond the assumption that inhabiting on hold is a form of space where protection and care become control, these ambivalent practices of resistance show how interactions between displacement and urbanity generate opportunities to live beyond the shelter and legitimate people's own right to overcome a dictated and controlled life.

Notes

[1] 'Hold' in English means both to take something in the hands and arms, to hold someone in a place so they cannot leave; it also means to maintain, to support, to create spaces of maintenance. In this way, while holding is both associated with care and a place of non-return (Sharpe, 2016), it represents an 'environmentally safe and just space' (Rendell, 2022: 201), yet 'something like care as a way to feel and to feel for and with, a way to tend to the living and the dying' (Sharpe, 2016: 139)

[2] The Haussmanian zoning was an urban renovation programme commissioned by Napoleon III between 1953 and 1870. It involved the demolition of entire neighbourhoods that were

considered overcrowded and unhealthy to build the Parisian homogeneous architecture we know today. The demolitions involved consistent evictions and displacements in the areas considered slums.

3   La Zone is an area of slums and informal dwellings that proliferated around the external periphery of the city from 1871, occupying the voids created by the deconstruction of the Enceinte de Thiers, the last defensive wall to be demolished in the city. The inhabitants of la Zone, named 'zoniers', were workers driven out by the transformations of the city under the Second Empire, as well as peasants and poor populations displaced by the real estate speculation that followed Haussmann (Fijalkow, 1998). The *bidonvilles* of Nanterre and Saint-Denis served to host marginalized communities in the city during the second half of the twentieth century, inhabited by immigrants and internally displaced people who arrived in the capital due to the urge of labour force for the reconstruction or by remnants of the Algerian war.

4   This chapter, drawing from fieldwork in 2022, was written before the developments at Porte de la Chapelle carried out for the 2024 Olympic Games in Paris. The developments led to further displacement and increased control measures in the neighbourhood, as well as a significant mobilization of migrant support networks across the city.

5   According to numbers provided by the prefecture, around 105 were evacuated in December 2021, with more than 200 people in their proximity. However, local associations assisting people on the move in the camp declared that a much higher number of people were sheltering there. In fact, the administration's available quantitative data only account for those who were sheltered following an evacuation, but this information may not be fully representative as it omits those people who purposely chose to avoid – or escape from – institutional aid and recognition.

References

Agamben, G. (1998) *Homo Sacer: Sovereign Power and Bare Life*, Stanford University Press.

Agier, M. (2002) 'Between war and city: towards an urban anthropology of refugee camps', *Ethnography*, 3(3): 317–41.

Agier, M. (2008) *Managing the Undesirables: Refugee Camps and Humanitarian Government*, Polity Press.

Agier, M. and Le Courant, S. (2022) *Babels: enquêtes sur la condition migrante*, Éditions Points.

Altin, R. (2020) 'Silos in Trieste, Italy: a historical shelter for displaced people', in T. Scott-Smith and M.E. Breeze (eds), *Structures of Protection? Rethinking Refugee Shelter*, Berghahn Books, pp 199–209.

Amigoni, L., Aru, S., Bonnin, I., Proglio, G. and Vergnano, C. (2021) *Debordering Europe: Migration and Control Across the Ventimiglia Region*, Palgrave Macmillan.

Aradau, C. and Tazzioli, M. (2020) 'Biopolitics multiple: migration, extraction, subtraction', *Millennium: Journal of International Studies*, 48(2): 198–220.

Arendt, H. (1951) *The Origins of Totalitarianism*, Penguin.

Awan, N. (2016) 'Introduction to border topologies', *GeoHumanities*, 2(2): 279–83.

Boano, C. and Astolfo, G. (2020) 'Inhabitation as more-than-dwelling: notes for a renewed grammar', *International Journal of Housing Policy*, 20(4): 555–77.

Boano, C. and Bianchetti, C. (2022) *Lifelines: Politics, Ethics, and the Affective Economy of Inhabiting*, Jovis Verlag.

Butler, J. (2015) *Notes Toward a Performative Theory of Assembly*, Harvard University Press.

Butler, J., Gambetti, Z. and Sabsay, L. (2016) *Vulnerability in Resistance*, Duke University Press.

Bouagga, Y., Barré, C., Barnier, S. and Babels (2017) *De Lesbos à Calais: comment l'Europe fabrique des camps*, Le Passager clandestin.

Coutant, I. (2018) *Les migrants en bas de chez soi*, Seuil.

Crawley, H. and Skleparis, D. (2018) 'Refugees, migrants, neither, both: categorical fetishism and the politics of bounding in Europe's 'migration crisis', *Journal of Ethnic and Migration Studies*, 44(1): 48–64.

De Genova, N. and Tazzioli, M. (eds) (2022) 'Minor keywords of political theory: migration as a critical standpoint', *Environment and Planning C: Politics and Space*, 40(4): 781–875.

Della Porta, D. (ed) (2018) *Solidarity Mobilisations in the 'Refugee Crisis': Contentious Moves*, Palgrave Macmillan.

Derrida, J. (2000) 'Hostipitality', *Angelaki*, 5(3): 3–18.

Di Campli, A. and Bianchetti, C. (2019) *Abitare la differenza*, Donzelli Editore.

Fijalkow, Y. (1998) *La construction des îlots insalubres, Paris, 1850–1945*, l'Harmattan.

Hanappe, C. (2018) *La ville accueillante – Accueillir à Grande-Synthe: questions théoriques et pratiques sur les exilés*, Editions du PUCA.

Haraway, D. J. (2016) *Staying with the Trouble. Experimental Futures*, Duke University Press.

Harvey, D. (2005) *Paris, Capital of Modernity*, Routledge.

Hilal, S. and Petti, A. (2018) *Permanent Temporariness*, Art and Theory Publishing.

Jordan, J. and Minca, C. (2023) 'Makeshift camp geographies and informal migration corridors', *Progress in Human Geography*, 47(2): 259–79.

Katz, I. (2019) 'En route', in A. Pieris (ed), *Architecture on the Borderline*, Routledge.

Katz, I. (2022) 'Camps by design: architectural spectacles of migrant hostipitality', *Incarceration*, 3(1). https://doi.org/10.1177/2632666322 1084586.

Katz, I. (2023) 'Borderzone departure cities: jumping-off urbanism of irregular migration on the edges of Europe', *Antipode*, 55(5): 1608–33.

Katz, I., Parsloe, T., Poll, Z. and Scafe-Smith, A. (2018) 'The bubble, the airport, and the jungle: Europe's urban migrant camps', in H. Brankamp (ed), *Camps Revisited: Multifaceted Spatialities of a Modern Political Technology*, Rowman & Littlefield, pp 61–82.

Lendaro, A., Rodier, C. and Vertongen, Y.L. (2019) *La crise de l'accueil. Frontières, droits, résistances*, La Découverte.

Malkki, L.H. (2002) 'News from nowhere: mass displacement and globalised "problems of organization"', *Ethnography*, 3(3): 351–60.

Martin, D. (2015) 'From spaces of exception to "campscapes": Palestinian refugee camps and informal settlements in Beirut', *Political Geography*, 44: 9–18.

Martin, D., Minca, C. and Katz, I. (2020) 'Rethinking the camp: on spatial technologies of power and resistance', *Progress in Human Geography*, 44(4): 743–68.

Mastromarino, S. (2022) *Inhabiting Spaces of Holding: Practices of Reception and Rejection in Greater Paris and at the French–Italian border*, MSc thesis, Politecnico di Torino.

Mastromarino, S., Boano, C. (2023a) 'Makeshift borders in Porte de la Chapelle: strategies of imperfect weak inhabitation across Paris's Boulevard Périphérique', *UOU Scientific Journal*, 5: 124–37.

Mastromarino, S. and Boano, C. (2023b) 'Vallée de la Roya and its opaque infrastructures of transit. Inhabiting the border', *field*, 9(1): 47–63.

Mastromarino, S. and Boano, C. (2024) 'Inhabiting through interstitial opacity: protective negotiations of suspended existence across Paris's liminalities', *lo Squaderno*, 67: 35–8.

Minca, C. (2005) 'The return of the camp', *Progress in Human Geography*, 29(4): 405–12.

Minca, C. (2015) 'Counter-camps and other spatialities', *Political Geography*, 49: 90–2.

Minca, C. (2022) 'Makeshift camp methodologies along the Balkan route', *Area*, 54(3): 365–73.

Minca, C. and Collins, J. (2021) 'The game: or, "the making of migration" along the Balkan route', *Political Geography*, 91: 102490.

Ministère de l'Intérieur et des Outre-Mer (2022) *Les principales données de l'immigration en France au 20 janvier 2022*, Ministère de l'Intérieur et des Outre-Mer.

OFPRA (2022) *Rapport d'activité 2021*. Office français de protection des réfugiés et apatrides.

Ramakrishnan, K. and Thieme, T.A. (2022) 'Peripheral humanitarianism: ephemerality, experimentation, and effects of refugee provisioning in Paris', *Environment and Planning D: Society and Space*, 40(5): 763–85.

Rendell, J. (2022) 'Site-writing as holding', *Journal of Architectural Education*, 76(2): 201–10.

Sanyal, R. (2011) 'Squatting in camps: building and insurgency in spaces of refuge', *Urban Studies*, 48(5): 877–90.

Sanyal, R. (2012) 'Refugees and the city: An urban discussion', *Geography Compass*, 6(11): 633–44.

Sanyal, R. (2014) 'Urbanizing refuge: interrogating spaces of displacement', *International Journal of Urban and Regional Research*, 38(2): 558–72.

Sharpe, C.E. (2016) *In the Wake: On Blackness and Being*, Duke University Press.

Simone, A. (2016) 'The uninhabitable?', *Cultural Politics*, 12(2): 135–54.

Squire, V. (2020) *Europe's Migration Crisis: Border Deaths and Human Dignity*, Cambridge University Press.

Tazzioli, M. (2020) *The Making of Migration: The Biopolitics of Mobility at Europe's Borders*, Sage.

PART IV

Extinction

9

Place Wounding and Becoming-Extinction in Baghdad after the 2003 US-led Invasion

Sana Murrani, Dhirgham Alobaydi, and Ula Merie

Introduction

The 2003 US-led invasion of Iraq marked a transformative moment for Baghdad, fundamentally reshaping its urban landscape and societal fabric. Beyond immediate destruction, the invasion set in motion cascading processes of violence, displacement, and environmental degradation, leading to what we describe as a protracted and iterative process of place-wounding. This chapter critically examines these transformations through the lens of extinction, a concept (Dawson, 2016) that underscores the irreversible erasure of spatial, ecological, and socio-political systems. It theorizes place-wounding as a process of *becoming-extinction*. Becoming extinct spatially in the context of Baghdad manifests in both symbolic and material senses as places and people collide with the trauma of war and violence, where processes of becoming-extinction operate across structures and scales of power and difference that emerge from within practices of place-making through an endless desire to seek refuge in the face of forcible acts of displaceability. We argue that spaces of becoming-extinction, while demonstrating rupture and impairment, also provide new spatial possibilities that are constantly open-ended, negotiated, and reimagined.

Rooted in the framework established in a deep-mapping research project across Iraq that examined the creative ways in which Iraqis responded to the trauma and violence of war, destruction, and displacement between 2003 and 2023 (Murrani, 2024), this chapter aligns with the broader thematic objectives of *Displacement Urbanism* with a focus on *extinction*. We argue that Baghdad's post-2003 urban trajectory epitomizes the violent interplay between systemic rupture and the emergent adaptive spatial practices that followed, perpetuated in an endless cycle of being, resisting, negotiating, and becoming – a type of becoming-extinction.

We engage with place-wounding as a process of negotiating and a product of spatiality, similar to Kearney's (2017) characterization of 'cultural wounding'. Place-wounding in this instance is the product of violence and harm inflicted onto place, as they become intertwined with the ecology of the place itself (2017: 1). In the context of Baghdad, place-wounding is entangled with different expressions of spatiality: that of destruction and reconstruction, of complex networks of internal displacement and the seeking of spaces of refuge, and of the creation of new cities that lack the substance of urbanity. Holbraad et al (2019: 1) describe critical rupture following Spinoza's 'dual aspect' of rupture as inherently negative, yet at the same time able to 'act as a positive or dynamic impulse towards escape, redirection, reconstitution and sometimes renewal', allowing a destructive and generative potential to emerge. They affirm that rupture, as a process, negates dominant narratives of modernity – including, for example, notions of resistance (2019: 18). This dual aspect of rupture goes beyond the dialectics of one condition against another, instead engaging with the plurality of difference and all forms of disruption to power.

To critically engage with the layered dynamics shaping Baghdad's trajectory post-2003, this chapter employs a multidimensional framework underpinned by case studies, which is structured around three interconnected axes of displacement urbanism: ruptures of power; palimpsestic spatial wounding; and homing, housing, and more-than-dwelling. This framework offers a lens through which to comprehend how various degrees and scales of 'difference' (Young, 2011) converge to shape the city's present condition and future trajectory through palimpsestic practices. By focusing on these nuances of difference, we underscore the need for a holistic approach to urban recovery – one that seamlessly integrates socio-spatial, geopolitical, and environmental justice as inseparable elements in reimagining Baghdad's wounded landscape and envisioning a just spatial future. Edward Soja (2010) asserts that injustice is manifested within and through geography, hence justice is materially spatial. As with spatial justice, spatial practices are inherently connected to the intertwined trauma of spatial violence embedded in the city, so any approach to urban recovery has to engage with the degrees and layers of injustices inflicted onto and born out of the city.

Przybylinski (2023: 191–2) articulates justice in spatial terms by identifying overlapping connections between concepts of space that are simultaneously 'absolute', 'relative', and 'relational'. He highlights the flexibility of scale and its critical role in 'examining how space is produced'. Przybylinski (2023: 192) emphasizes the importance of considering a 'politics of scale' in constructing our analyses, asserting that 'scale serves both as a measure for bounding analyses and as a concept to explain certain socio-spatial processes'.

Echoing this perspective, we align with feminist philosopher Iris Marion Young (2011), who proposes that justice should transcend the mere equitable distribution of wealth, land, and territory by instead embracing frames of difference that are akin to Przybylinski's 'politics of scale'. Stanley (2009: 1000–4) further elucidates that frames of difference can serve as analytical tools for 'difference-making', which 'takes place not only in space through the relational positioning of objects in space and in relation to already coded spaces, but also draws on spatial tropes, categories, and imaginaries to construct and create difference'. Consequently, difference-making becomes a facet of the 'politics of scale' (Przybylinski, 2023), where scale is pivotal in locating 'justice' (Young, 2011) spatially by embracing difference within various social agencies.

Within the fissures of trauma-ridden geographies, place-making practices are another categorization of difference-making. These practices transform into acts of political activism and an embrace of otherness and 'otherwise' (Caruth, 1995). This necessitates re-theorizing the processes of place-making and remaking within the context of war and violence as acts of making-otherwise. Recognizing that space and social relations are both shaped by and actively shape just and unjust frames of difference enables us to integrate this analytical framework to disrupt processes of *becoming-extinction*. By focusing on the degrees and scales of difference, we can better understand the nuanced ways in which *becoming-extinction* operates, allowing for more effective interventions toward justice, resilience, and recovery in wounded urban landscapes such as that of Baghdad.

The methodology underpinning this chapter adopts a multifaceted, reflexive approach that integrates lived experience with thematic conceptualization of case studies to critically engage with the complexities of the urban transformation in Baghdad over 20 years since the 2003 US-led invasion. Positioned within the ethics of insider research, this approach leverages the authors' roles as citizens, spatial practitioners, and researchers, offering a nuanced perspective on the socio-spatial and ecological challenges faced by the city over two decades. We actively engage with our positionalities and observations through a framework for reflexive qualitative research, providing a unique lens through which to analyse the volatile wounds that have reshaped the city's socio-spatial fabric. Immersed in its landscapes and social networks, we have witnessed the material and symbolic scars of displacement urbanism, from the erection of blast walls to the proliferation of the so-called informal settlements and displacements in camps on the peripheries of spatiality and society.

This insider perspective enables us to engage with reflexive ethnography to observe and document the everyday practices of Baghdadis navigating fractured spaces. Urban case studies serve as tools to ground our methodology, offering situated accounts of Baghdad's spatial encounter with extinction. By focusing on specific sites, such as the Green Zone, Sadr City, and the Basmaya Residential Project, we unpack the rupture interwoven into processes of place-wounding, trauma, and extinction. Through these case studies, we employ a multiscalar approach, analysing how localized phenomena, such as the militarization of streets or the encroachment of informal settlements on green belts, reflect broader socio-political and global environmental dynamics.

To ensure the validity and robustness of our findings, we employed reflexive triangulation (Flick, 2004), corroborating our observations across multiple data sources and analytical lenses. This iterative process facilitates a deeper understanding of the spatial dynamics of place-wounding and extinction as they come into friction with difference-making and place-making practices, while minimizing biases inherent in insider research. The findings presented in this chapter build upon and extend previous research conducted by the authors. Key contributions include Rashid and Alobaydi's (2015) analysis of territorial politics and sectarian violence; Murrani's (2016, 2023, 2024) examination, exploration, and mappings of creative place-making in trauma geographies across different scales of spatiality in Baghdad and across Iraq; Merie's (2021) investigation into the reshaping of national identity through emerging urban forms; and Merie and Murrani's (2024) framing of spatial justice and urban heritage as critical tools for fostering sectarian reconciliation in the city of Baghdad.

Baghdad's fabric of rupture

This axis examines how pre- and post-2003 political strategies institutionalized spatial violence and reinforced socio-spatial inequalities. These political agendas redefined spatial hierarchies within the city, transforming neighbourhoods into exclusionary enclaves and zones of abandonment, planting the seeds for becoming-extinction. The post-2003 US-led invasion alone created ripples of systemic violence and cycles of rupture. These socio-spatial and political forces, as previously explored, highlight a dialectic meaning to rupture (Murrani, 2024). Rupture as both a force of destruction and a catalyst for new – albeit precarious – spatial orders allowed the space for new political agendas to emerge, influencing decisions about reconstruction, resource allocation, and power dynamics within the city. Yet, drawing on the theorization of rupture (Holbraad et al, 2019), the pre- and post-2003 political strategies can be seen as deliberate acts of reconstitution that manifest in the dismantling of one urban order to construct another, rooted in exclusionary and divisive logics.

The 2003 US-led invasion on the ground, followed by the collapse of the Ba'athist regime and the creation of a spatial power vacuum, the implementation of de-Ba'athification policies that created multiple degrees of rupture in the fragile social makeup of the entire country, and the deployment of urban strategies involving walling big parts of the city – which will be the focus of this axis of ruptures – all collectively reconfigured Baghdad's geography and its socio-political relations, embedding patterns of disposability and exclusion into the city's spatial and symbolic geography. Following the fall of Saddam Hussein's regime in April 2003, the occupying forces led by the United States established a Coalition Provisional Authority (CPA), which immediately introduced a walling strategy as a critical component of its security and governance approach in Baghdad. The strategy was designed to control the city, protect the occupying forces, and mitigate escalating violence. However, these ostensibly temporary measures generated far-reaching ruptures and damaging impacts on Baghdad's social, spatial, and political fabric. As the CPA grappled with rising insurgencies and sectarian violence from within nearby neighbourhoods, the rapid deployment of blast walls (Figure 9.1), checkpoints, and other barriers fundamentally reconfigured the city, creating zones of exclusion, fear, and displacement.

Figure 9.1: Blast walls in the centre of Baghdad

Source: Authors

Figure 9.2: Fortified Green Zone and official buildings behind the walls

Source: Authors

The Green Zone became the epicentre of the CPA's authority and the starting point of the walling strategy. Encircled by T-blast walls, the Green Zone (Figure 9.2) is a 3.5 square-mile area in central Baghdad, originally housing government buildings, foreign embassies, and military installations, as well as the main presidential palace, before becoming an isolated enclave for the occupying forces and their allies (Windhauser, 2022). Outside its fortified perimeter lay the Red Zone, an increasingly fragmented and volatile urban space for nearby local Baghdadis. The physical separation between the two zones exemplified the sharp division between those who wielded power and privilege, and the broader Iraqi population left to navigate the consequences of occupation and instability. Walls quickly proliferated across Baghdad, enclosing hospitals, government offices, and entire neighbourhoods. Checkpoints were established at key intersections, restricting movement and creating additional layers of surveillance and control. These walls were justified by the CPA as necessary measures to protect infrastructure and reduce violence; however, their presence deeply exacerbated social and sectarian divisions.

The Ba'athist regime, led by Saddam Hussein for over 40 years, maintained oppressive policies that included a semblance of centralized control over the city's spatial organization. When Baghdad was captured by the occupying forces in 2003, its fall unleashed competing forces vying for power, many of which redefined space through violence, dispossession, and exclusion. As Mona Damluji (2010) explains, the walls not only served as barriers but also as physical manifestations of policies such as de-Ba'athification, which excluded Sunni communities from political power and later inflamed sectarian tensions. They further disrupted the city's physical connectivity and deepened mistrust and hostility between communities (Rashid and Alobaydi, 2015).

Framed as a necessary step toward democratization, another degree of difference-making, de-Ba'athification – the dismantling of the Ba'athist political structure (Pfiffner, 2010) – created further place-wounding in the city. Properties and institutions once controlled by Ba'athist officials were seized and redistributed, often informally, leading to the emergence of unregulated enclaves that reflected the shifting power dynamics. This redistribution not only deepened existing inequalities but also redefined Baghdad's spatial identity (Merie and Murrani, 2024), embedding rupture and exclusion into the city's geography. The systemic marginalization of Sunnis and other groups institutionalized disposability within Baghdad's urban fabric. Mixed ethnic and religious communities that had coexisted for decades were systematically segregated as walls further delineated Shia and Sunni enclaves. This fragmentation contributed to the early waves of internal displacement, with thousands of families forced to abandon their homes in the face of escalating violence and ethnic cleansing.

The walls also profoundly ruptured Baghdad's urban everyday life. Al-Naimi (2020) highlights the contrast between the insulated Green Zone, with its uninterrupted electricity, hospitals, and leisure facilities, and the deteriorating Red Zone, where residents grappled with intermittent power, unmaintained sewage systems, and mounting waste. Pavements became congested with generators, checkpoints delayed commutes, and the once-fluid movements of urban life were replaced by an atmosphere of lawlessness and frustration. These divisions mirrored the broader collapse of social cohesion in Baghdad, turning the walls into enduring symbols of foreign occupation and control. Analysis of the political geographies of walls in conflict zones such as Belfast and Jerusalem shows how these structures create 'place-based sovereignty' by dividing communities and reconfiguring power dynamics (Till et al, 2013). In Baghdad, the walls facilitated acts of violence, protests, and resistance while fostering an environment of placelessness on their edges. Tuan (1979) describes such landscapes as 'landscapes of fear', where the omnipresence of barriers intimidates and alienates residents, amplifying feelings of deeply entrenched rupture of security and political unpredictability while simultaneously symbolizing the broader marginalization of these communities, reinforcing cycles of exclusion and vulnerability. As Eyal Weizman (2017) observes in his work on frontier architecture, such tactics mutate urban environments into instruments of domination, transforming cities into surveilled and contested war zones.

Though many of Baghdad's walls were removed following the tapering of sectarian violence in 2017, their legacy endures in the city's social and spatial structures. Murrani (2016) examines how Iraqis responded to these barriers with adaptive and creative interventions, turning walls into canvases for resistance and coping with their disruptive ever-changing presence. However, the material absence of walls does little to address their lasting impacts. The scars they left on Baghdad's urban fabric – visible in fragmented neighbourhoods and weakened social ties – continue to shape the city's attempts at recovery. The walling strategy exemplifies how temporary security measures can produce enduring consequences of erasure and extinction. Their impermanence masked the long-term harm they inflicted, including the deepening of ethnic and religious fault lines that fractured Iraqi society, leading to full-blown sectarian violence. Ultimately, the walling strategy not only disrupted Baghdad's spatial order, but also redefined its social and political landscape, leaving a legacy of division and fear that persists to this day.

Prior to and during Saddam Hussein's regime, Iraq's political elite and governing structures were led predominantly by Sunni Muslims. This sectarian imbalance reflected a long history of systemic oppression against Shia Muslims; the ruling government sought to suppress its influence and disassociate Iraq from the Shia-dominated Iranian government. These dynamics were deeply embedded in the country's political history and manifested in various forms of marginalization and silencing of Shia communities across the country. The Green Zone served as a powerful symbol of rupturing, deliberately emphasizing the injustice of historic political and religious oppression and exclusion. Its fortification and isolation epitomize how political decision-making sowed the seeds of extinction of Baghdadis' complex yet fragile and once diverse socio-spatial, religious, and political structures, creating a stark divide that is out of sync with time and place between governance and the everyday spatiality across the city. Through this analysis, we argue that such policies operationalized a political urban rupture towards becoming-extinction as both a tool of vertical spatial violence (Graham, 2004) and an outcome of displacement urbanism.

Palimpsestic spatial wounding

If the violence of the walling strategy in Baghdad can be expressed as an imposed 'vertical geopolitics' (Graham, 2004), then the sectarian violence that followed and that engulfed the city between 2003 and 2017 must be viewed as 'spherical violence' (Elden, 2013), defying the Euclidean physical dimensions of geography and geopolitics. Elden (2013) reminds us to visualize power volumetrically in a three-dimensional spherical space that is associated with the geopolitics of territory, border, aerial bombing, urban violence, political exclusion, and social marginalization. Through layers, this axis explores the aftermath of political rupture on the socio-spatial dimensions of compounded trauma and wounding, situated in a spherical volumetric space of violence as experienced through a specific case study situated in the heart of Baghdad: Sadr City.

Originally developed in the 1950s to accommodate Baghdad's growing working-class population, Sadr City was envisioned as a modernist solution to urban overcrowding. However, its marginalization under Saddam Hussein's regime, due to the religious and political allegiances of its neighbourhoods when it was renamed Saddam City (despite being predominantly home to Shia Muslims), marked the beginning of its layered wounding. The inequities of allocation of land within Sadr City led to a sense of heightened deprivation among many similar poor neighbourhoods (Makiya, 1998). People deemed loyal to the powers running the country before the Saddam era were given plots of land that were much larger (around 400–600 m^2) than those in other, predominantly Shia, neighbourhoods such as Sadr City, where large families of seven to ten members were given plots as small as 100 m^2 (Pyla, 2008).

Davis (2007) pulls out the dialectics of violent planning tactics such as the Army Canal highway in Baghdad that divides multiple neighbourhoods to the east of the Tigris River, in criminalizing the urban poor to justify segregating areas within cities. Davis refers to Sadr City as 'one of the world's largest slums – [residents] taunt American occupiers with the promise that their main boulevard is "Vietnam Street"' (Davis, 2007: 205). Sadr City (Figure 9.3) emerged as one of the poorest enclaves situated on the eastern periphery of Baghdad, struggling for years with a lack of sufficient infrastructure, primarily the absence of sanitary water and a working sewage system. The enclave, segregated from the rest of the city by the introduction of the Army Canal highway (a 'corridor of violence'), was rife with unemployment, driving young men to organize a militia group, the Mehdi Army.

Between 2003 and the onset of sectarian violence in 2006, the Mehdi Army retaliated against the US occupation using any means possible, including suicide car bombs, also killing and terrorizing Iraqi civilians. Davis argues that the criminalization of the poor in Sadr City by the West has staged an Orientalist urban warfare between the 'civilized world' in the West versus the 'terrorists' nests of Islamic cities' – the 'Eastern Other' (Davis, 2007: 206). Inside the enclave, unequal distribution of resources led to overcrowding, inadequate infrastructure, and widespread urban displacement, disproportionately affecting vulnerable groups such as

Figure 9.3: Sadr City neighbourhood showing the ad hoc development of properties

Source: Authors

low-income families, women, and children. Many were forced to either leave in pursuit of limited employment or education opportunities or to join the expanding informal settlement sector inside the enclave (Davis, 2007). Under the Ba'athist regime, these populations were stigmatized as disruptive, ignorant, and uneducated, reinforcing cycles of social isolation and rejection. To counter this, Sadrist families formed tight-knit spatial communities, fostering mutual support and resisting sociocultural marginalization. They also encouraged relatives to relocate from other regions, creating cohesive tribal and social networks.

Attempts to address such enclaves, particularly on the outskirts of Sadr City along the eastern side of Canal Army, were often thwarted by the Ba'athist regime. Informant reports frequently led to the cancellation of relocation permissions (Alobaydi et al, 2019). Adding to their plight, a 1957 law restricted property ownership to those born in Baghdad before that year, directly targeting groups who had migrated after that date. Over time, displaced families divided their limited plots further, resulting in overcrowded and inadequate living conditions (Davis, 2007). This escalating pressure on land and resources amplified social unrest, especially under Ba'ath rule. The 2003 invasion brought a dramatic shift in power from Sunni Ba'athists to Shia Sadrists, fundamentally altering Baghdad's socio-political landscape. Sadr City became the largest Shia community and an influential political force, intensifying demographic and mobility shifts across the city. The fall of the regime also triggered the occupation of former Ba'athist properties, which were subdivided and taken over by regime opponents and revolutionaries (Alobaydi, 2017). This unplanned development transformed the city's urban fabric, increasing density and displacement (Rashid and Alobaydi, 2015). Emerging social networks among these groups, often rooted in tribal and clan ties, further reconfigured Baghdad's physical and social structures.

After the 2003 US-led invasion, Sadr City became both a refuge for displaced Shia populations and a symbol of resistance against external occupying military forces. This dual identity transformed the neighbourhood into a contested space, where over the years each new wave of violence inscribed additional layers of trauma onto its urban fabric. In Sadr City, each layer is evident in the militarization of its streets and the fortification of its boundaries, which reinforced its physical and symbolic separation from other parts of Baghdad. These processes of spatial wounding disrupted the neighbourhood's connections to the broader urban fabric, contributing to the broader extinction and trauma of Baghdad's pluralistic identity.

Geotrauma, as Pain (2021) articulates, is the mutual and ongoing clasp of trauma with place. This framework foregrounds the relational nature of trauma to place, emphasizing how the socio-spatial contexts of communities hold, perpetuate, or transform the impacts of violence. Pain (2021: 974) writes that 'the spatial contexts and relations around traumatized people, communities or nations may variously hold trauma in place, contribute to retraumatization, or help to establish freedom and the rebuilding of life after traumatic events'. In this framing, trauma becomes simultaneously timeless – etched into the body – and spatial, as it intersects with the environment and social structures. This is synonymous with the way Kearney (2017) describes 'place, cultural and environmental wounding' as the moment when violence and harm is inflicted on a place, affecting its relationship with its local ecological environment. In Sadr City, geotrauma and place-wounding act as a palimpsest of layers and traces of becoming-extinction, reflecting the cumulative impacts of marginalization, neglect, and violence that are constantly in friction with people and place. These physical and symbolic wounds reveal the palimpsestic nature of the neighbourhood's transformation, where past traumas persist even as new traumas are inscribed.

The concept of the 'palimpsest' offers a powerful framing and methodological tool for understanding such geotrauma and spatial wounding. Kimberly A. Powell (2008: 6) explores how the palimpsest can be instrumental in analysing the ways the built environment encapsulates the social, cultural, and historical narratives of a place, highlighting the intricate relationships between material, visual, and social experiences. The term 'palimpsest' has been adopted across various disciplines within the humanities, arts, and social sciences, extending beyond its original association with ancient manuscripts – a fact that underscores its metaphorical strength and possibilities (Powell, 2008: 7). Sarah Dillon (2007: 4) further delves into the semantic nuances between 'palimpsest', 'palimpsestic', and what she terms 'palimpsestuous'. She explains that 'palimpsestic' refers to the layering process that produces a palimpsest, while 'palimpsestuous' describes the resultant structure and the reemergence of underlying scripts. By employing the concept of the palimpsest as both a framing and methodological approach, we can deeply understand spatial wounding in contexts such as Sadr City emerging as the epitome of palimpsestuous geotrauma and spatial wounding, where layers of trauma and history overlap, revealing the complex interplay of past and present wounds etched into the urban fabric.

Despite the profound wounding inflicted on Sadr City, its residents have demonstrated remarkable resilience, adapting to their circumstances in ways that highlight the dialectical depth of rupture. For example, public spaces in Sadr City, although degraded, continue to serve as vital sites of interaction and solidarity. Informal economies and mutual aid networks provide critical support for residents, demonstrating how spaces of exclusion and wounding can also become sites of agency and survival. These practices reflect the palimpsestuous nature of Sadr City, where layers of trauma and adaptation interact to shape its evolving identity.

These processes are visible in the overlapping scars of sectarian violence and urban marginalization as they collide with community adaptation. The palimpsestic framework enables us to move beyond singular narratives of destruction or resilience, instead recognizing the neighbourhood's dynamic and layered identity in spherical and volumetric strata. Becoming-extinction in Sadr City is not a singular event, but rather a process that unfolds across temporal and spatial scales. It is a slow (Nixon, 2011) version of spherical violence – incremental, iterative, and invisible, only appearing from within the collapse of any familiar structure, be it political, social, or spatial.

However, as emphasized before (Murrani, 2024), extinction within a palimpsestic framework is never total or complete. Traces of past structures persist alongside the scars of violence, shaping how Sadr City's residents navigate their wounded environment. These traces reveal the dialectical nature of extinction, where trauma and resilience coexist within the same spatial and temporal context.

Homing or housing: the antithesis of displacement?

The third axis of analysis addresses the concept of housing as a critical site of socio-spatial justice in Baghdad, exploring how the interlinked notions of homing, refuge-making, and more-than-dwelling reveal the layered dynamics of housing as a tool for urbanism – particularly under ecological collapse and politically motivated planning policies that lack commitment to adequate housing strategies. Baghdad's housing crisis is inextricably linked to the broader socio-political upheavals and ecological degradation that have shaped the city's recent history. Decades of violence, coupled with unregulated urban expansion, have created an acute housing shortage, estimated at over three million units across Iraq (Al-Hafith, et al, 2021). This deficit is exacerbated by the destruction of existing housing stock during bombardment, sectarian violence, and insurgencies, resulting in a significant influx of internally displaced persons (IDPs) estimated at over six million IDPs (IOM in Iraq, 2022). The inadequacies of Baghdad's urban planning and housing policies have left displaced populations with limited options, driving the proliferation of informal settlements, IDP camps, and poorly conceived state-led housing projects.

Moving beyond the traditional view of home as merely a site, notion, or place, Paolo Boccagni (2022: 14) adds the suffix '-ing' to the word 'home' to acknowledge the inherent 'mobility' in its meaning. This expanded concept encompasses 'home as a place', 'home in the making', and 'home as becoming'. As both an analytical category and a practice, 'homing' captures the experience of home as an ongoing, open-ended process that may never result in complete and stable fulfilment, particularly for those with fragmented life and housing trajectories (Boccagni, 2022: 14). The oscillating tension between 'homecoming' and 'becoming home' represents the essence of 'homing' as an 'ontological struggle towards inclusion, recognition, and achievement of the ability to make oneself at home' (2022: 14). Boano and Astolfo (2020: 569) argue that the meaning of dwelling should be re-centred within the 'rubric of *inhabitation*'. They suggest that this shift contributes to the much-needed reorientation of dwelling to include intersecting forms of caring, repairing, and envisioning the future. Inhabitation is presented as a relational practice occurring in marginal and fragile environments, constituted by multiple incremental and transformative acts ultimately aimed at holding and resisting marginalization. In Baghdad, these negotiations occur within a deeply fractured urban landscape, where practices of refuge-making are situated amidst environmental precarity and inadequate state-led responses. In this regard, homing, refuge-making, and more-than-dwelling in Baghdad are always marked by layered trauma and violence, representing a counter-narrative to the systemic failures of formal housing policies and reflecting the broader dynamics of displacement urbanism, wherein populations displaced by violence and socio-political instability forge new ways of living within an increasingly hostile landscape.

The informal settlements that have emerged on the outskirts of Baghdad, known locally as *ashwaiat* (Figure 9.4), reflect the immediacy of the housing crisis. These settlements are characterized by their unplanned nature, occupying the porous boundaries between displacement urbanism and formal housing. They represent attempts by displaced populations to create a sense of home in the absence of state support, embodying the concept of homing as they construct makeshift shelters, often with limited access to basic services such as water, electricity, and sanitation. The informal nature of these settlements means they are constantly at risk of demolition or further displacement, perpetuating cycles of vulnerability, exclusion, and extinction. Built on agricultural land and in green belts, these settlements contribute to the degradation of critical ecosystems, exacerbating the environmental precarity that defines much of Baghdad's urban landscape. This interplay between displacement and environmental degradation mirrors Nixon's (2011) concept of 'slow violence', where the cumulative impacts of incremental environmental damage unfold over time, obscuring their catastrophic consequences.

Figure 9.4: Informal housing (*ashwaiat*) on the outskirts of Baghdad

Source: Authors

A more structured and planned response to the housing crisis comes in the form of modern-day cities that have sprouted on the outskirts of Baghdad. The Basmaya Residential Project, one of Baghdad's flagship post-2003 housing initiatives, stands in stark contrast to the informal settlements. Intended to provide thousands of housing units to alleviate pressure on Baghdad's urban infrastructure, the project has been critiqued for failing to adequately address the socio-economic realities of the displaced populations it was meant to serve. Built on former agricultural land, Basmaya's construction has exacerbated the city's ecological fragility by erasing green belts crucial for mitigating extreme temperatures, water scarcity, and air pollution. This environmental impact is compounded by Basmaya's peripheral location and unaffordability, which have alienated displaced populations, failing to integrate them into Baghdad's socio-spatial fabric. Numerous unfinished housing projects like Basmaya litter the rural and urban landscapes of the city. The majority of these developments are built on former agricultural land that was repurposed after deforestation practices changed the areas from agricultural use to urban development (Figure 9.5). By prioritizing modernist aesthetics and a globalized vision of urban development through acts of environmental extinction, such projects further neglect the localized needs of Baghdad's displaced populations and contribute to the processes of becoming-extinction. The concept of becoming-extinction captures

Figure 9.5: Deliberate acts of deforestation of a former date palm farm

Source: Authors

the hidden yet pervasive nature of urban extinction, wherein displacement, environmental degradation, and socio-political exclusion intersect to erode both the physical and cultural fabric of the city.

While Basmaya symbolizes the planned exclusion inherent in state-led housing initiatives, IDP camps represent the reactive and precarious nature of Iraq's response to displacement. Established as temporary shelters, these camps have evolved into permanent spaces of marginalization, where displaced populations face ongoing socio-environmental vulnerability. After the massacres perpetrated by members of the so-called Islamic State in Iraq and Syria (ISIS) in northern Iraq, 2.5 million Iraqis lost their homes in that region alone and were forcibly displaced into IDP camps in the Kurdish region of Iraq. More than 25 camps were established for IDPs by 2015 (Figure 9.6). The notion of 'refuge-making', as articulated by Murrani (2024), provides a lens through which to understand the microgeographies of displaced populations within these precarious environments. Despite the systemic neglect that characterizes both informal settlements and IDP camps, displaced populations engage in practices of refuge-making that reflect their resilience, embroiled in everyday processes of becoming-extinction. These processes and practices, while constrained by the structural conditions of displaceability and lack of means for return, reveal the potential for new forms of spatiality to emerge from the ruins of violence and environmental collapse.

This micro-scale interconnectedness of housing, environmental degradation, and displacement is further compounded by the global climate emergency, which has intensified Baghdad's ecological vulnerabilities, making Iraq the fifth most vulnerable country on the climate vulnerability

Figure 9.6: One of the 25 camps set up in the Kurdish Region, Kabarto Yazidi IDP camp in Duhok, north of Iraq

Source: Photo courtesy of Shahab Sameer, reproduced with permission

index. Rising temperatures, prolonged droughts, deforestation and increasing water scarcity are just a few contributing factors. Additionally, we must acknowledge foreign companies' intensified operations across the country in oil drilling and gas flaring – such as by BP and Shell – which resumed immediately after the collapse of the regime in 2003 (Kennard, 2023). This continuation of colonial extractivism has further depleted and debilitated a country already on its knees. Nixon's (2011) environmental 'slow violence', enacted in Iraq, was accelerated through environmental destruction due to war, violence, and displacement but continues to play out due to foreign acts of extractivism that embody the degrees of power and difference of injustice discussed by Young (2011). These acts have pushed the country's socio-ecological systems towards collapse, amplifying the challenges facing displaced populations.

Addressing Baghdad's housing crisis requires a paradigm shift that centres the voices and needs of displaced, local, and marginalized communities. Sustainable housing solutions, equitable resource distribution, and the restoration of ecological systems must form the foundation of Baghdad's recovery, ensuring that spaces of refuge transform into spaces of regeneration and inclusion. By recognizing the interconnectedness of the roots of displacement, housing, and environmental justice, Baghdad can begin to envision a future beyond the cycles of exclusion and extinction that have long defined its urban landscape. This future must be rooted in an ethics of care (Till, 2012), where the preservation of ecological systems and the promotion of social resilience are treated as inseparable imperatives in the pursuit of socio-spatial justice.

Returning to the concepts of homing, refuge-making, and more-than-dwelling as frames of difference, we acknowledge that displaced populations are not merely passive victims, but active agents navigating, negotiating, and reshaping their environments. Their practices of homing and more-than-dwelling represent critical forms of resistance and adaptation that challenge the degrees of injustice they face. By embracing these frames of difference, we gain a deeper understanding of how displaced communities strive for inclusion, recognition, and the ability to make themselves at home, even amidst adversity. This perspective underscores the importance of incorporating their voices and experiences into strategies for urban recovery and social justice.

Conclusion: Integrated narrative of becoming-extinction

The protracted shifting geography of Baghdad, shaped by the intertwined processes of rupture, palimpsestic spatial wounding, and homing with housing, reveals a complex iterative tapestry of spatial (in)justice. Through the exploration of these three axes, we have demonstrated how systemic violence, socio-political upheaval, and environmental degradation coalesce to produce a landscape marked by becoming-extinction. Soja's (2010) concept of spatial justice is particularly salient here, emphasizing that justice and injustice are spatially manifested in the organization of space as both a medium and an outcome of social relations and a critical lens for power and difference.

In Baghdad, becoming-extinction has become akin to a rite of passage for individuals navigating trauma geographies daily. The pervasive cycles of violence and displacement have entrenched forms of spatial injustice that manifest in the physical and symbolic erasure of communities and environments. Yet, through the cracks of these injustices inflicted upon them, the creative ingenuity and resilience of Baghdad's residents emerge as practices of homing, refuge-making, and more-than-dwelling, demonstrating how people actively resist and reconfigure spaces of exclusion and marginalization, forging new spatial possibilities that are open-ended, negotiated, and reimagined.

The concepts within the three axes converge to illustrate the dialectical relationship between becoming-extinction and spatial (in)justice. By integrating frames of difference and scales of (in)justice, we underscore the necessity of a holistic approach to urban recovery – one that embraces local and global socio-spatial, geopolitical, and environmental justice as inseparable dimensions for reimagining Baghdad's wounded landscape. As Soja (2010) asserts, achieving spatial justice requires recognizing and addressing the socio-spatial dynamics that produce inequality and marginalization. *Becoming-extinction* in Baghdad is not merely a narrative of loss, but one of persistence and transformation. People's actions exemplify how space and social relations are both shaped by and actively shape just and unjust frames of difference (Young, 2011), enabling the disruption of processes leading to extinction to collide with geographies and materialities of place. In acknowledging the resilience and agency of Baghdad's inhabitants as a palimpsest, we affirm that within spaces of becoming-extinction there exists the potential for new forms of spatiality. These are spaces where inhabitants' creative practices forge paths towards a more just and resilient urban landscape, contesting, negotiating, and imagining alternative trajectories of displacement urbanism that have long defined the city. The interplay of the three axes thus provides a comprehensive understanding of the complexities of Baghdad's urban transformation, emphasizing the critical role of spatial justice in envisioning and actualizing a future beyond cycles of exclusion and extinction.

References

Al-Hafith, O., Satish, B., and Wilde, P. (2021) 'A review of the Iraqi housing sector problems', *ACES: International Conference on Architectural and Civil Engineering 2020*, Cihan University.

Al-Naimi, S. (2020) '"Intensities, part 1: in search of Baghdad". A digital forum for conversations about buildings, spaces, and landscapes', *Platform: Provocative Timely Diverse* (blog). Available from: www.platformspace.net/home/intensities-part-1-in-search-of-baghdad-1 baghdad-1?rq=Baghdad [Accessed 2 August 2025].

Alobaydi, D. (2017) A Study of the Urban Morphological Processes of Baghdad: Implications and Guidelines for Urban Design and Planning in Middle Eastern Cities, PhD thesis, University of Kansas.

Alobaydi, D., Bonnie J.J., and Templin, J. (2019) 'Iraq's tough governance setting: examining the importance of self-sacrifice over institutions to public service motivation', *Journal of Contemporary Iraq & the Arab World*, 13(2): 181–203.

Boano, C. and Astolfo, G. (2020) 'Inhabitation as more-than-dwelling: notes for a renewed grammar', *International Journal of Housing Policy*, 20: 555–77.

Boccagni, P. (2022) 'Homing: a category for research on space appropriation and "home-oriented" mobilities', *Mobilities*, 17(4): 585–601.

Caruth, C. (ed) (1995) *Trauma: Explorations in Memory*, Johns Hopkins University Press.

Damluji, M. (2010) 'Securing democracy in Iraq': Sectarian politics and segregation in Baghdad, 2003–2007', *Traditional Dwellings and Settlements Review*, 21(2): 71–87.

Davis, M. (2007) *Planet of Slums*, Verso.

Dawson, A. (2016) *Extinction: A Radical History*, OR Books Alternative Publishing.

Dillon, S. (2007) *The Palimpsest: Literature, Criticism, Theory*, Continuum.

Elden, S. (2013) 'Secure the volume: vertical geopolitics and the depth of power', *Political Geography*, 34: 5–51.

Flick, U. (2004) 'Triangulation in qualitative research', in U. Flick, E. von Kardorff and I. Steinke (eds), *A Companion to Qualitative Research*, Sage, pp 178–83.

Graham, S. (2004) 'Vertical geopolitics: Baghdad and after', *Antipode*, 36: 12–23.

Holbraad, M., Kapferer, B., and F. Sauma, J. (eds) (2019) *Ruptures: Anthropologies of Discontinuity in Times of Turmoil*, UCL Press.

IOM in Iraq (2022) Data website. Available from: https://iraq.iom.int/iom-iraq [Accessed 2 August 2025].

Kearney, A. (2017) *Violence in Place, Cultural and Environmental Wounding*, Routledge.

Kennard, M. (2023) 'BP extracted Iraqi oil worth £15bn after British invasion', *Declassified UK* (blog). Available from: www.declassifieduk.org/bp-extracted-iraqi-oil-worth-15bn-after-british-invasion [Accessed 2 August 2025].

Makiya, K. (1998) *Republic of Fear: The Politics of Modern Iraq*, University of California Press.

Merie, U. (2021) 'Heritage, architecture and the establishment of national identity', in *The Iraqi Cultural Heritage is a Symbol of Identity and a unified of citizenship Conference Proceedings*.

Merie, U. and Murrani, S. (2024) 'Baghdad behind walls: Mapping urban heritage for spatial justice', *The Middle East Journal*, 77: 306–28.

Murrani, S. (2016) 'Baghdad's thirdspace: between liminality, anti-structures and territorial mappings', *Cultural Dynamics*, 28(2): 189–210.

Murrani, S. (2023) *Mapping the Unseen: Harnessing Indigenous Knowledge Through Participatory Mapping to Address Displacement and Housing Challenges in Post Invasion Iraq*, London School of Economics.

Murrani, S. (2024) *Rupturing Architecture: Spatial Practices of Refuge in Response to War and Violence in Iraq (2003–2023)*, Bloomsbury.

Nixon, R. (2011) *Slow Violence and the Environmentalism of the Poor*, Harvard University Press.

Pai, R. (2021) 'Geotrauma: violence, place and repossession', *Progress in Human Geography* 45(5): 972–89.

Pfiffner, J.P. (2010) 'US blunders in Iraq: De-Baathification and disbanding the army', *Intelligence and National Security*, 25(1): 76–85.

Powell, K.A. (2008) 'Remapping the city: palimpsest, place, and identity in art education research', *Studies in Art Education*, 50: 6–21.

Przybylinski, S. (2023) 'Spatial justice', in J. Ohlsson and S. Przybylinski (eds), *Theorising Justice: A Primer for Social Scientists*, Bristol University Press, pp 191–204.

Pyla, P.I. (2008) 'Baghdad's urban restructuring, 1958: aesthetics and politics of nation building', in S. Isenstadt and K. Rizvi (eds), *Modernism and the Middle East: Architecture and Politics in the Twentieth Century*, University of Washington Press, pp 97–115.

Rashid, M. and Alobaydi, D. (2015) 'Territory, politics of power, and physical spatial networks: The case of Baghdad, Iraq, *Habitat International* 50: 180–94.

Soja, E. (2010) *Seeking Spatial Justice*, University of Minnesota Press.

Stanley, A. (2009) 'Just space or spatial justice? Difference, discourse, and environmental justice', *Local Environment*, 14: 999–1014.

Till, K.E. (2012) 'Wounded cities: memory-work and a place-based ethics of care', *Political Geography*, 31(1): 3–14.

Till, K.E., Sundberg, J., Pullan, W., Psaltis, C., Makriyianni, C., Celal, R.Z., Samani, M.O., and Dowler, L. (2013) 'Interventions in the political geographies of walls', *Political Geography*, 33: 52–62.

Tuan, Y.-F. (1979) *Landscapes of Fear*, Pantheon Books.

Weizman, E. (2017) *Hollow Land: Israel's Architecture of Occupation*, Verso.

Windhauser, B. (2022) 'Walled in, out of sight: the contested urban environment of Baghdad', *Journal of Illicit Economies and Development*, 4(3): 370–81.

Young, I.M. (2011) *Justice and the Politics of Difference*, Princeton University Press.

10

Top-Down Disaster Preparedness and Grassroots Environmental Endurance in 2010s Turkey

Eray Çaylı

Introduction

In May 2012,[1] a law was issued in Turkey dubbed 'the Disaster Law'.[2] Still in force, this law proclaims its objective as disaster-proofing Turkey's building stock. When drafting it, the government developed a media discourse that emphasized a specific type of disaster: earthquakes (Milliyet, 2011).[3] Turkey sits on tectonically active ground and witnessed two major earthquakes in 1999 that shook the country's northwest – its most densely populated region (Güzel, 2016). But such specificity is absent from the Disaster Law. It avoids qualifying what a 'disaster' may entail and prescribes redeveloping not only vulnerable sites but also undeveloped areas that it now terms 'safe for settlement'. Due to these characteristics, the law's purview has reached far beyond vulnerable regions or buildings, making it into an instrument for legitimizing construction activity (a cornerstone of Turkey's neoliberal economic model) and governing populations by rearranging urban space.

Turkey's Disaster Law is therefore contextualizable in relation to recent developments elsewhere in the capitalist world, where disaster risk is normalized as an omnipresent reality to govern societies and boost market economies. Critique has tended to situate such developments within two political paradigms: neoliberalism and coloniality. The neoliberalism paradigm, which has figured prominently in existing debates on Turkey's Disaster Law (e.g. Soytemel, 2017; Erol, 2019; Ergüven, 2020; Ay and Demireş Özkul, 2021), spotlights the speculative-developmentalist and rentierist financialization of risk (i.e. Schuller and Maldonado, 2016; Imperiale and Vanclay, 2021; Long and Rice, 2021). The coloniality paradigm, on the other hand, emphasizes the colonial origins of the categories of risk, rent, and development at work in neoliberalism (i.e. Bonilla, 2020; Rivera, 2022; Sou, 2022). It indicates that policies premised upon these categories have always affected the world's population unevenly along divides such as the (post)colony versus the metropole and the Global South versus the Global North. It is this paradigm on which I dwell in this chapter, while also not entirely abandoning the focus on neoliberalism.

Resonant with the coloniality–neoliberalism nexus is Michel Foucault's take on the postcolonial world order that began to be instituted in the mid- to late-twentieth century. Foucault argued that the postcolonial world order did not so much involve a complete eradication of colonialism as it saw methods of governance used until then in the colony begin to permeate the metropole (Foucault, 2003: 103). Spatially oriented scholars have questioned this argument, especially in terms of its socio-political flatness. Geographer Derek Gregory (2004) and anthropologist Ann Stoler (2016), for example, have decisively problematized the idea that colonialism and postcolonialism have uniform effects across each of the territories identified as a colony or a post-colony and that the posteriority suggested by the prefix 'post' entails a systemically socio-political paradigm shift. Turner (2018) has furthered this critique by questioning the hierarchization that persists in Foucault regarding the colony's lagging behind the metropole. He has questioned this hierarchization for methodologically reproducing Orientalist developmentalism and civilizationism (if in reverse). The Foucauldian framework still sees the colony as a pioneering model for methods that are then employed in the metropole. Moreover, it considers colonization a method that the monolithically imagined geopolitical entity of the Global North applies to the similarly imagined Global South and that only then boomerangs back at the former (Turner, 2018: 766). Turner's alternative to the Foucauldian framework is to focus on 'how seemingly disparate practices of colonial pacification and social civilizational work come together in novel, yet familiar, ways ... that not only draw from experiments in ... counterinsurgency ... but are also buttressed by older histories of social work's "civilizing mission"' (2018: 779).

Still, there is a caveat when focusing on historical continuities, which Turner unpacks via anthropologist Elizabeth Povinelli. Framing contemporary governance in terms of coloniality requires attention to the 'contingencies, shifting remobilizations and logics' at work in what Povinelli terms 'late liberalism', and particularly its 'cultural recognition' strategies (Turner, 2018: 772). These appear to have shifted from the way 'liberal states' throughout much of the twentieth century at best neglected and at worst cemented racism and patriarchy. They purport to break with colonialism's racial and gendered hierarchizations at long last. For Povinelli (2011: 22–7), though, these strategies sustain coloniality insofar as they approach the world through the colonially grounded lens of developmentalism, which compartmentalizes peoples and/or regions into 'developed', 'underdeveloped', and 'undevelopable' ones, deeming the last of these disposable. For Turner, this developmentalism permeates contemporary 'liberal' modes of governance to the effect of what he terms 'internal colonization', which 'draws on [the] orientalist ... demarcation between the civilized and savage' and denies the subjectivity of marginalized social groups (2018: 770–2). Grasping the geographically and historically uneven effects of coloniality, then, need not require hierarchization between discrete instantiations of colonial policy – that is, precedents versus antecedents. Rather, each of these instantiations depends on several others to come into existence in the first place – an interdependence premised on a *civilizationist developmentalism* that stratifies peoples and that runs through policies driven by or premised on coloniality, both past and present.

If there is dynamic interdependence between ongoing instantiations of colonially grounded policy, those disadvantaged by such policies are also part of this dynamicity. Insofar as the process is a continually evolving one, the political effects involved in it are an open question. How, then, might critique consider the civilizationist developmentalism of top-down disaster preparedness policies by working from their situated, embodied impacts on the populations they target? The question is particularly relevant in a world marked by the climate emergency and the pandemic, which have made more palpable than ever the inherently corporeal character of modern-liberal sovereignty (theorized by the likes of Foucault and Agamben as biopolitics). Today, a growing literature debates how this corporeal character might be repurposed for social justice (Anderson et al, 2020; Hannah et al, 2020; Sotiris, 2020) through life-affirming material-spatial practices of 'endurance' that not only survive the present but also build futures otherwise (Boano and Astolfo, 2020: 571). A prevalent tendency within this debate has been to locate endurance in the creativity of lay people who navigate neoliberal biopolitics by exploiting its imperfections or in the ancestral and/or grassroots knowledge through which colonized or anticolonial communities repudiate colonialist biopolitics' claims to scientific universalism and developmentalist standardization (Jon and Reghezza-Zitt, 2020; DeVerteuil et al, 2021; Normann, 2021; Sultana, 2022). How might practices of environmental endurance by communities disadvantaged by top-down disaster preparedness inform this existing debate?

Guided by this question, the chapter will proceed by focusing on two self-built neighbourhoods from opposite ends of Turkey: a racialized working-class neighbourhood in Istanbul; and a neighbourhood on the banks of the Tigris River in Amed/Diyarbakır, the unrecognized capital of Turkey's Kurdistan, where racialization is a region-wide phenomenon. Having already been displaced in the past to arrive in their current abode, both communities are threatened with a new episode of displacement due to the Disaster Law being used for designating their neighbourhoods as disaster risk areas. In conclusion, I argue that the developmentalism of the Disaster Law operates by overriding grassroots developmentalisms that already exist among the communities that it targets. The targeted communities, in turn, hold state-endorsed disaster preparedness answerable to its promises of order, safety and security, often by claiming to fulfil this promise better than the avowedly developmentalist state.

The coloniality of top-down disaster preparedness

As mentioned in the introduction, existing critique of Turkey's Disaster Law problematizes it largely as an instrument of neoliberal governmentality (Soytemel, 2017; Erol, 2019; Ergüven, 2020; Ay and Demireş Özkul, 2021), thus neglecting the law's colonial and racialized workings. These workings have become palpable since April 2016, which was when the government amended the Disaster Law as part of its violent counter-insurgency campaign in Kurdish towns and cities. The campaign was accompanied by localized states of emergency. Turkey's Kurdistan had already had a history of emergency rule: a region-wide state of emergency had been in force between the mid-1980s and the early 2000s, followed by nearly a decade of relative quiet and a semi-official peace process.[4] The process collapsed in 2015, giving way to all-out war once again, but this time with a marked urban-spatial character (Köse, 2017). In this new episode of violent counter-insurgency, the government declared localized emergency rule zones in Kurdish towns and cities that it saw as hotbeds of insurgency. That emergency rule was declared only where insurgents sheltered, suggested the authorities, indicated a wariness of repeating the indiscriminate measures of the past (Radikal, 2015). The fact, though, is that emergency rule has had impacts reaching far beyond the theatres of war, and an amendment that the government introduced to the Disaster Law in April 2016 has been significant in this respect.

The 2016 amendment involved a new clause that defined — effectively for the first time in the letter of the law — what 'disaster' might entail. Disaster risk areas could now be declared in 'places with insufficient planning and infrastructure provision, where public order and security have been disturbed to the extent of interrupting or altogether stopping ordinary life' or in 'areas where at least 65% of the building stock is unlicensed or violated the building code at the point of construction, regardless of any legalization granted retrospectively' (Uzunçarşılı Baysal, 2018). The clause was initially used for designating urban war zones in Turkey's Kurdistan as 'disaster risk areas' but then stretched beyond this martial context. As the fighting subsided, the clause began to be used for designating a handful of racialized neighbourhoods as 'disaster risk areas', although they were not among those subjected to localized states of wartime emergency.

The two neighbourhoods discussed in this chapter are both in this category. To avoid exacerbating the surveillance already unleashed on these neighbourhoods as part of the emergency rule, I pseudonymize them both, as well as the residents whose experiences I discuss. I refer to the neighbourhood in north-western Turkey as Hillgreen (designated a 'disaster risk area' in late 2016), and the neighbourhood in the Kurdish region as Rockwind (designated as such in mid-2017). At the time of writing, both neighbourhoods' designation as disaster risk areas has yet to yield the complete overhaul that is its ultimate objective, as negotiation and appeal processes are ongoing.

Commencing with Rockwind, situated in the city of Amed – also known as Diyarbakır in Turkish – unveils how urban inhabitants of a region long governed by colonially driven policies have experienced top-down disaster preparedness. Amed, the largest predominantly Kurdish city in Turkey, resides at the uppermost stretch of the Tigris Valley, gracing a hilltop that overlooks the river. The city embraces a historic district nestled within ancient city walls, acknowledged and protected by UNESCO. Throughout the twentieth century, Amed underwent profound demographic and physical transformations. At the dawn of the century, it harboured a substantial indigenous non-Muslim population, representing up to a third of the city's total, according to some estimations. However, the Armenian and Assyrian-Syriac genocides of 1915–16 that marked the Ottoman Empire's transition into modern Turkey and the various policies against non-Muslims that followed led to the near-complete disappearance of the city's non-Muslim population by the mid-twentieth century. Colonial borders crafted during World War I cemented Kurdistan's separation into four pieces that are now scattered across the nation-states of Turkey, Iraq, Syria, and Iran, while denying the Kurds themselves a state. In the late twentieth century, Amed experienced a population boom due especially to the state's counter-insurgency campaign against Kurdish guerrillas. The martial component of the campaign largely took place in the countryside, causing rural-to-urban migration, whether indirectly or directly (by way of the forced evacuation of villages that did not consent to recruitment by the state as guards against the guerrilla). Rural communities sought refuge in cities both by moving into historic buildings emptied out as a result of non-Muslim dispossession and by forming self-built neighbourhoods known in Turkish as *gecekondu*. Rockwind is a *gecekondu* neighbourhood that stretches between the banks of the Tigris River and the hilltop that is Amed proper. It hosts more than 1,000 homes, where around 10,000 people live.

The story of K, a resident of Rockwind in his late forties, mirrors the experiences of many in the neighbourhood. Like most residents, his family relocated to Rockwind after being evacuated from their village, part of the wave of 4,000 such evacuations conducted in the 1980s and 1990s during the state of emergency accompanying the army's counter-insurgency campaign in Kurdistan. Their settlement in the neighbourhood coincided with the construction of the first two dams on the Tigris, situated approximately 50 km upstream of central Amed.

By the turn of the millennium, the dams' reservoirs were fully impounded, with ripple effects beginning to appear along the riverbank. The floodplains of Rockwind ceased to be inundated, gradually transforming into solid ground. The impact of the dams extended beyond hydrology, influencing legislation as well. Early stages of dam construction coincided with a significant amendment to the Coast Law, piece of legislation enacted in 1984, which prohibited physical interventions along Turkey's coasts, including major riverbanks such as the Tigris, unless in the public interest.

Throughout the late 1980s, the Coast Law went through repeated amendments to enhance its protectionism – for instance, by expanding what a coast geologically entails and narrowing what qualifies as 'public interest' (Kurt, 2015). However, one amendment stood out as the exception to these protectionist changes. Enacted in August 1990, it bore the title 'The List that Specifies What Part of Our Watercourses are Identified as Rivers'. This amendment redefined the Tigris River's origin to be 100 km downstream from its headwaters, where the first two dams had been constructed. Significantly, central Amed lay midway along this stretch, meaning that the 1990 amendment effectively nullified the Tigris's river status along the city's riverbanks.

As the dams started operating and the floodplains dried up, several Rockwind families seized the opportunity to claim portions of the newly exposed land down the hill and began to cultivate gardens. However, unlike many of his neighbours, K pursued a passion for fishing rather than farming. His interest in fishing intensified in 2016 when the counter-insurgency campaign put out of business the small coffee shop that he had been running at the junction of the neighbourhood and the walls of Amed's historic city centre. He started finding solace with a group of fishing enthusiasts in Amed who had just founded an association dedicated to this activity. The association's name featured the phrase 'the protection of natural life'. The phrase was not mere tokenism, stresses K, but rather an imperative in mid- to late-2010s Tigris. It was an imperative especially for subsistence fishers due to the growing presence of an invasive species called the Prussian carp, which has come to plague the river over the past several years.

Introduced to Turkey in the 1980s by freshwater farmers, the Prussian carp made its way to the upper Tigris in the mid-2000s, reportedly due to a miscalculation by a fish farmer. Finding a perfect habitat in the shallow and narrow river waters caused by the newly constructed dams upstream, the Prussian carp blocked stronger species endemic to the uppermost Tigris from swimming downstream. In the late 2010s, it established itself as the dominant fish in the river. The Prussian carp has harmed subsistence fishing because it is widely considered tasteless and thus nearly impossible to sell, as well as being invasive.

Between 2016 and 2018, when K and his fellow members of the newly founded association prioritized combating the Prussian carp, they initially reached out to the local branch of the Agriculture Ministry, whose remit normally includes aquaculture. Indeed, the ministry's official documentation lists the Prussian carp as 'ecologically detrimental to inland waters' and instructs that this fish should be reported wherever it is spotted. However, there was no coordinated response from the local branch of the ministry to the fishing association's inquiry about the Prussian carp. The authorities admitted to a lack of resources and equipment. Unlike other branches, which possessed watercraft and necessary tools, this branch was ill-equipped to address riparian issues, as this stretch of the Tigris that skirts Amed is officially not designated as a river. Faced with governmental apathy, the association took matters into their own hands, procuring a dinghy and additional equipment to conduct expeditions aimed at capturing and disposing of the Prussian carp in bulk.

For K, the story of the Prussian carp is not unrelated to Rockwind's recent designation as a disaster risk area. The work he and his fellow fishers did on the Prussian carp is a duty that, in his words, 'the state has repeatedly failed and will continue to fail unless the longstanding conditions change'. The failure, moreover, is not simply because of neglect or indifference, but rather because the work the state *does* do undermines the duty it promises to uphold. To quote K. directly:

> If fish species are disappearing that's because the Tigris River is dying. And if the river is dying that's due to the dams. If you look at how much electricity these two dams produce, it's less than 2 per cent of what the country consumes, meaning the extensive damage they cause is not worth it – meaning there is a different objective at work here. The objective is to not let anyone live except one's own, just like what the Prussian carp does.

Top-down disaster preparedness in the 'metropole'

The idea that the work the authorities do undermines their own promises of safety and security also looms large in Hillgreen, the *gecekondu* neighbourhood in Istanbul to which I now turn. Encompassing approximately 150 ha and home to around 35,000 residents, the neighbourhood developed in the late 1980s. Its population increased exponentially following the 1980 junta's introduction of a neoliberal economic model that boosted land speculation, often through the construction of large-scale infrastructures such as the cross-continental bridge now adjacent to the neighbourhood (Gold, 1989). For much of the 1980s, successive administrations from across the political spectrum promised to legalize neighbourhoods such as Hillgreen, where squatter populations often grew by 'leasing' or 'buying' from the land mafia who operated in such parts of Istanbul (Yalçıntan and Erbaş, 2003). By the end of the decade, not only did these promises remain unfulfilled in Hillgreen, but the authorities also began to take an actively hostile attitude towards the residents. In 1989, law enforcement raided the neighbourhood, demolishing 500 homes.

Around this time, revolutionary youths began organizing in the neighbourhood. Denied their traditional political avenues by the 1980 military coup, these youths found a new platform in neighbourhoods such as Hillgreen, where long-marginalized residents were sympathetic to leftist ideology. With these youths on their side, Hillgreen's residents began to invite their relatives and political kin to move here – mostly from Alevi villages in central-eastern and central-northern Anatolia – to take part in the reconstruction effort. However, this effort was met with violence from the land mafia, highlighting the challenges faced by those organizing in the neighbourhood against state and capital interests.

An anti-mafia petition, signed in mid-1990, led to a police raid that lasted nearly 20 hours, where the officers killed a resident and wounded 11 others. Clashes between state-endorsed mafia and revolutionary left-backed residents continued for two years, at which point the police used the pretext of public safety to turn part of the neighbourhood's primary school into a precinct. Six months later, a seven-year-old pupil was run over by an armoured police vehicle in the school's backyard. A lawsuit launched by the residents managed to shut down the makeshift precinct. But a new and still intact one was set up in late 2001 after the police raided the neighbourhood and killed four residents as a follow-up to the state's violent countrywide crackdown on prisoners fasting until death against the introduction of solitary confinement (Bargu, 2014).

In 2002, a seismological report that Istanbul Metropolitan Municipality commissioned to the Japanese International Cooperation Agency confirmed Hillgreen's stable geological conditions. However, when the Disaster Law was issued in 2012, the neighbourhood was among the first to be designated a disaster risk area. The residents appealed against this decision and won, thanks to the evidence provided by Japanese report documenting Hillgreen's geological safety. In the mid-2010s, the neighbourhood continued to witness violence and the murder of its young residents, whether by the police or the mafia. One was killed by the police at home during a misaddressed dawn raid; another by the mafia in a different left-leaning neighbourhood while campaigning against drug sale and use. In December 2016, the neighbourhood was once again declared a disaster risk area, based this time on the then-recent amendment that, as discussed above, expanded the definition of 'disaster risk' to include disturbance of public order/security and informality of construction.

In response to the new designation of Hillgreen as a disaster risk area, residents have increasingly emphasized not only the neighbourhood's geological safety, as documented by the Japanese report, but also its architectural soundness. Unlike many other *gecekondu* neighbourhoods, Hillgreen has maintained a low-rise architectural characteristic over the years due to self-regulation of construction activity.

Since the outset, the neighbourhood has been parcelled evenly, comprising 120 m^2 land plots. Each house has a maximum of two storeys with a base area of 80 m^2, alongside 40 m^2 of outdoor space. The outdoor spaces are often back-to-back, enhancing privacy indoors and sociability outdoors. Houses are fully detached with a minimum 3 m gap between them. Many of these gaps are employed for pedestrian passageways, allowing circulation up and down the hills and preventing dead ends. There are three piazzas, four shops serving basic needs, and a cluster of sociocultural facilities. The residents have regulated not only these physical characteristics but also how buildings are used. They have ensured that no one sells or rents out houses, no already propertied resident moves into the neighbourhood, and no extensions are built (except to accommodate newlywed children leaving their parental homes) – structures that might block the breeze or sunlight enjoyed by others are especially unwelcome.

Architectural discourse sympathetic to *gecekondu* neighbourhoods such as Hillgreen often defends them on the basis of being built gradually, from the bottom up, in a needs-based manner, by inhabitants and without professional expertise (Ertaş, 2010; Erman, 2019). Hillgreen requires nuancing this familiar defence. A collaboration initiated in 2015 between the residents and a collective of volunteer architects, which aimed to explore the possibility of resident-led improvement in the neighbourhood, revealed that Hillgreen was, in fact, intentionally designed.

The design was the work of a group of engineers in their twenties who were members of a now-defunct volunteers' organization named the Association for Solidarity with *Gecekondu* Inhabitants, founded in September 1989. The association was established in response to the recurrent demolition raids targeting neighbourhoods such as Hillgreen around that time. Upon each demolition raid, members of the association would help the reconstruction effort. As the land mafia began to withdraw from Hillgreen around 1992, the engineers got to work parcelling out the land in equal portions, laying out the passageways and roads, and programming the facilities needed by the neighbourhood. They smuggled 1:500 scale maps out of the municipality, which enabled them to consider not only surface area but also topographical characteristics in laying out the neighbourhood. The process was remarkably different from the way many other contemporaneous *gecekondu* neighbourhoods were constructed, including left-leaning ones. In the words of a former association member involved in planning Hillgreen, 'other neighbourhoods that have seen revolutionary activity physically originate in enclosures and land speculation by the mafia. This has created a pattern of property ownership within a profit-oriented framework leading to the four- or five-storey buildings we now see in other politically comparable neighbourhoods'. Hillgreen, on the other hand, was shaped not *by* but *despite* the mafia and the profit-led approach to land it promoted, which at times meant countering the expectations and attempts of certain inhabitants prone to the lure of grabbing as much land as possible.

Conclusion

Recall the point raised at the beginning of this chapter regarding civilizationist developmentalism as the link that connects neoliberalism to coloniality. Neoliberal developmentalism's civilizationist inheritances from colonialism are reflected in the way states and international organizations continue to categorize peoples and regions into developed, undeveloped, and undevelopable ones – especially through policies avowing to protect communities and the public at large against environmental vulnerabilities. Such categorization reverberates across the Disaster Law's differential impacts in and on urban Turkey, as seen in the racialized neighbourhoods discussed above. Buildings are considered underdeveloped, whereas their residents are deemed undevelopable – hence the threat of displacement facing them as the Disaster Law divorces them from their neighbourhoods and excludes them from the public it avows to protect against disasters.

Still, the experiences of racialized neighbourhoods such as Hillgreen and Rockwind require reconsidering whether the criticism should be directed at the ideal of development itself or the interventions made by decision-makers in its name. In both neighbourhoods, communities have organized collective challenges against the differential impacts of top-down disaster preparedness. Here they have built on grassroots legacies of upholding a certain ideal of development as requiring autonomous organization against injustice, whether resulting from the operations of the land mafia, extractivist market forces, or their allies who occupy positions of authority.

These communities draw from their experiences of being threatened with displacement in the 1980s and 1990s, a period marked by the institutionalization of neoliberalism in Turkey. Despite this threat, they have forged new collective livelihoods throughout the 2000s and the 2010s by seeking to develop some order and structure in riverine ecosystems as well as the urban fabric. Their experiences, then, do not reject the ideal of development outright, but rather insist that this ideal can only be attained by working from situated and embodied experiences of being threatened by displacement and endurance in the face of this threat.

The Disaster Law's categorization of these communities is best understood through a category of *mis*development: that which has developed incorrectly according to the modern-liberal-colonial notion of development, rather than merely being undeveloped or undevelopable. As such, the challenges that Hillgreen and Rockwind have posed to top-down disaster preparedness are not tantamount to lay people creatively exploiting neoliberalism's cracks or local communities recovering knowledges that coloniality has suppressed. Rather, these challenges are constituted in laying a claim to the very promises of order, safety, and security featured in government policy and legislation. Think of the invasive fish species that Rockwind residents have hunted tens of kilometres upstream together with fishers from elsewhere in the city to make up for the authorities' neglect of their duty to do so. Consider, too, the collaborations with architecture and planning experts that Hillgreen's residents have had since 1989 up until today to ensure the architectonic soundness of their neighbourhood. Such practices of environmental endurance in the face of civilizationist developmentalism are markedly future-facing and assertive. While undoubtedly grounded in situated and embodied experiences of displacement by state-endorsed developmentalism, these practices do not rest their political claims simply upon references to pre-development origins or to being development's victims and outsiders. Rather, they assert communities' capability to fulfil developmentalism's promises better than the authorities have. In so doing, they throw the politics of displacement into sharp relief as one that seeks to foreclose the possibility of developing otherwise and to undermine already existing models of such development.

Notes

[1] This chapter is a revised version of the author's early publication in Greek: Çaylı, E. (2024) 'Η «φυσική καταστροφή» ως εθνική ασφάλεια στην Τουρκία: πώς η πρόληψη μπορεί να καταργήσει τον νόμο στο όνομα του νόμου', in S. Portesi and S. Stavrides (eds), *Κατοικώντας την εξαίρεση*, Futura, pp 235–47.

[2] This law is officially called 'Act (no. 6306) on the Transformation of Areas under Disaster Risk'.

[3] In this chapter, 'the government' stands for cabinets formed by the AKP (Adalet ve Kalkınma Partisi – in English, Justice and Development Party) and led for the most part by Recep Tayyip Erdoğan. The party rose to power in November 2002 and formed a series of majority governments until the 7 June 2015 general elections, when it lost its majority for the first time. Amidst a new episode of all-out war in Kurdish regions, as discussed in this chapter, the other parties failed to form a coalition, leading to a new round of general elections on 1 November 2015, where the AKP restored its majority. The government then legislated for a referendum to be held on 16 April 2017, where

a new executive presidential system was voted for. The vote was in favour of the new system, leading to a new presidential election held on 24 June 2018 and won by Erdoğan, who has since continued to lead Turkey with cabinet members he personally appoints.

4 This previous Kurdistan-specific state of emergency was inaugurated by way of a piece of legislation passed on 19 July 1987, to then be extended (and, in some cases, geographically expanded) 46 times for four months each until 30 November 2002, when it was shelved. The period witnessed vast human rights violations across the region. The official death toll included 5,105 civilians, 3,541 security personnel, and 25,344 guerrilla fighters. Moreover, 371 members of the armed forces and 572 civilians died in mine or bomb explosions, and 1,248 activists or politicians were extrajudicially killed. Eighteen died under custody and 194 were disappeared. Of the latter, 62 were later found in prisons. There were 1,275 complaints of torture recorded, 1,177 of which were investigated. In addition, 296 cases against civil servants were brought to court. Although 60 of these court cases resulted in convictions, only four sentences were carried out, with the rest being suspended (Türkiye İnsan Hakları Vakfı, 2004: 30–32).

References

Anderson, B., Grove K., Rickards, L., and Kearnes, M. (2020) 'Slow emergencies: temporality and the racialised biopolitics of emergency governance', *Progress in Human Geography*, 44(4): 621–39.

Ay, D. and Demireş Özkul, B. (2021) 'The strange case of earthquake risk mitigation in Istanbul', *City*, 25(1–2): 67–87.

Bargu, B. (2014) *Starve and Immolate: The Politics of Human Weapons*, Columbia University Press.

Boano, C. and Astolfo, G. (2020) 'Inhabitation as more-than-dwelling: notes for a renewed grammar', *International Journal of Housing Policy*, 20(4): 555–77.

Bonilla, Y. (2020) 'The coloniality of disaster: race, empire, and the temporal logics of emergency in Puerto Rico, USA', *Political Geography*, 78: 102–81.

DeVerteuil, G. and Golubchikov, O., Sheridan, Z. (2021) 'Disaster and the lived politics of the resilient city', *Geoforum* 125: 78–86.

Ergüven, E. (2020) 'The political economy of housing financialisation in Turkey: links with and contradictions to the accumulation model', *Housing Policy Debate*, 30(4): 559–84.

Erman, T. (2019) 'From informal housing to apartment housing: exploring the "new social" in a *gecekondu* rehousing project, Turkey', *Housing Studies*, 34(3): 519–37.

Erol, I. (2019) 'New geographies of residential capitalism: financialisation of the Turkish housing market since the early 2000s', *International Journal of Urban and Regional Research*, 43(4): 724–40.

Ertaş, H. (2010) 'The potential of Istanbul's unprogrammed public spaces', *Architectural Design*, 80(1): 52–57.

Foucault, M. (2003) *Society Must Be Defended: Lectures at the Collège de France, 1975–1976*, Penguin.

Gold, S. (1989) 'The costs of privatisation: Turkey in the 1980s', *The Multinational Monitor*, 10(10): 34–9.

Gregory, D. (2004) *The Colonial Present: Afghanistan, Palestine, Iraq*, Blackwell.

Güzel, Ö. (2016) 'The last round in restructuring the city: urban regeneration becomes a state policy of disaster prevention in Turkey', *Cities*, 50: 40–53.

Hannah, M.G., Hutta, J.S., and Schemann, C. (2020) 'Thinking through COVID-19 responses with Foucault: an initial overview', *Antipode Online*, 5 May. Available from: www.antipodeonline.org/2020/05/05/thinking-through-covid-19-responses-with-foucault [Accessed 1 March 2024].

Imperiale, A.J. and Vanclay, F. (2021) 'The mechanism of disaster capitalism and the failure to build community resilience: learning from the 2009 earthquake in L'Aquila, Italy', *Disasters*, 45(3): 555–76.

Jon, I. and Reghezza-Zitt, M. (2020) 'Late modernity to postmodern? The rise of global resilience and its progressive potentials for local disaster planning (Seattle and Paris)', *Planning Theory & Practice*, 21(1): 94–122.

Köse, T. (2017) 'Rise and fall of the AK Party's Kurdish peace initiatives', *Insight Turkey*, 19(2): 139–66.

Kurt, S. (2015) 'Historical progress of laws and regulations on coastal use in Turkey', *Eastern Geographical Review*, 20(33): 91–110.

Long, J. and Rice, J.L. (2021) 'Climate urbanism: crisis, capitalism, and intervention', *Urban Geography*, 42(6): 721–27.

Milliyet (2011) 'Yasa çıkıyor, röntgende çürük çıkan bina 5 ay içinde yıkılacak', 24 December. Available from: www.milliyet.com.tr/ekonomi/yasa-cikiyor-rontgende-curuk-cikan-bina-5-ay-icinde-yikilacak-1479786 [Accessed 1 March 2024].

Normann, S. (2021) 'Re-living a common future in the face of ecological disaster: exploring (elements of) Guarani and Kaiowá collective memories, political imagination, and critiques', *Human Arenas*, 5: 802–25.

Povinelli, E. (2011) *Economies of Abandonment: Social Belonging and Endurance in Late Liberalism*, Duke University Press.

Radikal (2015) 'Erdoğan: Meclis'e 550 milli ve yerli milletvekili gönderin', 20 September. Available from: www.radikal.com.tr/turkiye/erdogan-meclise-550-milli-ve-yerli-milletvekili-gonderin-1437713 [Accessed 1 March 2024].

Rivera, D.Z. (2022) 'Disaster colonialism: a commentary on disasters beyond singular events to structural violence', *International Journal of Urban and Regional Research*, 46(1): 126–35.

Schuller, M., Maldonado, J.K. (2016) 'Disaster capitalism', *Annals of Anthropological Practice*, 40(1): 61–72.

Sou, G. (2022) 'Reframing resilience as resistance: situating disaster recovery within colonialism', *The Geographical Journal*, 188(1): 14–27.

Sotiris, P. (2020) 'Against Agamben: is a democratic biopolitics possible?', *Critical Legal Thinking*, 14 March. Available from: https://criticallegalthinking.com/2020/03/14/against-agamben-is-a-democratic-biopolitics-possible [Accessed 1 March 2024].

Soytemel, E. (2017) 'Urban rent speculation, uncertainty and unknowns as strategy and resistance in Istanbul's housing market', in G. Erdi and Y. Şentürk (eds), *Identity, Justice and Resistance in the Neoliberal City*, Palgrave Macmillan, pp 85–115.

Stoler, A. (2016) *Imperial Durabilities in Modern Times*, Duke University Press.

Sultana, F. (2022) 'The unbearable heaviness of climate coloniality', *Political Geography*, 99: 102638.

Turner, J. (2018) 'Internal colonisation: the intimate circulations of empire, race and liberal government', *European Journal of International Relations*, 24(4): 765–90.

Türkiye İnsan Hakları Vakfı (2004) *2003 Türkiye İnsan Hakları Raporu*, Buluş.

Uzunçarşılı Baysal, C. (2018) 'İmar Barışına mahalleden bakmak: kim/ler için bu barış?' *Evrensel*, 15 June. Available from: www.evrensel.net/haber/354964/imar-barisina-mahalleden-bakmak-kim-ler-icin-bu-baris [Accessed 1 March 2024].

Yalçıntan, M.C. and Erbaş, A.E. (2003) 'Impacts of *gecekondu* on the electoral geography of Istanbul', *International Labor and Working-Class History*, 64: 91–111.

PART V

Endurance

11

Beyond Destitution and Deprivation: Interrogating the Modalities of Endurance by Self-Settled Refugees in Arua City, Uganda

Peter Kasaija

Introduction

The realities of Maria, Mzee Mapesa (pseudonyms), and the South Sudanese refugees retold in this chapter exemplify the contrasting spatio-temporal trajectories that characterize the lives of close to 10,000 self-settled refugees currently living in Arua City, Uganda. The majority fled their homes involuntarily because of war and ethnic conflict in their homelands. For over three decades, refugees have flowed continuously across the border to Uganda from the Democratic Republic of the Congo (DRCongo) and South Sudan. They find themselves in a state of limbo and exposed to multiple challenges, including food insecurity, personal safety, and climate change impacts. Furthermore, refugees were captive to a context where the existing policy, legal, and institutional regime was configured by humanitarian rather than development approaches to meet their needs. Provisionality underpinned this outdated approach in the form of short-term solutions, including food rations/cash, temporary shelter, water supply, sanitation, and small plots of land for subsistence. These interventions are important, but they are inadequate to resolve difficult questions regarding how to manage the transition from refugee status to citizens in local development processes. Such critical questions need to be foregrounded in the ongoing discourse on protracted displacement to ensure the agency of self-settled refugees as important players in changing their situation from *being* destitute to *becoming* self-reliant and productive individuals with greater command over their futures is harnessed in meaningful ways.

This chapter employs the Theory of Change (ToC) framework to examine how new and older refugees who voluntarily leave refugee settlements navigate their new environments across space and time – or rather, how endurance is configured in the lives of these refugees. By moving out of the refugee settlements and self-settling in the urban centres of Koboko and Arua City, refugees are making a political statement, especially in the absence of formal policy, legal, and institutional support.

Endurance in this context is conceptualized as the intersection of disposability and displaceability, two conditions that characterize the everyday lives of self-settled refugees who are differently positioned temporally in a context where their spatiality has been delegitimized by the prevailing policy, legal and institutional regime. By moving out of the camps to urban centres such as Arua City where their presence is not recognized by law, these refugees are deemed to forfeit settlement-based humanitarian assistance. At the same time, Arua City Council cannot plan for and extend social services to them because it lacks both the material resources and the legal mandate to do so. Therefore, self-settled refugees living in Arua City have inadvertently been rendered disposable by this policy and legal regime. I draw from the experiences of three refugees positioned at different temporal nodes in their lives' historical trajectories. This aids in making the case for alternative conceptual and practical approaches to the spatialities of refugees in place-making and inhabitation in the context of protracted displacement.

Protracted displacement and the temporal materiality of 'invisible' inhabitation

Within the context of protracted displacement, one of the most pressing challenges that both practice and research urgently need to address is the phenomenon of refugees voluntarily or otherwise, moving out of designated protected settlements to urban areas in an attempt to be more self-reliant, especially in the Global South (Crawford et al, 2015). Evidence suggests that this trend of refugees relocating to urban areas in search of livelihood opportunities in places such as West Nile, Uganda is growing (Refugee Law Project, 2005; Hovil, 2007; Capici, 2021; Cities Alliance, 2021). After the relevance of humanitarian aid[1] has diminished, it is gradually replaced by the demand for development support to economically equip refugees to build sustainable livelihoods (Omata, 2023). Refugees were being proactive by seeking opportunities outside the designated settlements to secure self-sufficiency, and dignified and respectable lives. These refugee movements from designated settlements, or directly from conflict-affected homelands to urban areas, remain inadequately accounted for in current research. The agency of refugees in reshaping space across time through the everyday while enduring different challenges is almost non-existent in local decision-making and planning processes (Brun and Fábos, 2017). They are still largely approached as 'out of place', or what Steigemann and Misselwitz (2020) refer to as 'permanently temporary' bodies. By extension, the complex material conditions that underpin their lived realities remain obscured. These conditions impact the broader trajectories and pathways of their communities in ways that research, policy, and practice are yet to fully grasp.

The materiality of the everyday for self-settled refugees in the context of protracted displacement embodies the tangible aspects of their daily lives (Montaser, 2020). This includes the resources to which they have access or otherwise, such as shelter, food, clothing, and healthcare, as well as the physical spaces they inhabit, which are canvases upon which they create a semblance of home and belonging. In this context of protracted displacement, the materiality of the everyday is an essential aspect of life for self-settled refugees (van Liempt and Staring, 2021). However, their material realities go beyond the need for food, water, education, healthcare, and shelter – they also entail the mental and emotional impacts of protracted displacement. All these affect their health and productivity. Recognizing these realities challenges prevailing knowledge, policies, and practices for addressing protracted displacement. Examining such materiality should shed light on the ways in which displaced persons adapt to their surroundings, negotiate access to resources, and maintain a sense of agency and dignity. This deeper understanding can inform more relevant policies and interventions that take into account the complex dynamics of long-term displacement.

Various aspects of materiality play a crucial role in shaping the socio-economic integration of self-settled refugees. Through their daily routines, self-settled refugees interface with these aspects to find restoration, assert their agency, and claim control over their lives. Where self-settled refugees are not formally recognized by existing policy and legal frameworks, or are essentially 'invisible', the challenges associated with their material realities are amplified.

Invisibility in this context is deployed to refer to the lack of recognition by administrative authorities and being excluded from local planning processes because they are not citizens. Effectively, such systems become implicated in the 'othering' of self-settled refugees. Yet, self-settled refugees are visible, which exposes the irrationality and impracticality of such systems. Self-settled refugees go about their everyday routines, struggling to make livelihoods for themselves as urban residents alongside the citizens, consuming services as well as contributing to the development of their respective communities. They actively explore and exploit socio-economic possibilities between the interstices of visibility and invisibility, ascribing and projecting their future aspirations on space through informal livelihoods, building and sustaining social networks linked by shared solidarities – linguistic and cultural, among others. Non-recognition of their spatiality has reinforced the lack of access to economic opportunities through restrictive policies, complicating self-settled refugees' attempts to become self-reliant. Subsequently, as they navigate daily life, self-settled refugees grapple with vulnerability, precarity, and uncertainty. They juggle present pressures with yesterday's traumas arising from the loss of vital social networks. These trigger social disconnection, isolation, and internal turmoil, which contribute to demotivation, a sense of hopelessness, and lately, attempted suicide. Nonetheless, despite having many opportunities foreclosed to them, self-settled refugees are demonstrating remarkable resilience and resourcefulness as they act in various ways to restore what they have lost, regain a sense of control, and re-establish a sense of belonging in their new localities (Brun and Fábos, 2017; Albers et al, 2021). The material dimensions of places where self-settled refugees seek to make new homes become important physical anchors amidst the transience of displacement. How self-settled refugees navigate their new localities is crucial for their social integration (Steigemann and Misselwitz, 2020). The everyday practices of inhabitation in new places or host communities not only contribute to the physical and emotional well-being of self-settled refugees, but also serve as means of resistance and resilience against the restrictive policies and circumstances they face.

It is argued that self-settled refugees, especially those who are living invisible lives where they lack recognition, are heterogeneous when considered across the temporal dimension. New and older refugees face different kinds of challenges in relation to barriers, risks, and threats in their new environments; therefore, their modes of urban inhabitation contrast significantly. Yet, these geographies have largely remained under the radar. This chapter provides alternative understandings of inhabitation rendered invisible by the politics of displacement. Protracted displacement is constituted by both spatial and temporal dimensions. The latter binds past, present, and future through moments and events in space. However, policy discourses appear to overlook this. Similarly, just as time has been overlooked in the policy discourse, the heterogeneity of this group[2] also appears to be unaccounted for. Such policy 'blindness' has limited opportunities for engaging with the nuances of self-settled refugees' lived realities and how these generate diverse experiences of inequality, exclusion, and vulnerability. This book chapter seeks to contribute to debates that critically interrogate the above materiality of inhabitation by self-settled urban refugees in relation to their everyday acts of endurance. To this end, the chapter mobilizes insights from Arua City, West Nile, Uganda to capture the nuanced modalities adopted by self-settled urban refugees to rebuild their lives while navigating various challenges across temporalities.

Subsequently, the findings should inform and promote more contextually relevant policy and decision-making processes that connect with self-settled urban refugees' lived realities and, ultimately, re-energize efforts to respond to the growing challenge of protracted displacement and its multidimensional facets, especially in the Global South.

Customizing Janzen et al's (2022) theory of change (ToC) framework, the chapter examines three different modes of invisible inhabitation to offer critical insights into the complex socio-spatial and temporal experiences of self-settled refugees in Arua City. More broadly, it provides an alternative perspective for understanding how endurance unravels within the context of displaceability and disposability. Seen through the lens of the framework's three ecological levels across different timelines[3] of different inhabitation modes, the heterogeneous lived realities and experiences of displacement demonstrate how self-settled refugees transition from being in a cycle of destitution to becoming more resilient through the intersection of people, place, and time. This is set in an environment defined by the tripartite framework of neoliberal humanitarianism, displacement governance, and associated development politics, which has rendered them 'out of place'.

Setting the scene: Arua City and the geopolitics of protracted displacement

Arua City lies in a region that has experienced multiple geopolitical identities. At one point, it was part of Congo Free State before returning to Anglo-Egyptian Sudan in 1909 and subsequently being annexed to Uganda. In this sense, the city's history is somewhat poetic when juxtaposed with its reputation as a node for forced displacement of Congolese and South Sudanese refugees fleeing armed conflict in their homelands. Self-settled refugees had relatively unrestricted access to public services, including education and healthcare, to enable a relatively decent and respectable life in Arua City. From a 2023 survey,[4] a sizeable proportion of the resident refugee population is mainly concentrated in the central division, in the parishes of Tanganyika, Kenya, Pangisa, Adalafu, and Bazar (Figure 11.1). A group of Congolese refugees engaged in an FGD validated this information: 'The refugees are in Oli, Airfield, Oboloko, Pangisa, Pajulu ... let me say all this area [is] full of refugees ... it seems everywhere you go you find refugees ...'

Evidence suggests that self-settled refugees and local communities have largely coexisted and co-created dense social networks and productive exchanges. However, both latent and overt tensions remain between them. Nonetheless, Arua City is a convergence node where these groups are creating a complex urban socio-cultural tapestry. The city is both sanctuary and home for thousands fleeing conflict in the DRCongo and South Sudan.

Figure 11.1: Snapshot of refugee demographics for Arua City in numbers and gender

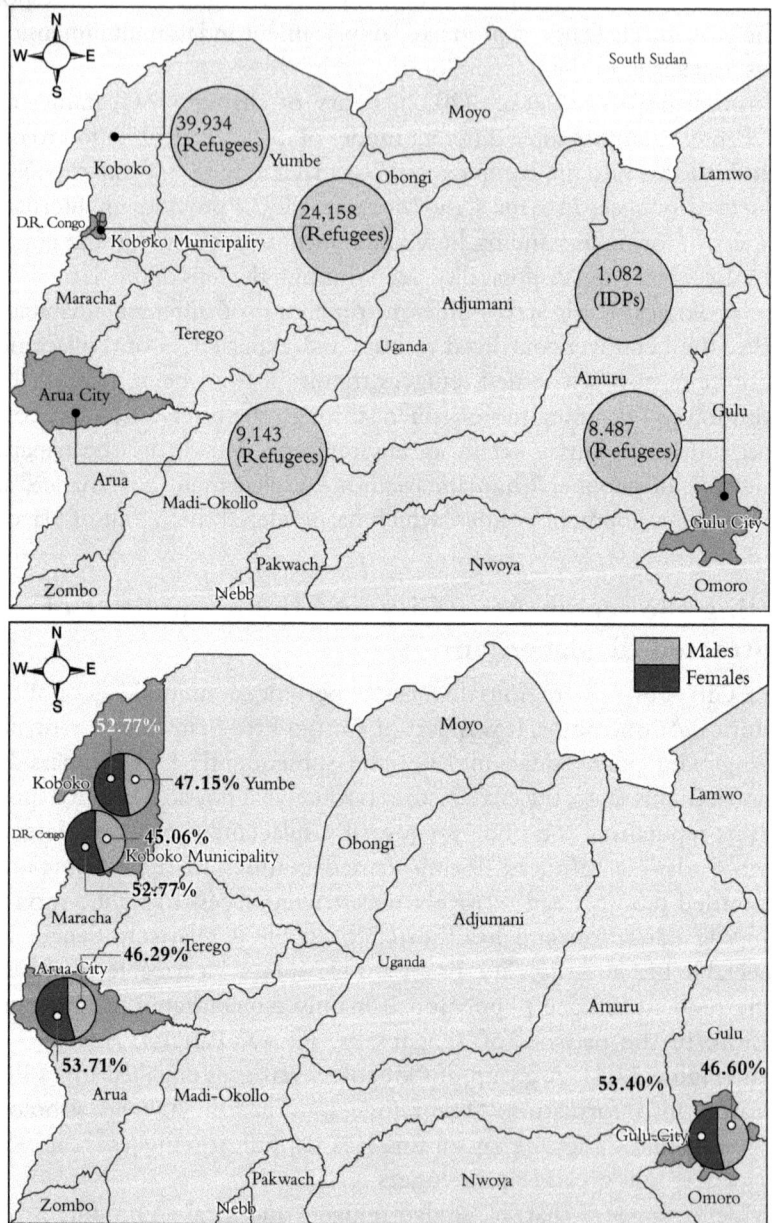

Source: Urban Action Lab (UAL), Makerere University (2023), reproduced with permission. Data are drawn from a survey undertaken by VNG and UNCDF in collaboration with UAL, in 2023. Data are included in the report *Localized Analysis: A Review of the Effects of Urban Refugees and Forced Migrants in Cities and Urban Settings of Northern Uganda: Case of Arua and Gulu Cities and Koboko Municipality*. Urban Action Lab, June 2024. Not published.

It has witnessed war, socio-cultural mobility and intersectionality, stability, prosperity and wealth concurrently throughout its history:

> We have suffered several cycles of war and conflict ... This is just a refugee and migration belt ... expect conflict to break out anywhere and then another cycle of movement will begin ... (FGD Participant, ACC, June 2023)

War in DRCongo and South Sudan, fuelled by ethnic rivalries coupled with regional power politics, predatory capitalism, and humanitarianism, has directly impacted Arua City. It has contributed to a continuous cycle of displacement, severely impacting development and loss of lives and livelihoods (Crawford et al, 2015; Policinski and Kuzmanovic, 2019; Wiggins et al, 2021). The city is a base for multiple agencies providing relief, protection, and other forms of short-term support for refugees. However, the traditional humanitarian approach they employ has come under scrutiny, with calls for coupling it with local economic development towards more durable and sustainable solutions (Nutz, 2017; Levine and Becton, 2019; Strand, 2020).

Historically, the humanitarian sector has largely operated in a silo manner, with minimal linkages to the mainstream development sector and markets. Yet humanitarianism does not operate in a void. Humanitarian actors are being compelled to engage with the development realm and its attendant modalities[5] to ensure refugees are genuinely supported to attain meaningful rights and opportunities towards full and dignified self-reliance. This will ensure more seamless transitions for self-settled refugees while avoiding the complications of creating parallel systems. Changing the entrenched demarcation between the humanitarian and development realms presents a significant challenge. However, small steps are being made in this direction.

Contrasting realities of different refugees living in Arua City

Evidence shows that several of Uganda's urban centres are hosting sizeable refugee populations driven by multiple push factors, including armed conflict. Arua City, the largest urban centre in the West Nile region, stands out in this regard. Refugees living and working in the city had become normalized. Besides being restricted from participating in democratic electoral processes, refugees live side by side with locals, engaging in the same everyday struggles to secure livelihoods and social services, and to realize their respective future aspirations. Yet, ironically, these realities remain in tension with the country's refugee policy, legal, and institutional framework. Uganda's official refugee policy has long been lauded as an exemplar for other nations across the world. However, while legally recognizing formally registered refugees[5] as eligible for humanitarian support, it is conspicuously silent about self-settled refugees living outside the formally designated areas.

This lacuna has rendered self-settled refugees in urban centres such as Arua City 'invisible' yet 'visible', confining them to a state of limbo. Subsequently, self-settled refugees have to negotiate multiple challenges emanating from the personal/micro-, community/meso-, and exo-systems that comprise the socio-environmental macro-system in which they live. These include personal psychological challenges and struggles to meet everyday needs, socio-spatial injustices rooted in systematic inequalities, exclusion and exploitation, power imbalances, and ethnic, gender, and linguistic differences. Within this context, refugees under 'invisible habitation' intersect with 'place' and 'time' to profoundly impact their own distinct lived experiences. They have also contributed to (re)shaping how space is (re)produced and the resulting urban motifs' configuration, socially, spatially, economically, and environmentally. To demonstrate these realities, this section draws from the experiences of 'new arrivals', who had lived for less than five years in Arua City, 'intermediate arrivals', and 'older arrivals', who had spent more than five years and ten years respectively in Arua City, to facilitate a critical examination of the increasingly complex and nuanced geographies of protracted displacement.

Maria's story

Maria (not her real name) is a Congolese refugee in her thirties[6] and a single mother[7] of six.[8] She left a designated refugee settlement with her family and moved to Arua City. She has lived in the Central Division for about three years so is a relatively 'new arrival'. Her life's experiences typified the struggles of new arrivals:

> Women who are not married are not trusted ... questions will be asked [as to how] such women found their way to this town ... So these are some of the challenges where society's perception of women is different from their [male] counterparts ... (KII, local official, ACC, May 2023)

Before she attempted suicide, she had limited social networks for support and struggled to secure a decent livelihood for her family. Personally, she grappled with psychological and mental challenges that impacted her ability to take good care of her children, according to her personal accounts:

> One time I [did not] have money because I was very sick ... I had gone to Kampala for radiotherapy treatment [supported by] UNHCR but the landlord could not sympathize with me ... he chased my children [out of the house and] they slept outside for three days ... At my son's

school, there [is a teacher] who [was very hostile] to me ... they chased my boy and [when I called] to talk to her she answered; 'You madam, am I the one who [sent] the cancer to attack you? You get out of [the school] with your boy if you can't pay [the fees]!' I was really so traumatized I don't know what to answer to that woman. I switched [the phone] off. They had taken my UGX150,000 [which was] the only money I had. My son didn't sit for exams [because I couldn't pay] the UGX400,000. (KII, Maria, Congolese refugee, May 2023)

She struggled with depression, self-esteem, and self-confidence. These appeared to be rooted in unresolved trauma, and a sense of loss, guilt, and fear from living with armed conflict in her homeland. An official summed up the depth and gravity of such psycho-social trauma:

We have a very big challenge, you see these parents are traumatized and this trauma is shifted to the children, and these children shift this trauma to the host community ... so we are likely to experience trans-generational trauma that we will struggle with over time which I think people are unconscious about ... some of these [refugees] witnessed [killings], some of them have killed ... this is very complex ... there needs to be checks and balances ... a proactive response that the humanitarian agencies need to support for example a robust mechanism to counter trans-generational trauma that is going to impact society over time. (KII, NGO official, Arua City, May 2023)

Nonetheless, Maria remained hopeful about a better future for her family. Aside from her fragile physical health, her outlook on life disguised the fact that she had contemplated suicide and was also undergoing monthly chemotherapy at the Mulago National Referral Hospital in Kampala, 300 km south of Arua City. Maria's treatment was financed by UNHCR. Whenever she travelled to Kampala for treatment, she made arrangements with friends to help look after her children.

The above narrative partly resonates with the Refugee Law Project (2005) regarding the key pull factors that draw refugees from the designated settlements to urban areas. The promise of access to reliable healthcare and education opportunities for their children, financial services, efficient communication services (e.g. telephone and internet), which are not readily available in the refugee settlements, is a major pull factor for refugees. This is partly aided by local authorities, who do not exclude refugees from accessing these services, despite the logistical challenges:

All the services are being shared with the migrants ... I would like to give you a live example: if there's a cholera outbreak in Tanganyika ward, are you going to say you will first treat the citizens before others? So they share services equally. The existing services in these areas are accessed by all regardless of status in terms of citizenship ... only that they are overstretched. (KII, local official, ACC, May 2023)

Maria and her family lived in a single-room tenement,[9] which she rented for less than UGX30,000 (approximately US$8) per month using her meagre earnings as a hairstylist. Housing was generally very expensive for the urban refugees, with costs rising to UGX200,000 for two- or three-bedroom housing units. Despite the relatively high costs of rental housing, households such as Maria's were dependent on it for their survival. Her large family faced exploitation by landlords and other associated challenges:

> [When] you come looking for a house to rent, if the land lord sees you have about five, six or seven children, they increase the rent, claiming [high occupancy increases costs] for toilet emptying ... if you don't pay, they will tell you 'leave our house' ... all of us as Congolese and South Sudanese experience these challenges. (FGD, Maria, Congolese refugee, May 2023)

Maria could not fully support her family to secure at least two meals a day, water, fuel and energy, sanitation, healthcare, and education. She was reliant on monthly rations from the refugee settlement. She had no productive household assets. Like many other urban refugees in her situation, moving to the city meant she had to make some difficult tradeoffs. In the refugee settlement, she had access to a small plot of land for subsistence in addition to the monthly rations from WFP. She therefore had to trade access to these privileges for her hopes for better livelihood opportunities and social services. In Arua City, she could not access a free plot of land, as in the refugee settlement. Her account encapsulates her everyday struggles:

> One time [I was very] sick and paralyzed... I could not walk ... [officials came] and wrote my name [and said] they were going to bring for [me food] ... I waited for that food and waited but it was [not delivered] ... I was supposed to pay money for my children's fees but I didn't have money. They couldn't go to class [so] I decided to sell my clothes [so that we get food] during the time of COVID-19. (FGD, Maria, Congolese refugee, May 2023)

Living in Arua City implied that reliable healthcare and education services were relatively nearer to Maria and her family. It also ensured that Maria was within reach of other vital social services, including churches, mosques, and community centres, police/security, city council administration, and the UNHCR offices within a 5 km radius. As a refugee, she could not participate in local democratic elections; however, she played a nominal role in neighbourhood meetings convened by local leaders (LC1) to address domestic/social conflict, crime, and insecurity.

Self-settled South Sudanese refugees

The second case considers groups of self-settled South Sudanese who had lived for more than five years in Arua City and their attempts at socio-economic stabilization. According to various local leaders, a significant number of South Sudanese refugees who had lived longer in the city than new arrivals such as Maria had attained a level of social integration. They established close social ties with the local communities, intermarriages ensued, and mixed families thrived. They also had relatively unrestricted access to some public services, which accorded them a relatively decent and respectable life. According to one local official, South Sudanese refugees intermarrying with local communities in Arua City also came with other important dimensions of protracted displacement, such as dual citizenship:

> Even those that have stayed here long enough, some have dual citizenship, others have even intermarried ... I think that's one way of integrating them. Our people have married their daughters and vice versa so in the process, we become relatives. (KII, local official, ACC, May 2023)

Some of the self-settled South Sudanese refugees with personal resources bought land, built houses, and made homes in attempts to rebuild their lives:

> Some of them especially those who have some relatives and those who are well off have actually bought plots and built houses ... others rent. Some [are living with] relatives ... but we do not have [the] data on that. (KII, local official, ACC, May 2023)

In these attempts to rebuild their lives, these refugees had to interface with the complex socio-cultural, economic, and political dimensions of land access and ownership. Unlike new arrivals such as Maria, and the majority whose choices were limited to rental housing for their shelter needs, South Sudanese refugees with resources to acquire land for building had to navigate the various dimensions of land, which was not 'just a commodity or a means of subsistence' (Lund et al, 2006). They had to engage with the challenges of land rights and tenure in a context where delivery mechanisms operated largely outside formal markets. Evidence reveals that these refugees employed a combination of informal and quasi-formal approaches to access land.

Within the above approaches, two tactics were prominent. The first tactic included negotiating with locals who were willing to sell land to them (either through leasehold or freehold[10] arrangements). Once agreeable terms were reached with landlords, the refugees proceeded to purchase land, followed by house construction:

> A number of them (refugees) have acquired land through leasehold as one of the ways of integrating them. Those that I have mentioned have built and have agreements. (KII, local official, ACC, May 2023)

They exploited their connections to relatives abroad in Europe and the United States to mobilize the finances they needed to buy the land and build houses:

> Many of them are [living] in informal settlements apart from a few who have capacity and ability to buy land and build their own houses. Some of them, especially the Sudanese they ... like good housing, I think they are supported by their sons and daughters who [live abroad] ... (KII, local official, ACC, May 2023)

The second strategy was more elaborate. Here, some self-settled refugees exploited their social networks to purchase and own land by proxy, according to a local leader:

> Like I said there are those who own buildings under leasehold but there [are] also those who own land in the names of others. It's a number of them. (KII, local official, ACC, May 2023)

Under such arrangements, they worked through trusted locals, who bought land on their behalf. This helped them to circumvent the possibility of being rejected since there were some locals with negative attitudes towards the refugees, who were against selling them land. Furthermore, proxies were useful for negotiating fairer prices to avoid exploitation. The latter was attributed to misconceptions that refugees[11] had cash, which they received from NGOs and other sources. These modalities of accessing land were largely bureaucracy-free, low cost, and highly responsive to needs of refugees. Following the land-acquisition process, the self-settled refugees then proceeded to undertake self-built house construction to make homes for themselves. Given their non-citizen status, they could not access formal housing finance, so they fully shouldered the financial costs by relying on personal resources and support from family and close friends. Self-settled refugees employed local artisanal labour to undertake house construction incrementally.[12] Few, if any, had formally approved house plans or occupancy permits.

With the support of the city's local leadership, some self-settled refugees had negotiated access to land in the city to set up a market. In this way, self-settled refugees were offered opportunities to engage in trade and entrepreneurship, which were critical for securing dignified, gainful, and sustainable livelihoods for self-reliance. The market also presented other net benefits, including the contribution of refugees to local economic growth and development through tax revenue, widening the pool of entrepreneurial skills, stimulating local production, expanding critical value chains, and creating employment opportunities for locals. A local official said:

> I've just told you a number of them have built here including residential and commercial buildings. There's a market here called [the] Sudanese fish market in the central division. It's one of the biggest where [Arua City] council actually generates revenue. The fish is [from South Sudan] and the market is run by the Sudanese and there's a lot of market in Congo. (KII, local official, ACC, May 2023)

Mzee Mapesa's story

The third case study draws attention to Mzee Mapesa (not his real name), a self-settled Congolese-Tutsi refugee in his mid-sixties who fled DRCongo with his family during the 1990s. He lived in a refugee settlement for a couple of years before moving to Arua City more than 20 years ago.

Initially, life was very hard. He got work as a trader, built a decent life for himself, and exploited his social networks to secure a small plot of land in Ayivu Division, where he built. His family could afford healthcare and education services since he made a decent living as a trader. Being able to access social services and engaging in the urban economy owes much to the local authorities' attempts to promote socio-economic inclusion of refugees:

> Our city is a city of trade and industry...where you have the mind of entrepreneurship, either a migrant or a refugee in this city you can flourish, you can actually be better. That's one of the ways, by supporting them but also the refugees are not discriminated from social services like the schools and health facilities, they enjoy the same services like the [citizens] enjoy. When you go to our schools like Arua Republic, you may even find half or more students are refugees. (KII, local official, ACC, May 2023)

Mzee Mapesa was fluent in Swahili, which was widely spoken in this region, making self-settling relatively less challenging. Over time, he had built strong social networks within the local community where he lived among the Congolese refugees in Arua City. He was highly respected and trusted by the Congolese community, which eventually selected him to lead an association under which they had mobilized themselves. The association held its meetings at his home. It served as a platform for providing both personal and collective welfare support for its members, representing the members who fell afoul of the law and acted as a voice for their engagement with local decision-makers.

Mzee Mapesa and his family lived in a three-bedroom unit built on the small plot he bought. When the family first moved to Arua City, they had to rent for several years before Mzee Mapesa built the house. By moving into their own house, the family were able to divert resources to the children's education and Mzee Mapesa's business. His wife stayed at home attending to the family's care needs and other domestic demands. As an established trader, Mzee Mapesa was relatively better off than many other self-settled refugees in Arua City. His resilience as a self-settled refugee was reflected in his decision to turn down an offer to migrate to Europe for better prospects:

> Some people approached me … they came and asked [me] if [I wanted to stay] here in Africa [or go] abroad … [I] told them it is better to stay in Africa because we Africans who go abroad as refugees, [it is like] slavery … It is better for us to work here and the tax that they [take] from us should remain here in Africa to develop Africa than us going to work as slaves abroad … [the government] should open up companies where refugees here should work … and the taxes remain here in Africa than going to be used outside. (FGD, Mzee Mapesa, Congolese refugee, May 2023)

It is against these contrasting backgrounds that different self-settled refugees accumulated diverse experiences in Arua City as invisible inhabitants. Through their daily struggles, they were active participants in remaking and co-producing place, in a context where governance systems for development and humanitarianism infrastructure remained largely disconnected – yet, ironically, were innately bound because they operated within the same space.

Invisible inhabitation through the lens of the theory of change

Survival: from attempted suicide to grappling with identity

Starting with Maria's case, three key events illustrate how her experiences were shaped by the three intersecting ecological levels of the theory of change (ToC) as entry points for a critical analysis of her life's trajectory; first, her personal psychological and livelihood struggles that triggered a suicidal attempt (micro-system); second, her joining a local Congolese association (meso-system); third, the ramifications of the governance system on her identity as an 'outsider' in relation to claiming recognition, access to social services, and other important material and institutional support for a dignified, respectable, and fulfilling life (macro-system). All these factors converged to generate the complex life motif of Maria as a new arrival in Arua City.

Given that Maria had spent less than five years in Arua City, her journey as a self-settled urban refugee was still in its infancy. Despite having been in the city for a relatively short period, evidence suggests that Maria's condition was not static – indeed, far from it. When considered alongside the factors that influenced the micro-, meso-, and macro-systems, a chain of events was perpetually in motion, linking her past and present. When Maria attempted suicide, this event had multifaceted impacts on her personally, communally, and in the wider macro systems. It unmasked the systemic decay of collective care, support, and empathy from a community system perspective. It amplified the centrality of community systems in enabling meaningful social connections to minimize isolation, manage refugee-to-refugee or refugee-to-host community conflict, and address segregation, discrimination and xenophobia, exposing refugees to the danger of being 'othered'. It also raised equally pertinent questions about the capacities of macro policy and institutional frameworks to fully empower the local city administration to provide the necessary psychosocial support in the form of counselling and other material assistance to address such critical issues. Despite evidence showing the gravity of this challenge (Bukuluki et al, 2021; United Nations High Commission for Refugees, 2022), the current system appears to remain inadequately equipped to address it.

Joining a local Congolese association

After attempting suicide, Maria confided in other fellow Congolese refugees. They encouraged her to join a Congolese association, which enabled her to secure assistance from a group which she identified with and with whose members she shared a sense of solidarity.[13] In this association, Maria found solace through their connected histories from their homeland and present experiences. This association can be categorized as an urban-based self-help group (Kara et al, 2022), which operated informally and was sustained by members' contributions. It supported Congolese families to raise resources for funerals and also acted as a platform for representing their collective demands when engaging with local authorities.

Such refugee-led institutions are increasingly drawing attention in research as important nodes of social organization, which self-settled refugees both draw upon and contribute to in pursuit of their interests that state or local governments and other agencies are unable to address (Easton-Calabria and Pincock, 2018; Pincock et al, 2021). They are alternative means through which refugees can claim their rights. Being in proximity to the refugees, these organizations are better able to build trust, treat refugees with more dignity, and be more accessible, less bureaucratic, and better positioned to articulate the challenges faced by refugees (Easton-Calabria and Pincock, 2018; Kara et al, 2022; Kara, 2023; Vuni et al, 2023). Despite this, they appear to remain on the margins of decision-making in the broader displacement governance domain and are inadequately resourced, among other barriers. However, their proximity to the realities of refugees suggests they are critical for shaping outcomes at the personal, community, and macro-levels.

Grappling with identity

Key challenges faced by self-settled refugees such as Maria include negotiating identity in an environment characterized by prejudice, phobias, stereotyping, discrimination, and exclusion. Therefore, protracted displacement in this context plays a very important role in impacting how self-settled refugees (re)make socio-cultural (i.e. ethnicity, language, gender, religion), geographical (i.e. adaptation to urban life), and political (i.e. ethno-nationalism, refuge-ness, citizenship) identities for their own benefits or to protect loved ones. For Maria, making a life in Arua City through the everyday alongside local communities involved acts of articulating or even concealing certain identities to procure psychological, social, or material benefits. It was a process of living between the interstices of visibility and invisibility. Refuge-ness had to be navigated strategically because it was an undesirable social label that accentuated socio-cultural stratification between non-citizens and citizens. Maria had to navigate everyday life through multiple identities[14] in a context where these identities could either enhance access to opportunities or amplify specific vulnerabilities.

For an urban refugee such as Maria, the concept of identity, without appearing to oversimplify its intricacies, obviously cuts across the personal, communal, and broader macro-system levels. On a personal level, it manifested in the way Maria had to negotiate religion, social beliefs, social class, ethnicity, physical and mental health, gender, marital status, skills, personality, and critical life experiences. Another important aspect with which Maria had to contend was her position in the community where she lived. Her personal wellbeing was closely linked to how she had been welcomed, received, perceived, or even (mis)understood for the few years of her existence, interaction, and transactions as an integral part of Arua City's urban ecosystem. In other words, her connectedness to the local community – her neighbours, other families, her peers and friends, leaders, elders – with whom she shared certain values were equally important elements that shaped her identity. Being disconnected from the local community in these multiple ways meant only a partial and incomplete form of identity for which Maria could not be able to satisfactorily attain self-actualization, meaning, respect, or a wholesome life.

Resource mobilization, land access, and self-built housing by South Sudanese refugees

For the second case, attention is drawn to three interconnected acts as the entry points for a critical analysis of the experiences of self-settled South Sudanese: first, the acts of mobilizing financial resources to purchase land and build houses; second, how the refugees negotiated access to the land they required; and third, the acts of undertaking self-built housing investments.

Certainly, these acts of inhabitation by self-settled refugees who had spent more than five years living in Arua City contrasted significantly with those of new arrivals such as Maria. Through these intertwined acts, the refugees' struggles to make homes as they sought to restore their lives and ensure some continuity invariably influenced micro-, meso-, and macro-systems in different ways. Time was an important dimension through which these acts, reflecting their hopes, dreams, and aspirations, left behind permanent 'footprints' of their presence despite being invisible under the prevailing policy and legal regime. Such 'footprints' also exemplified the self-settled refugees' adaptability, ingenuity, and agility.

Mobilizing resources for life rebuilding

Self-settled South Sudanese refugees demonstrated remarkable resourcefulness in seeking out alternative financial sources beyond their own savings to fund land purchases, construct self-built housing, and settle their families. Remittances from relatives abroad were a particularly important source of finance in this regard. This embodies another important dimension of self-settled refugees within the broader context of protracted displacement: the issue of cross-territorial financial flows and their impacts, both short and long term, especially on local host refugee economies. These processes essentially involved refugees drawing upon savings from previous livelihoods and incomes generated from productive activities elsewhere. By using these resources to fund land purchases, house building, and settling their families, such refugees directly and indirectly impacted the micro-, meso-, and macro-system dynamics of cities such as Arua.

Land access

For any given context, including protracted displacement and the associated geographies of humanitarianism, access to land is one of the most critical issues, given its centrality as an asset for subsistence and productivity. Beyond procuring critical basic needs (food, water, energy, etc.), accessing land by self-settled refugees brought them into contact with its various dimensions. By negotiating access to land either directly through leases, freehold, or through proxies, self-settled South Sudanese refugees had inadvertently been drawn into the different dimensions that this asset embodied. Land is not just an economic asset or commodity;[15] it embodies familial and social ties, belonging and identity (Lund et al, 2006), from a micro-system perspective. Self-settled refugees who had procured land were therefore drawn into a space where they had to engage with the burdens and benefits of land straddling the micro-, meso-, and macro-system TOC levels. At the micro- and meso-system levels, they had to negotiate issues including conflict, competing claims, legitimacy, discrimination, and recognition of market dynamics (informal and formal processes of land transfer), development (securing financial resources to add value to it), and its servicing (extending critical infrastructure) to ensure productivity, stable livelihoods, and settlement (Nkurunziza, 2007; Lawry et al, 2017; Schneider et al, 2020). At the macro-system level, these acts by refugees presented unprecedented challenges for policy, legal, and institutional frameworks that regulated land-governance systems.

Self-built housing

Equally, when self-settled South Sudanese refugees undertook self-built housing to create homes for their families using different financial sources, the impacts went far beyond the micro-system level. Self-built housing was underpinned by multiple processes, both visible and invisible, which ranged from sourcing building materials and hiring workers to managing all manner of activities from laying down the substructure and superstructure, installing utilities, and completing internal fixtures and other finishings for habitability. It is a highly demanding process (Centre for Affordable Housing Finance Africa, 2019). Therefore, such investments brought into sharp relief the manifold qualities – personal strengths, social networks and broader understanding of the local construction sector – that were needed for such undertakings. Self-settled refugees who took on this kind of investment were profoundly impacted at a personal level while the implications also extended to the meso- and macro-systems. On a personal level, undertaking such investments reflected elements of inner strength, self-determination, and perseverance. More importantly, it reflected forward thinking on the part of the refugees as they envisaged possibilities of becoming better, of transcending the limits of their current realities by deliberately acting to improve their material conditions to meet certain innate aspirations. At the meso- and macro-system levels, such actions inevitably enrolled the wider community through the engagement of local labour, skills, expertise, and resources, which impacted the local economy.

Socio-economic stability and self-reliance

In the last case, two scenarios from the life trajectory of Mzee Mapesa, an older arrival, were drawn on to provide valuable insights into the character of endurance in this context; the first scenario looks at Mzee Mapesa's leadership position and role in the Congolese refugee association; for the second scenario, we examine Mzee Mapesa's decision to turn down offers to migrate to Europe and instead remain in Arua City.

Leadership role in the Congolese refugee community

Mzee Mapesa was chosen to lead a local informal association of self-settled Congolese refugees living in Arua City because he was highly respected in his community and his experience was highly valued. As the association's leader and because of the roles he took on, his impact was felt across all the three ecological levels. At the micro-system level, he touched the lives of the members by providing personal guidance and advice to vulnerable refugees such as Maria. Mzee Mapesa also helped to advocate for the rights of the association's members and their well-being. Moreover, he mobilized resources and coordinated support for new arrivals. He also coordinated interventions for promoting self-reliance and sustainable livelihoods for the members of the association. Realizing these roles entailed managing the delicate internal dynamics within the association to ensure inclusivity, representation, and effectiveness. His position required him to assist the group to negotiate external challenges, including socio-cultural barriers, discrimination, and stigma, whilst also managing tensions and conflicts between the association and the host community, and the South Sudanese refugee community.

Furthermore, Mzee Mapesa's remit entailed negotiating complex political landscapes, which involved engaging state actors such as the city government, the Prime Minister's Office, other security agencies,[16] local NGOs, UNHCR and other development actors to advocate for refugee rights. Only through the engagement of these state and non-state actors could he amplify advocacy for the rights and well-being of his association's members. It was a delicate balancing act that required Mzee Mapesa to continuously juggle the needs of the association with the interests of the above multiplex of actors. Given his position, it was clear that Mzee Mapesa accumulated significant socio-political networks and power, and this raises critical questions about how he used that power to further both the collective interests of the association and his personal interests.

Social integration and resistance to change

In the midst of global migration challenges, there are instances where refugees opt to remain in their host communities rather than seek better opportunities abroad. Mzee Mapesa was a perfect example of this when he declined an offer to relocate to Europe. This decision was pivotal for the trajectory of his life and that of his family. Personally, through this decision Mzee Mapesa was able to consolidate his social networks in the local community. These networks offered stability and security for raising his family, enabling them to settle and build a decent livelihood in Arua City. Clearly, he rationalized and valued what such stability and security offered more than the uncertainty of moving abroad. Additionally, these networks enabled Mzee Mapesa and his family to attain some level of socio-cultural integration and a sense of identity, belonging, and support, given their history as refugees. With such integration, Mzee Mapesa and his family were better equipped to negotiate their new environment and engage meaningfully in activities that contributed to their personal development, wellbeing, and growth. Perhaps more importantly, this decision helped them to maintain ties with kin back in their homeland in neighbouring DRCongo.

The implications of such a decision also extended to the meso- and macro-system levels in various ways. At the meso-system level, it implied that the socio-cultural networks and other related support mechanisms[17] were functioning to some extent. Therefore, self-settled refugees such as Mzee Mapesa had the self-belief and determination derived from the support networks of the host community to confidently make a life for themselves. This scenario resonates with research that has found social support plays a key role in the successful settlement of refugees (Alegría et al, 2017). At a macro-system level, this decision also suggests that the multiple agencies in the region had created a relatively conducive environment that enabled self-settled refugees to thrive even with a policy that did not recognize their presence. More pertinently, it appears they had indirectly facilitated the agency of the self-settled refugees towards some level of self-reliance.

Conclusion: Endurance as a 'continuum' of in-place making and habitation

Current research shows that refugees have adopted various modalities of endurance to navigate multiple challenges while also attempting to harness the opportunities available to them in different localities within the broader context of displacement (Schweitzer et al, 2007; Hovil, 2015; Betts et al, 2020). However, it has yet to engage with some of the more granular dimensions of how endurance unfolds among different categories of self-settled refugees. This chapter has drawn attention to this knowledge gap by spotlighting the realities of different categories of self-settled refugees. The cases presented and discussed here form the basis upon which an alternative conceptualization for codifying the modalities of endurance for different categories of refugees is proposed. From a critical analytical perspective using the ToC, I propose bundling the modalities of endurance into three categories based on the temporal positioning of different self-settled refugees: first, survival and adaptation for new arrivals; second, post-survival and agency for change for intermediate arrivals; and third, self-determination and resistance for older arrivals. This bundling affirms that the convergence of time and place profoundly impact the everyday experiences and ultimately life trajectories of different self-settled refugees. Despite inhabiting the same place, new, intermediate, and older self-settled refugees faced different personal, socio-economic, and material challenges when viewed through the lens of the ToC. Subsequently, these challenges defined the pathways that they followed in relation to their everyday acts of inhabiting place. The outcomes were starkly diverse experiences. I briefly expound on each bundle to define how the above diverse life experiences unfolded within this context.

Survival and adaptation

The first bundle of endurance modalities applies to self-settled refugees who were relatively new in their respective host communities. More often, life for them was a daily struggle to secure the basics, including food, shelter, water, energy, healthcare, and education. Beyond these material demands, such self-settled refugees also faced immense psychological pressures, given the lack of social networks available to cushion them and ease the process of settling in. More precisely, the lives of new arrivals were largely circumscribed by personal crises, emotional turbulence, material precarity, scarcity, and vulnerability, as well as socio-cultural barriers including discrimination.

When situated along the space–time continuum, self-settled refugees such as Maria, who exemplified these modalities of endurance, were closer to destitution and deprivation. In this phase of in-place making and inhabitation, the everyday acts of self-settled refugees such as Maria were defined by survival and adaptation more than anything else. Their lives were characterized by struggles to get from one day to another, coupled by efforts to cultivate resilience through building community networks to enable them better navigate their unfamiliar new environments. Being able to survive and adapt were critical if they were to build the resilience required to transition beyond this phase.

Post-survival and agency for change

This category of endurance aptly captures the experiences of self-settled refugees who had spent more than five years in Arua City. Having had more time to settle into their new environments than the new arrivals like Maria, these refugees had attained some stability and life was less of a struggle. For intermediate arrivals whose life experiences resonated with this phase, the reclamation of agency was a driving force behind their attempts to reassert control over their lives. For some cases, as exemplified by some South Sudanese refugees in Arua City, in a bid to establish some continuity and belonging, intermediate arrivals exercised their agency to create anchors to which their old traditions, culture, and customs could be moored. This was realized through acts such as procuring land and undertaking self-built housing. Additionally, self- settled refugees in this phase of life tended to have acquired some confidence and assertiveness. Thus, they were able to take the initiative to exercise their agency for independence, mobilizing economic resources to empower themselves, be more self-reliant, strengthen socio-cultural stability, and exercise ingenuity in their attempts to take charge of their future. For this category of self-settled refugees, when situated along the time–space continuum, they had become relatively settled and achieved some socio-economic stability. Here, their everyday lives thrived, and the modalities of endurance were more than just about survival as they accessed vital productive resources such as land, established homes as spaces of comfort, restoration, and belonging, and developed a sense of home.

Self-determination, socio-political embeddedness, and empowerment

The third category resonates mostly with self-settled refugees who had lived for more than 10 years in Arua City. Self-settled refugees such as Mzee Mapesa were far advanced in their journey as refugees seeking to establish and cultivate social networks, and claim a sense of belonging while concurrently pursuing their own aspirations. They appeared to have adapted and integrated relatively well in their new environment and attained some level of personal restoration, self-actualization, and determination. They had built meaningful livelihoods, which afforded them a level of economic self-reliance. Perhaps more importantly, taking on leadership roles unmasked another dimension of socio-political embeddedness, which offered individuals like Mzee Mapesa some of the privileges of power. Such power could then be deployed and exploited to meet either collective group interests as self-settled refugees or the personal interests of those holding such positions of responsibility. With such privileges of power, the same individuals could also exercise their agency to mobilize their communities to collaborate with state or non-state actors in the promotion of mundane but vital public health policies[18] for refugee communities, or to act as nodes for enforcing both local and national security policies.[19] On the negative side, these positions of power also created possibilities for individuals to use their influence to resist policies that were deemed not in line with either their personal interests or the collective interests of their communities.

Deepening our approach to engage with the above dimensions of protracted displacement opens up opportunities and possibilities to better account for the nuanced complexity and heterogeneity underpinning such processes. Such an approach is a useful starting point to inform more effective policy and decision-making to address the challenges associated with protracted displacement, especially in a world where social, political, environmental, and economic upheaval and disruption are increasingly becoming recurring features of everyday reality.

Notes

1. Including shelter, water, medicines, and food.
2. Beyond basic demographic characteristics such as ethnicity, gender, age, literacy levels, skills, or economic status.
3. These are conceptualized as the inception period, intermediate period, and period of integration.
4. This was undertaken as a collaboration between VNG International, UNCDF, and Makerere University's Urban Action Lab (UAL).
5. Specifically, those in Kampala, the capital, and the 13 designated refugee settlements in different parts of the country.
6. The average age of self-settled refugees living in Arua City is estimated to be 32 years.
7. Data suggest that households headed by single mothers were the third largest category after those headed by male heads with spouses and those headed by female heads with spouses.
8. Data suggest that average household size of urban refugee households living in Arua City was eight members. All the data referred to herein, unless stated, are drawn from a survey undertaken by VNG and UNCDF in collaboration with the Urban Action Lab (UAL), Makerere University in 2023. It is yet to be published.
9. This form of housing, locally known as *Muzigo*, is the second most popular among urban refugees after detached standalone housing, according to the VNG/UNCDF (2023) survey data.
10. Under Uganda's land laws, refugees or non-citizens are not supposed to own land under the freehold option. However, some local leaders who were interviewed claimed that some refugees had actually secured freehold titles although without definitive proof.
11. South Sudanese refugees were especially targeted, partly due to the now-publicized evidence of South Sudanese political and economic elites as well as other profiteers exploiting from the protracted South Sudan political crisis and Uganda's hosting of refugees to divert public resources (NECC, 2020; HRC, 2021).
12. Starting with the foundation, the erection of the walls and internal partitions, and finally, roofing, installation of internal fixtures, finishing, electrical wiring, and plumbing works.
13. Such as language, food, and other cultural traditions.
14. That is, as a Congolese refugee, a woman, a single mother with no assets, and as a Christian.
15. Although this is highly unlikely, given that non-citizens are not permitted to own land in Uganda in perpetuity.
16. Including the Resident City Commissioner (RCC), District Security Officer (DISO), the Uganda Police Force (UPF), and the military.
17. Such as the extent to which refugees were welcomed and treated, and the prevailing attitudes of local communities – especially positive attitudes.
18. Such as state-sanctioned immunization and other public health protection and promotion programmes.

[19] Including the resolution of tensions and conflicts within the self-settled communities they represented or between different refugee groups (e.g. the Congolese and the South Sudanese in the specific case of Uganda).

References

Albers, T., Ariccio, S., Weiss, L.A., Dessi, F., and Bonaiuto, M. (2021) 'The role of place attachment in promoting refugees' well-being and resettlement: a literature review', *International Journal of Environmental Research and Public Health*, 18(21): 11021.

Alegría, M., Álvarez, K., and DiMarzio, K. (2017) 'Immigration and mental health', *Current Epidemiology Reports*, 4(2): 145–55.

Betts, A., Stierna, M.F., Omata, N. and Sterck, O. (2024) 'The economic lives of refugees', *World Development*, 182: 106693.

Brun, C. and Fábos, A.H. (2017) Mobilizing home for long-term displacement: a critical reflection on the durable solutions. *Journal of Human Rights Practice*, 9(2): 177–83.

Bukuluki, P., Kisaakye, P., Wandiembe, S.P., and Besigwa, S. (2021) 'Suicide ideation and psychosocial distress among refugee adolescents in Bidibidi settlement in West Nile, Uganda', *Discover Psychology*, 1(1): 3.

Capici, V. (2021) Refugeehood in Uganda's Rapidly Urbanizing Cities: An Investigation of the South Sudanese Refugees' Use of Assets and Community Self-reliance to Overcome Humanitarian Protection Challenges in Arua City, Northern Uganda, MA thesis, Lund University.

Centre for Affordable Housing Finance Africa (2019) *Housing Investment Chronicles in Uganda Six Individual Household Stories Housing Investment Chronicles Uganda*. Available from: https://housingfinanceafrica.org/wp-content/uploads/2025/01/Uganda-Housing-Investment-Chronicles_Individual-Household-Stories.pdf [Accessed 2 August 2025].

Cities Alliance (2021) 'Uganda'. Available from: www.citiesalliance.org/countries/uganda?keys=&page=1 [Accessed 2 August 2025].

Crawford, N., Cosgrave, J., Haysom, S., Walicki, N., Crawford, N., Cosgrave, J., Haysom, S., and Walicki, N. (2015) *Protracted Displacement: Uncertain Paths to Self-reliance in Exile*, Internal Displacement Monitoring Centre.

Easton-Calabria, E. and Pincock, K. (2018) 'Refugee-led social protection: reconceiving refugee assistance', *Forced Migration Review*, 58: 56–60.

Hovil, L. (2007) 'Self-settled refugees in Uganda: an alternative approach to displacement?' *Journal of Refugee Studies*, 20(4): 599–620.

Human Rights Council (2021) *Human rights violations and related economic crimes in the Republic of South Sudan*, United Nations.

Janzen, R., Taylor, M., and Gokiert, R. (2022) 'Life beyond refuge: a system theory of change for supporting refugee newcomers', *Refuge*, 38(2): 1–21.

Kara, A. (2023) 'Meaningful participation means refugee-led organisation (RLO) inclusion'. Available from: https://odi.org/en/insights/meaningful-participation-means-refugee-led-organisation-rlo-inclusion [Accessed 2 August 2025].

Kara, Y.A., Getachew, A., Gitahi, M., and Ramazani, U. (2022) *Refugee-Led Organisations in East Africa: Community Perceptions in Kenya, Uganda, Ethiopia and Tanzania*, Refugee Studies Centre and Refugee-Led Research Hub, Oxford University.

Lawry, S., Samii, C., Hall, R., Leopold, A., Hornby, D., and Mtero, F. (2017) 'The impact of land property rights interventions on investment and agricultural productivity in developing countries: a systematic review', *Journal of Development Effectiveness*, 9(1): 61–81.

Levine, S. and Becton, G. (2019) 'Blending market and humanitarian support for refugees in Uganda', Partnership for Economic Inclusion. Available from: www.peiglobal.org/knowledge-center/facing-challenges-blending-market-and-humanitarian-support-refugees-uganda [Accessed 2 August 2025].

Lund, B.C., Odgaard, R., and Sjaastad, E. (2006) *Land Rights and Land Conflicts in Africa: A Review of Issues and Experiences*, Danish Institute for International Studies. Available from: https://pure.diis.dk/ws/files/68278/Land_rights_and_land_conflicts_in_Africa_a_review_of_issues_and_experiences.pdf [Accessed 2 August 2025].

MoLHUD. (n.d.) 'USMID program'. Available from: https://mlhud.go.ug/projects/usmid-program [Accessed 2 August 2025].

Montaser, M.S. (2020) 'Investigating self–settled Syrian refugees' agency and informality in southern cities: Greater Cairo – a case study', *Review of Economics and Political Science*, 9(5): 454–71.

National Economic Crime Centre (2020) *Amber Alert: South Sudan: Illicit Finance Risks*. NECC. Available from: www.nationalcrimeagency.gov.uk/who-we-are/publications/428-amber-alert-south-sudan/file [Accessed 2 August 2025].

Nkurunziza, E. (2007) 'Informal mechanisms for accessing and securing urban land rights: The case of Kampala, Uganda', *Environment and Urbanisation*, 19(2): 509–26.

Nutz, N. (2017) *A Guide to Market-based Livelihood Interventions for Refugees*, International Labour Organization.

Omata, N. (2023) 'The role of developmental "buzzwords" in the international refugee regime: Self-reliance, resilience, and economic inclusion', *World Development*, 167: 11.

Pincock, K., Betts, A., and Easton-Calabria, E. (2021) 'The rhetoric and reality of localisation: refugee-led organisations in humanitarian governance', *Journal of Development Studies*, 57(5): 719–34.

Policinski, E. and Kuzmanovic, J. (2019) 'Protracted conflicts: The enduring legacy of endless war', *International Review of the Red Cross*, 101(912): 965–76.

Refugee Law Project (2005) *'A Drop in the Ocean': Assistance and Protection for Forced Migrants in Kampala*, Refugee Law Project. Available from: www.refugeelawproject.org/files/working_papers/RLP.WP16.pdf [Accessed 2 August 2025].

Schneider, F., Feurer, M., Lundsgaard-Hansen, L.M., Myint, W., Nuam, C.D., Nydegger, K., Oberlack, C., Tun, N.N., Zähringer, J.G., Tun, A.M., and Messerli, P. (2020) 'Sustainable development under competing claims on land: three pathways between land-use changes, ecosystem services and human well-being', *European Journal of Development Research*, 32(2): 316–37.

Schweitzer, R., Greensland, J. and Kagee, A. (2007) 'Coping and resilience in refugees from the Sudan: a narrative account', *Australian and New Zealand Journal of Psychiatry*, 41(3): 282–8.

Steigemann, A.M. and Misselwitz, P. (2020) 'Architectures of asylum: making home in a state of permanent temporariness', *Current Sociology*, 68(5): 628–50.

Strand, A. (2020) 'Humanitarian–development nexus', in *Humanitarianism: Keywords*, Brill.

United Nations High Commission for Refugees (2022) 'Analysis of suicide incidents'. Available from: https://data.unhcr.org/ar/documents/download/98223 [Accessed 2 August 2025].

van Liempt, I. and Staring, R. (2021) 'Homemaking and places of restoration: belonging within and beyond places assigned to Syrian refugees in the Netherlands', *Geographical Review*, 111(2): 308–26.

Vuni, F.J., Iragi, B., and Vidal, P. (2023) *Refugee-Led Organisations: Towards Community-Based Accountability Mechanisms*. Refugee Studies Centre. Available from: www.rsc.ox.ac.uk/publications/refugee-led-organisations-towards-community-based-accountability-mechanisms [Accessed 2 August 2025].

Wiggins, S., Levine, S., Allen, M., Elsamahi, M., Krishnan, V., Mosel, I., and Patel, N. (2021) *Livelihoods and Markets in Protracted Conflict: A Review of Evidence and Practice*, ODI Global.

12

Calais as a Zone of Care: Reimagining an Urban Migration Hub Between France and the United Kingdom

Kieran Tam and Irit Katz

Introduction

Situated on the cusp of the European continent and at the narrowest point of the English Channel separating the United Kingdom and France, for centuries the city of Calais has been a contested hub of human and material movement. The opening of the Channel Tunnel in 1994 significantly altered the relationship between the two landmasses of Great Britain and Continental Europe, for the first time creating a physical link between the two. This was just one of many successive evolutions in the history of this fluctuating borderscape. Decoupled from physical, geographical bounds such as the Channel, between 1347 and 1558 it was pushed far into the continent, placing Calais and its surrounding area under the rule of the English monarchy for over 200 years. Even today, 'juxtaposed' border controls have established British short-term holding facilities (SHTF) and British border controls within defined zones on French soil (Welander, 2021). In these little pieces of England scattered across Calais, everything is British, including time-zone, telephone numbers, signage, paperwork, and staff (Bosworth and Vannier, 2019). Over time, the Anglo-French border has proven to be fluid and ever-changing. Calais has become a place of many conflicting dualities: defence and reception, hospitality and hostility, development and decline.

In recent years – most notably during the so called 'refugee crisis' from 2015 to 2016 and the rise and fall of the infamous 'Calais Jungle' makeshift migrant camp (Katz, 2017) – Calais has been marred by a humanitarian crisis on its doorstep caused by the institutional abandonment of those 'on the move'. Contemporary narratives frame the status of Calais as a migratory place of transit as unique to our time, reflective of a siloed and isolated understanding of the history of the border. These narratives portray the presence of people-on-the-move as something to be eradicated while wilfully ignoring Calais's rich migratory urban history composed of centuries of human movement. Placed within a global context, this approach embodies a broader political and humanitarian crisis in the hospitality of the forcibly displaced (Katz, 2023). It demonstrates a crisis of the imagination, urban and political, and an inability to envisage alternative ways of engaging with human movement in and through cities such as Calais. Drawing on the authors' research and voluntary experiences in Calais – Tam's experiences as a volunteer and his research primarily through 'sensory ethnography' (Pink, 2012) and participant observation and the spatial research conducted by Katz in the 'Jungle' camp in Calais and other camps in Northern France between 2015 and 2017 (Katz, 2017, 2019, 2023) – this chapter seeks to reimagine Calais's relationship with the border and the people who live in and pass through it. It explores the ways in which radical geopolitical and spatial imagination could offer Calais a vision for alternative future configurations, roles, and identities in which people-on-the-move are not abandoned and discarded but rather embraced as part of the very identity and workings of Calais.

The constant flow of people and goods between Great Britain and the European continent has long been facilitated by regular ferries, trains, and vehicles crossing the Channel (Heddebaut, 2001). However, miles of fencing and vast swathes of border infrastructures built around Calais's port area and tunnel entrance allude to the darker realm of militarization and the illegalization of migrants by the Anglo-French-European border enforcement regime, where people-on-the-move have been forced into adopting more dangerous and clandestine routes (Akkerman, 2019). This phenomenon is also seen in many other areas of increased differential control and the restriction of borders across the globe (Hansen, 2014). Over time, as Great Britain and Continental Europe have become more intricately intertwined, England and France have begun to 'overlap' in their borderscapes (Heitzman, 2014: 277), which in turn are evolving into one 'shared space' (Morieux, 2016). This is evident in the 'juxtaposed' controls already established and the United Kingdom's significant role in transforming the French coast into the militarized borderland it is today. Successive arrangements between the United Kingdom and France have seen the British government commit over £232 million between 2014 and 2023 to strengthen policing and militarization of the border (Gower, 2023). However, the potential of this 'shared space' remains acutely unfulfilled, as Britain stops short of providing decriminalised and genuinely safe routes for asylum seekers to the United Kingdom. Despite increased measures to prevent 'illegal' entry, people continue to arrive and become trapped at the border, sometimes with fatal consequences (Hagan, 2020). There is a critical need for a major shift in political thinking about Calais to the thousands of migrants that still pass through it on their way to Britain. It is therefore crucial that Calais is imagined otherwise: as a hospitable city instead of the hostile borderscape it has become.

Situated within a body of literature that focuses predominantly on the violence of the state (Boyle, 2017; Davies et al, 2017; Rullman, 2020), camps and precarious shelters (Hanappe, 2017; Gueguen-Teil and Katz, 2018; Katz, 2019; Hagan, 2020), and humanitarian and solidarity practices (Rigby and Schlembach, 2013; Sandri, 2018), this chapter applies care ethics to investigate how the situation at the border can be imagined otherwise. Drawing attention to the ways in which violence is spatially (Herscher and Siddiqi, 2017; Van Isacker, 2019) and structurally (Davies et al, 2017) manifested, we argue that humanitarian interventions, although helpful in supporting the survival of people-on-the-move, have a limited capacity to alleviate their suffering. We further contend that there is a risk of humanitarians perpetuating hegemonic power imbalances (Belloni, 2007; Fassin, 2007) and becoming part of acts of bordering at both human and urban scales. Deindustrialization and the decline of tourism in Calais have, over recent decades, thrown the city of Calais into socio-economic decline and urban disrepair, exasperated by the municipality and state's violent campaign against people-on-the-move (Kelemen, 2021; Schmidt, 2021). To address the double failure of both governmental and non-governmental interventions, we propose the urgent replacement of the violence–humanitarian nexus with an expansive ethic of universal care. Employing literature on care ethics (Tronto, 1998; Noddings, 2012; Puig de la Bellacasa, 2017), maintenance and repair (Mattern, 2018), urban refuge (Oomen, 2019), and political imagination (Arendt, 2014), we speculate on alternatives to the current approach to Calais's border crisis.

States of violence: violent states

Since 1999, more than 400 people have been killed in their attempts to reach the United Kingdom, a third of whom have died in the vicinity of Calais (Galisson and Lambert, 2020). This is the result of a 'necropolitical border regime' (Williams, 2015) funded by the UK government and enforced by the French state in a form of 'structural' violence, which is systematic and 'shows up as unequal power and consequently unequal life chances' (Galtung, 1969: 171). In Northern France, structural violence manifests through the exposure of people-on-the-move to brutal conditions resulting from both state action and state withdrawal (Davies et al, 2017) – or, in Mbembé's (2003)

Foucauldian language, 'letting die'. 'Spatial violence', meanwhile, is enacted through the militarization and securitization of the borderscape, the regulation and restriction of humanitarian spaces (Williams, 2015), and 'refugee urbicide' (Davies et al, 2017), 'domicide' (Van Isacker, 2019), and 'active violence against makeshift materialities' (M. Hagan, 2021: 2). The violence faced by people-on-the-move in Calais has been widely documented, involving the securitization of the border, routine evictions, the destruction and confiscation of shelter, the banning of food distribution, the slashing of water tanks, and the refusal to provide services such as rubbish collection from their living sites (Human Rights Watch, 2021). These are the violent actions and inactions experienced by people-on-the-move every day, perpetuated by a violent state.

Observations made through Tam's period of fieldwork in Northern France reveal how, through neglect and securitization, violence is spatially engrained into the urban fabric of Calais. Throughout its history, the city of Calais has been perpetrator, witness, and victim to centuries of war and violence, evidence of which remains in the crumbling forts, bunkers, and batteries built between the thirteenth century and World War II. Even into the twenty-first century, security barriers, detention facilities, high-tech surveillance systems, and other militarized border technologies continue to dominate the urban landscape as state and municipality continue their manufactured war against the imagined threat of illegalized migration. Meanwhile, the rest of Calais's urban fabric is deteriorating, falling victim to the slow structural violence of neglect. The city's buildings suffer from the indiscriminate effects of austerity and disrepair, and its streets are characterized by greying walls covered in grime and peeling paint, punctuated by seemingly permanently shuttered windows, presenting a series of streetscapes that are cold, defensive, and unwelcoming. People-on-the-move who have been pushed further to the periphery remain visible through the traces of life they leave behind: discarded sleeping bags, tarpaulin sheets, mattresses, and empty food packaging where the municipality refuses to pick up refuse. Meanwhile, pockets of public land, left unmaintained, are now overgrown with weeds and littered with rubbish.

Spatial and material languages of security infiltrate the everyday lives of Calais's embedded and transient visitors, with the daily sight of convoys of police and military vehicles and a slew of surveillance systems. Quality of life in Calais has been sacrificed by the state in the name of border security, with people-on-the-move used as scapegoats (Kelemen, 2021; Schmidt, 2021). Intimidation tactics used by the police, such as the stalking of people-on-the-move, regular patrols, and the lingering threat of physical violence, have made it nearly impossible for them to comfortably use public spaces without the fear of retribution (Human Rights Watch, 2021). Spaces under bridges and flyovers where people would previously have found shelter have been made inaccessible through the erection of barbed wire fencing, the woodlands in which they camped are being flattened, and open fields are being churned up to make them uninhabitable (Louarn, 2021; Oberti, 2021). Meanwhile, large boulders are manoeuvred into place by the municipality to prevent humanitarian organizations from accessing distribution sites or refilling water points (Schmidt, 2021). In this way, authorities are employing a 'scorched earth policy' (Calais pour la Climat, 2020), designed to encroach on the spaces in which people-on-the-move are forced to find shelter and receive aid. For the past seven years, evictions have become a key part of this migrant-deterrence toolkit employed by the state, constituting a form of 'domicide', defined by Van Isacker (2019: 614) as the 'intentional elimination of contentious spaces and forms of inhabitance' through 'coerced abandonment', the physical destruction of shelter, or the prevention of construction. Since 2018, routine eviction operations have been carried out every 24 to 48 hours in the city as part of a zero-tolerance policy designed to destroy any living sites created by people-on-the-move, described by the government as fixation points before they grow into established makeshift camps (Human Rights Watch, 2021). Many people, however, return to the same place until another eviction team comes along a couple of days later, in a vicious domicidal cycle of destruction and reconstruction.

Despite a steady increase in the number of evictions in Calais between 2019 and 2021, the number of people-on-the-move living in and around Calais has risen significantly (Louarn, 2020; Human Rights Watch, 2021). The strong desire of many to reach the United Kingdom is reinforced by pre-existing familial and community ties or the underlying legacies of colonialism, such as a common language, perceived shared histories, and illusions of welcome, stability, and new beginnings. For others, the United Kingdom is a last resort, the end of the line where attempts to claim asylum elsewhere in Europe have failed (Hagan, 2020; CNCDH, 2021). In the absence of other viable, safe routes, people-on-the-move will inevitably continue to pass through Northern France to reach the United Kingdom, no matter the risk, jumping trains and lorries or using so-called 'small boats' organised by human smugglers who have capitalised on our governments' inaction (Gower, 2023: 7).

Violent spaces in disguise

Since the 1990s, the spatialities of migrant living environments have fluctuated between the makeshift and the institutional (Martin et al, 2019), corresponding to different approaches to border governance over time. Over the past three decades, people-on-the-move have endured violence through their forced induction into 'state-controlled circuits of mobility' (Van Isacker, 2019: 609), often justified by the authorities using 'paternalistic humanitarian narratives' (Van Isacker, 2019: 613).

In 1999, an old warehouse next to the newly opened Channel Tunnel entrance in Sangatte was repurposed and used as a reception centre to respond to an increase in migrant arrivals. Similarly in 2016, a large portion of makeshift settlements in the 'new Jungle' were demolished and cleared to make way for a provisional reception centre (Camp d'Accueil Provisoire, or CAP), composed of over 100 shipping containers. Both centres were fenced and gated, and entry became conditional on biometric registration in order to enforce the Dublin III Regulation, effectively denying the right of those registered to claim asylum in the United Kingdom and their right to a dignified wait in France. Both centres were temporary and were closed not long after they were opened.

In the makeshift camp of the Jungle, people-on-the-move were excluded not only spatially from the city but also through the withholding of services by the state, creating a form of 'violent inaction' (Davies et al, 2017). To fill the gap, citizens from all over Europe stepped in to act, creating a wave of new grassroots humanitarian groups (McGee and Pelham, 2018; Sandri, 2018), many of which continue to operate today. In a remarkable demonstration of resourcefulness, the Jungle's inhabitants, with the help of humanitarian architects and volunteers, constructed living spaces, shops, restaurants, schools, religious spaces, and various other self-built structures out of timber and tarpaulin sheets (Katz, 2017; Mould, 2018). Auto-construction enabled people to partially reclaim their identities as active agents, rather than the victims and illegals they had been depicted as being, performing 'acts of citizenship' in defiance of the state (Boyle, 2017). However, despite the Jungle's cultural and social richness, the high turnover of its inhabitants rendered it spatially extremely volatile and constantly in a state of 'unmaking' and 're-making' (Mould, 2018: 393), perpetually overshadowed by the lingering threat of eviction and clearance (McGee and Pelham, 2018; Sandri, 2018). The erection of the CAP container camp in 2016 signified the government's quickly dissipating tolerance of the Jungle's existence; by the end of the year, demolition squads had dismantled and bulldozed every structure on the site.

Indeed, the condition of displacement in Northern France exists in a state of violence, perpetuated by a violent state. While violence is most visibly and overtly directed at migratory bodies, it has also been inflicted on them indirectly through intimidation and threats of violence, destruction of their shelters and possessions, the restriction and regulation of their mobilities, and their abandonment and enforced precarity. In the past, institutional camps provided by the state in Sangatte and the 2015 Jungle have only served to facilitate the structurally violent regulation of the identities and lives of people-on-the-move forced to trade autonomy for shelter. At the same time, through abandonment and enforced precarity in makeshift camps, the state has inflicted latent and indirect biological violence on them.

A minimalist conception of humanitarianism restricts intervention to the saving of lives and temporary relieving of suffering in times of crisis (Fassin,

2007; Skinner and Lester, 2012; Ticktin, 2014, 2016). This is supported by Williams' (2015: 17) description of an unfolding 'minimalist biopolitics', where governmental and NGO humanitarian interventions merely 'hold off death', preserving and maintaining biological life but stopping short of enabling dignified living. State governments are no stranger to the use of humanitarianism as 'the handmaiden of their imperialist and militarized interventions' (Williams, 2015: 14). The British government has capitalized on recent deaths in the Channel to pursue an agenda of increasingly violent and Draconian measures to further police and militarize the border and criminalize border-crossing despite claiming humanity, generosity, and fairness (Home Office, 2021).

However, governmental appropriation of humanitarianism to legitimize border violence and control also manifests in subtler, more covert ways. In Calais, where food distributions were banned between 2020 and 2022 (ECRE, 2020), the organization La Vie Active has been contracted by the state to be the sole 'legal' provider of hot meals to people-on-the-move (Carreterro, 2020). However, food distributed by the organization has been reported to be both insufficient in quantity and insufficiently adapted to people's needs in terms of type and timing (Human Rights Watch, 2021). This claim was reinforced in 2023, when three consecutive months of the food distribution ban in 2020 were overturned by the administrative court in Lille, citing the insufficient quantity of La Vie Active's provision (Pall, 2022). Furthermore, state-administered spaces such as short-term reception shelters (*centre d'accueil et d'examen des situations*, CAES) are increasingly being used as part of an effort to 'govern more bodies ... and more spaces' (Williams, 2015: 11). In 2021, the organization Afeji was commissioned by the state to accompany people seeking respite from exposure to the brutal conditions of makeshift living sites to CAESs in Lille (Afeji Hauts-de-France, 2021). This is what Van Isacker (2019) describes as a 'carrot and stick' approach, where domicide is used to drive people-on-the-move into circuits of state migration governance. People who wish to stay for longer than one week in shelters must agree to make an asylum claim in France or leave. It cannot be denied that organizations such as La Vie Active and Afeji provide necessary services to people-on-the-move in Northern France, but they have also become complicit in the enforcement of the state's violent border regime (Rieff, 2002; Williams, 2015; Van Isacker, 2019).

Even for humanitarian groups independent of the state, the capacity of the minimalist, emergency humanitarian model to effectively counter the brutal violence of Anglo-French borderwork has proven to be limited. Local humanitarian groups provide a wide range of different services to the communities of people-on-the-move, including material aid such as shelter and clothes, cooking ingredients and equipment, hot food, potable water, and WASH facilities, as well as medical support, legal advice, internet connectivity, emergency accommodation, and women-only spaces. Humanitarian vehicles shuttle backwards and forwards from the donations' warehouses to the distribution sites in a daily routine that Hagan (2018) describes as a daily 'performance' of the camp. The distribution site becomes a shared space where the worlds of people-on-the-move and volunteers collide. However, while the volunteer presence regularly extends beyond the distribution site into migratory living spaces, most people-on-the-move are actively prevented from entering volunteer spaces, though steps are being taken to dismantle these practices. In this way, fluid mobile networks of aid are carved into spaces that separate the volunteer from people-on-the-move, while drawing distance between 'us' and 'them', as well as 'here' and 'there' (Tinsley, 2021), which can be seen through the problematic mainstream portrayal of people-on-the-move as helpless and desperate, and of volunteers as 'saviours'. However, by reattempting Channel crossings, building and rebuilding shelters, and through protests, memorials, and squatting, migrants perform daily acts of citizenship and continuously make claim to meaningful lives (Katz, 2023). In doing so, they shed notions of helplessness and demonstrate an agency and resilience that must be accounted for in future imaginings of the border.

Universal care and the power of imagination

Constrained by the humanitarian model, practices of care at the border in Northern France remain conceptually narrow and restricted. While the diverse humanitarian involvement has been effective in supporting the survival of migrants at the border, many people-on-the-move still experience extreme everyday suffering at the hands of the state. The humanitarian model also fails to address the needs of the local population, who have suffered decades of socio-economic decline due to deindustrialization and globalization, and after 30 years of the protracted crisis in border management are growing tired and frustrated (Kelemen, 2021).

Humanitarian approaches such as the 'humanitarian–development nexus' (Zetter, 2014; Strand, 2020) acknowledge that the responsibility of hosting displaced populations usually falls on already marginalized communities, seeking to remedy this by simultaneously engaging in the support and development of the host community. A survey of Calais residents conducted by the humanitarian collective La Voix Commune (2021) demonstrates that while many remain empathetic towards the plight of people-on-the-move, many are also exhausted by their presence and demonstrate feelings of powerlessness against the situation and the abandonment by the state. In carrying out this survey, humanitarian groups in Calais have shown a willingness to engage with the local population, who are often dismissed by volunteers as unsympathetic and racist. For migrant-oriented care work to be supported by the local population, it must also be seen to address their own local needs.

The common understanding of the notion of 'care' largely revolves around 'caregiving' and 'caring about' (Tronto, 1998). The former refers to the transaction of aid and support, whereas the latter refers to the emotional concern that often enables it. Through their work, the humanitarian organizations in Calais engage in these forms of care at the very least. However, these two facets make up just two of Tronto's (1998) 'four phases of care', which further include 'caring for' – the assumption of responsibility to meet identified needs – and 'care receiving' – an active response of attentiveness and receptiveness that enables the provider of care to assess whether the needs of care have been met (Noddings, 2012). Where the caregiver is in control of the knowledge or resources needed by the care receiver, power imbalances can arise and care receivers might be coded as 'helpless victims' (Van Leeuwen, 2018).

Ethical care, in contrast, is built on the foundations of equal power relations, where the perspectives and wishes of the cared-for are considered and they are respected as active agents in their own care (Van Leeuwen, 2018). Ethical care is relational and reciprocal, meaning that the 'carer and cared-for are not permanent labels but names for roles accepted in encounters' (Noddings, 2012: 53), rejecting notions of dependency in favour of interdependency (Chatzidakis and the Care Collective, 2021). Whereas the goal of humanitarianism is to preserve life and facilitate survival, an 'ethic of care' recognizes care as being a 'species activity that includes everything that we do to maintain, continue, and repair our world so that we can live in it as well as possible' (Tronto, 1998: 16). Chatzidakis and the Care Collective, 2021 (2021: 5–6) advance a model of 'universal care', which involves the establishment of 'political, social, material, and emotional conditions that allow the vast majority of people … to thrive'. The emergency situation of the humanitarian acting in solidarity (Millner, 2012; Rigby and Schlembach, 2013; Squire, 2018), or 'solidarian', is indicative of the limitations of humanitarianism and the need for the application of a broader, more equitable ethics of care at the border – a kind of 'universal care' that could allow all people, tourists and locals, people-on-the-move and volunteers, to flourish. This requires us to imagine Calais otherwise as a border city in various political, ethical, and spatial manners.

Speculating on the politics and urban spatialities of universal care at the border provokes not only 'political and ethical imagination' (Puig de la Bellacasa, 2017: 7), but spatial imagination as well. Hannah Arendt (2014: 43) writes that 'the force of imagination … makes the others present and thus moves in a space that is potentially public, open to all sides'. In order to create more political options of existing with one another, she argues, 'one [needs to train] one's imagination to go visiting' (2014: 43) and see 'alternative scenarios for past, present, and future realities' (Musih, 2021: 2). Spatial and political imagination is a skill that must be trained in order to enable us to conceive new realities that transcend the boundaries of what we know and break free of entrenched social, political, and economic systems.

By interrogating alternative futures for Calais's relationship with migration, this chapter seeks to be a part of this collective effort.

Imagining the borderscape in Northern France through universal care and its related spaces could enable the city of Calais and its embedded community to reinterpret its past, current, and future socio-political and spatial situations. This could encourage its recovery from decades of socio-economic and urban stagnation and the wounds inflicted by border securitization and militarization, simultaneously allowing spaces of solidarity and aid – which currently exist as small and networked sites of resistance – to be reimagined as part of Calais's fabric and grow into legitimized, shared spaces integrated into the city's urban strategy.

Over the past decade, the municipality of Calais has responded to years of urban deterioration and degradation by funding the redevelopment of key areas in the public realm. However, in many of these redeveloped sites, pockets of potential urban greenery are paved over by sterile slabs of grey stone, blockaded by defensive bollards and interventions hostile to the city's illegalized people-on-the-move, who remain explicitly excluded from urban participation. When read alongside the city's scorched-earth policies, these hostile interventions speak of a deep desire to cleanse the city of its migratory history and restart with a blank slate. However, as Hagan (2020: 177) puts it, 'as long as the cliffs of Dover lie across the water from Calais and the European asylum system continues to fail, [people] will be drawn to this border zone'.

Calais's history as a place of blurred boundaries, constant transit, and solidarity spaces challenging the order of the nation-state makes it an opportune site for the testing of other ways of thinking about municipal identity and urban membership that could eventually be expanded and adapted at a national scale, similarly to other 'sanctuary cities', 'cities of welcome', or 'cities of refuge' across the Global North (Darling, 2010; Bagelman, 2013; Delvino, 2017; Bazurli, 2019; Kaufmann, 2019; Oomen, 2019; Fischer and Jørgensen, 2020). Such schemes seek to legitimize the presence of people irregularized and illegalized by the state, recognizing the importance of their contributions to the vitality of urban socio-economic life in a way based on presence and participation. In Calais, this could become part of a new narrative of the city.

Narratives of sacrifice, rescue, and protection are baked into Calais's municipal identity, represented through its prized monuments and heritage sites, including Rodin's *The Burghers of Calais*, the Monument des Sauveteurs, the lighthouse, and the city's various forts and previously defensive moats. Rekindling this protective spirit through the establishment of an institutionally supported special care zone (SCZ) within the city limits, which will prevent policing, identifying, and controlling people-on-the-move while embedding expanded practices of care, could reclaim and forge new socio-political narratives of respite and restoration: that of the city, its local residents and new arrivals who have just endured dangerous migratory journeys. The creation of a protected sanctuary would allow both embedded and transiting residents to enjoy de facto urban 'cityzenship' (Oomen, 2019) and access public services based on their presence within these bounds and their active participation in urban life. Whereas 'zones' (special economic zones, free trade zones, etc.) have previously been employed to 'incentivize growth' and 'jumpstart economies' (Easterling, 2012), the SCZ could instead become a 'legal instrument' (Easterling, 2012), prescribing and prioritizing 'care logics' over 'border-zone logics' or 'market logics' where 'care work may be valued highly and care resources distributed equally' (Chatzidakis and the Care Collective, 2021, p 77). Here, the role of shared, public space in fostering 'care across difference' (Chatzidakis and the Care Collective, 2021), engendering 'reciprocity' (Darling, 2011) and promoting 'conviviality' through 'coexistence' (Zaman, 2020) is necessary for creating a Calaisien 'ecology of care' (Mattern, 2018). This might include practices of mobile commoning (Sheller, 2021), including practices of cohabitation between locals, volunteers, and people-on-the-move, offering different forms of collectivized living (Katz, 2023).

In Northern France, a growing network of *citoyen hébergeurs* (citizen hosts), and organizations, such as Maria Skobtsova House and La Maison Sésame, now host people-on-the-move in home-like settings, affording the most vulnerable a stable and protected environment in which to stay (E. Hagan, 2021). La Maison Sésame near Dunkerque engaged its residents in a collective renovation project to convert a large family home and a farm into spaces of refuge, education, play, horticulture, maintenance, and repair (Maison Sésame, 2020a). The house is open to all, regardless of legal status or intended duration of stay, and is described as a space to be 'built as its inhabitants pass through it' (Maison Sésame, 2020b). Kreichauf et al (2020) suggest that infrastructures such as these not only transform the people who go through them but are also transformed by them. Spaces such as La Maison Sésame, self-described as a 'citizens' initiative of hospitality' providing 'a stopover on the migration journey' (Maison Sésame, 2020b) could offer a starting point from which the SCZ could be scaled up.

Squats in border cities and shared homes such as these have illustrated how the commoning of space also requires the negotiation of shared responsibilities (Katz, 2023). Studies have shown that through the collective maintenance of defective infrastructures, social and political bonds are drawn between the people engaged in the process (Mattern, 2018). As these spaces have shown, the sharing of responsibilities allows for interdependencies to be drawn between different actors, challenging narratives that migrants will be a drain on their host communities. Similar social and moral contracts could underpin the conditionality of urban hospitality within the SZC, further encouraging embedded and transiting residents to participate in and contribute to their shared urban environment during their residency. The requisition and redistribution of land by the municipal authorities in order to build on infill sites or redevelop and reuse derelict homes, shops, restaurants, and hotels could lead to the sprouting of an expanded network of shared accommodation, solidarity kitchens, public wash facilities, and community centres. Migrant solidarity groups could occupy these spaces on the condition that they repair these sites prior to occupation and maintain them throughout, creating an urban strategy predicated on principles of care.

Through this approach, we seek to provoke thoughts and new imaginaries on how urban membership can be afforded to people-on-the-move through a politics of presence and fostering welcome, belonging, and interdependence through shared spaces and collective responsibilities. In the same way that the violence of the border has spread into the everyday spaces and lives of the people who live in and pass through Calais, the caring relations described have the potential to be radically rescaled and redrawn at an urban scale. For the time being, this exercise in imagination stops short of abolishing the border, but seeks to envisage the emergence of a mainstream counter-culture of universal care, giving Calais a second lease on life and the opportunity to recover from decades of urban decline while embracing the past histories and future inevitabilities of its role as a migratory transit point.

Conclusion: Imagining Calais beyond humanitarianism

For 30 years, the city of Calais and the French state have consistently found themselves unable to cope with the presence of people-on-the-move stuck at the border. In denying the city's inevitable role as a migratory transit point, they have become complicit in the manufacturing of today's crisis in border management. This chapter has asserted that Calais can no longer deny its migratory reality and must develop a different approach to it in order to address its fragility through practices and ethics of care.

As people continue to go to extreme lengths to make it to the United Kingdom, it has become obvious that the French government's multi-scalar strategy of deterrence through structural and spatial violence does not work (Katz, 2023). Humanitarian groups have intervened to challenge and mitigate the effects of this enforced precarity, but the spaces within which they can operate are increasingly being encroached upon by the state. At the same time, many humanitarian groups also embed practices in their work that draw boundaries between volunteers and people-on-the-move, resulting in instances of spatial bordering at both human and urban scales. Nonetheless, the emergence of the solidarian and solidarity spaces indicates an acknowledgement of these shortfalls and injustices. Solidarity practices grounded in egalitarian logic, rejecting the infantilization of the migrant figure and defiantly challenging the violence of the border regime, indicate how more ethical caring relations might be drawn between people of different mobilities.

Due to the failures of the Sangatte Centre and the 2015 Jungle, the state has since been reluctant to renew policies of reception. However, these previous attempts to accommodate people-on-the-move failed because they neglected to acknowledge migrants as capable, agentive contributors to their environments. Instead, these interventions saw them as solitary bodies to be constrained, stored, and hidden from view. As the state's strategies of deterrence become increasingly untenable, the government now has the opportunity to look to alternative approaches to confronting the ongoing realities of the border situation. As we have argued, it is indeed possible to reimagine the violent-humanitarian border as one of universal care and to see that existing spaces of care and collectivized living have the possibility to be expanded and redrawn at an urban scale. Inspired by existing cities of refuge, we argue that by engaging with a politics of presence and affording people-on-the-move's urban membership within SCZs, Calais could become a testing ground for policies promoting welcome, belonging, and interdependence. Combined with an urban strategy prioritizing shared spaces and a collective responsibility to repair and maintain the urban environment, this could give the city the opportunity it desperately needs to undergo radical urban transformation and recover from decades of urban decline, while creating an environment in which its embedded and transitory inhabitants can thrive as opposed to just survive. Imagining this spatial-political and social change could be the beginning of making it an actual possibility for the future of Calais.

References

Afeji Hauts-de-France (2021) *Par tous les temps, l'Afeji Hauts-de-France accompagne la mise à l'abri des migrants.* Available from: www.afeji.org/par-tous-les-temps-lafeji-hauts-de-france- accompagne-la-mise-a-labri-des-migrants [Accessed 9 December 2021].

Akkerman, M. (2019) *Hunted. Detained. Deported. UK–French Co-operation and the Effects of Border Securitisation on Refugees in Calais,* Stop Wapenhandel & Care4Calais.

Arendt, H. (2014) *Lectres on Kant's Political Philosophy*, Chicago University Press.

Bagelman, J. (2013) 'Sanctuary: a politics of ease?', *Alternatives: Global, Local, Political*, 38(1): 49–62.

Bazurli, R. (2019) 'Local governments and social movements in the "refugee crisis": Milan and Barcelona as "cities of welcome"', *South European Society and Politics*, 24(3): 343–70.

Belloni, R. (2007) 'The trouble with humanitarianism', *Review of International Studies*, 33(3): 451–74.

Bosworth, M. and Vannier, M. (2019) 'Blurred lines: Detaining asylum seekers in Britain and France', Journal of Sociology, 56(1): 53–68.

Boyle, M. (2017) 'Shelter provision and state sovereignty in Calais', *Forced Migration Review*, 55: 30–2.

Calais pour la Climat (2020) *Destruction systématique de la végétation à Calais: ça suffit!* Available from: https://calaispourleclimat.fr/2020/11/18/destruction-systematique-de-la- vegetation-a-calais-ca-suffit [Accessed 8 January 2022].

Carreterro, L. (2020) *Calais: les distributions de nourriture de la Vie active deviennent mobiles.* Available from: https://www.infomigrants.net/fr/post/27836/calais--les-distributions-de- nourriture-de-la-vie-active-deviennent-mobiles [Accessed 9 December 2021].

Chatzidakis, A. and the Care Collective (2021) *The Care Manifesto: The Politics of Interdependence*, Verso.

CNCDH (2021) *Opinion on the Situation of Exiled Persons in Calais and Grande-Synthe*, Commission Nationale Consultative des Droits de L'Homme.

Darling, J. (2010) 'A city of sanctuary: the relational re-imagining of Sheffield's asylum politics', *Transactions of the Institute of British Geographers*, 35(1): 125–40.

Darling, J. (2011) 'Giving space: care, generosity and belonging in a UK asylum drop-in centre', *Geoforum*, 42: 408–17.

Davies, T., Isakjee, A. and Dhesi, S. (2017) 'Violent inaction: the necropolitical experience of refugees in Europe', *Antipode*, 49(5): 1263–84.

Delvino, N. (2017) *European Cities and Migrants with Irregular Status: Municipal Initiatives for the Inclusion of Irregular Migrants in the Provision of Services*, City Initiative on Migrants with Irregular Status in Europe.

Easterling, K. (2012) *Zone: The Spatial Softwares of Extrastatecraft*. Available from: https://placesjournal.org/article/zone-the-spatial-softwares-of-extr astatecraft [Accessed 9 January 2022].

ECRE (2020) *France: Ban on Food Distribution in Calais City Centre Appealed to Council of State, Police Dismantles Makeshift Camp.* Available from: https://ecre.org/france-ban-on-food-distribution-in-calais-city-centre- appealed-to-council-of-state-police-dismantles-makeshift-camp [Accessed 9 December 2021].

Fassin, D. (2007) 'Humanitarianism as a politics of life', *Public Culture*, 19(3): 499–520.

Fischer, L. and Jørgensen, M.B. (2020) ' "We are here to stay" vs "Europe's best hotel": Hamburg and Athens as geographies of solidarity', *Antipode*, 53(4): 1062–82.

Galisson, M. and Lambert, N. (2020) *Observatory of Deaths at the Borders: France, Belgium, UK*. Available from: https://neocarto.github.io/calais/en [Accessed 22 October 2021].

Galtung, J. (1969) 'Violence, peace, and peace research', *Journal of Peace Research,* 6(3): 167–91.

Gower, M. (2023) *Irregular Migration: A Timeline of UK–French Cooperation*, House of Commons Library.

Gueguen-Teil, C. and Katz, I. (2018) 'On the meaning of shelter: living in Calais's Camps de la Lande', in I. Katz, D. Martin and C. Minca (eds), *Camps Revisited: Multifaceted Spatialities of a Modern Political Technology.* Rowman & Littlefield, pp 83–98.

Hagan, E. (2021) *Interview about Refugee Women's Centre*. interview, 23 September.

Hagan, M. (2018) *The Jungle 'Performance': Recreating a Refugee Camp on the Fly*. Available from: www.newsdeeply.com/refugees/community/2018/09/07/the-jungle-performance-recreating-a-refugee-camp-on-the-fly [Accessed 24 December 2019].

Hagan, M. (2020) 'The Contingent Camp', in T. Scott-Smith and M.E. Breeze (eds), *Structures of Protection?*. New York: Berghahn Books, pp 111–121.

Hagan, M. (2021) 'Precarious encampments in hostile border zones: the methodological challenges of and possibilities for studying contingent camps', *Area*, 54(3): 355–64.

Hanappe, C. (2017) 'A camp redefined as part of the city', *Forced Migration Review*, 55: 33–34.

Hansen, R. (2014) 'State controls: borders, refugees, and citizenship', in E. Fiddian-Qasmiyeh, G. Loescher, K. Long and N. Sigona (eds), *The Oxford Handbook of Refugee and Forced Migration Studies*, Oxford University Press, pp 253–65.

Heddebaut, O. (2001) 'The binational cities of Dover and Calais', *GeoJournal*, 54(1): 61–71.

Heitzman, M. (2014) '"A long and constant fusion of the two great nations": Dickens, the crossing, and *A Tale of Two Cities*', *Dickens Studies Annual*, 45: 275–92.

Herscher, A. and Siddiqi, A.I. (2017) 'Spatial violence', in A. Herscher and A.I. Siddiqi (eds), *Spatial Violence*, Routledge, pp 1–9.

Home Office (2021) 'Home Secretary's Speech on Channel deaths'. Available from: www.gov.uk/government/speeches/home-secretarys-speech-on-channel-drownings [Accessed 2 January 2022].

Human Rights Watch (2021) *Enforced Misery: The Degrading Treatment of Migrant Children and Adults in Northern France*, Human Rights Watch.

Katz, I. (2017) 'Between bare life and everyday life: spatializing Europe's migrant camps', *Architecture_MPS,* 12(2): 1–20.

Katz, I. (2019) 'En route: the networked mobile border camps of Northern France', in A. Pieris (ed), *Architecture on the Borderline: Boundary Politics and Built Space*, Routledge, pp 119–37.

Katz, I. (2023) 'Borderzone departure cities: jumping-off urbanism of irregular migration on the edges of Europe', *Antipode*, 55(5): 1608–33.

Kaufmann, D. (2019) 'Comparing urban citizenship, sanctuary cities, local bureaucratic membership, and regularisations', *Public Administration Review*, 79(3): 443–6.

Kelemen, N. (2021) 'Discussions on Fort Risban and the migrant situation in Calais', interview, 3 March.

Kreichauf, R., Rosenberger, O. and Strobel, P. (2020) 'The transformative power of urban arrival infrastructures: Berlin's Refugio and Dong Xuan Center', *Urban Planning*, 5(3): 44–54.

La Voix Commun (2021) *Etude Harris*. Available from: www.calais-m.fr/etude-harris [Accessed 29 July 2021].

Louarn, A.-D. (2020) 'In Calais, at least 1,200 migrants are on the streets, twice as many as last summer'. Available from: www.infomigrants.net/en/post/25590/in-calais-at-least-1200- migrants-are-on-the-streets-twice-as-many-as-last-summer [Accessed 23 October 2021].

Louarn, A.-D. (2021) 'In Calais, the prefecture extends the ban on the distribution of meals to migrants'. Available from: www.infomigrants.net/fr/post/30754/a-calais-la-prefecture- prolonge-l-interdiction-de-distribution-de-repas-aux-migrants [Accessed 14 March 2021].

Maison Sésame (2020a) 'Les Lieux: our spaces'. Available from: https://maisonsesame.org/les-lieux [Accessed 9 January 2022].

Maison Sésame (2020b) 'Notre Approche: our approach'. Available from: https://maisonsesame.org/qui-sommes-nous [Accessed 9 January 2022].

Martin, D., Minca, C. and Katz, I. (2019) 'Rethinking the camp: on spatial technologies of power and resistance', *Progress in Human Geography*, 44(4): 743–68.

Mattern, S. (2018) 'Maintenance and care'. *Places*, November. Available from: https://placesjournal.org/article/maintenance-and-care [Accessed 14 January 2022].

Mbembé, A. (2003) 'Necropolitics', *Public Culture*, 15(1): 11–40.

McGee, D. and Pelham, J. (2018) 'Politics at play: locating human rights, refugees and grassroots humanitarianism in the Calais Jungle', *Leisure Studies*, 37(1): 22–35.

Millner, N. (2012) 'Sanctuary sans frontières: social movements and solidarity in post-war Northern France', in R.K. Lippert and R. Sean (eds), *Migration, Citizenship and Social Movements*, Routledge, pp 57–70.

Morieux, R. (2016) *The Channel: England, France and the Construction of a Maritime Border in the Eighteenth Century*, Cambridge University Press.

Mould, O. (2018) 'The not-so-concrete Jungle: material precarity in the Calais refugee camp', *Cultural Geographies*, 25(3): 393–409.

Musih, N. (2021) 'Bridging memories: Training the imagination to go visiting in Israel/Palestine', *Visual Studies*, 38(3–4): 512–22.

Noddings, N. (2012) 'The language of care ethics', *Knowledge Quest*, 40(4): 52–6.

Oberti, C. (2021) 'Razed woodlands prevent migrants from sheltering around Calais'. Available from: www.infomigrants.net/en/post/29002/razed-woodlands-prevent- migrants-from-sheltering-around-calais [Accessed 14 March 2021].

Oomen, B. (2019) 'Rights, culture and the creation of cosmopolitan cityzenship', in R. Buikema, A. Buyse and A. Robben (eds), *Cultures, Citizenship and Human Rights*, Routledge, pp 121–36.

Pall, E. (2022) *Migrants à Calais: la justice annule des arrêtés anti-distribution de nourriture*. Available from: https://france3-regions.francetvinfo.fr/hauts-de-france/pas-calais/calais/migrants-a-calais-la-justice-annule-des-arretes-anti-distribution-de- nourriture-2638260.html [Accessed 4 September 2023].

Pink, S. (2012) *Doing Sensory Ethnography*, Sage.

Puig de la Bellacasa, M. (2017) 'The disruptive thought of care', in *Matters of Care: Speculative Ethics in More Than Human Worlds*, University of Minnesota Press, pp 1–24.

Rieff, D. (2002) *A Bed for the Night: Humanitarianism in Crisis*, Council on Foreign Relations.

Rigby, J. and Schlembach, R. (2013) 'Impossible protest: no borders in Calais', *Citizenship Studies*, 17(2): 157–72.

Rullman, H. (2020) *Fort Vert: Nature Conservation as Border Regime in Calais*, Statewatch.

Sandri, E. (2018) '"Volunteer humanitarianism": volunteers and humanitarian aid in the Jungle refugee camp of Calais', *Journal of Ethnic and Migration Studies*, 44(1): 65–80.

Sheller, M. (2021) *Commoning Mobilities: Mobility Justice, Public Space, and Just Transitions*. Available from: www.publicspace.org/multimedia/-/post/commoning-mobilities- mobility-justice-public-space-and-just-transitions [Accessed 4 September 2023].

Schmidt, C. (2021) 'Interview about Human Rights Observers', September.

Skinner, R. and Lester, A. (2012) 'Humanitarianism and empire: new research agendas', *The Journal of Imperial and Commonwealth History*, 40(5): 729–47.

Squire, V. (2018) 'Researching precarious migrations: qualitative strategies toward a positive transformation of the politics of migration', British Journal of Politics and International Relations, 20(2): 441–58.

Strand, A. (2020) 'Humanitarian–development nexus', in A. De Lauri (ed), *Humanitarianism: Keywords*, Brill, pp 104–6.

Ticktin, M. (2014) 'Transnational humanitarianism', *Annual Review of Anthropology*, 43: 273–89.

Ticktin, M. (2016) 'Calais containment politics in the "Jungle"', *The Funambulist*. Available from: https://thefunambulist.net/magazine/05-design-racism/calais-containment- politics-jungle-miriam-ticktin [Accessed 2 January 2022].

Tinsley, J. (2021) 'Interview (Mobile Refugee Support)', interview, 31 October.

Tronto, J.C. (1998) 'An ethic of care', *Generations: Journal of the American Society on Aging*, 22(3): 15–20.

Van Isacker, T. (2019) 'Bordering through domicide: spatializing citizenship in Calais', *Citizenship Studies*, 23(6): 608–26.

Van Leeuwen, B. (2018) 'To the edge of the urban landscape: homelessness and the politics of care', *Political Theory*, 46(4): 586–610.

Welander, M. (2021) *The Politics of Exhaustion and Migrant Subjectivities: Researching Border Struggles in Northern France in 2016–2019*, PhD thesis, University of Westminster.

Williams, J.M. (2015) 'From humanitarian exceptionalism to contingent care: care and enforcement at the humanitarian border', *Political Geography*, 47: 11–20.

Zaman, T. (2020) 'Neighbourliness, conviviality, and the sacred in Athens' refugee squats', *Transactions of the Institute of British Geographers*, 45(3): 529–41.

Zetter, R. (2014) *Policy Brief: Reframing Displacement Crises as Development Opportunities*, Roundtable on Solutions.

Conclusion:
The Impossible Task

Camillo Boano

Displacement occupies a central position within the policy and planning agendas of nation-states, academic institutions, and international organisations alike. The term is employed to articulate the consequences of crises and their spatial dimensions, large-scale movements of people, and the persistent challenge of meeting the fundamental needs of millions who are compelled daily to escape violence, disaster, and environmental degradation. It is frequently juxtaposed with initiatives aimed at developing long-term responses, regulating mobility, and managing the arrival of displaced populations. Within these debates – spanning concerns of security, governance, and control, alongside the principles of freedom of movement, inclusion, and participation – the intertwined notions of refuge, shelter, and inhabitation remain of paramount importance.

This book seeks to conceptualise displacement not as a particular absence, location, or category within migration studies, but rather as a generative process of territorial production – an urbanism in its own right – despite its conventional association with forms of life existing out of place. It wishes to contribute to other debates that have recently discussed displacement as urbanism directly (Huq and Miraftab, 2020; Soedberg, 2021; Lichtman and Traganu, 2024; Watt and Morris, 2024), while reframing displacement as urbanism, questioning its productive tensions with forms of exhaustion, extinction, extraction, and expulsion.

Displacement produces territories, landscapes, and regions not as the sole outcome of territorial operation, biopolitical or capitalist, extractive or violent, securitarian or humanitarian, but as form of resistance, acceptance, and inevitable agency – fragile and precarious at most. However, such production – being an urbanism – is not a sole question of spatial practices. Rather, due to its planetary scale, it becomes a more ontological one: a way of being, a world-making issue generated by the complex and interrelated processes of global-scale economic and political organization with endless local and subjective variations, as we argued in the Introduction.

Life, resistance, spatial practices, new beginnings, or simply some form of what we had in the past called 'inhabitation' (Boano and Astolfo, 2020), are also produced or set in motion by displacement, manifesting 'a critical presence by doing and undoing, by giving up and resisting erosion, debility, reorganizations of spaces and capture'.

Across the different chapters, the new normal global ontological conditions of being displaced are confronted with the agent-ful embodied action of making place, replacing, and emplacing bodies, communities, and objects through stories, cases, and spatial narratives.

This concluding chapter is not returning to each narrative, nor is it attempting to universalize the learning that comes from reading each territory and its experiences. Our aim is not to offer a universal definition of displacement urbanism – albeit in a composite representation – nor a form of space made by the multiple forces of displacement, nor the one spatialized by agencies of resistance, or spatial practices. While stemming from this obvious articulation, we think displacement urbanism being a register or interrogation, a dispositive to 'assemble', able to depict the crisis of inhabitation and presence. We assembled the stories from each chapter – each with its own distinct narrative – into a structure defined by a constantly unsettled relationship between them. Anna Tsing (2020: 24) suggests that assemblages are 'are open-ended gatherings. They allow us to ask about communal effects without assuming them. They show us potential histories in the making.' In the same way, this book shows histories and spaces of a crisis of inhabitation and how different individuals and communities hold together different agencies – oppression and liberation, exhaustion and endurance, uninhabitability and inhabitation – as conditions of possibility, questioning the apparent opposition between being displaced and making place.

What is such crisis? And what is its foundational element? For Ernesto de Martino, a pioneer of cultural anthropology in Italy, when the crisis is generalized – as perhaps it is in the present – there is a risk of what he calls 'cultural apocalypses' – that is, 'the risk of not being able to be in any possible cultural world' (de Martino, 1977: 15). If displacement is a form of crisis, or is generated by crisis, crisis is exactly such impossibility to 'be in any world'; the crisis of displacement is therefore an impossibility to be, to be inhabiting, but at the same time it is 'the loss of worldliness itself, of that which allows humans to make a world ... makes it difficult to inhabit' (Consigliere, 2014: 14). Displacement is a worlding process, even if violent, precarious, fragile, exposed to suffering, but it makes space, territories, geographies and, therefore, possible modes of inhabitation (Boano and Astolfo, 2020).

All the places discussed in the book, from Istanbul to Yangon, seem to tell a story of those practices that spatialize life without the promise of stability (Tsing, 2020: 24), where inhabiting is weaving relationships, making the world 'fragile, imperfect, and far from idyllic, but undoubtedly alive' (Consigliere 2014: 114) as well as an ongoing experimentation, an imprecise effort in generative feeling, an ongoing and unfinished art of noticing and learning (2014: 114). It is a series of possible alliances with other little hangings-together, with realities lost, suppressed, marginalized, with realities fantastical, incomprehensible, and implausible, that shape 'unhinged' territories (Thomas and Masco, 2023), always 'in touch with other worlds underway and yet to be made' (Savransky, 2021: 2).

All the places discussed in the book, from Paris to Baghdad, seem to make clear the production of borders. Protection takes different forms, and territory – rural and urban – becomes itself a dispositif of control and rejection of the migrant, a refuge but at the same time a threat, a hospitable place but also a repulsive one: an infrastructure used to 'continue to maintain, a boundary between the white spaces ... and the Black spaces of migrant lifeworlds on the margins' (Raeymaekers, 2024: 127); an urbanism, a product of a spatial politics of racial differentiation and of managing difference through spatial dispersal (Hawthorne, 2021: 5). Earlier work mobilized the figure of *Lifeline* (Boano and Bianchetti, 2022) as both a prospective and an attunement, a correspondence with ecological thinking of spaces. Not a reparative infrastructure but a space for a 'subjectivity that is always subjectivity-in-brokenness – if brokenness means a subjectivity that is not just shaped but constituted by the external world's force' (2022: 10). Lifelines are lines, nesting, gatherings, where some form of protection is in place: infrastructures, membranes, ambient; ecologies and spaces in which life and death, health and suffering, exile and capture, proximity and distance, solidarity and abandonment, freedom and dependence are constantly at stake. Lifelines are those spaces where the world and life intertwine, mingle, twist in a constant resistance – awkward and fragile – to the mechanisms of capture, exploitation, and creation of social and environmental precariousness.

Somehow, for us and all the authors who participated in the book-making, displacement urbanism is not a thing, an essence, or a case. Instead, it must be understood as a perspective, a way of situating research in the ontologies of its everyday fragility of Southern urban practices in a place that is culturally and politically riddled with heavy colonial patinas (Stoler, 2016) – a being on the periphery and a colonial matrix marked by forms of racial capitalism, aggressive extraction, and imperial infrastructure. A focus, a strategic re-centrality, a politics of space understood not as product or mere representation, but rather as spatial practices – as practices at the origin of urban thought and action.

Displacement as a practice has a set of logics that make it effective and necessary to achieve certain results in the specific historical and spatial contexts of urbanization – its pressures, violences and political economies. To take the productions of space in displacement seriously is to see displacement not only in its tensions with the settlement, in the logics of law and planning, or simply in the material forms of housing, but as a mode of practice that embraces uncertainty, measures itself against limited temporalities, and works to move forward incrementally in every way possible. This mode of practice is claimed here as an equal possibility for action – for policies, programmes and plans – and not just for subaltern urban residents.

To paraphrase Deleuze and Guattari's (1987) conceptual pair of 'territorialization' and 'deterritorialization', displacement urbanism is a sort of deterritorializing counter-device that deactivates the proprietary claims of the territorializing settlement. The non-finiteness of displacement urbanism, its continuous becoming, assembling, reacting, resisting, organizing itself, dismantles modern and Western dualist thinking that tends to transform space into a controlled, legible object, devoid of grey areas. There are no empty zones. A zone of contamination, exchange and conflict: *nepantla*, a Náhuatl word that Gloria Anzaldúa (1987) uses to describe those spatial, temporal or psychic crises that occur in situations of transition. Always a threshold.

Displacement urbanism, its space, its assemblages, requires a new articulation in which we move from reasoning about *forms of living* and spaces conceived in terms of production systems to another elaborated according to *generative processes*. The two analyses differ first by their principle: freedom for the one, dependence for the other. The generative system involves agents, actors, living beings with distinct capacities to react. It does not derive from the same conception of materiality, does not have the same epistemology, and does not carry the same politics. The generation does not pursue a project of emancipation, but moves according to the virtues of dependence. Thinking with displacement urbanism might help us with thinking on an ontology, on a space, and on a city capable of making us abandon the modern emancipatory project to discover the virtues of dependence.

Therefore, displacement urbanism is not just one of the many forms of urbanisms; it is also a device of non-representation, where thought is aimed primarily at trying to decolonize our imaginary. This does not imply a frontal critique of modernity, a pragmatic inclination to 'solve' displacement, but it suggests some form of autonomy from the dominant form of modernity and city.

A coda

This book was a long time in the making – exceptionally long for several reasons, some beyond our control, other due to mistakes and difficult choices. Long after we started an even darker moment in our present emerged. The darkness of war is growing ever deeper, when the abyss of destruction, of impossible return, of desperate flights in search of safer places, has become a grim necessity. It is not just a denial of space, of difference – whether historical, political, or religious – but a brutal annihilation that extends from Gaza to Lebanon and elsewhere. Displacement and its urbanism are not fading away in the irrelevance of research and academic writing. War seems to have become a project of emptiness, of absence, of nothingness.

'There's no point in what I'm doing if the house is burning. And yet, it's precisely when the house is burning that one must carry on as usual, doing everything with care and precision – perhaps even more diligently, even if no one notices.' So writes Giorgio Agamben in a short pamphlet titled *When the House Burns* (2022: 1). This is not a metaphor, but words that convey the impossibility of living, that make visible this project of annihilation – and at the same time, point to a possible stance.

War is not someone else's project. The annihilation of Gaza is no longer just a suspicion, but an explicit, intentional strategy of total destruction, carried out with cold, technical violence. The scale of it is horrifying and there is no need to mention the numbers again. What is left is just rubble: 'There is no geography anymore, except that of proximity, nor any historical time: civilization is a vague memory, rendered useless by the urgency of survival, and it expresses itself only through what remains of practical teachings' (Berlant, 2011: 10). Water, shelter. It's a constant friction that Lauren Berlant (2011: 10) calls 'crisis ordinariness': that exhausting horror of the complexities of staying 'attached to life'.

The project of uninhabitability is the systematic making of life impossible in every form, leaving only the fragile spectres of exile and *sumud*.[1] This is not new. Displacement is even impossible here. What seems crucial to underline is that this project of annihilation implies – at least as I understand it – the impossibility of finding refuge, of seeking out safe places. Even the ruins, the so-called safe zones, the tunnels, the hospitals, have become uninhabitable. Today, perhaps more than ever, war strips us of the very idea of refuge. This is the mantra of these days: there are no more safe places. What is to be done? How do we survive? How do we remain subjects – agents? How do we refuse? Perhaps we need to halt the 'extraordinary capacity of people to go on refusing the terms of defeat, and to insist on life at all costs … To believe in life, to live –despite everything' (Abourahme (2024).

Displacement unfolds in the very moment of escape. To think about it means looking beyond a narrative of time (be it dramatic, exceptional, prolonged, or linear), and instead reading of its ecological and therefore relational conditions: recognizing difference, multiplicity, change, and movement. Escaping capture, of displacement and the complete annihilation, is being imaginative, courageous, and creative of the ways in which individual and groups are holding up, are making spaces, and repoliticizing such efforts.

Note

[1] *Sumud*, which translates from Arabic as 'steadfastness' or 'steadfast perseverance', is a commonly used term to describe the everyday non-violent resistance of Palestinians against the Israeli occupation. Over time, the concept of *sumud* has taken on various meanings and forms, evolving through different phases of the Palestinian struggle against

ethnic cleansing. Rather than being a rigidly defined term, it represents a continuum of resistance goals and practices that adapt to the shifting dynamics of oppression and resistance, encompassing a broad spectrum of cultural, ideological, and political values and actions. For more, see www.palquest.org/en/highlight/33633/sumud.

References

Abourahme, N. (2024) 'In tune with their time', *Radical Philosophy*, 216: 13–20.
Agamben, G. (2022) *Quando la Casa Brucia*, Giometti & Antonello.
Anzaldúa, G.E. (1987) *Borderlands/La Frontera: The New Mestiza*, Aunt Lute Books.
Berlant, L. (2011) *Cruel Optimism*, Duke University Press.
Boano, C. and Astolfo, G. (2020) 'Inhabitation as more-then-dwelling: notes for a renewed grammar', *International Journal of Housing Policy*, 20(4): 555–77.
Boano C. and Bianchetti C. (2022) *Lifelines: Politics, Ethics and the Affective Economy of Inhabiting*, Jovis.
Consigliere, S. (2014) *Antropo-logiche*, Colibrì.
De Martino, E. (1977) *La Fine del Mondo. Contributo alle Analisi delle Apocalissi*, Einaudi.
Deleuze, G. and Guattari, F. (1987) *A Thousand Plateaus: Capitalism and Schizophrenia*, trans B. Massumi, University of Minnesota Press.
Hawthorne, C. (2021) *Contesting Race and Citizenship: Youth Politics in the Black Mediterranean*, Cornell University Press.
Huq, E. and Miraftab, F. (2020) '"We are all refugees": camps and informal settlements as converging spaces of global displacement', *Planning Theory and Practice*, 21(3): 351–70.
Lichtman, S.A. and Traganu, J. (2024) *Design, Displacement, Migration: Spatial and Material Histories*, Routledge.
Raeymaekers, T. (2024) *The Natural Border: Bounding Migrant Farmwork in the Black Mediterranean*, Cornell University Press.
Soedberg, S. (2021) *Urban Displacements: Governing Surplus and Survival in Global Capitalism*, Routledge.
Stoler, A.L. (2016) *Duress: Imperial Durabilities in Our Times*, Duke University Press.
Tlostanova, M. (2023) *Narratives of Unsettlement. Being Out-of-Joint as a Generative Human Condition*, Routledge.
Tsing, A. (2020) 'When the things we study respond to each other: Tools for Unpacking "the Material"', in P. Harvey and C. Krohn-Hansen and K.G. Nustad (eds), *Anthropos and the Material*, De Gruyter, pp 221–44.
Watt, P. and Morris, A. (2024) 'Special feature: putting urban displacement in its place', *City*, 28(1–2): 161–88.

Index

References to figures appear in *italic* type. References to endnotes show both the page number and the note number (66n6).

A
acute violence 163
adaptation 267
Afeji 279
Agamben, G. 22, 73, 295
agency of change 267–8
agriculture 77, 81, 83
  see also farmers
Al-Naimi, S. 215
Algerian Accord 1975 170
Alto Hospicio *see* Iquique and Alto Hospicio
Amed 234
Andreucci, D. and Zografos, D. 26
Anfal campaign 173
Anthropocene 32
Anzaldúa, G. 294
Arab Spring 179
Arabization 169–70, 178
Arbat refugee camp 161, *162*
Arbat strip 161, *162*
Arendt, H. 281
arrival cities 39
Arua City, Uganda
  self-settled refugees 247–8
  case studies 254–60
  case study analysis 260–6
  endurance 266–9
  invisible inhabitation 249–51
  protracted displacement 248–9, 251–3, 262
  refugee demographics *252*
Ashti IDP Camp *182*
ashwaiat 222
assemblages 292
Association for Solidarity with *Geekondu* Inhabitants 238
asylum claims 278, 279
asylum seekers 83, 189–90, 196–7, 199, 274–5
augmented disposability 116, 119–21

auto-construction 64–5
auto-eviction 64–5

B
Baghdad
  becoming-extinction 209–10, 211, 220, 225–6
  housing 221–5
  place-wounding 210, 215
  spatial wounding 216–21
  walling strategy 212–16
bare life *see zoé*
Barzani, M. 168–9, 170
Basmaya Residential Project, Baghdad 223
becoming-extinction 209, 211, 220, 223–4, 225–6
Beller, J. 196
Berlant, L. 30, 295
Bernstein, H. 62
bidonvilles 194, 203n3
biodiversity 24
biographies 162–3
  territorial biographies approach 163–4
biopolitics 21–3, 26, 27–8
  of displacement urbanism 36–7
  minimalist 279
  and posthumanism 32–3
  and race 34–5
  reception, reflections and elaboration 28–33
biopolitics of surplus 23
biopower 32
bios 73
biovalue 29
Black African migrants 35–6
Black feminism 34–5
Black Marxism 23
Black Mediterranean, The (Proglio et al) 35–6
Boano, C. 56
Boano, C. and Astolfo, G. 221

297

Boccagni, P. 221
Boutry, M. 64
Braidotti, R. 27, 73
British colonialism 58, 60
British mandate 166
Burma *see* Myanmar
Butler, J. 29

C

Calais 273–4
  beyond humanitarianism 284–5
  spatial violence 276–80
  universal care and power of imagination 280–4
Calais Jungle 278
campamentos 139–41, 141–2, 151–2, 154–6, 157
Campbell, S. 56–7, 62
camps 13–14, 19–20, 22, 39, 73, 84, 224
  Calais Jungle 278
  Greater Paris 191, 192–4
  Delphine Seyrig 197–9, 201, 202
  Porte de la Chapelle 195–7, 201, 202
  Soixante AdaDa 199–200, 201, 202
  Kurdistan Region of Iraq (KR-I) 161, *162*, 170, 178, 179, 181–3
capitalism 29, 77
Capitalocene 25
care 280–4
  ethics of 225
'care receiving' 281
'caring for' 281
Carsten, J. and Bozalek, V. 25
Castel Volturno 72
  extraction 80–3, 84
  humanitarian aid 75–6
  migrant workers 74–5, 77–80
central government of Iraq (CGoI) 174, 176, 179, 181
Centre Humanitaire de Porte de la Chapelle 196
change *see* agency of change; Theory of Change (ToC)
Channel Tunnel 273
Chile
  migration to 143
  see also Iquique and Alto Hospicio
China
  forced resettlement 93–5, 102, 108
  population growth 91–2, 99
  resettlement neighbourhoods 95–9
  future settlements 105–8
  Suzhou Industrial Park (SIP) *96*, *97*, 99–105, 107
  urbanization 91, 92, 93
cities 39, 40, 56, 92
citizenship 80, 169, 192, 257
citoyen hébergeurs (citizen hosts) 283
civilizationist developmentalism 232, 239

climate apartheid 26
climate change 25–6
climate coloniality 26
climate crisis 224–5
Coalition Provisional Authority 213, 214
Coast Law, Turkey 235
Colline du Crack 196
colonial displacement 23–4
colonial extraction 25–6, 225
colonialism 58, 60
coloniality 230–2
  of top-down disaster preparedness 233–6
community 262
  see also Congolese refugee community
community systems 261
compensation 61–2, 94, 104
Congolese refugee community 260, 261–2, 265
Cooper, M. 29
Corboz, A. 163
cordon sanitaire 170–2
Cornish, G. 63–4
COVID-19 27
crack dealers 196
crisis 292
'crisis of reception' 200
crisis ordinariness 295
critical rupture 210
cultural apocalypses 292

D

daily displacement squeeze 61–4, 65
Damluji, M. 215
Darling, J. 22, 39
Davis, M. (2006) 65
Davis, M. (2007) 217
de Martino, E. 292
death
  as nonlife 32
  slow 30–1
Death by Landscape (Wilk) 17
debilitation / debility 30–1, 61, 62, 65
debt 63, 65
deforestation 223
degeneration 126
Delaney, D. 38
Deleuze, G. and Guattari, F. 294
Delphine Seyrig 191. 201, 191, 197–9, 201, 202
developmentalism 232, 233, 239
difference-making 211, 215
Dillon, S. 220
disability 61–3
  see also debilitation / debility
Disaster Law, Turkey 230, 233, 237, 239, 240
disaster-preparedness 233–9
displacement
  colonial 23–4
  forms of 55–6

INDEX

internal 215
migrant women 150, 152, 153, 155
protracted 248–9, 251–63, 262
and urbanism 18–19
see also forced displacement; urban displacement
displacement squeeze 3, 61–6, 65–6, 66n5
displacement urbanism 1–2, 41, 291–2, 293–4
  biopolitics of 36–7
  manifold dimensions of 37–9
  see also urban displacement; urban/displacement relationship
disposability / displaceability 3, 55, 79, 115–17
  Fikirtepe 119–21, 124–5, 126
dispossession 15, 20–1
domicide 277, 279
drug dealers 196

E

earthquakes 230
Elden, S. 217
empowerment 268–9
endurance 32–3, 248, 266–9
Erdoğan, R.T. 123
ethical care 281
ethics of care 225
ethnic groups, Syria and Iraq *180*
ethnic segregation 215
evictions 64–5, 152–4, 198, 201, 277
excess 4
excess capital 77
excess population 72–3
exclusion 80
exhaustion 32–3
expansion by expulsion 21
extinction *see* becoming-extinction
extraction 1, 3, 56, 64, 80–3, 84, 116
  colonial 25–6, 225
extractivism 156–7, 225
Extraordinary Reception Centres (CAS) 83

F

family reunion 154
farmers 93–5, 102, 108
  see also agriculture
Fassin, D. 31
Figure of the Migrant, The (Nail) 21
Fikirtepe 119–31, 131n3
  scrap dealers 119–20, 121–3, 126–9
  undocumented migrants 125–6, 129
fishing 235–6
food distribution 279
Forbes, E. 64–5
forced displacement
  Kurdistan Region of Iraq (KR-I) 163–4, 169, 172, 174, *184*
  Myanmar 58–9

forced evictions 152–4
forced migration 200
forced resettlement 93–5, 102, 108
Foucault, M. 21, 32, 33–4, 231
  see also biopolitics
France 275–6
  asylum seekers 189–90
  see also Calais; Greater Paris
Free Trade Zones (FTZs) 141

G

Gaza 295
gecekondu neighbourhoods 117, 118
  Fikirtepe 119–31, 131n3
  scrap dealers 119–20, 121–3, 126–9
  undocumented migrants 125–6, 129
  Hillgreen 236–9, 240
  Rockwind 234–5, 236, 239
genocide 173
geontopower 32
geotrauma 219–20
Gillespie, A. 23
global warming *see* climate change
Glück, R. 17
Gonzalez, R. 26
Greater Paris 194–5
  Haussmanian zoning 194, 202–3n2
  refugee camps 191, 193–4
  Delphine Seyrig 197–9, 201, 202
  Porte de la Chapelle 195–7, 201, 202
  Soixante AdaDa 199–200, 201, 202
Green Zone, Baghdad 214, 215, 216
Gregory, D. 231
Gregotti, V. 163
gross domestic product (GDP) 99, 107, 139
Guyer, S. 27

H

Habeas Viscus 34–5
Hagan, M. 282
Harvey, D. 20, 31, 77
Haussmanian zoning 194, 202–3n2
healthcare 254–6
Hillgreen 236–9, 240
Hoffman, D, 65
Holbraad, M. 210
home-making 14
homing 221, 222, 225
Homo Sacer (Agamben) 22
homogeneity 97–9
housing 221–5, 238, 256
  self-built 264–5
  social 142
  temporary 196
  see also rental housing
housing market 139, 141
  informal (*tegurios*) 143–50, 156, 157

humanitarian aid 75–6, 77, 81, 83, 84, 174–6, 253
humanitarian interventions 275, 278–80
  universal care and power of imagination 280–4
humanitarian organizations 277
humanitarianism 31
  beyond humanitarianism 284–5

I

identity 262–3
imagination 281–4
immunity 22
inclusion 80
informal housing market (*tegurios*) 143–50, 156, 157
informal settlements (*ashwaiat*), Baghdad 222
informal settlements (*campamentos*) 139–41, 141–2, 151–2, 154–6, 157
  see also La Zone
infrastructural violence 163, 172, 173
infrastructure, people as 40
inhabitation 221–2
  invisible 250–1, 254, 260–6
injuries 61–2
injustice 210
insider research 211
Intergovernmental Panel on Climate Change (IPCC) 24–5
internal displacement 215
internally displaced persons (IDPs) 178, 181, 221, 224
intimidation tactics 276
invisible inhabitation 249–51, 254, 260–6
Iquique and Alto Hospicio 137
  forced evictions 152–4
  informal housing market (*tegurios*) 143–50, 156, 157
  informal settlements (*campamentos*) 139–41, 141–2, 151–2, 154–6, 157
  urban development 139–42
Iraq
  expansion of ISIS *180*
  modernization 166–9
  National Housing Programme *168*
  US-led invasion 209, 212–13, 219
  see also Baghdad; Kurdistan Region of Iraq (KR-I)
Iraq-Iran war 172–4
Iraqi-Kurdish Peace Accord 1970 169
Islamic State of Iraq and Syria (ISIS) 179, 224
  expansion of control *180*
Istanbul
  disaster-preparedness 236–9
  urban transformation crisis 117–19
  Fikirtepe 119–31, 131n3
Istanbul Metropolitan Municipality 237

J

Janzen, R. 251
justice 211
  spatial 210

K

Kawergosk Refugee Camp *182*
Kearney, A. 219
kinopolitics 21
Kreichauf, R. 283
Kurdish Front 172
Kurdish Regional Government (KRG) 176, 178, 179, 181, 183
Kurdish revolt 170
Kurdistan 160–1
Kurdistan Democratic Party (KDP) 170, 172, 176
Kurdistan Region of Iraq (KR-I) 161
  1950-91 166–74
  1991-2011 174
  2011 to present 179–83
  Arbat strip *162*
  prior to World War I 164–6
  between World Wars 166
Kurdistan, Turkey, top-down disaster preparedness 233–6
Kyed, H. 63

L

La Maison Sésame 283
La Vie Active 279
La Zone 194, 203n3
labour protection 61–2
land access 257–8, 263–4
land allocation 217
land appropriation / land grab 59, 60, 63
land exhaustion 62
land expropriation 93
land redistribution 284
landscape 17
landscapes of fear 215–16
Lemke, T. 28
Les Midi du Mie 199, 202
Les Restos 198
life
  precariousness of 29–30
  as surplus 29
  see also biopolitics; nonlife; *zoé*
lifelines 293
Lotus Village 97

M

mafia 237
maintaining 14
Martin, D. 193
materiality 249
Maung, M.L. 64, 65
Mbembe, A. 80, 275–6
Mbembe, J.-A. 32, 34

Mediterranean 35–6
Mellino, M. 77
Merie, U. 212
Mezzadra, S. 64
Mezzadra, S. and Neilson, B. 80, 81, 82
migrant families 141
migrant solidarity groups 284
migrant women
  forced evictions 152–4
  informal housing market (*tegurios*) 143–50, 156, 157
  informal settlements (*campamentos*) 151–2, 154–6, 157
migrant workers 15, 25, 56–7, 74–5, 77–80, 80–3, 125, 129
  see also racialized labour
migrants 21, 35–6, 39
migration 22, 30, 143
  forced 200
Minca, C. 30
Minera, C. 22
minimalist biopolitics 279
modernization, Iraq 166–9
money lending 63
'multicrisis' events 200
Murrani, S. 212, 216, 224
Myanmar
  auto-eviction 64–5
  daily displacement squeeze 61–4, 65–6
  dual displacement machine 59–60
  forced displacement 58–9
  necroeconomy 56–8

N

nail houses 94
Nail, T. 21
necroeconomy 56–8
necropolitics 22, 26, 32, 34, 37
neo-apartheid regimes 23
neoliberal capitalism 29
neoliberal governance 118
neoliberalism 230–1
nepantla 294
Nixon, R. 163, 225
no-fly zones 174, *175*
Nolan, R. 34–5
nonlife 32
Nwe, T.T. 55

O

oil drilling 225
Oil-for-Food Programme (OFFP) 176, 177
ordinary suffering 31–2
othering 26, 249
Otsuki, K. 163

P

Pain, R. 219
palimpsest 220
palimpsestic 220
palimpsestuous 220
Paris *see* Greater Paris
Patriotic Union of Kurdistan (PUK) 170, 172, 176
Pedreño, A. 77
people as infrastructure 40
place-making 14, 211
place-wounding 210, 215
  see also spatial wounding
planned service life 104
Plantatiocene 25
police violence 237, 276
political economy of human deployment 40
political imagination 281–4
politics of scale 210–11
population growth 91–2, 99, 142
Porte de la Chapelle 191, 195–7, 201, 202
post-survival 267–8
postcolonial capitalism 77
postcolonial world order 231
posthumanism 32–3
poverty 107–8
Povinelli, E. 24, 31–3, 231–2
Powell, K.A. 220
power 217, 268–9
precariousness / precarity 29–30
primitive accumulation 20–1
Project X 32–3
property ownership 219
protection-seeking 14
protracted displacement 248–9, 262
  geopolitics of 251–3
Prussian carp 235–6
Przybylinski, S. 210–11
psycho-social trauma 255
Puar, J.K. 30, 61
'putting out' 56–7

R

race 34–6
racial displacement 23–4
racialization 3, 26, 75, 141, 145
racialized labour 77–8, 80–1, 84
racialized neighbourhoods 234–9
racialized territories 82–3
racism 33–4, 157
Rashid, M. and Alobaydi, D. 212
reception centres 196
recycling 32–3
Red Zone, Baghdad 214, 215
reflexive triangulation 212
refuge-granting 14
refuge-making 222, 224
refugee camps *see* camps
Refugee Law Project 255
'refugee/migration crisis' 200
  see also Calais
refugee urbanism 39–40

refugees 22, 39, 165, 170
  see also self-settled refugees
relief programmes see humanitarian aid
religious segregation 215
rental housing 139, 141, 256, 257
  informal (tegurios) 143–50, 156, 157
repairing 14
resettlement, China 93–5, 102, 108
resettlement neighbourhoods
  China 95–9
  future settlements 105–8
  Suzhou Industrial Park (SIP) *96, 97*, 99–105, 107
resource mobilization 263
Reyneri, E. 77
Rhoads, E. 59
Rockwind 234–5, 236, 239
ruins 12–13, 72
rupture 210, 212–16

S

Saddam City see Sadr City
Sadr City 216–21
safe routes *175*
Santiago de Chile see Iquique and Alto Hospicio
scale, politics of 210–11
scrap dealers 120, 121–3, 126–9
Seethaler-Wari, S. 19
self-built housing 264–5
self-determination 268
self-exploitation 62
self-managed informal settlements 154–6
self-settled refugees 247–8
  case studies, analysis 254–66
  endurance 266–9
  invisible inhabitation 249–51
  protracted displacement 248–9, 251–3, 262
  refugee demographics *252*
Settlements Rehabilitation Programme (SRP), UN 176–7
Sharma, A. 23
shelter-home 14
short-term holding facilities (SHTF) 273
sickness 31
Sierra Leone 65
Simone, A. 40
simple displacement squeeze 3, 66n5
slavery 58
slow death 30–1
slow violence 163, 225
Smith, S. and Vasudevan, P. 33
social cooperation 64
social housing 142
social networks 219, 250, 251, 258, 259, 265–6
socio-political embeddedness 268
Soixante AdaDa 191, 199–200, 201, 202
Soja, E. 210, 226

Solidarité Migrants Wilson 198, 202
solidarity practices 284–5
South Sudanese refugees 257–9, 263–5, 268
Soviet Union 98
spatial figures 12–14
spatial imagination 281–4
spatial justice 210, 226
spatial practices 14
spatial tensions 14–16
spatial violence 276–80
spatial wounding 216–21
  see also place-wounding
special care zones (SCZs) 282–3
Special Economic Zones (SEZs) 91, 92, 107
spherical violence 217, 220
squats 283–4
squatters 60, 62–3, 64–5, 237
Stanley, A. 211
Steigmann, A.M. and Misselwitz, P. 249
Stoler, A. 231
storytelling 162–3
structural violence 116, 275–7
suffering 34, 35
  ordinary 31–2
suicide 10, 250, 254, 255, 260–1
Sultana, F. 26
sumud 295, 295–6n1
surplus
  biopolitics of 23
  life as 29
surplus capital 77
surplus value 20, 23, 26, 29
survival 260–1, 267
Suzhou Industrial Park (SIP) *96, 97*, 99–105, 107
Sykes-Picot Agreement 166
Syria 179
  expansion of ISIS *180*
Syrian refugees 179, 181

T

Talabani, J. 170
Tanzimat Acts 1839 165
temporary housing 196
territorial biographies approach 163–4, 183
Thailand 56–7
Theory of Change (ToC) 248, 251, 260, 264
Tongli 97
transnational agriculture 77
trauma 16, 31, 255
  see also geotrauma
Tronti, M. 66
Tronto, J.C. 281
Tsing, A. 292
Tuan, Y.-F. 215
tugurios 143–50

INDEX

Turkey 170
  Coast Law 235
  Disaster Law 230, 233, 237, 239, 240
  top-down disaster preparedness 233–9
Turner, J. 231

U

Uganda
  self-settled refugees 247–8
  case studies 254–60
  case study analysis 260–6
  endurance 266–9
  invisible inhabitation 249–51
  protracted displacement 248–9, 251–3, 262
  refugee demographics 252
UN Habitat Settlements Rehabilitation Programme (SRP) 176–7
UN Security Council 174
uninhabitability 295
unions 61–2
United Kingdom 274–5, 277
universal care 280–4
urban displacement
  biopolitical frames 21–3
  colonial, racial and violent displacement 23–4
  and violence 21, 22–3
  see also displacement urbanism
urban/displacement relationship 18–19
urban extinction 224
Urban Planning and Design Research Institute of China 98
Urban Planning Regulation of China 1984 93, 98
urban transformation crisis
  Istanbul 117–19
  Fikirtepe 119–31, 131n3
urban turn 19–20
urbanism 28
  see also cities; displacement urbanism; refugee urbanism
urbanization 19, 38, 178
  China 91, 92, 93. *see also* Suzhou Industrial Park
Utopia 56, 196, 198

V

value extraction *see* extraction
Van Isacker, T. 279
Vatter, M. 29
violence 15–16, 21, 22–3, 31–2, 172, 173
  acute 163
  frames of 163
  infrastructural 163, 172, 173
  slow 163, 225
  spatial 276–80
  spherical 217, 220
  structural 116, 275–6
  see also police violence
violent displacement 23–4
visa documentation 145

W

Wai, P. 60
Walby, C. 29
walling strategy 213–16
war 295
Watson, G. 29
Weheliye, A.G. 34
Weizman, E. 216
When the House Burns (Agamben) 295
Wilk, E. 17
Williams, J.M. 279
Win, Y.N. 61–2
Worker Journal, The 61
workers' unions 61–2
World Bank 91
Wright, M. 37

Y

Yangon
  auto-eviction 64–5
  daily displacement squeeze 61–4, 65–6
  dual displacement machine 59–60
Yazidi IDP camps 181, 183
Yiftachel, O. 55
Young, I.M. 211, 225

Z

Zaw, Y.K. 62
zoé 3, 4, 73, 75, 79, 80, 83, 84
zoé politics 73

www.ingramcontent.com/pod-product-compliance
Lightning Source LLC
Chambersburg PA
CBHW051527020426
42333CB00016B/1820